A GRAMMAR OF CONSENT

Library of Religious Philosophy

Thomas V. Morris, editor

Volume 6

A GRAMMAR OF CONSENT

The Existence of God in Christian Tradition

AIDAN NICHOLS, O. P.

University of Notre Dame Press

Notre Dame   London

Library of Congress Cataloging-in-Publication Data

Nicholas, Aidan.
  A grammar of consent: the existence of God in Chris-
tian tradition / Aidan Nichols.
      p.   cm. – (Library of religious philosophy; v. 6)
  Includes bibliographical references and index.
  ISBN 0-268-01026-9
  1. God – History of doctrines. 2. Philosophical theology.
3. Catholic Church and philosophy. 4. Catholic Church –
Doctrines – History.   I. Title. II. Series.
BT98.N45   1991
231'.042 – dc20   90–50978
                                                         CIP

We need a clue into the labyrinth which is to lead us to Him. . . . He has made this path of thought rugged and circuitous above other investigations, that the very discipline inflicted on our minds in finding Him may mould them in due devotion to Him when He is found.

> —John Henry Newman, *An Essay in Aid of a Grammar of Assent*

One torch lights another. . . . It is best to learn from others; it gives a touch of creatureliness.

> —Baron Friedrich von Hügel, *Letters*

CONTENTS

PREFACE

Today, in the Western countries at least, believers in God live for the most part within a culture that is shot through with skepticism in religious matters and with a practical atheism where all decisions of moment are concerned. It may sound paradoxical to say that an environment of this kind can be of great help to the reflective believer in his or her life of faith. Yet such skepticism and practical atheism can equally easily act as a stimulant as it can as a depressant or dissolver. This particular mental milieu that we share is not so much the product of a more or less successful refutation at the level of theory of the allegation that God exists. Much more is it the result of an imaginative collapse, the breakdown of a worldview. Now to some extent, an imaginative collapse can only be remedied by an imaginative renaissance. That was the implication of an earlier study, *The Art of God Incarnate*, whose subtitle was meant to indicate the close relation of *Theology and Image in Christian Tradition*, though with particular reference to *visual* images, so vital in both Catholicism and Orthodoxy.[1] The picture of the world that empiricists (professional or not) have forced upon us makes it difficult, imaginatively difficult, to sense the palpable pressure of God in our experience. But we are not obliged to accept this picture, and almost any creative use of the imagination takes us over the edge of its canvas. The practical breakdown of the theistic worldview is a sickness for which philosophy, too, can offer a therapy, if not a complete cure. The twentieth-century Spanish philosopher Ortega y Gasset once suggested that it is precisely at these moments of the disintegration of some great view of the world, of some major interpretative framework for existence, that philosophy comes into its own.[2] When an overall framework of meaning, itself created by an interplay of experience and reflection, begins to

ix

break down in people's imaginations the most useful philosophizing is done.

The example that Ortega y Gasset gives, which will be familiar to many, is that of Socrates and his enemies, the Sophists. At a time when the traditional ethics of the Greek city-state were in the melting pot, the Sophists had begun to use the time-honored language of ethical commendation ("This is good"; "that is right") in a quite new way. In place of telling us what reality around us is like, pointing out the values embedded in the real, awaiting our discovery and delight, the Sophists used moral terms as counters or weapons. They set out to manipulate their hearers in the interest of the speaker's own rise to fame and fortune. The crisis of life and thought was Socrates' opportunity. Only through a breakdown of traditionally accepted ways could just those conditions be created that would nurture a person of his or her qualities. Putting the old tried and tested values on a new and better foundation, demonstrating their rational intelligibility, required the kind of distance that the Sophistic crisis provided. Some things cannot be seen properly if you are too close to them, just as a painting needs to be viewed from some distance. There is no necessary virtue in having your eyeball up against the brushwork. Perhaps the retreat of theism in our own society provides a parallel opportunity to stand back and take a fresh look at its rational resources.

It is worth noting that Socrates was not concerned simply to restate the old beliefs in fresh and more reasonable ways. He also wanted to purify them, by stripping away forms of expression or associated and less worthy ideas that detracted from the value of those traditional beliefs. The Christian philosopher can find an encouraging analogy here also. The value of philosophy to the Christian lies primarily, it may be said, in what it can offer by way of purifying and enriching our image of God, our sense of God. (I have offered some suggestions for the role of philosophy within theology elsewhere, in the second section of *The Shape of Catholic Theology*.)[3] Not all philosophical writing can serve this purpose, of course: and yet we should not be too quick to dismiss the services, *malgré eux*, of even atheistic philosophers in criticizing our taken-for-granted, perhaps time-desecrated rather than time-hallowed, images of God. The kind of philosophizing that I have in mind is that which remains in touch with the origins of philosophy, those origins that even now appear in the word *philosophy*, "the love of wisdom." All great philosophy possesses not only system, coherent organization, but also vision, penetration into human life and into the mystery of being, the dark and dizzy fact that there is something rather than nothing. Great philosophers, in brief, have great souls. The use of philosophy to the man or woman who is embarked on the quest for God consists in the confrontation between his or her own sense of God, on the one hand, and the sense of God that is located and lived with in the great-souled, on the other. Not normally the product of books that describe such a confrontation, faith in God can be touched, and touched up, by a meeting with the philosophers and may even, in certain circumstances, be ignited by that encounter.

Written into the structure and argument of this book is a principle not usually met with in religious philosophy: the communion of saints. That, in John Donne's words, "no man is an island" is generally regarded as too commonplace a thought to suggest something as elevated as a philosophical method. Similarly, the claim, as in T. S. Eliot's evocation of Little Gidding, that "the communication of the dead is tongued with fire beyond the language of the living," seems too remote a piece of dogmatic theology to guide the philosophic hand. Nevertheless, I believe that if we are to stand any decent chance of discerning the presence of God in the most basic facts of our human experience we cannot afford to be individualists in splendid isolation. We have to be on the alert for experiential cues for the apprehension of God as these are offered to us in the life and thought of a whole range of lovers of wisdom in the past. In that portion of the Catholic church that I happen to know best, the bit belonging to the British Isles, we have the twin advantages of a continuous Catholic Christian tradition, stretching back ultimately into the Roman world, and a wider cultural context where response to the word *tradition* is on the whole favorable, despite the best efforts of the Utilitarians and their crew. Having written these words in Norway, where Catholic Christianity has had to be reconstructed haltingly and painfully from scratch, and where the relation of those alive today to the riches of the medieval Catholic past can be rebuilt only in a literary way, the merits of the British situation seem obvious. But in practice, obsession with contemporary experience, surely one of the greatest of all limiters and a real sickness of the life of the mind, is as widespread among the spiritual descendants of Anselm, Scotus, and Newman as it is anywhere. This is sad, for each age has its blindspots, and only the oblique angle of the historian's view from the past as he or she relives it can identify them.[4] Contact with the living past, by which is meant in this context the past in all its latent powers of spiritual fruitfulness for the present, is the best cure for intellectual myopia.

In the last fifty years the members of the Dominican Order, to which I belong, have contributed a good deal to this process of *ressourcement*, the refreshing and renewing of the life of faith by broader and deeper acquaintence with the theological resources of the past. My *Yves Congar* was intended as an act of homage to one such attempt.[5] In the later 1960s and 1970s it sometimes seemed as if this movement had served its purpose and finished its work. Theological activity, both of the heavy and the popular varieties, began to address itself purely to what were taken to be the most pressing contemporary problems, a type of thinking summed up in the formula, "The world sets the agenda." Only with the coming of a new decade in the 1980s could one see clearly that what might be called "*Newsweek* theology" was in fact a capitulation of the most dramatic and abject kind to the last generation's radical inability to be taught by the living past. Such matters as social justice and the future of the third world, the disposition of roles between men and women in society, the fate of our common environment—these are, certainly, weighty human issues, and possibly, even probably, Christian theology may have light to shed on them over and above the ordinary workaday resources of human ethics and common sense. But to let such questions as these become the dominant motif of Christian proclamation and Christian believing is to fuddle, and eventually to destroy, the Christian pattern. For traditional Christianity has a unity, the unity ultimately of a Face. You cannot rearrange the features of a face without making its bearer wholly unrecognizable. Christians do no service to their own age if they forget that with their Master they belong to all the ages. Not least, their resources consist in the riches of the faithful generations that preceded them, hence the peculiar actuality of such historical theologians as Hans Urs von Balthasar (about whom I hope to write a full-length study) and Joseph Ratzinger (whose work I have described in *The Theology of Joseph Ratzinger: An Introductory Study*).[6] The distinguished English (in fact, Scottish) Dominican into whose hands I made my first vows, the late Father Ian Hislop, once described the purpose of the Order of Preachers as "the theological articulation of contemporary experience." Without wishing to deny an element of truth in that claim, I think it fairer to describe that purpose as, rather, "the contemporary articulation of theological experience." The "pre-Conciliar Church," when all is said and done, includes the apostles.

This book has been written, quite deliberately, not so much as an exercise in personal ingenuity as an exploration of the tradition of Christian philosophy. To my mind not one theological movement among many, *ressourcement* is the enduring character of the Christian life of reflection. The office of the Spirit of truth in the Christian community, as St. John's Gospel indicates, is to *remind* disciples of all that the Christ has said to them. Yves Congar, O. P., in his massive study of the experience of the Holy Spirit in the Church, writes that "le chrétien est un homme précédé," "the Christian is essentially a man who has predecessors."[7] In this way, one likes to think, the life of the Dominican friar is simply a paradigm of the basic Christian life in one of its essential facets. He lives by theological contemplation, by adoration of the inexhaustible Source of meaning from which the Church has lived and experienced down the centuries. He sends himself to school with the mysteries of God, Christ, and the Church, through the sacred liturgy – itself a deposit of the corporate past – and through study, all animated by a personal search for God. (In my *Yves Congar*, I have tried to bring out these dimensions in an account of one theologian's work.)[8] Since he has the right to preach precisely as part of an *ordo*, an order, a community and tradition, he has something fortunately richer than his own meager individual resources of reflection to offer those who are hungry for the Word of God. "No thinker is the sun and the sunlight, for this is the Truth itself, infinite, utterly mysterious, always new yet older than man."[9] If truth has no judges at least it has witnesses. In this spirit, Friedrich von Hügel saw the theological enterprise as essentially an interrogation of witnesses, and I shall draw this preface to an end by making some words of his my own. He is introducing the first edition of his great study, *The Mystical Element of Religion* :

And I thus trust that the book may turn out to be as truly Catholic in fact as it has been in intention; I have striven hard to furnish so continuous and copious a stream of actions and teachings of Christian saints and sages as everywhere to give the reader means of correcting or completing my own inferences; and I sincerely submit these to the test and judgment of my fellow Christians and of the Catholic Church.[10]

I should like to make mention of two relatively recent books that have helped me in writing this text: Rowan Williams's *The Wound of Knowledge* (London, 1980) and Noel Dermot O'Donoghue's *Heaven in Ordinarie* (Edinburgh, 1979). Their combination of, on one hand, a willingness to be taught from the deepest sources of Christian wisdom, the saints and the mystics, with, on the other hand, a concern for a proper philosophical rigor seems to me to indicate the most hopeful way forward for Christian thinking in the near future. More remotely, I am happy to return fraternal thanks to those English Dominicans of Blackfriars, Oxford, who had the ungrateful task of introducing some elements of philosophy into my head; and above all to Father Fergus Kerr, then prior of Blackfriars, who taught us that philosophy and contemplation belong together and who kindly read and helpfully commented upon this book in its first draft. It only remains to thank my brethren of the Dominican community in Oslo for their hospitality, friendship, and generosity in allowing me time and space enough, within the round of conventual duties, to prepare the materials for this book. Lastly, I wish to thank Jeannette Morgenroth Sheerin of the University of Notre Dame Press in the most wholehearted way possible for the great care with which she has refined this material for publication. I dedicate the book, though conscious of its shortcomings, to the memory of John Henry Newman, in whose oratory at Littlemore I celebrated the Mass for the first time in my priestly life, and whose anniversary year we are now keeping.

Blackfriars
Cambridge
Easter, 1990

ACKNOWLEDGMENTS

The author and publisher are grateful for the following permissions to reprint:

The Scottish Journal of Theology, published by the Scottish Academic Press, for an earlier version of chapter 1: "John Henry Newman and the Illative Sense," in vol. 38.3 (1985), pp. 347–368. © The Scottish Academic Press 1985.

The Downside Review, for an earlier version of chapter 4: "Anselm of Canterbury and the Language of Perfection,: in vol. 103.352 (1985), pp. 204–214.

New Blackfriars, for an earlier version of chapter 10: "Gabriel Marcel, Philosopher of Mystery: A Centenary Appraisal," in vol. 70.828 (1989), pp. 289–300.

The Chesterton Review, for an earlier version of chapter 11: "G. K. Chesterton's Argument for the Existence of God," in vol. 12.1 (1986), pp. 63–73.

Aitken and Stone, Ltd., publishers of *The Poems of St. John of the Cross*, translated by Roy Campbell, © 1979, for the use of the translation of "Noche oscura."

Constable and Co., Ltd., publishers of Helen Waddell's *Mediaeval Latin Lyrics*, © 1948, for the translation of "O mea cella."

INTRODUCTION: THE VOICES
OF EXPERIENCE

The aim of this book is to show how we can reasonably assent to the existence of God and, indeed, respond to God's presence in the depths of our experience. The fundamental contention is that human experience, when its inner order and coherence are drawn out by reason, proves to have a theistic order and coherence that are only fully explicable in terms of the reality of God. In this sense the title of this book, *A Grammar of Consent*, points back to the work done by John Henry Newman in his *Essay in Aid of a Grammar of Assent.*[1] Newman, as I shall show in the next chapter, highlighted the proper form that an argument for God's existence should take. This is neither deductive nor, in any strict, formal sense, inferential, as theological rationalists would hold; nor is it couched purely in terms of religious experience straitly so called, as many of their extreme opponents would allege. It is, rather, a cumulation of experiential cues (many of them apparently secular in character) that indicates the reasonableness of assent to the proposition, "God exists," although, in the nature of things, these cues cannot compel that assent. Yet this is not simply a restatement of Newman's *Essay*. I part company from Newman where the content of the argument for God's existence is concerned. I believe that Newman was mistaken in concentrating his energies so exclusively on one aspect of our experience, our awareness of moral obligation. There is, it seems, an irreducible plurality and a richness in the experiential indicators of God, just as there is in the texture of experience itself. Particular writers in the history of Christian philosophy, because of their particular backgrounds or biographies or temperaments, have illuminated now one, now another, aspect of this total

1

experiential field or flow that is the life of humankind. What we need to know is that these various pointers to a transcendence implicit in experience, yet going beyond it (as the word *transcendence* itself suggests), really do aim in the same direction. We need not simply a grammar of *assent* but a grammer of *consent*. The chapters of this book will try to unfold such a consenting harmony among the various voices who will be speaking through them.

The text will offer, then, in the first place, a sketch of the rational form of that thinking which issues in religious assent (introduction and chapter 1): here the aim is to show that the kind of thinking that leads to an affirmation of God's existence is reassuringly like the thinking that we employ in many everyday judgments about ourselves, our friends, those we meet, and the common world we share. As grammar derives the laws of language from everyday use, so a grammar of assent to the propositions of religion will try to show that religious thought is intimately related to the thought processes of everyday life. Second, the book will contain an apologia for the case that the concept of God, which religious thinking produces, has application in reality (chapters 2 to 11). The areas of experience that prove to be theistically evidential are more spacious than we may have suspected. The whole essay will also constitute something of a phenomenology of belief. The views adopted here on the subject of theistic belief involve an evocation of the inner "feel" of that belief, its experiential consistency. The grammar is in one sense unitary: it sees Newman's exposition as a substantially correct account of the nature and limits of reason in regard to religion. In another sense, however, the grammar is as manifold as the writers it describes and the readers into whose hands it may fall. As Newman saw, the personal reading of experience is indispensable in all assent to God.

PRIOR DISPOSITION AND EXPERIENCE

In speaking of the evidences of revealed religion, Newman stressed in both his Anglican and his Catholic periods the importance of prior disposition, of the attitudes that each spectator brings to the allegedly revelatory event. In the case of the evidences of natural religion, i.e., of the affirmation that God exists, Newman rarely touches on the possible analogues of such states of mind and heart as he took to be the individual's *praeparatio evangelica* before opening the Gospels, hearing the Word preached, assisting at the liturgy or studying the history of the Catholic church. I would like to suggest that a suitable analogue, where the basic affirmation of God's existence is concerned, lies in a certain confidence in our own experience. I shall try to explain myself.

The quest for religious truth has often been imagined as a journey, perhaps a mountain climb or, again, a pilgrimage. In terms of that metaphor, Catholic teaching has it that some at least of the resources we need for the journey are already given in our ordinary experience. We do not need to appeal to the authority of some revelation before we set off. Indeed, it is hard to see what sense we could make of the gift from without of a map unless we had first decided from within that there was a goal, and that a journey thither was worth the making. The tracks already lead out and up in a variety of directions.

Signposts and markers abound. The supplies that any traveler needs are available around us in the form of experiential confirmation or feedback to reassure us that we are progressing to some purpose. In the light of this metaphor, the problems of the person who is seeking to know if there is any ontological basis to religion, any foundation in reality for its claims, are twofold.

First of all, he or she must have sufficient confidence to trust his or her own experience, for this is a person's basic resource. By *experience* here I mean what at an unsophisticated level the man or woman in the street means by this word; or again, at a more reflective level, what a novelist might mean by it. I do not mean what philosophers of an empiricist bent have coerced that mauled and suffering word into signifying, for, as Donald Nicholl has written,

> No illusion has produced more baneful effects on modern thought than that which maintains all our experience to be sense-experience. The reason for this limitation is not far to seek; it arose from the prestige given by philosophers to seventeenth century physical science. Having noted the success of this science, which successfully used instruments in order to record impressions of the world, they tried to build up a picture of the world from the sort of impressions which are recorded on instruments. They tried to turn themselves into instruments receiving "impressions" (which an instrument, by the way, does not do), in order to work out what the world would look like if they themselves were instruments and not human beings. For this reason the Humians talked interminably about sense-data, as though sense-data were the original material upon which human beings have to work in order to construct a picture of the world. . . .

It is not surprising that the picture of the world presented by Hume (and his positivist successors) is not one which human beings recognise as the one in which they live.[2]

Theism cannot survive the adoption of materialist or empiricist accounts of knowing whose conceptual apparatus leads one to see reality as "a mechanistic" congeries "of elements, a bundle of un-thinking, purposeless, insignificant bits of matter or sensation."[3] But then no satisfactory account of human man's experience can survive those epistemologies either. An account of experience, like theism, depends on our approaching reality as "a molar, totalistic, meaningful whole . . . which contains many levels of meaning, and which different sorts of analysis can dissect in different ways."[4]

The absolutely indispensable condition in the search for the foundations of religion is a fundamental confidence in the capacity of the mind to take in the realities around it and within it—whatever shape these may prove to have. One must take one's own experience of the world *au sérieux*. Any other posture, indeed, will prove suicidal. Systematic skepticism or doubt must eventually saw off the branch on which they are sitting, for skepticism and doubt of this variety are as vulnerable to a dose of healthy skepticism and doubt as are any other theories of human knowledge. Sensitivity to the force of experience, on the other hand, leads us to uncover within experience itself all kinds of indications of further dimensions to the real. By it own weight, experience can propel us beyond itself into the sphere of a surrounding and undergirding reality, even though that reality cannot necessarily be felt on our pulses at any given moment.

The second prerequisite for the person who starts out on the religious quest is this: the person must not only trust his or her resources but also count and take stock of them. As I suggested in the preface, it is shortsighted in the extreme to believe that we can contextualize and interpret our experiential resources entirely by ourselves, as self-sufficient individualists. Since human beings know themselves primarily through the forms they produce (forms that vary from a philosophy to a sonnet to a scratched image in a catacomb), the possibilities of human experience can only be done full justice when we look back into the treasury of forms of our past. As the late nineteenth-century German philosopher Wilhelm Dilthey saw, contemporary life must be directed for its own possibilities to the forms fashioned by earlier generations where they are accessible to what he called *die verstehende Besinnung*, "comprehending recollection." In one sense we have no choice in this. The very language we speak has a powerful, if subtle, control over the scanning of reality, the interpreting of experience. And language, as Ludwig Wittgenstein so forcefully reminded us, is nothing if it is not public, corporate, and inherited.[6] But the very fact that each individual human being has a distinctive use of language, a personal voice, even though the distinctions between our favored idioms and images may be infinitesimal in certain cases, implies that our shared use of language does not in itself guarantee that we shall interpret our experiences in solidarity and communion with others. This is true whether the others in question are others who speak our own particular language, or whether they are others who have irradiated some aspect of human life through their writings (as with the figures we shall be considering in this book), or whether, finally, they are all the other language users of the earth, all the sons and daughters of Adam and Eve. It is only too painfully obvious that we can use language selectively to buttress and confirm our own prejudices and to disallow or discourage attitudes and evaluations that we find unfamiliar or uncongenial. For the most part, this is not a matter of bad faith; it is simply that we are not *educated* enough, in the most primary sense of that word: we are not sufficiently "drawn out" from our own individuality and practical egocentrism to be able to place our experience in the ampler interpretative context that awareness of what others have lived, thought, and suffered always gives.

This book will try to enable people to take stock of their experience of the world by placing various crucial aspects of experience in the interpretative contexts offered by a number of seminal thinkers of the past. In so doing it will hope to respond to that other need of the person in the search for the foundation of religion—the confidence that if only the cues of experience are followed up they will lead to ever-increasing illumination, to a condition where our experience becomes, so to speak, more palpably itself. This may sound thoroughly esoteric: in fact it is a commonplace. To have the experience but miss the meaning is a leitmotiv of the human condition. Fortunately, so is the discovery that experience takes on new clarity and depth when resituated with the benefit of hindsight. Our first impressions of a foreign country, the initial impact of a poem, the primordial stirrings of sexual desire in an adolescent—all of these are enhanced and enriched by the understanding that follows on picking up the cues that they first gave us. We come to grasp the meaning of our experiences by accepting an interpretative context for them. But that interpretative context, or the approximate direction in which to find it, is normally suggested by the very character of the experiences themselves. We take them not simply as hard facts but as pointers, cues, signs. In "The Dry Salvages," one of his *Four Quartets*, T. S. Eliot spoke of the moments of sudden illumination that punctuate human living. We may have the experience, he pointed out, yet miss the meaning. But he held out the possibility of our subsequent drawing close to the meaning in a way that both re-creates, "restores" the original force of the experience and enlarges, reshapes, re-forms it, rendering it transparent to an object greater than our hearts, "beyond any meaning/We can assign to happiness." Nor, so Eliot insisted, is this "past experience revived in the meaning" a matter, merely, of one individual's experience, or even that of an individual generation; it is, rather, the experience "of many generations."[7]

We shall be trying then, to make sense of vital aspects of experience; and we shall be doing that by deliberate exposure to what other people in the tradition of philosophical reflection in the Christian Church have made of those aspects of experience. Their subject matters are, to the best of my knowledge, constants of human living; they cannot but have some relation to our own lives. Obliquely, then, the reader is asked to carry out a reflection on her- or himself and her or his own experience. This is an "over-the-shoulder" kind of looking, for our object out front consists in a gallery of living images, men who have lived out experiences related to our own but have lived them out with an intensity and fidelity to their implications, their meaning, which in all likelihood enormously surpass any such qualities of which we might boast.

INTERPRETATIVE CONTEXTS

If this were all, though it would be much, it might well leave us in a somewhat disintegrated state. For shall we not finish with a series of disconnected partial readings of experience, a set of discreet interpretations of distinct aspects of life, not always an easy fit one with another? Will not the traveler be faced with a bewildering variety of possible tracks in wildly divergent directions? This will indeed be our situation unless we can suggest an overall context for our limited contexts, a view of what it is to produce a context for experiences that might suggest how to come by a context for experience *as a whole*. For it is here, as Wolfhart Pannenberg has insisted, that the question of God has its source.[8] It is here too that Newman's *Grammar of Assent* is invaluable; for it shows how one modality of reason, the most familiar in everyday life, works by sifting like and unlike fragments of evidence until in and through them it seizes a conclusion larger then they are. How else, Newman will ask, "does the mind fulfill its function of supreme direction and control, in matters of duty, social intercourse and taste?"[9] And in the pause that follows on his rhetorical question, he tells us:

> It is natural, then, to ask the question why ratiocination should be an exception to a general law which attaches to the intellectual exercises of the mind; why it is held to be commensurate with logical science; and why logic is made an instrumental art sufficient for determining every sort of truth, while no one would dream of making any one formula, however generalised, a working rule at once for poetry, the art of medicine, and political warfare. [10]

If the mind is thus possessed of an architectonic power to form the materials of awareness into a single and unified judgment that transcends them, it is possible to suppose that what we do with impressions of half-a-dozen types when we finally judge our next-door neighbor to be an honest man may have an analogue in a wider realm. Perhaps the equally varied aspects of human experience that strike us as signals, as somehow pointing beyond themselves, may also be gathered into a pattern. In such a case, the pattern would be *there*, woven into the cloth of the world, but its presence would be detected by a kind of reasoning closer to skill or art than to strict formal inference. In forming a context for experience as a whole, in raising the question of transcendence, it may be that "the practised and experienced mind is able to make a sure divination that a conclusion is inevitable, of which his lines of reasoning do not actually put him in possession."[11] In this "one complex act both of inference and of assent" Newman awarded a high place to symbol and image. They enabled us, he thought, to apprehend in a fashion he termed *real*, contrasting this with *notional*, what is being proposed to us in the language of religion. Thus of conscience, for him the principal quarry for theistic evidence, he could write: "Conscience, too, teaches not only that God is, but what he is; it provides for the mind a real image of him, as a medium of worship."[12] And again of Jesus of Nazareth, whose life is seen as the central revelation-bearing moment in Christianity, when he departed this world he was

> found, through his preachers, to have imprinted the Image or idea of himself in the minds of his subjects individually; and that Image, apprehended and worshipped in individual minds, becomes a principle of association, and a real bond of those subjects one with another, who are thus united to the body by being united to that Image; and moreover that Image, which is their moral life when they have been already converted, is also the original instrument of their conversion.[13]

In other words, Newman sees reason and imagination as working in tandem in engagement of the mind with the real.

We have here an account of what it is to be intelligently responsive to experience that, according to Keith Ward,

> allows an approach to reality which, though cognitive, yet depends essentially upon imaginative symbolism and creative personal response to what is apprehended. The very nature of such an approach would rule out the possibility of a detached experimental concern, which would be necessarily manipulative rather than responsive and interactive. . . . So, as one holds oneself prepared to discern a non-material source of values one may find that certain events or experiences do convey to one an apprehension of such a source, which may give a clue to the significance of one's life. . . . . Concepts which spring from situations in which some transcendent reality is mediated become images which one can use to evoke specific reactive attitudes and emotions, and which may be in some sense confirmed and amplified by personal experience.[14]

But the distinctive note of Newman's approach, echoed throughout this book, is the need to let such "apprehensions" or interpretations of experience rub off one on another. "I prefer to rely," he wrote, "on (the argument of) the *accumulation* of various probabilities."[15] As G. K. Chesterton wrote, one elephant having a trunk may be an accident; all elephants having trunks must be a conspiracy. In chapter 1, I shall offer a fuller account of Newman's essay, crucial to all that follows since that will presuppose the correctness of Newman's remarks on the form that argument to God's existence should take. It is, or should be, a matter of convergent probabilities, where various aspects of our experience take on a depth and coherence and yield themselves to an intelligible account of their being as they are only when we refer them to God as to their ground and goal. This concern with form is not to be set aside impatiently as formalist: a recent writer has gone so far as to say that, "basically, the inadequacy of traditional natural theology lies not in the areas of experience chosen as theistically evidential but in the elucidation of the way in which they count as evidence."[16] This is, perhaps, overstated, for those "areas of experience" are further flung than is often suggested, as chapters 2 to 11 of this book will show. For the argumentative form (perhaps better, persuasive form) adopted will be filled here with a very different content from that Newman gave it. In practice, Newman concentrated almost exclusively on the evidence of our moral experience as the sign par excellence in our world of a divine reality. I propose that Newman's form may be filled with a much richer, more generous, human experiential content than he gave it. I suggest that various figures in the history of reflection on God have pointed to diverse areas of experience and practice and reflection, all of which must be taken into account in exploring the foundations of theism. The history of Christian thought (for it is with that theism which has developed within the Christian religion that I am best acquainted) can itself be seen as constituting cumulative and convergent evidence for the reasonableness of belief in God. In this sense it is not so much one individual's personal assent to God which is our problem and model, but the consent of a variety of persons. Of course, in the end we have to decide to add our voice to that consent. But in so doing, the consent itself plays a vital role in extending our awareness of the range and variety of possible signals of the transcendent in our experience.

THE WRITERS' VOICES

The inflection of these various voices is diverse. The different approaches suggested occupy different points in the spectrum of formal and informal logic. Some have a "hard" logical form, other a "soft." Some aspects of our experience yield to a more rigorous representation in reflection; others can only be expressed and illumined by some kind of persuasive discourse. It is living that is prior to thinking, although living is, for human beings, already saturated with intelligibility: there is no *brute* experience. But because living is prior to thinking, it is only right that each aspect of experience should itself

prompt the style of reflection we adopt in its regard. It is in this sense
that I would take the protest of the Newman scholar John Coulson:
"Plato's distinction between responsible and irresponsible philosophis-
ing is particularly necessary nowadays; and I suggest the philosophis-
ing is irresponsibly conducted when it is divorced from the claims of
our experience and is reduced to the level of a puzzle which we contemplate in the unmoved manner of a fish in an aquarium."[17] Similarly, while pointing out that religion is larger than religious experience,
Gabriel Daly, O.S.A., in his study of Catholic modernism and its
aftermath, has chronicled the lamentable effects of the virtual outlaw-
ing of an appeal to "experience as a factor in religon, theology, and
spirituality."

> The victory of integralism resulted in the virtual exclusion of the term
> "experience" from the Roman Catholic theological vocabulary. . . . As
> several of the modernists had pointed out, lack of an immanent dimen-
> sion in theology and spirituality inevitably produces a coarsening of reli-
> gious outlook. It is only when we have appreciated the implications of this
> spiritual malnutrition that we are in a position to evaluate much that is
> happening by way of reaction in the Roman Catholic Church of today.[18]

The recovery of some more satisfactory integration of reason and
feeling in theology later this century must be set to the everlasting
credit of the Church in France. In a representative product of that
theological renewal, Régis Jolivet, then dean of the Institut Catholique
in Paris, wrote that argument for the existence of God, if it is to do
justice to its subject, must be forever trembling into awareness of the
presence of God; God is first a problem and then a mystery for our
knowledge; in reality he is first of all mystery, and it is we who are the
problem. By being separated through excessive abstraction from the
living experience that they imply, the proofs of God's existence can
only seem cold and dry, a conceptual game. Their roots must be kept
intact if they are to flourish, and the soil into which these roots go
down is "the presence of God in everything that exists and especially
in the spiritual and moral life"; and he goes on to say that the question is more a matter of "uncovering" God than of "proving" God:

> We only "prove" what is absent; the present which at first is veiled or dis-
> guised, is uncovered. . . . Our knowledge of God presupposes that at first
> he is hidden and mysterious, and when achieved it realises that it is never
> finished, and that the discovery of God is never-ending.[19]

And he remarks, in words that Newman would have rejoiced to hear,

> The fact must not be disguised that all these arguments in connexion with the existence and nature of God remain inadequate to translating and rendering explicit in conceptual terms (as they try to do) our deep human experience. They have no chance of convincing us except insofar as they awaken or re-awaken in us the sense of a creative and vivifying presence.[20]

So far, the writers alluded to have at least in common the Christian faith. In this book, the choice of philosophical figures from within the Christian tradition (as distinct from another theistic community, such as Jewry, where another gallery could have been brought together in such people as Moses Maimonides, Martin Buber, and Emmanuel Lévinas) is deliberate. But the implications of that choice could easily be overrated as well as underrated. I am not implying that Christian revelation is the necessary key to a sound theism at this most elementary (if fundamental) level. For a Catholic writer, that position is, arguably, ruled out of court by the definitions of an ecumenical council, the First Vatican Council of 1870:

> The same Holy Mother Church holds and teaches that God, the beginning and end of all things, may be certainly known by the natural light of human reason, by means of created things, "for the invisible things of him from the creation of the world are clearly seen, being understood by the things that are made" (Romans 1:20).[21]

It is surely clear enough that there are other theistic traditions than the Christian, notably the Jewish, the Islamic, and certain varieties of the Hindu, not to mention segments of the religions formerly known as primitive and now more usually referred to as "traditional." To these may be added the personal syntheses of individuals. On the other hand, I do not think that Christian revelation is wholly irrelevant to the philosophy of religion. In a well-known passage in his *Memorial*, Pascal opposes the "God of the philosophers and scholars" to the God of Christian revelation, "the God of Jesus Christ." Surely this will not do either. No direct appeal can be made to faith in a purely rational enquiry: so much may be conceded, and to that extent Pascal's schism in the conceptualizing of God is justified. When the Christians of the second century called Christianity "our philosophy" they did not mean that their religion was itself a form of philosophical exploration. They used the phrase with a certain irony intended to convey that in an age when philosophy, as the search for beatitude through wisdom, was seen as an all-embracing way of life their ultimate commitment was to the person of Christ as himself incarnate Wisdom. But the mainstream Christian tradition has found that there is a distinctively Christian way of exercising reason, a "Christian philosophy," just as the mainstream philosophical tradition in the West has found that its discussions have been usefully extended and enriched by the intellectual initiatives of believers, so that Christianity may be said to have opened up new philosophical perspectives for culture at large. Insofar as believers base their affirmations on revealed religion they remain purely and simply believers. Should they find that some at any rate of their beliefs are capable of being laid out in rational terms they become philosophers also. And if they find that some insight, which can be shown to be genuinely philosophical, to stand up on its own legs, so to speak, is owed by them to their Christian faith, there is really no contradiction (*pace* Pascal) in calling them Christian philosophers. It seems likely, for example, that the notion of personhood is the fruit of Christian philosophy. And as we shall see, Pascal himself, despite his outburst in the *Memorial*, is not the last impressive example of the species. Maurice Blondel, a modern disciple of Pascal, answered his master when he wrote that "the philosopher does not find in the thought of a living and transcendent Truth, which possesses itself and gives itself, a theory incapable of standing up to criticism; he can reconcile the God of Abraham and of the Gospel with the most stringent demands of reason."[22] The mood of the sentence is odd (Blondel says the philosopher "does not" where we should expect "need not" and "can" where we should suppose "may," but the sentiments are unexceptionable. The primary relation of Christianity to philosophy, or of revelation to reason, that is presupposed in this book, then, is that Christianity (revelation) can open up for philosophy (reason) perspectives on the way things are that may then be claimed (one hopes gratefully) by the recipient in its own right.[23]

No apology will be made for the choice of various thinkers from the *past* of the Christian tradition as the starting-points for the various avenues of approach here displayed. Thus Jaroslav Pelikan concludes his study, *Historical Theology*: "The historical process needs to be seen by Christians as a medium of growth, not as a source of embarrassment."[24] More strongly, Karl Barth has this to say:

There is no past in the Church, so there is no past in theology. "In him they all live." Only the heretic, indeed only the arch-heretic, the one who is totally lost even for God's invisible Church, could really belong to the past and have nothing more to say to us. And we are in no position to identify such arch-heresy. . . . The theology of any period must be strong and free enough to give a calm, attentive and open hearing not only to the voices of the Church Fathers, not only to favourite voices, but to all the voices of the past. . . . We cannot anticipate which of our fellow-workers from the past are welcome in our work and which are not. It may always be that we have especial need of quite unsuspected (and among these of quite unwelcome) voices in one sense or another. So history, the history of the Church, of doctrine and of theology enters the theological work-shop and becomes a theological task.[25]

Contact with tradition is vital to every human generation because of the need for keeping open all possible imaginative options. We must not allow ourselves to get imprisoned within the terms of reference of contemporary presentations of what is, and is not, real. This is not just a matter of noticing that certain arguments have been worked out by our predecessors (the customary and, so far as it goes, wholly adequate defense of the study of the history of philosophy). It is also a question of openness to cues for fresh ways of interpreting the business of being human. At the present time, orthodox believers belong to what the sociologists call a *cognitive minority*. Their worldview does not receive much in the way of sustenance and support from society at large. This lack of confirmatory signals from others can certainly undermine religious faith, unless a person is especially strong willed. We should not imagine that *aggiornamento* and "coming out of the ghetto" are processes in which no milk is spilt: what is spilt may even, from time to time, be cream. In itself the fact that a proposition is entertained as true, or false, by a majority of one's contemporaries is not a reason for holding it to be true, or false. Nevertheless, the pressure to conform leads ineluctably towards reductionism and finally apostasy if nothing is done to resist it by suitable strategies. Playing something of the same role here that Peter Berger has ascribed to the sociology of knowledge as a discipline, awareness of tradition can free us from the tyranny of the present and relativize the relativizers. So often there is a kind of pernicious double standard at work in the way people evaluate the belief systems of the past. The past, from which tradition comes, is relativized in terms of this or that sociohistorical

analysis, yet the present is graciously endowed with a curious immu-
nity to such relativization: "Truths can be discovered or rediscovered.
Truths can also be lost or forgotten again. History is not the night in
which all cats are grey, but neither is it a giant escalator ascending to
the point at which we happen to stand."[26]

In the course of his fascinating essay, *A Rumour of Angels*, Berger
points out that while such appeal to tradition may help us to render
more supple our sense of "cognitive fit" as we size up the world around
us, this is not really enough by itself to undermine reductionism and
relativism. Ludwig Feuerbach prophesied correctly in the nineteenth
century that in the modern period men and women would come to
see the sense of God as one gigantic projection of humankind's own
sense of itself: humankind writ large. Sociology, psychology, and various other disciplines all have their own pet version of this "religion-
is-nothing-but . . . " approach to things. However, so Berger goes on,
what appears as a human projection in one frame of reference may
appear as a reflection of divine realities in another. And he concludes
with a suggestion that suits perfectly the temper of this book:

> It would seem that any theological method worthy of the name should be
> based on this possibility. This most emphatically does not mean a search
> for religious phenomena that will somehow manifest themselves as differ-
> ent from human projection. Nothing is immune to the relativisation of
> socio-historical analysis. Whatever else these phenomena may be, they
> will also be human projections, products of human history, social con-
> structions undertaken by human beings. The meta-empirical cannot be
> conceived of as a kind of enclave within the empirical world. . . . The
> theological decision will have to be that "in, with and under" the immense
> array of human projections, there are indicators of a reality that is truly
> "other" and that the religious imagination of man ultimately reflects.[27]

PLAUSIBLE OBJECTIONS

I would like to finish this introduction by putting forth two plausible objections to the approach of this book. First of all, it may be said
that a grammar of consent is an impossible plum pudding of a confec-
tion. The reader is being offered a quite bewildering variety of different philosophical voices—divergent philosophical approaches laid
end to end without any real attempt to cope with their intrinsic lack

of fit. Can we make use of a variety of metaphysical systems simultaneously without suffering from chronic pains in the head? Shall we not end up with a sort of theologian's nonsense verse, a work where each word may be meaningful but not in the way the author has arranged them? To this there are two replies.

First, I am not suggesting that the reader should attempt to adopt simultaneously all the metaphysical systems espoused by the various figures described in this book. To do so would indeed be intellectual suicide and perhaps a very good way to send oneself to Bedlam. All I am proposing is that we should attend as carefully as possible to what they have to say about particular aspects of human experience that for them were crucial in the approach to God. Their illumination of these is partially, though not perhaps wholly, distinguishable from their wider speculative systems (where they had such). Thus, for instance, one may accept Kant's account of moral obligation while preserving a prudent reticence about his theory of knowledge. But further, the objection in some cases may be based on the supposition that there is a final and perennially true metaphysical system in a quite straightforward sense—if only we could find it. Frederick Copleston, S. J., in his book *Religion and Philosophy*, remarks that in one sense there must be such an animal, but in another sense there could never be. He points out that some propositions must be true if we are to speak of a world of finite things at all. They express what he calls "the logical scaffolding of the world."[28] If a coherent arrangement of such propositions could reasonably be described as a metaphysical system, that a perfectly true metaphysical system exists is indeed a possibility. But the statements of such a system would scarcely be intellectually exhilarating. There remains another, and complementary, view of what a metaphysical system might be. A philosophical vision may well be founded on the assumption that some feature or features of the world—which could conceivably be absent or other than they are—provide a key or keys to the nature of reality as a whole. In this sense the request for a final metaphysical system is hopeless and counterproductive. For it is always possible to focus attention on other features of the world and so to construct a rather different worldview. Such worldviews are persuasive invitations, invitations to see the world in ways in which it cannot be taken for granted that we do in fact see it. (Notice here that it is not assumed that these worldviews are mere *bliks*, perspectives adopted without explicit reference to their rational resources.) In the clash or dialectic

of various attempts to gain conceptual mastery of the transcendent—
the Ground and Goal of our experience, we have a witness, Copleston
thinks, to the divine transcendence itself as well as to the limitations
of the human mind. *Deus semper maior.* Copleston concludes by suggesting that the dialectic of systems also bears witness to the fact that
human effort alone cannot draw back the veil that hides the transcendent. It will be removed only where God discloses himself to humankind through his own initiative in revelation. The mind's own
exploration of existence, which leads in theism to the apprehension of
the transcendent God, should be seen as propaedeutic to revelation, a
preparing of the ground, and not as an alternative to revelation. The
natural relationship to God that we explore in philosophy turns out
to carry a summons to a more personal, intersubjective kind of relationship, the relationship of grace which we explore in theology.[29]
The God who allows himself to be known in our exploration of the
general structures of existence then positively discloses himself to us
through the particularities of his living images in persons and events
in history. The God of the philosophers is indeed the same God as the
Father of Jesus Christ, but he is known in two different fashions. In
the Letter to the Romans Paul affirms that "ever since God created the
world his everlasting power and deity—however invisible—have been
there for the mind to see in the things he has made" (Romans 1:20).
Yet Paul also affirms in the same letter that this is finally poor stuff
when compared with the full vision of the glory of God disclosed in
the mercy and faithfulness of Jesus Christ, "the love of God made visible in Christ Jesus our Lord" (Romans 8:39).

A second objection might run as follows. The claim of this book is
that theistic philosophy has a greater coordinating and synthesizing
power for our experience than has any atheistic or nontheistic
worldview. Theistic philosophy can bring into mutually illuminating
relationships a wide variety of forms of human experience. In the
now-hackneyed phrase of the later Wittgenstein, it unites a whole
series of "language games." Very well; but in seeking so many different
routes of assent to God, does not this approach fail to ensure that
what is being assented to is really the same object? Is the grammar of
consent not in fact a cacophony, because the conversation it contains
is proceeding at cross-purposes? E. L. Mascall has warned against the
sophistry of implicitly assuming "a minimal definition of God in arguing for his existence and a much more ample definition in discussing
his nature."[30] In these pages there will be no formal discussion of the

divine attributes; but in the course of tracing the movement of thought that carried each of the authors described here to the conclusion that God exists, a view of God's nature will be progressively constructed for those who can read between the lines. As Ward has written: "The various strands of the concept of God elucidate the various areas of experience within which an attitude of response to a transcendent ground of experience seems to find some objective correlate."[31] But this may also be seen from the other end of the telescope: reflection on various areas of experience indicates the strands that must be woven into our concept of God. How may we rule out a polytheism that would see in each of these evidential areas the manifestation of one divinity among others? At least one of the key areas we shall be looking at, that mapped by Immanuel Kant, indicates the centrality of the concept of an absolute moral value and purpose, such as only a unitary image of the divine could sustain (see chapter 8). There is a confluence here between what has come to be a "given" of philosophical rationality, namely that the Source and Goal of all things must itself be one (else we should need to posit a Source and Goal for the divinities that participate in transcendent being) and the religious tradition of Judaeo-Christianity which, at least in modern times, first presented the philosophers with its own unification of the images of transcendence around the central notion of an absolute moral demand and enabling power.[32]

1

JOHN HENRY NEWMAN AND THE ILLATIVE SENSE

Our first task must be to set forth more fully the basic structure of argument to the existence of God that this book will presuppose. As already indicated, that structure is laid out in its fundamental form in John Henry Newman's *Essay in Aid of a Grammar of Assent.* In the succeeding chapters, the reader will be asked to exercise his or her illative sense on the various experiential materials, relevant to the theistic case, that the study of now one, now another, writer in the tradition highlights. Thus the first prerequisite is to clarify what faculty this may be that the reader is invited to use.

In this chapter, I shall consider, first, in what sense Newman (1801–1890) may be called a natural theologian; second, I shall give an account of the notion of the illative sense within the developing pattern of Newman's thought; finally, I shall suggest that by a unilateral concentration on moral experience – the "voice of conscience" – Newman failed to do justice to the full significance of his own argumentation. The point of the illative sense is not that it helps us to identify any one experiential content or area of reflection that might lead us to theistic belief, but that it provides an overall context in which a variety of experiential strata and argumentative strategies may be displayed. Newman was, perhaps, too dominated by a sense of his personal history in the realm of fundamental belief in God to identify and correct the individualism that in dogmatic theology proper he would have avoided. Our theistic materials do not lie simply within our own breasts but in an inter-rogation of the entire theistic tradition as it is mediated to us by the classic texts of our predecessors.

REVELATION AND RATIONALITY

The intrinsic ecclesiastical interest of Newman's career has tended to overshadow his original contribution to natural theology. The feeling—the general belief among those who know something (but not very much) about Newman and the philosophy of religion—is that one who was so thoroughly a churchman, and so consumed by the principles involved in intra-ecclesiastical debate, both ancient and modern, will not have much to offer outside the *particular* theological world born of Christian revelation. For natural theology may be defined as what human experience *in general* can do to point us to its own transcendent ground and meaning. But this feeling is not justified. Christian revelation may be in a position to serve philosophy and not just to exploit it or even, as has happened in some historical situations (Tertullian's Carthage, Savonarola's Florence, Luther's Wittenberg), to serve notice of summary expropriation. With the late Etienne Gilson,[1] one can hold that revelation can be of use to philosophy by helping it to identify areas of reflection likely to prove rewarding in the exploration of being and the manifestation of being, meaning.

But even those who subscribe to this position in principle do not find a major role in the story of Christian philosophy for Newman the preacher, ascetic, would-be reformer of the Church of England, and finally cardinal priest of the Church of Rome.[2] The theme that holds together the distinctive moments of his life seems to be ecclesiological rather than philosophical. The silver-voiced Oxford preaching, the controversial journalism, the eventual gesture of submission to papal authority in the person of Father Dominic Barberi as the English rain thundered its disapproval on Littlemore; then the sacramental ministry among the Birmingham poor; the physically withdrawn but impassioned involvement in the Catholic politics of the day: the unity of these lies in a life-long passion for one idea. What and where is the Church of Jesus Christ? What are its proper structures and what the authentic inner spirit which should inspire them? These are manifestly extraphilosophical questions, but they possessed Newman's mind. Yet this is not, in fact, the end of the story.

At the close of his *Essay on the Development of Christian Doctrine,* Newman sums up his account of the Church as moving continually between "slumber" and "restoration," yet preserving an unmistakable identity through many transformations. He goes on:

Such were the thoughts concerning the "Blessed Vision of Peace," of one whose long-continued petition had been that the Most Merciful would not despise the work of His own Hands, nor leave him to himself, while yet his eyes were dim, and his breast laden, and he could but employ Reason in the things of Faith. And now, dear Reader, time is short, eternity is long. Put not from you what you have found; regard it not as mere matter of present controversy; set not out resolved to refute it, and looking about for the best way of doing so; seduce not yourself with the imagination that it comes of disappointment, or disgust, or restlessness, or wounded feeling, or undue sensibility, or other weakness. . . . Time is short, eternity long.[3]

These are, admittedly, the tones of a preacher, and a preacher who takes as his text the great orthodox dogmas of God, Christ, and the Church. This is true even though Newman set his materials in a context of intellectual inquiry, in that perspective of the historically developmental character of human understanding which he did as much as any Victorian thinker to open up. It is at least intelligible, therefore, that the editor of Newman's *Letters and Diaries*, the late Stephen Dessain of the Birmingham Oratory, could write:

The fundamental interest of Newman's life is his devotion to the cause of Revealed Religion. He was led to accept it whole-heartedly as a boy, and to seek out its full and balanced content. This devotion gave his life its unity. It led him to become the leader in a movement to re-invigorate and supernaturalise the Church of England; it caused him to abandon it for the Roman Church; it made him try to remedy various deficiencies he found there, and to moderate excesses. In many of his efforts he failed at the time, but history has vindicated him, and the Catholic movement of reform has hailed him as a prophet. He was always a herald of forgotten truths.[4]

But the passage I have cited from Newman's essay on the development of doctrine should give us pause. Newman writes, he tells us, as one who "could but employ Reason in the things of Faith." Among the various ways in which religion was rationally commended in the age of romanticism, Newman's nuanced sense of the relation between philosophy and religious belief stands out for its sanity. Not the least aspect of his prophetic quality or of his heralding forgotten truths lies

in his stress on the need to approach "Revealed Religion" as a reasoning animal.[5]

For Newman, we find revelation in a direction already suggested by
the life of ordinary experience and the life of reason, which consists in
reflection on that same experience. As reasoning beings, we can and
must seek to integrate our experience at the level of understanding.
We have to try to discern its deep structure, to see whether there may
be a significant form latent within it. And when we do this, or so
Newman considered, we find that this form points beyond itself to the
mystery that we name "God."

THE "UNIVERSITY SERMONS"

The primary source for Newman's reflections on the rationality of
religious belief is his *Essay in Aid of a Grammar of Assent*. But the
themes that he laid out there in a more rigorous philosophical form
he had already stated many years previously in his *University Sermons*.[6] Between 1839 and 1841 Newman preached five sermons on the
relation of faith and reason before the University of Oxford. Newman's
concern in these homilies is to communicate a wider and juster view
of this relationship than the currently favored one that was preoccupied with evidences. In an apologetic tradition dating back into the
previous century, the rational basis of Christianity was excogitated
out of a set of objective data or evidences: for the existence of God,
these might be found in the design of the hummingbird or the human
eye; for the divinity of Christ, in his miracles and fulfillment of proph-
ecy. But the evidence, as Newman pointed out, can be seen in many
lights and appears more or less convincing with every change of
observer. What is seen, in the sense of what appears on the retina,
does not oblige the reasoning mind to surrender to God in faith.
What *does* make for the acceptance of Christianity, for the Christian
interpretation of these evidences, is the existence of prior dispositions
in the person. These dispositions, while they cannot be created by
reason, can be judged by reason and found not unreasonable: "A
judge does not make men honest, but acquits and vindicates them; in
like manner Reason need not be the origin of Faith, as Faith exists in
the very persons believing, though it does test and verify it."[7] The
assumption that reason must be the inward principle of action in religious inquiries or conduct is "the mistake of a critical for a creative
power." It is a confusion, to take up Newman's own simile, between

the power of poetry and the art of criticism, a case of mistaken identity, one might say, as between Keats and the editor of the *Edinburgh Review*.

In these sermons Newman is not engaged, in fact, in persuading to belief in God. He is presupposing that and going on to encourage a positive and wholehearted response to the truth-claims of Christian orthodoxy as he then saw it, "the promise of the Gospel." Naturally enough, therefore, his account of the "previous notices, prepossessions, and (in a good sense of the word) prejudices"[8] necessary to educe from the evidences of revealed religion their transcendent dimension already presumes acceptance of God's existence. Newman is concerned primarily with the man or woman who affirms the existence of God but is in a quandary as to whether this God has revealed himself personally in history. This is the man or woman who will be convinced by the evidence if he or she enjoys certain antecedent dispositions, among which Newman lists "love of the great Object of faith, watchful attention to him, readiness to believe him near, easiness to believe him interposing in human affairs, fear of the risk of slighting or missing what may really come from him."[9] Nevertheless, Newman is clearly working towards a distinctive view of the interrelation of three factors—disposition, evidence, and reason—which he will find serviceable in the analysis of a still more fundamental religious act, the affirmation that God exists.

One of the rare points in these homilies where Newman speaks of the evidences of natural (as distinct from revealed) religion, and so of the evidence for God's existence (as distinct from God's self-communication), comes in a passage on two modalities of human reason that anticipates the argument of the *Grammar of Assent*. What Newman calls "implicit reason" here may be paraphrased as the attempt to do intellectual justice to the entire texture of our experience. Of its operation he writes:

> The mind ranges to and fro, and spreads out, and advances forward with a quickness which has become a proverb, and a subtlety and versatility which baffle investigation. It passes on from point to point, gaining one by some indication; another on a probability; then availing itself of an association; then falling back on some received law; next seizing on testimony; then committing itself to some popular impression, or some inward instinct, or some obscure memory; and thus it makes progress not unlike a clamberer on a steep cliff, who, by quick eye, prompt hand, and firm

foot, ascends, how he knows not himself, by personal endowments and by practice, rather than by rule, leaving no track behind him, and unable to teach another.[10]

The implication of the comparison with mountaineering, an increasingly popular pursuit after the Lake Poets, is clear. Through its sifting of experience, the "living spontaneous energy" of the implicitly reasoning mind can strike out towards conclusions, just as a fell-walker strikes out towards the hilltops of the Cumbrian countryside.

Contrasted with implicit reason is Newman's "explicit reason," which turns out to be the analysis of this whole movement of spontaneous interpretation of experience. Within that analysis particular kinds of conceptual or causal linkage as studied by more conventional logic and metaphysics have their rightful place.

When the mind reflects upon itself, it begins to be dissatisfied with the absence of order and method in the exercise, and attempts to analyse the various processes which take place during it, to refer one to another, and to discover the main principles on which they are conducted, as it might contemplate and investigate its faculty of memory or imagination.[11]

This second-order activity enables us to understand the type of rationality that attaches to many of our judgments in ordinary life, on matters great and small. A good instance thereof is Newman's homily itself.

Yet it is implicit reason that is crucial in living and for which formal qualifications in logic, while certainly not useless, are not decisive either. "All men have a reason, but not all men can give a reason." The significance of evidence, of discrete moments in experiential flow, will depend partly on whether we are judging it by implicit or explicit reasoning. It will be one thing as caught in the play of implicit reason, where it is connected to, and illuminated by, other aspects of our experience, whether direct or by testimony. It will be quite another thing when, withdrawn from that flow, the evidences are set up as objects of independent and isolated inspection. Then a datum will have a much weaker power to arrest our intellectual attention. Similarly, in the religious realm, an atomism of privileged facts is no adequate basis for the act of faith. So Newman affirms that "whereas mere probability proves nothing, mere facts persuade no one; . . . probability is to fact, as the soul to the body; . . . mere presumptions may have no force, but . . . mere facts have no warmth."[12] A grasp of human beings' structure as knowing agents enables us, therefore, to say that not all assertions that transcend experience, but that the materials of experience prompt us to make, are abuses of reason. They will not be beyond reason simply because they go beyond the evidence.[13] Reason itself tends to exceed the evidence: if it did not—and this remained Newman's conviction throughout his life—human living would be rendered impossible.

THE "GRAMMAR OF ASSENT"

Early in 1870, some thirty years after the texts we have been exploring, Newman published his *Essay in Aid of a Grammar of Assent.*[14] He had been making drafts for such a work on the philosophy of religion for perhaps the entire intervening period.[15] The shift of apologetic interest from a defense of Christian dogma in the 1830s and 1840s to argument for the rationality of belief in God's mere existence at the turn of the 1860s itself reflects the changing religious world of Victorian England. At the start of Victoria's reign the Evangelical movement was at the height of its popular influence; by her middle years the varieties of unbelief among her subjects had multiplied bewilderingly. Newman himself seems to have seen the *Grammar of Assent* as his most intimately personal response to his age, the least ad hoc affair of all his works:

> What I have written has been for the most part what may be called official works done in some office or engagement I had made—all my sermons are such, my lectures on the prophetical office, on justification, my essays in the *British Critic* and translation of St. Athanasius—or has been from some especial call, or invitation, or necessity, or emergency, as my Arians, Anglican Difficulties, Apologia or Talks. The Essay on Assent is nearly the only exception. . . . I had felt it on my conscience for years, that it would not do to quit the world without doing it.[16]

Newman has puzzled many readers by this work, despite Aldous Huxley's accolade that "its analysis of the psychology of thought is one of the most acute, as it is certainly the most elegant, which has ever been made."[17] The book plunges into its subject without a word of introduction as to its author's purposes. But in fact Newman did explain his project elsewhere. In December 1877 his fellow Oratorian, the hymn-writer Edward Caswall, noted on the flyleaf of his own copy of the book the gist of a conversation with Newman about it: "Object of the book twofold. In the first part shows that you can believe what you cannot understand. In the second part, that you can believe what you cannot absolutely prove."[18] The book is indeed a diptych. One way of describing its twofold articulation is to say that in the first part, "Assent and Apprehension," Newman shows how personal, and particularly imaginative, acceptance of the dogmas of the Church is possible, even though the truths concerned are mysteries beyond the capacity of reason to understand completely; in the second part, "Assent and Inference," Newman suggests how we can rationally justify this personal and imaginative adhesion. We can use the materials of experience to come to an unconditional assertion of God's existence (and of the propositions of revealed religion) even when we would not be justified in concluding to these things by strict inference. It is with the second part of the *Grammar* that we are chiefly concerned here, but a glance at the first is necessary for an understanding of the whole.

REAL ASSENT: IMAGINATION AND DOGMA

Newman sets out by distinguishing assent, which is unconditional and personal, from inference, which is a logical procedure bound for the truth-value of its conclusions to the validity of the premises it assumes. He goes on to say that we cannot assent to what we in no sense understand. Yet the nature of our assent depends on whether the propositions placed before us for our minds to dwell upon express something *notional* or something *real*. *Real apprehension* is "in the first instance an experience of or an information about the concrete." *Notional apprehension*, on the other hand, takes place when for some, perhaps perfectly good, reason, the concrete has become the abstract; the particular, the general; and the image, a notion.

> It is plain what a different sense language will bear in this system of intellectual notions from what it has when it is the representative of things. . . . Thus it comes about that individual propositions about the concrete almost cease to be, and are diluted or starved into abstract notions . . . all that fulness of meaning which I have described as accruing to language from experience, now that experience is absent necessarily becomes to the multitude of men nothing but a heap of notions, little more intelligible than the beauties of a prospect to the short-sighted, or the music of a great master to a listener who has no ear.[19]

So there are two uses of propositions, each with "its own excellence and serviceableness": both the kind that evokes experiential flow, with its rich and concrete plenitude, and the kind that simply generalizes from limited aspects of this experience. But of the two, Newman hands the palm unhesitatingly to the first:

> Without the apprehension of notions, we should for ever pace round one small circle of knowledge; without a firm hold upon things, we shall waste ourselves in vague speculations. However, real apprehension has the precedence, as being the scope and end and the test of the notional; and the fuller is the mind's hold upon things or what it considers such, the more fertile is it in its aspects of them and the more practical in its definitions.[20]

The weakness of real apprehension and assent, or at least its apparent "imperfection," lies in its dependence on what is personally experienced. Such dependence may seem to threaten human intercourse and community as well as the possibilities of agreed tests and controls on our assertions which these provide. But this is an inevitable price to pay, since real apprehension is impossible without a personal exercise of imagination.

> We cannot make sure first, for ourselves or for others, of real apprehension and assent, because we have to secure first the images which are their objects, and these are often peculiar and special. They depend on personal experience; and the experience of one man is not the experience of another.[21]

Such images are not available except within a common culture of language and metaphor; yet by a paradox they are also personal to the point of incommunicability in actual use.[22] As Newman grew older, his view of imagination came to resemble that of S. T. Coleridge: the image is "translucent" to the greater concrete reality that it serves.[23] Imagination is, therefore, a means of access to truth. But it is also, and here the moral seriousness of Tractarianism adds a nuance to the Coleridgean "common tradition," a means to action. Real assent, viewed simply in itself, does not lead us to act, yet "the images in which it lives, representing as they do the concrete, have the power of the concrete upon the affections and passions, and by means of these indirectly become operative."[24]

Applying this to the sphere of religion, Newman remarks that a dogma, since it is a proposition, may stand for either a notion or a thing. The notion and the reality assented to are represented in the same linguistic act but serve as distinct interpretations of it.

> The proposition that there is one personal and present God may be held in either way; either as a theological truth or as a religious fact or reality. . . . It is discerned, rested in and appropriated as a reality by the religious imagination; it is held as a truth by the theological intellect.[25]

Imagination is therefore not only an analogy for belief; it is itself involved with belief. Not simply will and ratiocination but the power to form images and respond to them is taken up by grace to constitute Christian revelation and Christian believing. As a result, devotion (the imaginative response of the believer) and dogma (the reflective articulation of the theologian) are complementary and interdependent activities in the life of the Church. The same formula that "embodies a dogma for the theologian, readily suggests an object for the worshipper."[26] Thus the propositions of faith are valuable in their dogmatic aspect "as making clear for us the truths on which the religious imagination has to rest."[27] It is by means of the Church, the Scriptures, the sacraments, and indeed the sign of the crucifix "in every house and chamber" that "Christ lives, to our imaginations, in his visible symbols";[28] but without the ability to "hold" the same christological content "as a truth, by the intellect," the life of faith falls a prey to rationalism or to superstition.

> Theology may stand as a substantive science, though it be without the life of religion; but religion cannot maintain its ground at all without theology. Sentiment, whether imaginative or emotional, falls back upon the intellect for its stay, when sense cannot be called into exercise; and it is in this way that devotion falls back upon dogma.[29]

REAL ASSENT: RATIONALITY AND BELIEF

In the second part of the *Grammar of Assent*, Newman discusses not how the revelation of God in Christ, through Scripture and tradition, enters into our imaginative experience in the Church but whether or not the belief that does so is rationally justified. After all, as Newman himself points out, "When I assent to a proposition, I ought to have some more legitimate reason for doing so than the brilliancy of the image of which that proposition is the expression."[30] Nevertheless, in Newman's view, the kind of experience that gives us clear, rich, and fertile images for God is also the kind of experience to which we should look for validation of the claim that God exists in the first place.

Newman had told Caswall that this second wing of the diptych was meant to show that "you can believe what you cannot absolutely prove." By "you can believe" Newman meant "you have a legitimate intellectual right to believe," not "you have a psychological capacity for believing." Newman's aim was to explain how faith, either in its specifically religious sense or in the more general applications of the word in English usage ("I have faith in her veracity"), is a reasonable act even when based on something less than strict demonstration. Newman had in mind two classes of people. In the first was the educated person trained to evaluate evidence and handle argument. In any question beyond the trivial, the educated were encouraged only to give their assent when proof was forthcoming and to see the acceptance of more than was strictly, logically or scientifically, demonstrated as an offense against truth. This was the position of Newman's friend and correspondent William Froude, brother of the flawed Tractarian saint Richard Hurrell Froude, whose posthumously published *Remains* had underlined the unconventionality of the Oxford movement in matters of personal religion. William Froude wrote to Newman some years before the publication of the *Grammar*: "even the highest attainable probability does not justify the mind in discarding the residuum of doubt." And for good measure he added that any attempt to tip the balance of someone's judgment in the decision of faith by any other than rational considerations was "distinctly an immoral use of faculties." As the editor of the Newman-Froude correspondence put it, Froude "considered faith, as the theologians explained it, to be another word for 'prejudice'—i.e. as the formation of a judgment, irrespective of, or out of proportion to, the evidence on which it rests."[31] Newman paraphrased the objection in his own distinctive terms: "Thus assent becomes a sort of necessary shadow, following upon inference, which is the substance and is never without some alloy of doubt, because inference in the concrete never reaches more than probability."[32] His preliminary reply is to deny that in fact such a theory can be carried out in ordinary social practice:

> It may be rightly said to prove too much; for it debars us from unconditional assent in cases in which the common voice of mankind, the advocates of this theory included, would protest against the prohibition. There are many truths in concrete matter, which no one can demonstrate yet

every one unconditionally accepts; and though of course there are innu-
merable propositions to which it would be absurd to give an absolute
assent, still the absurdity lies in the circumstances of each particular case,
as it is taken by itself, not in their common violation of the pretentious
axiom that probable reasoning can never lead to certitude.[33]

If human nature is to be "its own witness," Froude's objection must be
dismissed by the common voice of "high and low, young and old,
ancient and modern," as continually expressed "in their ordinary say-
ings and doings."[34] What this appeal to the usage of the marketplace
implies will be explored in a moment.

Besides the learned and the rationalistic, Newman had a second
category of folk in mind. The vast majority of mankind accept without hesitating truths that they are incapable of explaining satisfacto-
rily or defending logically. The Christian faithful, the *plebs sancta
Dei*, are on the whole prominent among them. In the *University Sermons* he had already applied himself to the question, How might the
faithful, lacking as they usually do any formal theological education,
be saved from the charge of superstition? He had found the characteristically Romantic answer in holiness of heart. A right state of heart is
the eye of faith, keeping it from fastening upon unworthy objects.[35]
Now, without by any means neglecting this concern with the set of
will and feeling, he turned to meet a second secular challenge. He proposed to defend the mass of the faithful against the charge that they
were not simply superstitious but fideistic. W. G. Ward, the sharpest
logical mind of the Catholic Revival, put the difficulty with his customary pungency:

> No one can know for certain that God exists, except on grounds of rea-
> son; and no one can make any act of faith until he knows for certain that
> God exists. It is necessary, then, for all men without exception who would
> be saved, and not merely philosophers, to know certainly God's existence
> on grounds of reason. Yet to the enormous majority of mankind, such
> grounds of reason seem on the surface inaccessible.

And Ward goes on by way of reference to the main social strata of the
period:

> It would be very ludicrous child's play, that some labourer, or farmer, or
> tradesman, or even hunting country gentlemen, should explore such argu-
> ments for God's existence as are found in Catholic philosophical works;
> especially if you suppose him to explore them on the principle of judging

for himself and by the perspicacity of his own intellect, how far they can be vindicated against the objections.[36]

To both Froude's question and Ward's, Newman put the counterquestion: How are we to justify the ordinary assents and certitudes of life? Clearly enough, the great majority of them have neither resulted from, nor can they be proved by, inferential logic. Nevertheless, we would not easily be persuaded by a professional epistemologist that, for instance, our conviction that Britain is an island enjoys a merely probable status. Newman could afford to be prodigal with such examples:

> We are sure beyond all hazard of a mistake that our own self is not the only being existing; that there is an external world; that it is a system with parts and a whole, a universe carried on by laws; and that the future is affected by the past. We accept and hold with an unqualified assent that the earth, considered as a phenomenon, is a globe; that all its regions see the sun by turns; that there are vast traces on it of land and water; that there are really existing cities on definite sites, which go by the names of London, Paris, Florence and Madrid. We are sure that Paris or London, unless suddenly swallowed up by an earthquake or burned to the ground, is to-day just what it was yesterday, when we left it.[37]

The "real and necessary method" by which we are enabled to "become certain of what is concrete" is not formal logical sequence but something rather different.

> It is the cumulation of probabilities, independent of each other, arising out of the nature and circumstances of the particular case which is under review; probabilities too fine to avail separately, too subtle and circuitous to be convertible into syllogisms, too numerous and various for such conversion, even were they convertible.[38]

And appealing not so much to the grand-scale creative imagination of Schelling and the Schlegels which lies behind Coleridge as to a more modest model of disciplined imaginative looking, he suggests that the contrast between a *portrait* and a *sketch* might be a fair reflection of the relation between the "multiform and intricate process of ratiocination" in judging life in the concrete and the "rude operation of syllogistic treatment."[39]

In evaluating the case for a concrete truth, we "grasp the full tale of premises and the conclusion . . . by a sort of instinctive perception of the legitimate conclusion in and through the premises."[40]

The conclusion in a real or concrete question is foreseen and predicted rather than actually attained; foreseen in the number and direction of accumulated premises, which all converge to it, and as the result of their combination, approach it more nearly than any assignable difference, yet do not touch it logically (though only not touching it) on account of the nature of its subject matter, and the delicate and implicit character of at least part of the reasonings on which it depends.

Thus resuming the distinction made earlier in the Oxford Sermons, Newman continues:

It is by the strength, variety or multiplicity of premises, which are only probable, not by invincible syllogisms, – by objections overcome, by adverse theories neutralized, by difficulties gradually clearing up, by exceptions proving the rule, by unlooked-for correlations found with received truths, by suspense and delay in the process issuing in triumphant reactions, – by all these ways, and many others, it is that the practised and experienced mind is able to make a sure divination that a conclusion is inevitable, of which his lines of reasoning do not actually put him in possession.[41]

The architectonic faculty that in this way gathers up the fragments of experience into a single and unified judgment is called by Newman the *illative sense.*

The Illative Sense: Experience and Truth

Newman is not out here to manufacture from the common stuff of experience some arcane and hitherto unrecognized power. As he wrote, the illative sense "is a grand word for a common thing."[42] In several essays on the *Grammar of Assent*, Dessain drew his readers' attention to a passage in Willa Cather's novel, *Shadows on the Rock*, set in French Canada:

"When there is no sun, I can tell directions like the Indians."
　　Here Auclair interrupted him.
　　"And how is that, Antoine?"
　　Frichette smiled and shrugged.
　　"It is hard to explain, by many things. The limbs of the trees are generally bigger on the south side, for example. The moss on the trunks is clean and dry on the north side—on the south side it is softer and maybe

a little rotten. There are many little signs; put them together and they point you right."[43]

"They point you right": this is the heart of the illative sense. A whole host of features of experience conspire to "carry us into" (the original late Latin sense of *illatio*) the more spacious realm of a conclusion that is larger than any of them. The heaping together of tiny indications, none of which by itself is conclusive, produces certitude in ordinary human affairs. At some point there is a qualitative change in the quantitative amassment of evidence. Spread out the pieces of a jigsaw puzzle on a table, and it may be only probable that they are more than an accidental collocation. Fit them together and there will be no doubt. Newman himself, according to his first notable biographer, Wilfred Ward, once used the illustration of

a cable, which is made up of a number of separate threads, each feeble, yet together as sufficient as an iron rod. An iron rod represents mathematical or strict demonstration; a cable represents moral demonstration, which is an assemblage of probabilities, separately insufficient for certainty, but when put together, irrefragible.[44]

The application to religious belief is not far to seek. In Newman's novel *Loss and Gain*, the protagonist, the undergraduate Charles, finds himself confronted by just the dilemma exposed in Newman's correspondence with William Froude. In a carriage of the Great Western Railway, Charles enters into conversation with a Catholic priest who identifies him as an "Oxford man" by noting telltale features of his fellow traveler's demeanor. The ability to make such judgments is not a bit surprising, says the priest, for "a man's moral self is concentrated in each moment of his life; it lives in the tips of his fingers and the spring of his insteps. A very little thing tries what a man is made of."[45] This is the illative sense at work in an everyday world. Charles, who is struggling with the very problems of religious thought that Newman's career had raised, senses the relevance of the priest's remark to his own concerns. During the conversation, his obscure sense of a way forward becomes gradually clarified. His difficulty is exactly Froude's. "The evidence of revealed doctrine is so built up on probabilities that I do not see what is to introduce it into a civilised community, where reason has been cultivated to the utmost, and argument is the test of truth."[46] The priest points out that we can in fact quite properly give

our assent in cases where formal inference will never find reason enough
to bring us to a conclusion. Charles asks,

> "Do you mean that before conversion one can attain to a present abiding
> actual conviction of this truth?"
>
> "I do not know," answered the other; "but at least he may have habit-
> ual moral certainty; I mean a conviction, and one only steady, without
> rival conviction, or even reasonable doubt, present to him when he is
> most composed and in his hours of solitude, and flashing on him from
> time to time, as through clouds, when he is in the world . . . "
>
> "Then you mean to say," said Charles, while his heart beat faster, "that
> a person is under no duty to wait for clearer light?"
>
> "He will not have, he cannot expect, clearer light before conversion.
> Certainty, in its highest sense, is the reward of those who, by an act of the
> will, and at the dictate of reason and prudence, embrace the truth when
> nature like a coward shrinks. You must make a venture; faith is a venture
> before a man is a Catholic; it is a grace after it." [47]

"Certainty in its highest sense": Newman is speaking here, as the language of "grace" implies, of a supernatural state of the mind, and the
analysis of the act of faith in terms of reason and will is very much the
commonplace account of classical Latin Christian theology rather than
the personal tones of Newman himself. But it is arrival at the "habit-
ual moral certainty" which precedes the gracious act of faith itself that
is characteristically Newmanian, proceeding as it does by implicit reason working through the delicate instrumentality of the illative sense.
Of this, a major Newman scholar has summed up: "It is the mind in
its perfection, judging and correlating at the highest point of any
given individual; it concerns itself with principles, doctrines, facts,
memories, experiences, testimonies, in order to attain insights too delicate and subtle for logical analysis." [48] One illuminating way to see
Newman's concept of illation is to view it as a transposition into a
philosophical key of the sacramentalism of the English religious tradition. The illative sense actualizes our capacity to uncover, by a search-
ing and subtle attention to experience in its complexity, the sacramental
transparence of the world to God. We touch here on a presupposition
of Catholic Christianity consciously recovered by Anglicans in the
seventeenth-century renaissance of Christian Platonism, itself the suc-
cessor to the "long reign of Nominalism through the unmetaphysical
epoch of the Reformation." [49]

> The man that looks on glass
> On it may stay his eye,
> Or, if he chooseth, through it may pass,
> And then the heaven espy.[50]

Newman's writing conveys a peculiar sense of adequacy to experience that, given his limitations as an imaginative writer, is all the more noticeable in his philosophy of religion. He manages to combine an evocation of depth and multidimensionality with a feeling for what A. N. Whitehead called "presentational immediacy," the surface "given" of things. Jan Hendrik Walgrave, O.P., in his study *Newman the Theologian*, finds the key to Newman's fascination in his having at one and the same time a very Platonist and a very Aristotelian mind: "An extreme tension pervades Newman's thought, drawn as it was by two opposing tendencies of the English mind, namely, a Platonic longing for immaterial ideas and invisible realities, and the need for facts precisely perceived, recorded and verified."[51] It is hard to deny this character to the *Grammar of Assent*, which has it on one page that "We are in a world of facts, and we use them for there is nothing else to use. We do not quarrel with them, but we take them as they are";[52] and on another, speaking of the Christian religion, "Our communion with it is in the unseen."[53]

ILLATIVE MATERIALS:
A PROPOSAL FOR REVISING THE "GRAMMAR OF ASSENT"

So far nothing has been said about the particular experiential materials that the illative sense is to draw on in considering whether or not God exists. In point of fact, Newman restricted these materials rather rigorously to our experience of conscience:

> My true informant, my burdened conscience, gives me at once the true answer to each of these antagonist questions [arising from God's "absence . . . from his own world"]. It pronounces without any misgiving that God exists, and it pronounces quite as surely that I am alienated from him. . . . Thus it solves the world's mystery and sees in that mystery only a confirmation of its own original teaching.[54]

Conscience becomes here the point of insertion of the presence of God into the life of humankind: a presence discovered by the illative sense working on a variety of partial evidences from our awareness of moral situations. It seems possible to suggest that while the form of Newman's argumentation is eminently acceptable, the content is extremely restrictive and impoverished. Is it really the case that the only indications of the existence of God in experience are of this narrowly moral order? On the contrary, there is a rich variety of areas of experience that may well have theistic relevance. One thinks immediately of such experiences as wonder, hope, desire, joy—all of which have been held by different writers to carry metaphysical implications of an ultimately theistic kind.

Just as there is a need to break through the undue restrictiveness of Newman's illative materials, there is also a need to dismantle a certain autobiographical individualism that is presumably the root of the restrictiveness in question. It is true that the argument of the *Grammar of Assent* requires our interest in the query, "Who, in fact, is doing the reasoning?" in any given case, for its author holds that assent is always in form a uniquely personal act. But it does not require that the content of what a person takes as his or her illative materials should be individual. There is no reason why we should not regard the theistic assents of others—their grasping of transcendent reality through the particularities of experience—as among the materials on which our own illative sense can get to work. Partly this is because, where persons of outstanding moral and intellectual integrity are involved, we should be willing to let their judgments be indicators in our exercise of illation. This is the legitimate place of argument from authority. It implies no surrender of our powers of judgment, because in locating such people we have ourselves applied judgment to our impressions of their lives and writings. But more importantly, we can find our own existence and experience illuminated through their intersection with the texts that represent the illative judgments of others in their own particular approaches to God.

If, therefore, we take as our point of departure not just our own experience, as individuals or a generation, but that of a gallery of figures through the tradition of reflection on these matters, we shall secure a much richer supply of illative materials. A variety of our predecessors in the tradition reasoned to God as the condition of possibility for some variety of human experience, whether that be desire (Gregory of Nyssa), truth (Augustine), perfection (Anselm), transience (Thomas), the limits of action (Pascal), hope (Marcel) or joy (Chesterton). Their personal assent cannot be ours, yet the convergence of areas in which such men have come to make theistic assent provides us within an infinitely richer sense of the real in coming to our own judgment in the matter of belief in God.

It is sometimes forgotten that the sum total of partial and inadequate arguments is not the sum total of their inadequacies, despite what misleading metaphors may suggest. The agnostic Anthony Flew has remarked that "if one leaky bucket will not hold water there is no reason to think that ten can."[55] But to this Richard Swinburne has counterargued: "Clearly, if you join ten leaky buckets together in such a way that holes in the bottom of each bucket are squashed close to solid parts of the bottoms of neighbouring buckets, you will get a container that holds water."[56] To change the metaphor to one of Newman's own, the cable that is composed "of a number of separate threads, each feeble," is not itself feeble, but "as sufficient as an iron rod." What is wanted, therefore, is not simply a *Grammar of Assent* but a *Grammar of Consent*: an invitation to let one's illative sense explore the real through the media of various "consenting" theists. To respond to the invitation will not entail a minute dissection of logical forms but rather, in Newman's words, "a mental comprehension of the whole case and a discernment of its upshot."

Ever since F. D. Maurice, readers of the *Grammar of Assent* have been simultaneously excited by its promise and disappointed by its actual texture as a piece of writing.[57] Having held out to us the appropriate form for argument to God's existence, a form at once rational and imaginative, Newman's content seems thin gruel in comparison. The moral argument for God's existence, already laid out impressively in Kant, is certainly not dead.[58] But if moral experience alone can feed the illative sense in matters of natural religion (Newman has other materials to draw on where revealed religion is concerned), then the illative sense can scarcely claim to traverse the whole field of human experience. And yet the claim that it is a power that identifies convergences, uncovers clues, and synthesizes the various deliverances of experience surely supposes some such universality. An English philosopher of religion has written: "Basically, the inadequacy of traditional natural theology lies not in the areas of experience chosen as theistically evidential but in the elucidation of the way in which they count as evidence."[59] If this be so, to fit Newman's form to this ampler experiential content may well be just the job.

To trace in the midst of a variety of such materials interweaving theistic threads will be the best way to establish the rationality of belief in God's existence. It will also be to follow the line of development of Christian philosophy as now one, now another, thread glints into the light of historical day. There is no better place to begin such a search than in the Greek-speaking eastern Roman empire of the first Christian centuries, for it was there that men and women of the Gospel were first obliged, on any significant scale, to give a reason for the faith that was in them. The encounter between Christian faith and the philosophical resources of the Hellenistic world was already underway in the second century. A disparate group of writers, known to historians of doctrine as the Apologists, were its trailblazers. But the movement they initiated did not reach full intellectual maturity until the fourth century, that golden age of Greek Christian thought. For our first witness, therefore, we shall summon to the bar a philosopher-theologian of that period. Appropriately enough, Gregory of Nyssa, who is first in time among the figures dealt with in this book, is also the one who exposes the most basic, primordial, and so first in significance of its approaches to God. Were it not for the existence of a basic drive towards the infinite in human beings themselves, a fundamental yearning of the human spirit, a longing that the dream of God may be true, neither readers nor writers would be likely to concern themselves with religion at all.

2

GREGORY OF NYSSA AND THE
MOVEMENT OF ERŌS

Pagan Learning and Life in Christ

By any reckoning one of the greatest of the Fathers of the Church, Gregory of Nyssa (c. 330–c. 395) belonged to that fourth-century world where the enterprises of philosophy and theology were not as yet too nicely distinguished. Education—the process whereby we are drawn out and molded into awareness of the ultimate realities we have to do with, called by the Greeks *paideia*—was for Gregory both a matter of a share in the life of Christ and a question of appropriating the insights of the pagan philosophers. Werner Jaeger could write accurately that for the Cappadocian Father, "the formation of the Christian man, his *morphōsis*, is the effect of his unceasing study of the Bible. The form is Christ. The *paideia* of the Christian is *imitatio Christi*: Christ must take shape in him."[1] And in virtually the same breath, the distinguished classical scholar could also observe that "the way that" Gregory "approaches" his work as a writer and educator "shows him to be steeped in the great Greek philosophical tradition and its cultural ideas"; he made a "conscious attempt to arrive at a conception of the development of the human personality that could do justice to the highest demands of Greek educational philosophy."[2] In this he was building on foundations laid by the early Christian apologists, especially Justin.[3] In the language of Stoic philosophy, the world was permeated by a cosmic reason, *logos*, which gave all people the chance to glimpse the truth for themselves. What they perceived in fragmentary ways has been disclosed in its completeness in Jesus Christ, who is the Word, *logos*, made flesh. "All positive achievement before Christ,"

39

writes Robert Markus, "could thus be understood as part of his truth."[4] The Christian, listening to the logos, was prepared to find truth anywhere. In 362, when Gregory was about thirty years old, the emperor Julian the Apostate excluded Christians by decree from attendance at the pagan schools; we notice at once that it was Julian, not the Christians themselves, who thought that "the classics and the gospels could not go together."[5]

Gregory was by temperament more of a scholar than a bishop, in whom, as St. Thomas Aquinas points out, contemplation must needs be combined with action.[6] Von Campenhausen, in his collection of brief lives of the Fathers, regards Gregory as essentially an observer.[7] A man who knew how to see and who could turn his observations into reflections of a more universal sort, he remained a solitary spirit, poorly suited to life in a community. If there is justice in this judgment, it was a sign of the times that Gregory was called from the rhetor's teaching desk to the bishop's throne. Culture in that age was nourished on the rhetorical tradition, and the Church was struggling to draw to herself the living forces of the human spirit that the culture held. Despite the extremely public setting of Gregory's life, he does seem a loner, his correspondence strangely mute on his personal relationships. Gregory's task in the Church was a task of reflection, not the active task of his initially more famous brother Basil, the inspiring and organizing center of a web of ecclesial, monastic, and personal friendships. As V. W. Callahan writes of Gregory's relation to Basilian monasticism, "He undertook to interpret the philosophical, theological and mystical implications of the *Rules*."[8] But the scope of this statement may be extended. To make out the implications of all the human striving that went on in the cities of the late antique world as well as in the monastic settlements that followed Basil's code of life: this was Gregory's essential contribution to the life of the fourth century. From it he disengaged the theme of erōs, of humankind as desire. The human animal, as Gregory sees us, is a living flame of desiring, guttering when fed with the oil of any finite, created satisfaction and so pointing irresistibly towards an infinite satisfaction, namely, God.

Despite a lifelong devotion to his formally better-educated brother, Gregory had a freedom and originality that led him to strike out on an intellectual and spiritual path of his own. Plato, the middle Platonists, Plotinus, Philo, and Origen were his preferred sources, the finest products of the marriage of Plato's dialogues with the rest of Greek philosophy, Judaism, and Christianity.[9] Particularly striking is his high regard for the contemporary (and somewhat dangerous) representative of the pagan alternative in Antiochene Syria, Libanius.[10] But his was not a sunny synthesis of an altogether too easy sort. A. J. Malherbe and E. Ferguson wrote in the preface to their version of his *Life of Moses*:

> Gregory reflects an honest ambivalence in regard to pagan learning. He has some harsh things to say about its inadequacies and dangers. Very graphic is his figure of pagan education as "always in labour but never giving birth" (II.11). On the other hand . . . [he writes] "There are certain things derived from profane education which should not be rejected" in our striving for virtue (II.37). The spiritual meaning of the "spoiling of the Egyptians" is that God commands those participating through virtue in the free life also to equip themselves with the wealth of pagan learning (II.115). "Such things as moral and natural philosophy, geometry, astronomy, dialectic . . . will be multiplied when in time the divine sanctuary of mystery must be beautified with the riches of reason."[11]

No surprise, then, that Von Campenhausen could call Gregory the "most versatile theologian of his century."[12] Yet, profoundly intellectual as he was, it would be false to give the impression of a man cut off from the roots of ordinary human feeling, if not from the values of the human city. As a young man his career as a rhetor, denounced by Basil's closest friend and colleague, Gregory Nazianzen, made Gregory of Nyssa a professional expositor of the pagan classics, with their rounded and nuanced capturing of the myriad faces of man. He married, and while he deplored in his first book, *On Virginity*, the fact that he who was writing to defend consecrated virginity "should have put a foot into the affairs of this world,"[12] neither his marriage nor his rhetorship appear to have seriously retarded his religious development. He had the enduring bond of physical and spiritual brotherhood with his sibling Macrina, abbess of a convent on the river Iris in east-central Turkey. This relationship, too, gave him insight, this time into the new world of Cappadocian monasticism. The *Life of Macrina* is not simply, or even mainly, an evocation of individual events but, rather, in accordance with the canons of the art of biography in the Greco-Roman world, is more of a "unifying reading of the life of the hero, a vision and interpretation of the whole of his or her existence."[14] In that *Life* Gregory presents Macrina, in Jaeger's words, as "the very soul and living model of a monastic community,"[15] and she is also, as M. Pierre Maraval has shown in his exhaustive edition, a confirmation of Gregory's own account of human development.[16] It was, I suggest, precisely this combination of awareness of the world, with its own varied loves, and intimate acquaintance with the monastic life, with its *unum necessarium*, the love of God, that provided the impetus for Gregory's own philosophizing. His approach to God discovers transcendence through erōs itself – seeing all finite human desire and finite human loving finally purified and satisfied in an endless movement of loving desire towards God. The Absolute, for Gregory, is revealed in the simultaneous actuality of our manifold varied loves and our awareness that nothing finite will ever satisfy them.

In Gregory's eyes, the center of revelation is the person of Jesus Christ, but the perspective in which that figure is seen (our concern here, in the evaluation of fundamental resources for the religious quest) was suggested by a personal variant on the Platonist tradition. To say that revelation centers in Christ is to affirm that Christ is the answer to a question. First, however, we need to know what that question is. Transcendence is a human problem before it is a divine gift. The problematic that Gregory adopted was familiar enough in the thought-world of his time: the soul's need for effective deliverance from its own triviality, corruptness, and estrangement from its proper destiny. Humankind needs to be raised, purified, and brought back to its spiritual home, which for the Christian Platonist is God as creator and lord. The chosen metaphors of this scheme may strike us as unfamiliar, even bizarre, but what they express is intelligible enough. The essential thing about a human being is that he or she is unfinished, not in the sense of an evolutionary botch, which might have to be consigned to a cul-de-sac of cosmic history, but in the sense of an unfinished symphony, already bearing the marks of its own greatness and crying out for completion. For Gregory, human nature is not a closed system, for its most characteristic quality is its tendency towards the infinite. We realize our humanity in and through a vocation to a union with what is not ourselves. In this open-ended movement of erōs, desiring, this essential incompleteness at the heart of human living, a need to be complemented and fulfilled by what is not ourselves,[17] Gregory finds the point of insertion of the divine into the human.

In his attempt to state this view of humankind Gregory turned, as I have said, to the developed Platonism of his day for a suitable language and likely categories. Greek Christian writers show a variety of attitudes to the Platonist tradition. As I. P. Sheldon-Williams put the matter:

> Three attitudes towards pagan learning were possible for the Christian: uncompromising acceptance, which led to heretical Gnosticism; uncompromising rejection as shown by the early apologists and ascetics, favoured by the School of Antioch, and surviving into the Iconoclastic movement and into some forms of modern Protestantism; and controlled acceptance, the attitude of the Alexandrians and of the [Cappadocian fathers] . . . which produced the Christian philosophy. . . . This attitude acknowledges that the philosophical systems contained elements of truth, a fact taken for granted by the Alexandrians and openly asserted, with particular reference to Platonism, by the Cappadocians, while rejecting what is evidently falsified by the Christian Revelation.[18]

Among the Cappadocians we might turn for confirmation to Basil's essay, *To the Young Men, on the Subject of Pagan Literature*,[19] to Gregory Nazianzen's *Orations*[20] and, as we have already seen, to Gregory of Nyssa's *Life of Moses*.[21] For the last, following a recurrent line of thought in Platonism, humanity is a unique case. The human being is the only being who straddles two worlds, the world of sense and the world of mind. As Gregory remarks in his *Catechetical Oration* (a kind of résumé of Christian faith), humanity is *methorios*, "a borderline case."[22] As such we form the bridge and way of access from the one, to which we belong as animals, to the other which is ours by right as rational souls. Our being is inclusive of all the finite orders, for, on a principle virtually axiomatic in later Platonism, all higher powers include what is below them. So the human being as rational animal is the summation of the whole sensuous world; animal, vegetable, and inanimate matter are all involved in his or her making, which is the fruit of which the visible world is the seed.[23] But this inclusive being is not exclusive of reality higher still: we are the priests of this visible creation, the agents by which the universe is presented as a unity to the God who is supremely one.[24] This description of humanity as a microcosm of the macrocosm is interesting in its own right,[25] but Gregory was not himself primarily concerned with our relation to nature. Basil, who was much more inclined to natural philosophy and speculations about the cosmos,[26] had omitted an account of the creation of human beings in his *Homilies on the Hexaemeron* (the six-day creation of Genesis). He promised to write a separate treatise on humanity but constantly deferred it (as authors will) and never did so. Gregory had the chance to fill in this lacuna with his own treatise, *On the Creation of Humankind*.[27] But in fact the book's center of interest is very different.

DESCENT AND REASCENT TO GOD

Gregory used this essay to embark upon a Christian version of the Neoplatonist "myth" of the soul's coming forth from God and her return to him. I write the word *myth* in so-called scare quotes advisedly, because Gregory's affirmation of the biblical doctrine of creation, which sets the clearest of all possible boundaries between the creature and the creator, naturally makes the idea of the soul's emanation from God no more than a symbol of the creator-creature relationship. To be sure, Gregory is sufficiently impressed by the Platonists to see this making of humanity as taking place in two distinct moments, corresponding to the radical distinction between body and spirit in their thinking.[28] But complex and intriguing as Gregory's occasional cosmological speculations may be, and breathtaking as his boldness most certainly is in saying that humanity is so much the image of God as to differ from its prototype only as created does from uncreated,[29] his stress and his interest lie not so much with what is behind human existence as with what lies ahead of it.[30]

The soul's descent from God is seen as marked by three crises: from her first creation in the world of mind, she passes through a remaking in the world of sense, and this clothes her with the bodily passions necessary for life on earth. Finally, she undergoes the crisis of the fall, in which these passions become vicious rather than virtuous and take away her comeliness. The pattern of this dramatized account of the making of humanity is not, however, of any great moment to Gregory for its own sake. It is simply the shadow of the subject that occupies the forefront of his mind as a monk and pastor. This subject is the future return to God in the reverse direction, by purification, illumination, and finally personal union with him.[31] This is quite clear in his biography of Macrina whose "philosophical life" is said to consist in "liberation from the passions, and from that point on, an angelic life devoted to contemplation; it is also love.[32]

The movement of faith begins with a "desire and longing to share in what is good."[33] Its awakening begins with the apprehension of beauty about us. Purification from the vicious passions is a prerequisite of all honest apprehension of the real. We cannot see what is before us if we constantly mask the real with our lust, greed, and egoism. The role of the lovely, to kalon, is to awaken us from our egotistical slumbers. Equally important, however, is the process of illumination whereby we come to see the empirical realities around us as signposts to what they "imitate" and in which they "participate": "Through the beauty seen in all these" (the sky or the rays of light or any other beautiful appearance) "we would be led to a desire for that beauty of which the heavens tell the glory and the firmament of all creation proclaims the knowledge."[34] The deepest reality of things, on Gregory's account, is their fundamental likeness to God, the Father of lights, whose "rays" (aporroiai) or "activity in creation" (energeia), make them what they are. We are in the world of Plato's Symposium here.

> When, in search of the Beautiful, the uninstructed mind sees something in which there is an appearance of beauty he supposes that this . . . is beautiful in itself, and sees no need to search further. But he who has purified the eye of his soul . . . forgets the matter in which the Form of Beauty manifests itself and makes of the visible object a vantage-point from which to contemplate that intelligible Beauty by participation in which all beautiful things are beautiful.[35]

The soul will not be satisfied with less than "what is beautiful of itself and in itself; what is always beautiful, not sometimes beautiful and sometimes not; what is above addition and increase and incapable of any kind of change and transformation."[36] Humankind is in movement, and the driving force of this movement is erōs, the mind's desire for the real and pursuit of the whole, our unlimited openness to being, our need and thirst for fulfillment. Gregory compares the mind to a river making for the open sea:

> If it flows in all directions, it scatters itself by running towards what is pleasing to the senses and has no worthwhile force for its journey to the really good. But if it were called in from all sides, collected unto itself, brought together, it would move with its own natural energy and nothing would prevent it from being borne upwards and fastening itself upon the truth of reality. . . . The human mind, being constrained from all directions by self-control . . . will somehow be taken up by the nature of the movement to a desire for what is above, there not being any place for it to run to.[37]

All of this becomes quite clear when Gregory goes on to speak about humanity's destiny, our movement into perfect union with God.

Purification and illumination mean that we are now restored to a conscious relationship with our transcendent source and model. Reality, if we are genuinely open to the world around us, cannot but change us; and this is true above all of our relation to the supremely and incomparably real, God. The soul "will find the only thing that is worth longing for, and having come close to beauty, will become beautiful itself."[38] Gregory speaks of this as the restoration of the Image, as knowledge of God "by participation" in him, and as the return of humanity to the society of the Angels, the recovery of Paradise. Invoking this last metaphor, he writes:

> The soul rises again . . . and moves about in the world of mind, the world above this universe . . . where the Principalities dwell, and the Dominations, and the Thrones assigned to the Powers. She frequents the assemblies of the celestial beings . . . and mingles with their numberless throng, seeking her Beloved there . . . and . . . begins to question whether the very angels can apprehend him whom she loves. They give her no answer, but by their silence make it plain that he is inaccessible even to them. So . . . she abandons all that she has found there, and finds her Beloved in her very inability to grasp all that which he is.[39]

The awareness that the movement of erōs has no term is the dark knowledge of God. This knowledge consists in being aware that the true knowledge of God is to know "that our goal transcends all knowledge and is everywhere cut off from us by the darkness of incomprehensibility."[40] At first, this awareness makes the soul despair, until, as Gregory tells us, she discovers that to find God is to seek him without end,[41] and that "the true satisfaction of her desire consists in constantly going on with her quest and never ceasing in her ascent."[42] At this point, as Jean Daniélou remarked, "we are at the very heart of Gregory's spiritual doctrine."[43]

Daniélou's phrase should make us pause. Are we not dealing here with the life of the believer responding to the grace of Christ, rather than with some aspect of human experience accessible to Everyman? It is true that Gregory sees Christ and the Spirit of Christ as intimately involved in the process that we have just charted. He rejected the view of that theological rationalist Eunomius that in our struggle to find an infinite object commensurate with our desire the Holy Spirit merely helps us "by acclamation," applauding, as it were, from the front stalls. The Spirit, Gregory insists, actually wrestles with us, on our side; he is a "co-agonizer," a "coworker": hence the favor bestowed on the language of *sunergia*, cooperation, for the relationship between God and humanity.[44] On the other hand, Gregory is chary of any hint of divine determinism in that struggle's outcome. As he stresses in the *Catechetical Oration*, the human being is *autoexousios*, self-determining.[45] This would be difficult to reconcile with the notion of synergy, and harder still to square with the idea of grace in Latin Christianity, had Gregory possessed the view of will that the West has inherited from St. Augustine. For Augustine, will coincides with the power to form will's direction; and so to say that it is by grace that we move towards God is necessarily to say that the will itself must be re-created from within; the grace of the New Testament is a fresh interior love from the beginning, bestowed by God. But while Gregory's erōs is indeed a stream of willing, it is not the only element in the human constitution with a role of a crucial kind to play in the movement to transcendence. There is also the capacity for vision. *Prohairēsis*, "choice," for Gregory, is our capacity to block the power of seeing, so that we do not focus on the archetypal good that is present, to varying degrees, in the concrete objects before us.[46] The refusal to look at those objects in our human environment that would carry our erōs increasingly towards the divine soon becomes an active power making for darkness. As he says in the sermon *On the dead*, in the sinful, erōs degenerates into passion: our drives become self-serving. It is not, however, the will that needs to be recreated, for erōs is in itself a drive towards the infinite, towards that utterly attractive transcendent reality which he calls *to autoagathon*, "goodness itself." What "saves" us is God's clarification of our inner eye by showing the worthlessness of the objects that we have falsely divinized and by giving us in their place objects that mediate his goodness. This is why, in the *Life of Macrina*, the saint's pattern of life can be described in "philosophical," that is, universal human, terms almost until the very end; when on her deathbed, and in the liturgical context of her last moments, Gregory speaks of the object she sought as her "lover" (*erastēs*), Christ.[47] But the movement of erōs by which she sought that unique face[48] is, for Gregory, an aspect of humanity as such, of Everyman.[49]

Through the movement of erōs humanity finds itself from the very first embarked upon a journey, "a journey into infinity – not an abstract 'absoluteness' but an infinity of what Gregory simply calls 'goodness', an infinite resource of mercy, help and delight."[50] Our nature as a willing and desiring nature is extraordinarily mobile and endlessly dissatisfied.[51] Our "straining onwards"—to use Gregory's own preferred term, *epektasis*[52]—our tendency to surpass continually our own achieved satisfactions, tells us something about human subjectivity, but it also argues for a divine correlate in the objectivity of God. In the first place, then, it speaks to us of humankind: in his book *On Perfection*, Gregory comforts any reader disturbed by the instability of his or her own loves with the thought that this instability is in itself the clue to humanity's high destiny:

> Let no one be grieved if he sees in his nature a penchant for change. Changing in everything for the better, let him exchange "glory for glory," becoming greater through daily increase, ever perfecting himself and never arriving too quickly at the limit of perfection. For this is truly perfection: never to stop growing towards what is better and never placing any limit on perfection.[53]

Gregory bases these exhortations on the affirmation that "what appears so terrifying (I mean the mutability of our nature) can really be a pinion in our flight."[54] In the second place, however, the open-endedness of the movement of erōs tells us something about divine transcendence, not merely about our self-transcendence. As Ekkehard Mühlenberg has stressed, Gregory's search to formulate a proof of Infinite Spirit from the structure of finite spirit finds its terminus here.[55] Our infinitely mobile nature is such that when we turn towards the good "the movement forward never ceases because of the endlessness of the course to be traversed."[56] God's transcendence lies in his co-responding endlessness.[57] "His measure is his unmeasuredness," as Gregory delights to put it. Our *epithumia*, our condition as longing creatures smitten with *Sehnsucht*, derives from our ordering to this God who alone, through the endlessness of his own being, can grant us eternal life.[58]

Alien as Gregory of Nyssa's language may be to the twentieth-century West, his is not an approach to the existence of God that is incapable of being rendered in a more modern idiom and conceptuality. Copleston, in his essay *Religion and Philosophy*, has adopted a clearly Gregorian standpoint. He suggests that the search for a metaphysical ultimate, for one final ground of finite existence, is based on "an experience of limits, coupled with a reaching out" (cf. *epektasis!*) "towards that which transcends and grounds all limits."[59] In this act of self-transcendence we can see, he thinks, "an expression of the orienta-

tion of the human spirit to the divine reality."[60] God manifests himself
to us as the "attractive but hidden term or goal of a movement." If this
is not what Gregory means by the divine erōs, it is hard to see what
could be.

Copleston is not, of course, claiming that human individuals are
constantly adverting to a "love for a thing eternal and infinite"—to
use Gregory's language. At the level of conscious awareness we do
not, most of us, most of the time, share this love that he speaks of. Yet
it seems undeniable that in the course of most human lives advertence
to certain features of the finite world does spark off a kind of movement of transcendence, a nostalgia for eternity, a haunting sense of
the infinite. This nostalgia can certainly be brushed aside as irrelevant
to ordinary living; yet equally certainly it can be interpreted as the
eruption into everyday consciousness of the most fundamental orientation of the spirit of man. For man is essentially erotic: man is openness, wanting, and thirsting to be filled. Copleston concludes:

> It is in and through its own performance of the movement of transcen-
> dence that the spirit comes to recognise the meaning of its own striving.
> This knowledge is prefigured as it were in the structure of the spirit, but it
> is not there explicitly from the start. It is rendered explicit and appreci-
> ated only in the process of personal reflection which constitutes the rec-
> ognition of an already existing ontological relationship.[61]

If this is tough going, C. S. Lewis, the northern Irish historian of
medieval literature who became the best-known Christian apologist
of the contemporary period in the English-speaking world, has left us,
in his spiritual autobiography, *Surprised by Joy*, an excellent concrete
case. He tells us that as a child he came across Longfellow's epic poem,
The Saga of King Olaf. He was struck at once by these lines: "I heard a
voice that cried / Balder the beautiful / is dead, is dead."[62] He writes:
"I knew nothing about Balder; but instantly I was uplifted into huge
regions of northern sky. I described with almost sickening intensity
something never to be described (except that it is cold, spacious, severe,
pale and remote) and then . . . found myself at the very same moment
already falling out of the desire and wishing I were back in it."[63] From
this fading of what he childishly called "the Northernness," he should
have concluded, so he says, that the final term of this experience, "the
Desirable," merely "shone through" this system of mythology. As it
was, he identified it as an inner state that he must at all costs seek to
reproduce for its own sheer delight. Only years later, partly through

reading S. Alexander's account of mind in *Space, Time, and Deity* did Lewis realize that introspection merely contacts the residue of our intentional experiences, those experiences whereby we reach out to what is other than ourselves.[64] It is these other realities that leave a deposit within us, "like the swell at sea, working after the wind has dropped." The next remarks are so Gregorian that they may be cited in their wholeness:

> This discovery flashed a new light back on my whole life. I saw that all my waitings and watchings for Joy, all my vain hopes to find some mental content on which I could, so to speak, lay my finger and say, "This is it" had been a futile attempt to contemplate the enjoyed. All that such watching and waiting ever *could* find would be either an image . . . or a quiver in the diaphragm. I should never have to bother again about these images or sensations, I knew now that they were merely the mental track left by the passage of Joy—not the wave itself but the wave's imprint on the sand. The inherent dialectic of desire itself had in a way already shown me this; for all images and sensations, if idolatrously mistaken for Joy itself, soon honestly confessed themselves inadequate.[65]

And Lewis concludes:

> I did not yet ask, Who is the desired? Only, what is it? But this brought me already into the region of awe, for I thus understood that in deepest solitude there is a road right out of the self, a commerce with something which, by refusing to identify itself with any object of the senses, or anything whereof we have biological or social need, or anything imagined, or any state of our own minds, proclaims itself sheerly objective. Far more objective than our bodies, for it is not like them clothed in our senses; the naked Other, imageless (though our imagination salutes it in a hundred images), unknown, undefined, desired.[66]

At this point, then, we can say with some confidence that we have already identified an important experiential stimulus for the illative sense. The infinite erōs of the human spirit itself propels us towards God. Yet here the mind quite rightly pulls us up short. May not this orientation towards a postulated divinity be a trick of the cosmic powers, a fluke of the evolutionary process? May it not be a fantasy of a peculiarly endemic kind, turning up again and again to haunt the fitful repose of the human race in the world of things? Do we not also have a responsibility to our intellectual nature to face this possibility honestly and directly, and not just a duty to our affective nature to take the metaphysical implications of our emotional structure *au sérieux*? We must confront the question of the truth-value of claims to God's existence, not simply bask in their congeniality to our human nature. But here again, in this matter of our passion for truth we can ask, Is not this also a part of the theist's evidence? To study this second approach to God's existence we may turn from the world of the Greek Fathers to that of their Latin colleagues, and in particular to that giant among them, Augustine.

3

AUGUSTINE OF HIPPO AND THE LIFE OF SPIRIT

For Augustine of Hippo (354–430) – philosopher (in various phases Manichaean, Academic, and finally Plotinian), monk, presbyter, and ultimately bishop of a maritime city in the Roman province of Africa – God is to be found by reflection on the human spirit, a spirit as tumultuous and unsettled as Augustine's own personal history.[1] The finest activities of the spirit, he would have it, are only seen aright when they are seen as pointing towards God. Augustine is traditionally regarded as the *doctor cordialis*, the theologian whose gift it was to chart the hidden swell and surge of the heart of humankind. He is the man who seeks God because in the deep, personal center that the Latin Bible called *cor*, the heart, there is a restlessness that will not be satisfied until it finds an object spacious enough to give it house and home.[2] To this extent, I would link Augustine, despite the divergence in conceptual idiom, with Gregory of Nyssa and his movement of erōs (see chapter 2). But it is important to note that Augustine shows us the God present in the heart (roughly speaking, in the period of his writing as bishop of Hippo) only after he has satisfied himself that experience points us to the actual existence of this God in the life of the spirit (roughly speaking, in the period of his writing as a layman, in Italy). To schematize Augustine's development, we may say that, as a religious philosopher, he begins from our awareness of ourselves as spirit, that is to say, as knowing beings to whom the universe of truth lies open. The discovery of our nature as spiritual, in the most fundamental, if also to a degree prosaic, sense of that word, is the Augustinian way to transcendence. But this discovery and reflection on its implications opens up for the mature Augustine a whole new possibility of spiritual experience in a more pregnant and interesting sense.

Our feeling-response in various situations and to various events is now seen in, with, and through a relation to a God who draws us towards himself "by his own sweetness" through their agency. The *Confessions* are the evocation of such an Aeneid of the spirit, at once personal and typical. These two aspects of Augustine—the philosopher of the spirit and the teacher of the heart—must be kept together if the authentic balance of his teaching is to be preserved.

Augustine was born in the town of Thagaste, in the proconsular province of Africa, in the year 354.[4] He grew up in a world of farmers but chose instead a career as schoolmaster, which took him away from the land, and when he was forty years old the people of Hippo gave him a new vocation as bishop, which reinforced this; he would be a didact—distanced from, yet related to, his pupils. In Augustine's childhood, Roman Africa, like so many parts of the Roman Empire, was in serious economic decline, its civic monuments crumbling, its agriculture given over to a single crop, the olive, which required the minimum of tending, its non-Roman population increasingly disaffected with Roman rule. Yet to be a full citizen of a Roman town it was unnecessary to be rich: to be free and civilized was enough, and here the passport to success lay in a classical education. By 385, when he was thirty-one, Augustine would hold an imperial appointment as professor of rhetoric and be on the way not so much of transcendence as of preferment.

For the inside of Augustine's experience in youth and early manhood, we must turn first and foremost to the *Confessions*, and after that to his letters and homilies, especially perhaps the sermons on the psalms which he delivered in the basilica at Hippo and stenographers took down *viva voce*. The dominant figure in the *Confessions* after Augustine himself is Monica, his mother. A traditional African Catholic with the African tradition's fervent sense of the Church's set-apartness from the world, she was not, for all that, unoriginal. Her belief that a classical education, though pagan, would ultimately make her son a better Christian is notable. Even more so is her demandingness, which Augustine recognized in admitting an element of "unspiritual desire" in her devouring love for him.[5] Her flawed gift to Augustine was her determination, expressed both in her insistence that "a son of so many tears should not be lost"[6] and, by extension, in his ferocity as a controversialist in later years. In his magisterial biography, Peter Brown judged that "no thinker in the early Church was so preoccupied with the nature of human relationships; but then few environments would have impressed their importance upon Augustine as vividly as the close-knit world in which he had grown up."[7]

Augustine grew up, under Monica's ambitious reign, as a master of the spoken word. His world, as the historical imagination summons it before us, is a world full of sounds: the chanting of the psalms, the songs at harvest time that served him as a metaphor for the joy of salvation, and above all the conversation of his friends.[8] At one point in the *Confessions* he calls words "those precious cups of meaning":[9] he had come to find the sheer fact of intelligibility, the human being's transparence to the real, a source of explicitly religious inspiration. It seems clear that whatever Augustine himself may have felt, his period of sexual experimentation as a young man was a fairly modest affair; its importance for us lies in its liberation of the feelings of a person whose capacity for feeling was uniquely rich and powerful: herein would lie the secret of his gifts as monk, bishop, and preacher.

At the age of nineteen he began to take a serious interest in religion following his reading of a Ciceronian treatise, the *Hortensius*, in which the author had encouraged his readers to strive for blessedness through wisdom. The wise person is the one who knows where one stands in the universe, reveres the most Godlike part of oneself, the rational soul, and by it transcends the ambitious illusions of society.[10] To a young man of the fourth century with some residual Christian attachment, the word *sapientia*, "wisdom," would at once suggest Christ, for during that period Christ was represented customarily as the Teacher of Wisdom, garbed in the robe of a professional philosopher, often seated bearing a book, the book of eternal wisdom. Augustine had now found the form of his life: it was to be a search for the ultimate wisdom, and on this he would not renege. He had not yet, however, found its content. A closer inspection of the Bible, and especially the Old Testament, appalled him. His outrage at the "materialism" of Jewish history and the Jewish hope made him particularly vulnerable to Manichaeism, a radical offshoot of the Gnostic traditions of eastern Iran that was then flourishing in Africa.[11] For nine years he would be an *auditor*, "hearer" of the Manichee religion, accepting not only that matter, and so the body and history, were irredeemably corrupt, but also that the soul and God were themselves species of utterly refined matter, related to each other as parts to whole. Towards the close of this period he became increasingly skeptical of the cosmological speculations of his official mentors; but his connection with them, curiously, brought him into contact with the means of his eventual conversion to orthodox Christianity. In the aristocratic, senatorial circles of Rome, clinging tenaciously as these did to the old paganism, Manichees were regarded as useful allies against the Catholics. The prefect of Rome appointed Augustine professor of rhetoric at Milan, where a non-Catholic presence was urgently required.[12] The Milanese church was enjoying a superb renaissance of spiritual and intellectual power and hence of human and political influence. Clergy and laity, gathered around their bishop, Ambrose, sustained a high level of cultural achievement, borrowing the ideas of the Neoplatonist philosophers to reexpress Christian truths for their contemporaries.[13] And it was here, from Ambrose and behind him the *libri Platonici*, the "books of the Platonists," that Augustine would first find a satisfactory notion of the transcendence of God. The divine, he would come to see, precisely in virtue of its distinction from finite spirits, is relevant to the life of those spirits, singly and together.

Augustine's decision to enroll as a catechumen at Milan confirmed another notion, to withdraw with a group of friends to a temporary retirement for philosophical reflection, an experiment in the *beata vita*, where wisdom is happiness.[14] A text of this Cassiciacum period, the *Soliloquies*, is the first that will detain us. In this period Augustine is a Catholic Plotinian.[15] Like the great master of the Neoplatonist school, he sees the sensuous world irradiated by the nontemporal beyond of another world, which furnishes this world with a principle of existence and intelligibility that it otherwise lacks. This beyond was, for Plotinus, not beyond human intelligence, but the mind's access to it was in the last analysis mysterious and indescribable, though prepared for by philosophical reflection and an ascetic discipline of life. Augustine will eventually see the differences between Plotinianism and Christianity as at least as interesting as the similarities; but he will never forget the Plotinian vision of human life as an exile in a distant land, where the far-off music of our *patria* is nevertheless still audible. Much of the pathos of Augustine's preaching in later life flows from this. The Platonist tradition at large had seen humanity as in need of therapy: our mind needs healing, for a life too concentrated on the sensuous has wounded it. In these early years of his writing Augustine sees Christ as the invisible doctor, unknowingly desired by the Platonists. By an act of *clementia popularis*, "mercy for the multitude" (a piece of court language, it seems, drawn from imperial politicking), God sent his incarnate Word or Wisdom to the world, and this action still resonates through time and space, thanks to the preservation of the Scriptures in a catholic (universal) Church. By attention to the Word Incarnate, grasped through the mediation of the Bible in the Church, the inner eye of the mind can become clear again.[16]

If one takes the entire corpus of Augustine's writing, it becomes clear that he offers his readers a wide variety of approaches to the existence of God, even though it is the one that surfaces earliest, at Cassiciacum, which is the most characteristic of the man. Some of these approaches were to be drawn from Scripture, for instance, the argument, leaning on the first chapter of Romans, from the order of the world, a theme of Augustine's sermons.[17] Others he found in earlier Christian apologists, such as Lactantius; from them would come the argument "from the consent of peoples," the overwhelming testimony of humankind to the reality of the realm of the sacred, mentioned in the *Tractates on John*.[18] Yet others he found in the pagan philosophers, especially in Plotinus, whose *Enneads* Augustine knew through their translation into Latin by his fellow convert in Milan, Marius Victorinus. An example here would be the argument from the beauty of the world, seen as a kind of sacrament of a transcendent order, a thought that Augustine expresses in at least one celebrated passage of the *Confessions*.[19] But taken overall, he did not devote any very substantial part of his energies to developing these ways of approach to the divine. He settled instead for what was to become in the Western Christian milieux, where his writings were taken as faith's classical statement, the characteristic Augustinian approach to God.[20] By and large, he left aside these alternative routes to apprehending transcendence, in the words of Fulbert Cayré of the Augustinians of the Assumption, "not because he disdained them but because he went beyond them."[21] The approach that for him rendered experience most transparent to God was formulated in terms of the dependence of mind or spirit on God. Our awareness of the structure of mind, the "faculty of truth," is what carries us towards the affirmation that God is. Partly, this choice, to focus on the mystery hidden in our own interiority, can be explained by the kind of human being Augustine was. Subtle and perceptive where the inner life was concerned, it might be said of him, to invert the aphorism of the Parnassian poet Théophile Gautier, that Augustine "was a man for whom the *interior* world exists."[22] But partly, too, the choice reflects the pastoral and evangelical concern that marked Augustine. His driving force was the call to prosecute the vital union of every human being with God. Naturally, then, the most congenial approach to God's existence would be for Augustine one that led of itself to Everyman's self-gift to God. It would be one charged with what a later generation would call, in an increasingly debased language, alas, "existential" relevance. Ultimately, such a self-donation, Augustine thought, must be the work of God's grace, the love that the Holy Spirit sheds abroad in our hearts. But this supernatural union might be prepared by a less exalted natural proceeding, a kind of conversation of the mind with itself, a meditation that generates a knowledge and love of God as very Truth.[23]

Discussion of this interrelation between philosophy and theology[24] in Augustine has chiefly been couched in terms of the significance of his conversion or conversions.[25] On this a considerable literature has accumulated, and it does not seem likely that much further enlightenment will be gained by this method.[26] Instead, it may be useful to suggest how, in the great lines of Augustine's writing as a whole, philosophical and theological accounts of approach to transcendence can be seen as interrelated. While such an approach is chiefly by way of ideas' content, and not biography, biographical reference can scarcely be excluded. *In nuce*, the question to consider might be phrased in this way: Is Augustine better thought of, with Hegel, as a philosopher of spirit,[27] or, with baroque Catholicism, as the *doctor cordialis*, "teacher of the heart"?[28]

Philosopher of Spirit

Insofar as Augustine may be described as a religious philosopher (as distinct from a theologian), his thought takes its starting point from our awareness of ourselves as spirit, that is, as knowing beings to whom the universe of truth lies open. The discovery of ourselves as spiritual, in the most elementary sense of the word gives Augustine the basis for a rational approach to transcendence.[29] This emerges clearly enough from the Cassiciacum dialogues (*Against the Academicians*; *On the Happy Life*; *On Order*; *Soliloquies*), based as these probably were on actual conversations—some informal, others arranged for the benefit of his teenage pupils Licentius and Trygetius—that took place in 386/7 at the villa of Augustine's friend Verecundius in the foothills of the Italian alps, some forty miles to the northeast of Milan.[30] The *Soliloquies* are an apparent exception to this rule, as their name suggests, but a hint in *On Order* would justify us in regarding them as a kind of residue from one such "arranged conversation."[31] The general project of the Cassiciacum works is stated in Augustine's *Against the Academics*:

> No one doubts that we are impelled to learn by the twofold forces of authority and reason. I have determined henceforth never to depart from the authority of Christ, for I find none more valid. But as regards that which must be pursued with subtle reasoning, my disposition now is to long impatiently to apprehend the truth not only by faith but also with the understanding; and I am confident that meantime I shall find in the Platonists something that is not incompatible with our sacred things.[32]

In other words, having laid to rest the ghost of Academic doubt (i.e., systematic skepticism), he intends to work out a system of philosophy in which the fundamental aspects of Christian believing will be interpreted for the benefit of the understanding by following up clues supplied by Platonists. By 391, when Augustine returned to Africa from Italy, this project was essentially completed. Years later, in the *Retractations*, he would bemoan what by then seemed to him its imperfect permeation by the Gospel spirit—the early project's lack of a thoroughgoing theocentrism and its absence of eschatology, as well as its overheavy reliance on the duality of body and spirit (rather than of sin and grace) and its excessive indulgence towards the pagan philosophers.[33] Yet he would always remain a Platonist, albeit a Christian one.[34]

The first clear statement of Augustine's philosophy of spirit is found in the *Soliloquies*, which are among the writings of the year of his arrival at Cassiciacum, 386. The *Soliloquies* turn on the human ability to make judgments in the light of abiding principles of rational truth. Whence come the absolute criteria in whose light we judge the things about us? Augustine probes the answer of Christian faith in terms of its adequacy to the philosopher's question. Thus the prayer that opens the work is explicitly said to be made out of faith, hope, and charity; at the same time, the conceptualizing of divine transcendence as this prayer unfolds belongs to the philosophical idiom announced in *Against the Academics*: "Father of our awakening and of our illumination . . . the intelligible light in, by, and through which all intelligible things are illumined . . ."[35] The *Soliloquies* is an unfinished work, but the argument, suggested by Augustine's hostility to the skepticism of the New Academy, is that since rational principles do not depend for their truth on any contingent object, then their truth must be eternal and must inhere in a reality as eternal as itself. God is the "sun of the intellectual realm."[36] As sunlight is detected in its capacity to display sensible realities but, once detected, may then be looked at in itself, so reason begins by showing God in the reflected luminosity of rational disciplines of knowledge but then goes on to become the *adspectus*, or "attention," of the mind as it looks towards God himself.[37] What makes reason well advised to lean on divine authority is not any structural weakness in its cognitive powers but the practical deficiencies of the mind in actual use. Here we have for the first time a characteristic Augustinian contrast important for the relationship between philosophy and theology, namely, the contrast between human potential (on which Augustine is an optimist) and the actual human condition (on which he is a pessimist). Venality and indolence cause us in practice to fix our minds on the concerns of earthly life.

Augustine's fullest discussion of a philosophical approach to transcendence comes, however, in the *Problem of Free Choice*, written shortly before his return to Africa and based on conversations in Rome after Monica's death in 389. His interlocutor, Evodius, is concerned chiefly with the problem of evil (the work is among the first of Augustine's many anti-Manichaean treatises), but the dialogue contains a sustained digression on God's existence. Evodius has been saying that even his certainty that God exists comes to him through faith. Were an atheist to interrogate him on the subject, he would answer in terms of the authority of all those writers who testified that they lived with the Son of God, i.e., the evangelists.[38] Augustine agrees that, often enough, faith precedes understanding, but he will not allow that Evodius has told the whole story. Augustine draws attention to the phenomenon of shared truth. If we consider the principles of wisdom expressed in such maxims as "One ought to live justly" or "The better should be preferred to the worse," we realize that "you could not call this yours or mine or any man's, but it is present and offers itself in common to all who behold unchangeable truths like light which in wonderful fashion is both secret and public."[39] And Augustine continues:

> If this truth were on an equality with our minds, it would itself be subject to change. Sometimes our minds see it more clearly, sometimes less clearly, and as a result they admit themselves to be subject to change. The truth, however, abiding in itself, gains nothing when we see it more clearly, and

loses nothing when we see it less clearly, but, whole and sound, it glad-
dens with its light those who are turned towards it, and punishes with its
blindness those who are turned away from it.[40]

Evodius is to "embrace and enjoy" this truth. The language, though
strong, remains that of classical philosophy.[41] But then with a marked
shift in rhetorical inflection, Augustine adds that Evodius is thus to
"delight in the Lord, and he will give you your heart's desire." (Psalm
36: 4). After this allusion to the psalter, there follows a lyrical evocation of the blessedness that stems from embracing truth, and, citing
the words of the fourth Gospel on the truth that sets one free (John 8:
32), Augustine concludes: the truth

> is close to all its lovers throughout the world who turn towards it, and for
> all it is everlasting. It is in no place, yet nowhere is it absent; from without
> it admonishes us, within it instructs us. It changes all its beholders for the
> better; it is itself never changed for the worse; without it, no one judges
> rightly.[42]

In this treatise, we find a second sort of relation being established
between a philosophical and a theological account of transcendence.
In place of the notion of the *Soliloquies* that on practical grounds theology (faith with its authority) must supplement philosophy (reason),
here we find that the successful realization of Augustine's philosophical project brings about the need for theology, as is shown in the
change of rhetorical register.

The *Problem of Free Choice* offers an ontology leading up to a doctrine of spirit. But reflection on the doctrine of spirit sparks off a
movement of self-transcendence towards God that then requires a
modulation into a strictly theological key. The book's ontology is stated
in terms of three diverse and increasingly rich and comprehensive
modes of existence. First of all, one may speak of being itself, *esse*,
the foundation word that expresses our basic awareness of reality.
Second, there is life, *vivere*, which incorporates *esse* and adds a new
element of richness to it. Third, there is knowing, *intelligere*, which
contains the other two (as the activity of a living being) and renders
them self-aware.[43] Reality becomes more *comprehensive* because more
comprehending. Spirit, the mind of the intelligent creature, is located
at the summit of the hierarchy of being, glorious in its privilege of
knowing truth. But by a spontaneous movement of reflection, the

mind then turns in search of a transcendence that can ground itself. In this way, Augustine detects a pressure from the infinite in our "spiritual" (*geistig*) experience. At the lowest reckoning, the divine illumination of spirit, which grounds spirit's activity by regulating that activity, may strike us as nothing more than a sense of responsibility about higher norms, for instance the imperative to use precision in describing empirical data. Again, it may operate through our sense of certitude about our knowledge and judgments—or even a questioning after their validity, since in the nearly contemporary *On the True Religion* Augustine appears to regard the question about an ultimate ground of meaning as itself testifying to an awareness of that ground.[44] Such experiences, Augustine is saying, have aspects that indicate that in, with, and through them we are enjoying an obscure apprehension of God as truth.

Whatever one makes of such an argument, there is little doubt that it is a piece of philosophizing, and philosophizing of such a kind that it justifies my description of Augustine as a "philosopher of spirit," with its suggestion of some affinity between Augustine, in this regard, and G. W. F. Hegel (both, indeed, were indebted to Neoplatonism).[45] Put into a less exalted terminology, we can say that Augustine is drawing attention to the exceptionally strong way in which the authoritativeness of values strikes us in the case of the value of truth.[46] We feel that truth imposes its authority upon us. We sense a need to be receptive or even humble before the truth. Truth always outruns us and summons us to go beyond ourselves in a movement, then, of self-transcendence. But since a being is only what it is and cannot transcend its own limits, this self-transcendence can only mean response to an invitation to be taken beyond oneself.[47] We stand before an offer, an *act* of inviting. We begin to find ourselves engaged with the infinite in a relationship that can only be spoken of in quasi-personal terms. If truth as the authority of eternal being is experienced as calling us, as inviting us to response, then the language of the spirit must be replaced by that of the heart. This is what Augustine found himself doing vis-à-vis Evodius in *The Problem of Free Choice*. The paradigm of this shift is the shared vision of Augustine and Monica at Ostia. As Cayré saw many years ago: "With St. Augustine, the demonstration of God's existence has scarcely reached its term before the author begins to urge the soul to unite itself to God . . . to a reality at once so living and so personal that it welcomes with joy the gift of self that those who respond to it make."[48]

DOCTOR CORDIALIS

So far I have suggested, on the basis of the early dialogues, that the philosophical way to transcendence in Augustine yields to a theological way by one or another of two steps. Either the practical difficulties of embodied spirit in its effort to sustain spiritual activity makes recourse to the authority of faith necessary. Or else the exploration of finite spirit's relation to infinite Spirit finds itself transposed into a quasi-personal key and so becomes the description of a God-human relationship. On the one hand, in the *Soliloquies*, the practical failure of philosophical reason makes recourse to faith, and so to theology, a necessity. On the other hand, in *The Problem of Free Choice*, the very success of philosophical reason brings about a change of tonality to a theological key. From the Cassiciacum-Roman period, therefore, Augustine could take two principles that would be able to guide his theological reflection: first, the contrast between the potential of human resources and the miserable state of humanity's actual condition; second, the notion of God as initiating personal relationship with the human being who has been granted a preunderstanding of God through reflecting on the phenomenon of shared truth.

What determined Augustine's use of these principles (which have a pervasive force in his African writings), was, certainly, the changed environment into which he came on his return to Africa and the fresh set of tasks he found awaiting him. As Gerald Bonner has pointed out, Augustine moved from a world of Christian intellectuals, in which the resources of classical culture and philosophy might be taken for granted, into the world of the *rudes et simplices*, the unlettered Catholics of Africa. Bonner sees Augustine's episcopal ordination in 395 as crucial here: "For the rest of his life the Bible was to be his rule and norm. . . . A bishop has better things to do than to expound Cicero's treatises."[49] The mind of Augustine was significantly modified by his new situation as "pastor of souls." Confronted with the intractable problems of his people, and above all with the obstinacy of the Donatists, Augustine's preferred metaphors for the way to transcendence become, as Peter Brown has remarked, those of pilgrimage and way-faring:[50] in other words, they become more modest and discreet. The forces that prepare one to find final joy in God are now seen as lying preeminently in the subconscious region of the heart and as hidden in the unfathomable mystery of the grace of God (cf. the *Soliloquies*). At the same time, Augustine's stress falls increasingly on the divine

initiative found in the missions of the Son and the Spirit: these form
the way to the goal that the authors of the "books of the Platonists"
had espied (cf. *The Problem of Free Choice*).

The ecclesiology of the anti-Donatist writings and *The City of God*;
the anthropology of the *Confessions* and the *Tractates on John*; the doctrine of God in *On the Trinity*: the doctrine of grace in the anti-Pelagian
writings: all these are theological in a way in which the early dialogues
are not. Nevertheless, this shift of perspective does not derive simply
from a change of concerns, from philosophically minded and self-
employed layman to priest and bishop concerned with the exposition
of *sacra doctrina*. The change derives also from a natural outworking
of the internal logic of the early dialogues. The philosopher of spirit,
once his task is done, naturally transforms himself into a teacher of
the heart. As such, his controlling themes are inevitably those, on the
one hand, of the mystery of motivation and aspiration in the heart of
humankind, and, on the other, of the divine initiative mediated by
the trinitarian missions and finding its term in grace.

If this is so, then we can draw from this interrelation some guidance
in our choice of historical reconstructions of Augustine's development.
Those accounts of the various conversions which stress continuity
would seem to have the better claim on our attention, provided that
they do not elide all distinction between the mind of Augustine around
the time of his baptism (and so after the moral conversion) and the
mind of Augustine as African churchman. In the Cassiciacum-Roman
period Augustine is, in fact, a Catholic Plotinian as much as a Plotinian
Catholic.[51] Both terms are of equal defining force, as they must have
been for many people in that brief efflorescence of Christian Plotinianism in the Milanese Church. The mind's access to the beyond which,
for Neoplatonism, founds this world and gives its final meaning, is
both prepared for by philosophical reflection *and* enabled by the incarnate Word or Wisdom which is Christ. In such dialogues as the *Soliloquies* and *The Problem of Free Choice* we find Augustine confronting
the nature of the relationship that this "both . . . and" implies. As we
have seen, it is at once the failures and the successes of the philosophical way to transcendence that lead Augustine to give ever greater
weight to the divine economy and so bring his philosophical concepts
into the service of a theological vision based on Bible and Creed. Yet
the philosophy of spirit of the early Augustine is not simply subjacent
to, or assumed by, the theology of the mature Augustine. Rather, the
philosopher of spirit transforms himself, through the internal demands

of his own rational enterprise, into the doctor of the heart.[52]

The mutability of the spirit of man, Augustine's starting point in assenting to God, is now given unforgettable dramatic expression in terms of the story of the heart. Rowan Williams has essayed a summary of Augustine's mature anthropology in these words:

> The mystery of the depths of the self directs us beyond the world of clear and orderly sense experience but is itself only a stage on the road to the greater mystery of God; there is no substantial continuity of the soul and God. So there is no rest in mere self-awareness, because to know the self properly is to see it set in the midst of the vast landscape of God's workings, a landscape with no human map, trusting only to the hand of God. Once having glimpsed this vastness and heard the distant sounds of the "holiday of heaven" the spirit must live by hope, knowing as clearly as ever it will that nothing else can substitute for that vision and its delights.[53]

It would rest with a deeply Augustinian mind fifteen centuries later, the mind of Gabriel Marcel, to turn this theological theme of hope in the later Augustine into a new motif of philosophizing. But, as we shall see later in this book, Marcel never used this discovery, any more than did Augustine, to deny the presence of God in the depths of the self, a presence provisional, albeit, and obscure (see chapter 10). For humankind open to truth is in and through that very fact humankind open to God.

In considering thus the implications of our varied human ways of seeking truth or otherwise adverting to the demands of intellectual integrity, we have in Augustine's company found open before us a second avenue of experiential approach to God. Perhaps it would be more just to say, confining ourselves to the more strictly philosophical burden of Augustine's theism, that we took a further step along the road to transcendence. Between the conviction that there is a realm of reality above and beyond the play of sense, above and beyond the frailties of the finite spirit, and the full-blooded affirmation that our idea of God as the absolutely perfect Being is justified, a yawning abyss threatens to open along our path. Is our theistic language really the proper form of speech about transcendence? Does it block our further progress, or, on the contrary, provide a source of support in the religious quest? To help answer this question, we shall turn to a theologian of the early Middle Ages, a dominant figure in the intellectual renaissance that swept the Latin church in the twelfth century: Anselm of Canterbury.

ANSELM OF CANTERBURY AND THE LANGUAGE OF PERFECTION

THE "PROSLOGION" IN CONTEXT

Anselm of Canterbury (c. 1033–1109) is the typical monastic philosopher, so much so that his principal contribution to the philosophical tradition is today most easily available in English dress as part of an anthology of his prayers and meditations.[1] This is as it should be. Anselm's life is unintelligible except in terms of the search for transcendence, itself regarded as the heart and goal of the metaphysical enterprise by traditional philosophy in the West. At the same time, his philosophy cannot be placed until we recognize that we are dealing with a monk, a man of prayer and brotherhood. In his prayers, which are formal and highly structured but nevertheless deeply felt set pieces that initiated a fresh devotional style in the Latin church, it is characteristic of Anselm, as Richard Southern has pointed out, that he "moves from inertia to a vivid apprehension of the being and love of God."[2] This also happens to be the program of his philosophical masterpiece, the *Proslogion*, which he wrote in a single gust of inspiration in 1078.

Anselm was fortunate in his biographer, a member of what became eventually his own monastic family at Christ Church, Canterbury.[3] Eadmer's account of the political events of Anselm's episcopate, the *Historia Novorum*, has been hailed as "the first major Latin historical work in England since Bede and . . . one of the greatest achievements of Anglo-Norman historiography."[4] In a more personal chronicle, the *De vita et conversatione Anselmi archiepiscopi Cantuarensis*, Eadmer gives us an image of Anselm's childhood that is evidently meant to serve as a parable of the whole man. In his childhood in the Alpine foothills Anselm imagined heaven perched atop the snowcapped mountains

THE LANGUAGE OF PERFECTION

around Aosta: once in a dream, he scaled them and was graciously received at table by God, imagined as a great king.[5] As a youth, he took the way of many Italians in the eleventh and twelfth centuries, crossing the Alps to Burgundy, France, and Normandy in search of higher education. Here he would find not only *litterae humaniores* but also theology.[6] It is conjectured that Chartres and Fleury-sur-Loire may have been his magnets, but in time the reputation of his fellow Italian, Lanfranc, who was master of the Norman Benedictine school of Bec, drew Anselm farther north to the area of Rouen, then governed by Normandy's most celebrated duke, William the Conqueror.[7] Over thirty years later as abbot of Bec Anselm would be brought to Canterbury as archbishop by the Conqueror's son, William Rufus. He accepted with a reluctance that, in a monk of a house in the buoyancy of its founding generation, was probably not simulated. By this date, 1093, he had behind him his published prayers, identified from an anarchic manuscript tradition by the labors of André Wilmart,[8] and his philosophical writings, among which was the *Proslogion*. The later theological writings were produced in interludes of quiet in the turbulent politico-ecclesiastical history that followed the struggle over the episcopate's freedom of spiritual action or the so-called Investiture Controversy.[9]

For the intellectual resources Anselm brought to the search for transcendence we may look to the school of Bec itself as well as to his own writings. It is known that Lanfranc had offered a generous formation in the humanities, with a particular stress on logic.[10] The researches of D. P. Henry have shown that Anselm was familiar not only with the *logica vetus*, consisting of Aristotle's *Categories*, *Topics*, and *De Interpretatione*, but also the logical works of Boethius. The latter's logic, as expressed in his commentary on the *Isagoge* of Porphyry and therefore in effect a commentary on Aristotelian logic at one remove, was much concerned with "modal" concepts of possibility and necessity that would exercise Anselm also.[11] Anselm's theological master was undoubtedly Augustine.[12] The combination of sources is piquant and instructive. In the contemporary struggle between dialecticians and antidialecticians, Anselm was very much on the side of the former, those who saw the need for a rational exploration and systematization of the materials of revelation, against those for whom theology was simply a paraphrase of Scripture in the light of the Fathers.[13] The curious thing is that, while this is true, his proof of God's existence nonetheless issues from prayer and terminates in prayer.

The *Proslogion* is one of Anselm's Norman works, composed while prior at Bec. A prior's office was essentially that of domestic administrator, far removed from the international concerns of Anselm's later period, concerns reflected in correspondence with, among others, the king of Scots and the Crusader rulers of the Latin Kingdom of Jerusalem.[14] The human background of an Anglo-Norman house of this period would be very much that described by David Knowles in his *Monastic Order in England* – a highly organized conventual round of study, labor, liturgy, and fraternal coexistence.[15] This background is exceedingly relevant to the presuppositions of the *Proslogion*'s argument.

In the preface to the *Proslogion*, Anselm explains that, once finished with the brief treatise known as the *Monologion*, it occurred to him that this latter work "consisted in a connected chain of many arguments." He began to ask himself "if it would be possible to find one single argument, needing no other proof than itself, to prove that God really exists, that he is the highest good, needing nothing, that it is he whom all things need for their being and well-being, and to prove whatever else we need to prove about the nature of God."[16] After describing the mental struggle whereby at first he groped in vain for this "unique argument" and subsequently spent his energies in keeping the problem from tyrannizing over all his waking thoughts, Anselm goes on: "One day, when I was tired out with resisting its importunity, that which I had despaired of finding came to me, in the conflict of my thoughts, and I welcomed eagerly the very thought which I had been so anxious to reject."[17] It is Eadmer who records that the timing of this moment was the Office of Matins in the monastic liturgy at Bec.

> Suddenly, one night during Matins, the grace of God illuminated his heart, the whole matter became clear to his mind, and a great joy and exultation filled his inmost being. Thinking therefore that others also would be glad to know what he had found, he immediately and ungrudgingly wrote it on writing tablets and gave them to one of the brethren of the monastery for safe keeping.[18]

In the light of what has been said above concerning Eadmer's integrity as an historian, this section of the *Vita* can hardly be dismissed as conventional pious ornament. The *Proslogion* belongs in one sense, therefore, with the devotional writings that were written largely, as Southern remarks, for Anselm's fellow monks, though also to meet the increasingly articulate needs of laypeople with the time, inclination, and (presumably) financial wherewithal to adopt the religious practices of the monastic life.[19]

Of course the word once written takes on a life of its own beyond the control or even expectations of an author. The audience that the *Proslogion* eventually commanded was provided by the history of philosophy, rather than a monastic *conventus*. The significance of Anselm's discovery escaped his contemporaries, apart from the immediate reply it evoked from a fellow monk, Gaunilo of Marmoutiers,[20] and a reminiscence in the writings of Abbot Gilbert Crispin of Westminster.[21] As M. J. Charlesworth put it, "St. Anselm's *Proslogion* might have fallen stillborn from the scriptorium for all the influence it had upon his own intellectual milieu."[22] The thirteenth century, however, more than made up for the twelfth's lack of acumen in Anselm's regard, and a host of writers studied his "unique argument": William of Auxerre, the Dominican Richard Fishacre, the Franciscans Alexander of Hales and Bonaventure, through whom it became known to St. Thomas. In John Duns Scotus's version it passed into the mainstream of early modern philosophy, to Descartes and Leibniz. It was this third- or fourthhand paraphrase, it seems, that Kant attempted to refute, since when, and until fairly recent years, the argument came to be viewed as "a quaint and naïve mediaeval conundrum."[23] Once again, however, an Anselmian renaissance has succeeded an age of neglect, both in Continental and British writing. Its celebration is the interdisciplinary and international collection, *Spicilegium Beccense*, published in Paris on the nine-hundredth anniversary of Anselm's arrival at Bec.[24]

Prayer or Philosophy?

Several of the defenders of the "unique argument," and notably Anselm Stolz, have been at pains to rescue the *Proslogion* from the ravages of philosophical critics by claiming that its intention is essentially spiritual or mystical.[25] It is, they say, an essay in mystical theology, in the understanding, then, of the practice of prayer. To discover God as necessary perfection, as Anselm does, is to offer crucial counsel on how to pray. In praying, one must never be content with one's current images of God but strive constantly to transcend them towards a reality that is of its nature *semper maior*. It is true that prayer is the vital context of the argument. Indeed, as we shall see, to sever the argument entirely from this context is to lose its strictly philosophical force. The first and last chapters of the *Proslogion*, in particular, are entirely characteristic Anselmian meditations. Thus for instance, from *Proslogion* 1:

> Lord, I am not trying to make my way to your height, for my desire is in no way equal to that, but I do desire to understand a little of your truth which my heart already believes and loves. I do not seek to understand so that I may believe, but I believe so that I may understand; and what is more, I believe that unless I do believe I shall not understand.

But is it not a modern fallacy to suppose that a monastic and spiritual concern, such as Anselm's undoubtedly was, must necessarily exclude a philosophical and rational concern? We need not surrender to impaling on the horns of the dilemma that would have the *Proslogion* to be *either* spirituality *or* philosophy but on no account both. Professor E. L. Mascall has well said of Anselm in this connection:

> He believed by faith that God is supremely rational, and it therefore seemed obvious to him that, if only one could find out how to do it, it must be possible to prove the existence of this supremely rational being. He believed that God had shown him how to do this, and he could never thank him sufficiently for it. I think, therefore, that one key at least to the *Proslogion* is to be found in the fact that it could never occur to Anselm that there was anything irrational or anti-rational about faith and revelation.[26]

The relationship between faith and reason in Anselm is a complex one, partly because the question has not yet become a topic of discussion in its own right. He wished to hold *les deux bouts de la chaîne*, maintaining both that reason has a role to play prior to faith and within the realm of faith and that faith transcends reason, from which it follows that it cannot be on purely rational grounds alone that the mysteries of the faith are given lodging in the mind.[27]

Looking for confirmation more widely in Anselm's writing, we find him affirming in the *Soliloquies* that he accepts the teachings of Scripture in the hope that he will come more and more to understand them.[28] This is the classic sense of the Augustinian adage, *credo ut intellegam*.[29] Reason serves the life of faith by exhibiting the intelligibility of God and his decrees. In the *Cur Deus homo*, on the other hand, a novel and distinctively Anselmian note is struck. The interlocutor here is a monk who is not so much seeking reasons to confirm faith as *gaudium*, a joy that flows from one's realization that faith accords with reason, a spiritual joy of the intellect delighting in the truth.[30] And departing further still from the root Augustinian meaning of *credo ut intellegam*, the terms of the command "Believe that you may understand" that Anselm addresses to the monk in the *Cur Deus homo* may in fact be transposed at certain points. We thus find instead: "Understand so that you may believe." The skeptic is challenged to understand that God exists (the *Proslogion*), that he is supremely good and just (the *Monologion*) and that he has made provision for humankind's salvation in the only way possible (the *Cur Deus homo*). Jasper Hopkins warns that when we find Anselm saying that reason can never conflict with Scripture we should not take him to be asserting in doctrinaire fashion that he would not recognize any such conflict if brought to his notice.[31] Rather, he is making a prediction based, Hopkins suggests, on three factors. First, Anselm has, in fact, found himself able to resolve *prima facie* conflicts between reason and the Bible when he found them. Second, he recognized that adjudication in such conflicts is itself a rational undertaking. Third, he believed that human reason cannot, in principle, comprehend the full mystery of the Godhead revealed in Christ. He also works on the presupposition, noted by Mascall, that a rational God cannot reveal to humanity anything intrinsically irrational. And so the notion that reason and revelation never conflict is a structural principle for Anselm, set to work to interpret all the data of theology. Only if the consistent interpretation of those data by that principle became too costly would it be abandoned. Anselm never found it necessary to abandon it.[32] The *Proslogion* may very well be *both* prayer *and* philosophy.[33]

THE LANGUAGE OF PERFECTION

The fundamental objection, or at any rate the main feeling of discomfort, shared by readers of the *Proslogion* concerns the notion that an argument to God's existence could be deduced from a mere definition—the definition of God as necessary perfection, or in Anselm's own words, "that than which a greater cannot be thought." It smacks of the triumphant conjuror drawing a rabbit from a top hat. But "How did he do it?" is the response of a person who feels tricked by sleight of hand, rather than of the genuinely convinced enquirer. In recent years, however, it has been questioned whether this view of the treatise really corresponds to Anselm's intentions as embodied in the *Proslogion* as we have it.

At the start of the argument, Anselm attempts to identify the God *to whom he is in the course of praying* with what he calls "something than which a greater cannot be thought." But the point of the argument, in the first instance, is precisely to confirm this identification. As Richard Campbell has shown in his study of the *Proslogion*, the idea of necessary perfection cannot be construed as a definition playing its part in the logic of the argument as it unfolds, since it is itself one of the conclusions towards which the argument is to proceed.[34] Further, Campbell points out that the passage I have cited above from *Proslogion* 1, a passage which immediately precedes the "unique argument," is scarcely an example of the way a man arguing from a definition of God would be likely to speak. And finally, before ending the *Proslogion*, Anselm says in so many words that he must pass beyond this characterization of God as "that than which a greater cannot be conceived" since even this has proved inadequate to what he has found to be true in prayer. "Lord, you are then not only that than which nothing greater can be thought; you are something greater than it is possible to think about. For since it is possible to think that this could exist, if you are not that thing, then a greater than you can be thought; and that will not do."[35] Throughout the treatise, in fact, *God* is a proper name, a subject of address, and proper names do not have definitions. If definitions give the meaning of terms, proper names have no meaning. Their office is to refer, and this referential function is not necessarily connected with any descriptive import that some given proper name might (as in Guggles Radziwill) or might not (as in Joe Smith) convey. And so: "While Anselm says to God, 'You are that than which a greater cannot be thought,' that assertion cannot reasonably be taken as an answer to the absurd question, 'Who or what is meant by "you"?' "[36] Years ago, Stolz had realized that the celebrated Anselmian identification is no definition but rather a conclusion. But for him, as we have noted, it was no philosophical conclusion; it was the mystical issue of the monk's prayer life. For Stolz, Anselm simply presumes God's existence, wishing to pass over from pure believing to an experiential encounter with the ever-present God affirmed by faith.[37] But we have found already that this will not serve as an account of Anselm's view of the relationship between faith and reason. Moreover, it ignores the fact that the *Proslogion* is simply littered with argumentative connectives.

What then *is* the true starting point of Anselm's thought about God's existence? The Anselmian argument is founded upon the language of perfection. In the public realm, we use and find meaning in a language about perfection. We do not regard this use of language as utterly baffling, although it may sometimes strike us as curious or provocative. At the opening of the "unique argument," Anselm's interlocutor, the Fool of the Psalter (he who "has said in his heart: 'There is no God' "), overhears Anselm praying in this language. He is speaking of that than which nothing greater can be conceived, the unconditionally perfect. The Fool "understands what he hears, and what he understands is in his mind, even if he does not understand that it actually exists."[38] Anselm's speech act involves limit language that may be mysterious but yet is not totally incomprehensible. The Fool himself makes good use of this same language in formulating his objection to Anselm. As Ludwig Wittgenstein might comment, a person who knows how to use the language of perfection but denies that he can understand its significance does not know what he is saying, for "just as language allows us to speak of the unspeakable, so thought allows us to think of that which, in itself, surpasses the ability of thought to comprehend."[39] Anselm will go on from his initial speech act to argue that the whole realm of discourse that permits one to speak of God as that than which a greater cannot be conceived rules out the possibility of intelligently denying God's existence. He claims, in effect, that the use of the language of perfection opens up a path down which all language-using and meaning-laden beings are pointed, a path leading to the mystery of God.

> In coming to understand that the Fool's challenge to faith oversteps the limits of what can be thought, in this becoming aware of the bounds of the creativity of human thought, one finds faith and reason working together to point towards the pre-containing creativity of God who transcends human thought.[40]

How then does Anselm propose to show that the Fool's construction of the language of perfection is impossible, whereas his own imposes itself? The words "that than which a greater cannot be conceived" serve to specify an "intentional object," what Anselm calls something "in the mind," *in intellectu*. This object is not regarded as a mental item with some arcane autonomous existence of its own but simply as an intellectual mediation of some possibly existing reality.[41] Concepts are that by which we grasp the real, not mental impressions parallel to it. Anselm now goes on to claim that this "that than which a greater cannot be conceived" is not only *in intellectu* but also *in re*, in existence: "Surely that than which a greater cannot be thought cannot exist in the mind alone. For if it exists solely in the mind even, it can be thought to exist in reality also."[42] The crucial thing here is the meaning to be attached to *in re*. By *in re* Anselm means belonging to experience as a whole, which experience cannot but be informative about the realm of the real. It has become a commonplace here to drag in a cannon bearing the name of Kant with which to shoot down Anselm's enterprise. But curiously enough, as Campbell has shown, Kant's *Critique of Pure Reason* may here be turned to defense of the *Proslogion*'s argument in its authentic form. For while Kant was indeed to argue that existence is not a determining predicate (if it were, that which we say "exists" would no longer be the same something as what we spoke of before we made that assertion), nevertheless he did not regard the predicative use of *exists* as simply meaningless, mere vibration of the air. He saw it as a special kind of relational predicate whose task it is to locate what is thought of, or spoken of, in the context of experience at large.

> Though in my concept nothing may be lacking of the possible real content of a thing in general, something is lacking in its relation to my whole state of thought. Therefore through its existence (the object) is thought of as belonging to the context of experience as a whole.[43]

And so that than which a greater cannot be thought can be thought to exist in reality also, and this, Anselm now adds, "is greater." Existence is a valuational relationship, not just a brute fact. We have a preference for the actual, if only to complain of it.

> If then that than which a greater cannot be thought exists in the mind alone, this same that than which a greater *cannot* be thought is that than which a greater *can* be thought. But this is obviously impossible. Therefore, there is absolutely no doubt that something than which a greater cannot be thought exists both in the mind and in reality.[44]

Given the meaningfulness of the speech act from which we started, it appears self-contradictory to say that that than which nothing greater can be conceived is in the understanding only. It does not make sense to deny the purchase on reality of the language of unsurpassable perfection.

But which thing, or things, answers, or answer, to this description? To secure the identification of God with such a reality, Anselm must show that there is some characteristic true of this reality which is true only of God. And this he finds to be the unthinkableness of its not existing. Whatever this thing is, it is characterized by the sheerest ontological independence. If it failed to exist, or came into existence, or passed out of it, it must be dependent on something greater still, and that is contradictory. If it exists, and Anselm has by now established to his own satisfaction that it does, then it cannot not exist: "And this is you, O Lord our God. You therefore so truly are, O Lord my God, that you cannot even be thought not to be."[45] The God who is the Lord of the Church is also the God of the enquiring mind.

THE FIDUCIARY APPROACH TO LANGUAGE

Since the starting point of Anselm's argument is language-in-use, the *Proslogion* is not to be seen as an exercise in impersonal, purely logical, demonstration of the existence of God. In so far as Anselm sets out from the actual performance of a speech act his conclusions cannot be said to be either impersonal or logically entailed. Not all exhibition of the rationality of beliefs takes the form of logical demonstration. Campbell draws an instructive parallel here with a passage from the Wittgenstein of the *Philosophical Investigations*.[46] The comparison concerns language about external objects. Since language of its very nature inhabits a shared public realm, any denial of the existence of reality beyond the self, that is, of the existence of such a public realm, is at bottom unintelligible, precisely because any such denial must itself be made in language. In saying this, it is not being claimed that the existence of external reality is logically entailed by the language we use. Nevertheless, we are showing forth the reasonableness of our belief in that external reality. Similarly, in the *Proslogion*, Anselm shows how our capacity to use the language of absolute perfection makes it unintelligible to deny that such language opens out onto the realm of the real.

Our response to Anselm will depend, accordingly, on the degree of willingness we feel to take language on trust, to accept what John Coulson has called its "fiduciary" demands.[47] Language may have developed as it has just because of its aptness for disclosing features of reality. It always implies a commerce between the language user and the real. This need not mean that every description formulated in language must necessarily describe some real thing. But it will mean that using language involves, in and of itself, a turning to the real. Thus openness to learn from what is said something of what there *is* can be commended as a rational posture. Linguistic formulas can present us with distorted pictures of the real, but in the case of the language of perfection we can come to see, through the argument of the *Proslogion*, that the formulas of *this* language, at any rate, are not systematically misleading but rather the contrary.

As G. R. Evans has shown in her recent studies of Anselm, Anselm regarded language as divine in its origins and function.[48] The self-subsistent Word, which is God himself, is the ultimate and universal "language" from which ordinary speech is derived. In the *Monologion* Anselm proposes that all language ultimately derives from the great universal words in the divine Mind. The various languages that human beings use are doubtless derived from these words in complex and tortuous ways. Nonetheless, they gain their meaningfulness from their relation to the universal *verba*.[49] Such an archaic ontology of language naturally predisposes Anselm to that fiduciary view of language that thinkers as diverse as S. T. Coleridge and Martin Heidegger have embraced in very different ways. We are dealing here with a fundamental option of a kind that is capable of commendation but not of coercive proof, for the very good reason that it helps to establish the conditions on which what is to count as argument will obtain. The option is the view that language is in itself hermeneutic, revelatory of a world; that its action is comparable to that of symbol or sacrament in presenting in a concrete medium a reality otherwise inaccessible.

In Coleridge and Heidegger, the *lingua communis* grants us access to what is most fundamental in reality. In Coleridge's case, the fact of such a fiduciary approach to language is more striking than any great clarity, or even perhaps originality, in how it is presented.[50] Heavily indebted as he was to German romantic idealism, Coleridge's formulations are frequently more obscure than in their original sources. In the preface to *Aids to Reflection* he produced, nonetheless, the lapidary statement, "Words are not THINGS but LIVING POWERS, by which the things of most importance to mankind are actuated, combined and humanized."[51] Coleridge had already found the supreme exemplification of this idea in the verbal symbols of the Scriptures. In *The Statesman's Manual* the divinely inspired language of the biblical revelation is described as "the living educts of the imagination; of

that reconciling and mediatory power, which incorporating the reason in images of sense, and organizing (as it were) the flux of the
senses by the permanence and self-circling energies of the reason, gives
birth to a system of symbols, harmonious in themselves, and consub-
stantial with the truths of which they are conductors."[52] But in this
the divine action simply raises to a higher power the capacity of language to disclose the "things of most importance to mankind" that
Coleridge would discuss in Aids to Reflection, itself a manifestly philosophical, rather than theological, work, conceived, indeed, as a pocket
version of the Coleridgean synthesis of German and English philosophy. Coleridge's theological affirmations rarely lack a philosophical
correlate, or mirror image, in just this kind of way.[53] But the point
here is that for Coleridge, language, as the most sensitive of all the
instruments of the human mind, most fully realizes mind's basic relation
to reality, which is at once projecting—and to this extent, we must be
critical towards language and yet also receptive—and to this extent,
we must trust language to disclose the real and not to conceal it.[54]

The affinity of Coleridge with Heideggerian thought has been noted
by George Steiner.[55] But Heidegger's reflections on the epiphany of
being in and through speech acts come from a writer with greater
powers of prose organization. Although Heidegger's concern with language as the logos of being is a pervasive feature of his work, his central discussion of a fiduciary approach to the word is that found in the
essay collection, Unterwegs zur Sprache.[56] Pointing out that the prologue
to the fourth Gospel has licensed ancient Christian thinkers in speaking of the divine origin of language,[57] Heidegger develops his own
account of the primacy of the logos over man, in conjunction with the
philosophers and poets of German romanticism and their Symbolist
successors. For Heidegger, "man succeeds in speaking only insofar as
he corresponds with language."[58] Language is the "house of being," as
Heidegger insists in his conversation "Between a Japanese and an
Enquirer." Thus the wider realm of being in which humanity's life is
set is not subordinate to humanity but quite the contrary. Humanity
is humanity through its awareness of the logos, the language of being.

> The being of humankind is brought into its own by language, in such a
> way that it remains tributary to the very nature of language, the sound of
> silence. This happens insofar as language of its very nature as the sound of
> silence needs the speech of mortals in order to make the sound of silence
> audible to mortal hearing.[59]

For Heidegger, we need the poet to purify our sense of language so that we may find it in the self-disclosure of reality itself.[60]

My fragmentary discussions of two such complex thinkers are meant only to highlight the kind of approach to language on which the argument of the *Proslogion* makes most sense. We find the language of perfection in possession, in both Church and society. With the *logos* as with the law, possession must count for a very great deal. It is true that there are trivial and parasitic uses of the language of perfection in currency. For a rather gushing guest to tell his hostess that the Coupe Melba was "absolute perfection" is of no more metaphysical interest than it would be of religious interest had he told her it was "simply divine." Nevertheless, the language of perfection is not wholly debased in the secular community of speech. While our world is flatter than that of the medievals, a *scala perfectionis* still stands. Only the rungs — subatomic particle, atom, molecule, cell, organism, the human beings, society — are differently placed. And so long as the language of perfection remains a feature of our linguistic world, the Anselmian approach to God will remain of outstanding fascination.

Following up our third witness, then, we have come to see that theistic language is highly desirable for the intellectual ordering of our experience. Language about unsurpassable perfection enables us to place all other language, and at the same time it can be shown to possess its own internal rationale — given confidence in language in the first place. There is indeed a sense in which finite things are dependent for our capacity to evaluate them in speech on the infinite perfection of God, for the order in which valuational language places them has its standard in the unsurpassable, the divine. But is this to be the only sense in which we find talk of the world thrown back on talk about God? Is there to be no mention here of the perennial human experience of finding the very existence of the stuff of the world — not just language about the world — something that requires God for its sustenance? It is this cosmological approach to the existence of God that we find supremely exemplified in the greatest of the medieval doctors, Thomas Aquinas.

5

THOMAS AQUINAS AND THE
FRAGILITY OF BEINGS

For the tradition stemming from the great thirteenth-century Dominican St. Thomas Aquinas (c. 1225–1274), the central metaphysical problem is how to understand the nature and origin of finite beings. The key to this understanding is taken to lie in what is called their contingency, their nonnecessary character, bound up as this is with their essential limitedness and transience. I call this the *fragility* of beings. On this view and in this Thomist tradition, the existence of God offers itself as the final and sole adequate solution to the metaphysical search that this aspect of things precipitates.

God and Beings

If Newman's temperament was expressed in his youthful apprehension of "two luminously self-evident beings, God and myself," Thomas's may be summed up in a more cosmic adage, "God and beings." His writing has a submerged lyricism, a generosity in intake of the real, best expressed, perhaps, in the passage of the *Summa contra gentiles* where he describes, in a single sweep, the ordered structure of being, ascending in value in proportion to its own inwardness, or capacity for self-awareness.[1]

Thomas was born in the 1220s in the Roman Campagna, not far from Naples.[2] After a childhood spent as an oblate in the Benedictine abbey of Monte Cassino, having been dispatched thither by parents who saw in him a future abbot of that splendid institution, he passed his adolescent years in the newly founded imperial university of Naples. There he began his study of Aristotle under the aegis of one Peter of

Ireland. In the 1240s such university milieux were just the places where the infant Dominican Order was recruiting, and Thomas, to his aristocratic parents' dismay, fell victim to the Order's enticements as well as to his own stubborn persistence in seeking an answer to the question that he had put as a child to the monks at Monte Cassino and was still awaiting a reply: "What is God?" After some years of study at Cologne under Albert the Great, chiefly in philosophy, Thomas went to Paris to teach and study. The Capetian capital was to be his principal home, though he also spent considerable periods in Italy, in the service of the master of the Dominicans and of the pope. His energies, whose extent may be gauged by a glance at the authoritative Leonine edition of his works, begun in the late Victorian era and still not completed, were devoted principally to lecturing on the Scriptures and on the *Sentences* of the early Scholastic, Peter Lombard, a thematically ordered anthology of texts from the Fathers and church councils. Being a man who would never rest until a problem was securely resolved on the basis of first principles, Thomas, though primarily a theologian, did not neglect the metaphysical interests he had first shown at Monte Cassino. It is this aspect of his work that concerns us here.[3]

I can introduce his cosmological approach in no better way than by letting one of his modern disciples speak for him. The distinguished Anglican Thomist, E. L. Mascall, in his Gifford Lectures, *The Openness of Being*, offers to reproduce for us the basic metaphysical intuition at the heart of Thomas's account of the relation between things and God. Mascall points out that there are two fundamental characteristics of any of the extramental beings we perceive by our senses as a real thing, an *in-se*. First comes reality; second, contingency. By reality we mean a thing's character as enjoying concrete existence.

> Whatever causal relations it may have to other beings, it is not just a state of my mind or a figment of my imagination, nor is it an appearance or aspect of the absolute. It is something in itself, a being, an *ens*, an *in-se*. It confronts me, as the chestnut-tree confronted Antoine Roquentin in Sartre's novel *La Nausée*, in all its obstinate indifference to me and my desires, in all its ontological self-centeredness, its *densité*.

Although in my perception of it I can get into it with my own mind and, as the scholastic philosophers say, "become" it ("intentionally," in awareness, not "entitatively," in hard fact), it has nevertheless a core of impenetrability and resistance: it *exists*. And this existence with which it confronts me is not just a bare passive thereness. It is energy, activity—the fundamental activity without which any other activity is impossible.[5] Yet—and here is the second aspect of our experience of things as such—it is also contingent. There is in its own nature neither reason nor cause why it should exist at all. It is non–self-explanatory and non–self-existent. By no logical necessity does it exist. And this is true of whatever being we may have in mind. Norman Malcolm, in his memoir of Wittgenstein, recollected that the latter would refer to an experience best described by saying that "when I have it I wonder at the existence of the world. And I am then inclined to use such phrases as 'How extraordinary that anything should exist!' or 'How extraordinary that the world should exist!' "[6] For if the constituents of the world are contingent, the world itself must be so too, since the world's existence is nothing over and above the existence of its constituents. While St. Thomas's detailed formulation of this two-fold intuition into the simultaneous reality and contingence of things in his "Five Ways" of proving the existence of God[7] may be faulted, it seems that his essential point is valid. And from the perplexity at the nature of things that this intuition arouses, the move to affirm God, on his view, is made.

It is a moot point whether this move from the recognition of contingent being to the affirmation of the necessary being of God grounding it can rightly be called an *argument* at all. Perhaps what is at stake in Thomas's approach is, as I have hinted, a special kind of metaphysical intuition, a *contuition*, it has been called, of God-and-the-world-in-the-cosmological-relation.[8] The formalized articulation of the passage from beings in their fragility to the Ground of being is, we are told, only a kind of dialogue to prepare a human being for due sensitivity to this aspect of things. Mascall remarks that in all likelihood the comparative incapacity of modern people to see the world in this way is due "far more to the atrophy of a normal human faculty than to the emancipation of the human mind from the shackles of superstition and confusion."[9] Each of Thomas's ways to God moves in one form or another from existence to Existence, from what is to He Who Is. But if the civilized Western mind cannot now grasp the existence of He Who Is as the demonstrated conclusion of a process of metaphysical reasoning of this sort, may it not be that this kind of mentality is incapable of understanding the being of what is, the common nature of the finite things around us? The indigence and pathos that runs through being and attests to its radical contingency has somehow been lost to view. In our own century, the philosophy of Martin

Heidegger may be seen as an attempt to recover a juster vision of the fragility of beings, an antidote to that "forgetfulness of Being" in our culture, and so, possibly, a propaedeutic to a recovery of Thomas's understanding of the world.[10] And so I shall treat a theme of Heidegger's as a prologue to an account of Thomas.

Heidegger's analysis of contingency unfolds through the agency of the concept of nothingness.[11] "Human beings grasp nothingness with the assistance of the emotion of dread. Unlike fear, dread is directed towards no specific object. Bound up especially with our sense of the inevitability of our own death, it is the characteristic emotion we experience when what we are running away from in life cannot be specified. Nevertheless, we feel that this "something" is of a threatening nature. For Heidegger, such dread discloses an essential facet of the world. Dread reveals nothingness, and follows on our apprehension of the general character of existence, the totality of beings in their sheer thereness. We perceive that "there is 'nothing' to hold onto. While everything positive slips away, the only thing that remains and overwhelms us is 'Nothing'."[12] In the face of this experience "much of our striving to put forward positive interpretations and attitudes merely testifies obliquely to the abiding presence of Nothing, which we dread."[13] Being is intuited, but in the very moment we seem to have the very stuff of the world in the palm of our hand, a bottomless abyss opens up before us. This falling-away of what is, the being of the beings that actually are, reveals Nothing. Dread is the principal, but not the only, mood through which we recognize that this is how things are, as Heidegger himself says:

> In great desperation, for instance, when all weight tends to disappear from things and all meaning is obscured, then this question arises, be it only by a single stroke like a dull bell-sound resounding in existence and slowly dying away again. In heart-felt joy this question is there because here all things are transformed and stand around us as newly born in such a way that they may almost be conceived as not being rather than being or as being the way they are. The question is present in boredom where we are equally removed from desperation as from joy, and a hardened ordinariness spreads a desolation in which we are indifferent to whether the being is or is not, and thus again the peculiar question begins to sound: why is there being at all and not rather a nothing?[14]

In our concern with what can be listed and enumerated, classified and quantified, we overlook the significance of such experiences, which is the mysterious location of beings, all beings, between being and nothing.

This account recaptures in a fresh idiom what appears to be an experiential presupposition on the part of Thomas. For Thomas, metaphysics is born when a human being is stirred to see that the things around him or her do not exhaust being. One looks at things, not in their individual particularities but in the fact of their very existing, and sees, with surprise and a sense of shock, that they need not be. A necessary moment in adverting to this side of things is surely the kind of experience Heidegger has in mind. But for Thomas, as we shall see in a moment, the sense of the limits and transience of being in the beings there are does not necessarily lead to some sort of nihilism. That sense can be held together with a sense of the richness and positiveness of things, so long as this being of what is be seen as *derived* being, *participated* being. In marking off the various features of things in the effort to come to grips with that by which they sheerly and gloriously are, Thomas finds that we encounter their (and our) metaphysical foundation, namely, the ceaseless communication of the act of existence: "They are intrinsic differentiations of being, and being overflows into them and becomes determinate in them."[15] To disengage being from the finite order in this way is to see that the universe of being is a universe existing, so to say, by grace and favor. This or that thing is, certainly, but it does not itself constitute that *is*. Instead, it simply *has* that *is*.[16] It shares in being; it does not possess crown rights over being. To be a sharer in being is to be a receiver, to accept a gift from a source, from unparticipated existence, He Who Is, *ipsum esse subsistens*. Let a person grasp the most trivial thing in its sheer existing and he or she touches thereby the Cause of being. To see a creature as a creature—and here lies the heart of Thomas's metaphysics—is in itself to have brushed the Face of the Uncreated.[17]

At this point, taking up our stance before participated being, the being of beings, in due awareness of its radical contingency, we should find ourselves faced with a fundamental choice. On the one hand, we may, if we wish, refuse to admit that the finite and derivative thing before us has its being from God's being. In this case we have no option but to echo the judgment of atheistic existentialism that in the last analysis the world is absurd from the roots up. If things that have being do not have it from God, then the very revelation of being opens onto Nothing; "Nothing is being transfigured, caught in terror and dread, sickening the soul unto despair."[18] Alternatively, we may see in participated being the radiance of unparticipated being, the holy being that grants it its foundation.[19] It is the sense of holy being that has been largely forgotten and stands in crying need of recapture.[20] The appreciation of Thomas's account of the move from the creature to the Creator requires us not so much to sharpen our conceptual tools as to accept a pedagogy. We must be willing to unlearn and relearn our response to things, to cultivate a sensibility that will let us see being as the inexhaustible plenitude on which things draw, that within which their incalculable variety is deployed. Drawing together here the threads of both Thomist and Heideggerian thought, André Léonard would have us affirm the intimate interrelation of beings, being, and the subsistent Being of God himself: "God is Being as giver of all richness, while being is this very richness precisely as gift. This gift is so thoroughly given over, that it does not subsist in itself. It manifests its unlimitable transcendence only among the beneficiaries of its own self-givenness: namely, in the heart of beings, and in the human heart, in their unsounded depths."[21]

The mind's advertence to the fragility of beings, then, impels it to raise the problem of the Absolute. The dread that the existentialists speak of, what O'Donoghue has called "all those inner dulls and disquietudes of the spirit which are, as it were, the touch of nothingness,"[22] is evoked by our awareness of beings as manifesting the contingency, instability, and lack of self-sufficiency in the existing order. As such it partakes of the character of an intellectual act, and is not to be confused with the affective response that is its vehicle and accompaniment.[23] This encounter of the feeling mind with the transience of things is one of the enduring sources of humankind's poetic art. In this connection, it is worth recalling that for Thomas as for his philosophical master Aristotle, the stimulus to philosophizing is first and foremost wonder. And wonder is not so different a root from that possessed by poetry. An early medieval monk was no stranger to this wondering dread at the passing quality of beings.

> Vertitur omne decus secli sic namque repente
>   omnia mutantur ordinibus variis.
> nil manet aeternum, nihil immutabile vere est.
>   obscurat sacrum nox tenebrosa diem,
> decutit et flores subito hiems frigida pulcros,
>   perturbat placidum et tristior aura mare.

quare campis cervos agitabat sacra iuventus
  incumbit fessus nunc baculo senior.
nos miseri, cur te fugitivum, mundus, amamus?
  tu fugis a nobis semper ubique ruens.
te fugiens fugias, Christum nos semper amemus.
  semper amor teneat pectora nostra Dei.[24]

Helen Waddell has translated these lines of Alcuin – the Yorkshireman who became Charlemagne's librarian and tutor – in her collection of medieval Latin poetry:

So passes all the beauty of the earth.
Nothing remains in one immortal stay,
Bright day is darkened by the shadowy night,
Gay buds are stricken by the sudden cold.
A sadder wind vexes the quiet sea,
And golden youth that once would course the stag
Is stooped above his stick, a tired old man.
O flying world! that we, sick-hearted, love thee!
Still thou escapest, here, there, everywhere,
Slipping down from us. Fly then if thou wilt.
Our hearts are set in the strong love of God.[25]

Thomas's metaphysics are an attempt to render the whole of this poetic intuition in philosophical terms: not simply the fragility of finite beings, but also the solidity and inexhaustible fecundity of the being of God. God's hold on being is absolute, while the world's being, on the other hand, is constantly "slipping down from us."

It may be objected that such a poem is too different in style from Thomas's own crisp writing with its privileging of objectivity and rigor to serve as a suitable commentary on his work. Yet Thomas himself has styles of utterance that hint that behind that work there lies a fundamental intuition akin to the poet's. His approach to God "through the things that are made" is usually formulated, it is true, with pains-taking methodological clarity. He writes:

There can be two procedures in demonstration: one is through the cause, and is termed a proof for-the-reason-that; this type of argument works from what is prior in reality. The other is through an effect, and is termed a proof inasmuch-as; and this type of argument works from what strikes

us first. When an effect is better known to us than its cause then we proceed through the effect to the knowledge of the cause. From any effect we
can demonstrate the proper cause of its being, so long as the effect is more
palpable; because if the effect exists the cause must preexist, since every
effect depends upon its cause. Hence the existence of God insofar as it is
not self-evident to us is open to demonstration from those effects of his
that are known to us.[26]

Yet the insight animating this way to God is painfully human: "Man's
natural reason tells him that he is under a higher power because of the
deficiencies he feels in himself crying out for care and comfort. Whatever that higher power may be, it is what men call God."[27]

THE FIVE WAYS

A word should be offered as to the function of the Five Ways within
the organism of the *Summa theologiae*, Thomas's introduction to theology "for beginners."[28] It has sometimes been asked what possible
place there can be for this type of argumentation, which we should
unhesitatingly term philosophical, in what professes to be a summary
statement of theology. Thomas himself says, in the opening question
of the *Summa*, that the theology, strictly so-called, that belongs to the
sacra doctrina, "holy teaching," of revelation is distinct in kind from
the theology, so-called, that is part of philosophy.[29] Philosophy considers God solely in the light of what is discoverable by natural reason. What business have the Five Ways, then, in the preaching and
teaching of the Gospel of salvation? As the late Victor White, O.P.,
remarked, "These and suchlike questions haunt many besides the disciples of Karl Barth."[30] However, White offers us his own answer,
which also happens to be Thomas's.

> The *Summa Theologica* is not, as is sometimes supposed, a *pot-pourri* of the-
> ology and philosophy; it is wholly a *Summa* of theology concerned with
> the *Sacra Doctrina*, the Holy Teaching of salvation given by God's revela-
> tion. But *because* it is that, it can *use* philosophical argument for its own
> end—which is *homini salus*—the health or salvation of man [*Summa
> theologiae* I a. 1, 1]. It in no way substitutes a "natural theology" for reve-
> lation, nor does it appeal to reason for what only revelation can impart.
> But it is part of its own task to teach those who acknowledge no revelation
> at all—not indeed about the "God of Revelation" *as such*, but at least
> about such presuppositions (*preambula*), doubt or denial of which is an

intellectual obstacle to faith. Such supremely is the question, *An Deus sit?* — whether there is a God at all.[31]

Formally and intrinsically the Five Ways are philosophy; but their end and function in the *Summa* are purely theological.

How do the Five Ways serve this purpose? By reflecting on phenomena, on aspects of the reality around us, which reflection leads to the conclusion that *omnia abeunt in mysterium*, "all things lead down into a mystery," the intractable mystery of the fount of being that religion calls God.[32] As such, the Five Ways are quite different from the argument of William Paley, the eighteenth-century apologist and archdeacon of Carlisle, from the watch to the Watchmaker, a straightforwardly comprehensible cause.[33] The Five Ways also indicate that this mystery is no mere pool of ignorance in the mind of human beings, but something that the mind is compelled to affirm really *is*. The text of the ways is too lengthy to present *in extenso* here but may be consulted conveniently in the second volume of the English Dominican translation of the *Summa theologiae*.[34] Instead, I shall briefly indicate their character from the vantage point of their common integrating factor: a focusing on the fact of limit. This limitedness in what experience delivers to us can be of various kinds. According to the first way, limitedness may have to do with a thing's lack of complete actuality as fully itself, its being merely potentially itself at some point in its existence. Alternatively, as we find at the heart of the second way, it may belong to a thing's need for the resources of another thing to enable its own effective action. Then again, there is the kind of limit involved in a finite thing's being merely a possible, and not a necessary, existent, for everything subject to the processes of birth and decay can only be a possible thing; here we have the essence of the third way. Limit also enters into our experience of things insofar as their share in qualities of the real, such as goodness, is a matter of varying degree (the fourth way). Last of all, the fifth way, which considers purposiveness in things, also discloses aspects of limitation, since beings lacking in awareness cannot explain the direction involved in the finality, in the orientation to an end that they manifest. These ways are, we may take it, sample offers of the fundamental Thomist way, which is that of finding the infinite through meditation on the finite. It would not be going too far to say with Newman that they are "rather specimens and symbols of the real grounds than those grounds themselves."[35]

For Thomas and his modern disciples the sense of contingency appears to be itself the carrier of a sense of divinity.[36] The fundamental experience that Thomas tries to unfold in his Five Ways is that of a contuition of the dependence of the world with the God on whom it is so dependent. Creatures, despite their non–self-existence, do in fact exist: but we can only see this fact fully in the face if we see it as one side of a coin with two faces. The other face is that creatures are the objects of the incessant creative activity of the self-existent God. We may find it difficult or impossible to conceive of what self-existent being is like. But the intuition, and the argument that attempts to prompt it and unpack its content, does not require us to achieve this feat. If our capacity for wonder is functioning properly, we shall see that what is truly strange is that there should be any other sort of being than self-existing being, the "love which secures our breasts," in the language of Alcuin. With our blunted ontological sensibility, the need in reason for reason to require a divine foundation to things must itself be imaginatively commended. We can if we wish stay put on the horizontal level of simply observing the concrete limitations of things as and when they occur to us. We can refuse to advert to the universal condition of limit as such, and so not move to the vertical dimension of the source on which these things depend. Here the methods of strict inference will not take us far. According to Jacques Maritain, "The nerve of the proof, the formal principle of the demonstration, is the same in each of the five ways, to wit, the necessity of a first cause which is pure Act or Being, itself subsistent in its own right";[37] but this principle, on which all else depends, cannot itself be demonstrated in the strict form beloved of later and lesser Thomists. Thomas's arguments set out to show how finite being is non–self-explanatory, but there is, strictly speaking, no reason why it is so. It just is so, and this has to be appreciated. It seems obvious enough, from our poets if not from our philosophers, that there is a general question that human beings ask about the universe, and not simply about individual items within its system: Why is it so? The late Austin Farrer once spoke about the "vitality of the concealed motive" behind this question:

> It is nothing to be wondered at if the idea of the Supreme Existence in himself, outside and above the series of finites rising towards him, appears merely problematic to our minds; for the thought which erects the scheme places the supreme term outside the range of our experience. But in the

question, Why is it so?, pressed upon us by the contemplation of a finite existent, the finitising Infinite Cause makes his determinative act felt in the finite effect.[38]

In our exploration of the relation of the world to God there are two preeminent desiderata. The first is the cultivation of a contemplative sense that *omnia abeunt in mysterium*, the direct but mediated presence in all being of the One who is, in Thomas's words, "the source and goal of all things." The second is the awareness of how strange a thing it is to use human language, tailor-made for this finite world, to speak of transcendence. Formed in the medieval schools with their careful attention to speculative grammar, to logic and language, Thomas was able to keep in harness these two movements of the mind: a positive movement of the mind in touch with God through creatures; and a negative, self-disciplining movement of the mind aware that its formulations, in this one case, are unprepared by the rules of ordinary discourse. David Burrell, in his book *Aquinas: God and Action*, places this at the heart of his account of Thomas's theology.[39] The opening questions of the *Summa*, the so-called treatise *de Deo*, show us in one way after another how our discourse fails to represent God.[40] The end result of this enquiry does indeed deliver its object—we do not finish up empty-handed—but it does not do so in the way that the enquirer after the concept of God had anticipated. Instead, the place of God in our minds and lives is demarcated precisely by noting how various purported descriptions of God break down in practice. For what holds for the universe cannot hold for the "source and goal of all things." The Five Ways are just so many ways of showing that this phrase applies in reality. If some aspect of a thing that in fact exists demands a source and cause, then a fortiori that source and cause must exist. But these considerations are the merest propaedeutic to our encounter with God. In each of the Five Ways God is arrived at after the manner described, yet in himself God is unqualifiedly first, the "primal truth" as Thomas loves to call him. Nevertheless, calling the divine being "source and goal of all things" does us one sterling service. It nicely distinguishes God from the universe. The beginning and end of all things cannot himself be one of those things.

Thomas does not treat philosophy as a total explanatory framework within which religious questions may be pursued. So absolute a frame would be little less than a rack for the religious mind. Rather, it is for him a kind of intellectual therapy, an invaluable corrective to the vagaries of language, when with our finite words we must speak of the infinite Word and Wisdom of God. Burrell, whom I follow here, highlights in this connection the key Thomist concept of the divine simplicity; according to that concept, God is said to be personally all that he has by way of attributes:

> Aquinas needs to correct the spontaneous drift of our understanding in this regard by showing that simpleness in the case of God spells not imperfection but perfection, not incompleteness but undivided wholeness. Moreover, the limitlessness which follows upon simpleness does not have the overtones of chaos in this instance but of omnipresence. Similarly, the unchangeableness implied by simpleness here does not mark a divine indifference to change so much as it suggests a life not subject to the metric of time.[41]

This can be seen to be so because, for the philosophical analysis of human experience, God is known to be being, in the plenary sense of that word.[42] In one sense, indeed, "to be" is for Thomas a definition of *God*, offering us, insofar as it goes, an account of God's nature. But while "to be" is a phrase that really does signify God's act of existing, as He Who Is, it does not succeed in telling us whether this God does in all reality exist. For that, as we have seen, we must turn to our experience of the world around us. But in this case we are talking not about God as he is in himself but simply and solely of God inasmuch as he is the proper cause of those effects of his which we call the beings of our world. So for Thomas, we can know clearly *that* there is a God, for the fragility of beings is eloquent with this affirmation, yet we cannot know clearly *what* God is. On the other hand, knowing that God is "to be," that God transcends those beings in the world around us whose grasp on existence is but transient, shaken off like dew from the hedgerow, we can at the very least rule out of court all limited language in God's regard. We can practice what in the Christian East is the theology of the alpha privative (he is *not* this, *not* that), negative, or apophatic, theology, the way of unknowing.

In the Christian West, it has generally been understood that this way of alluding to God restrains and purifies a more positive, or cataphatic, way, based on what we know of the Creator in the creature. If the transcendent self-existent ground of contingent being has genuinely communicated himself in the existence of beings, then those beings embody in their infinitely lower mode of dependent being the perfections that in him are self-existent and unlimited. It is this onto-logical relation between God and God's creatures which makes it possible for both to be spoken of in the same language. Thomas noted that all terms to do with perfection enjoy a semantic structure that we can call analogous; that is, words like *one, good, lovely*, seem to hold together states of affairs in a wide variety of contexts. "Analogical expressions merit special attention because of their capacity to play many roles gracefully, that is, to perform their tasks effectively in quite unrelated contexts,"[43] and this leads to the suspicion that they in particular might prove useful in speaking of those things "whereof we cannot speak." These perfection expressions were later made into a doctrine, the doctrine of analogy, notable by its absence in Thomas's own sense of his theological tools.[44] His thinking is indeed profoundly analogical, but he used analogy analogously, letting each context suggest how a relationship to the divine might be displayed.

> The same term repeated over again does not always bear the same fixed sense, but receives an interior movement and modulation according as its position varies in the whole. Such terms are like living cells, not like bits of a mosaic; they are open and respond to one another, and while ever keeping their proper likeness and form can be shotted and shimmering with differences. They are not given the same name by the accident of the poverty of language, for that is mere equivocation (*aequivocum purum, a casu*) which is the occasion of fallacy, but in order to manifest mobile inner relationships by a designed equivocation (*aequivocum a consilio*, or *analogum*).[45]

Naturally, then, the later obsession with the strict analogy of proper proportionality, where the relation of perfection predicates to their subject is itself related mathematically to predicates of divine perfection to theirs, whittled away the vital metaphorical dimension in all this.

> Whether we use perfection expressions properly when we use them of God depends on an acquired skill: knowing how to respect the grammatical difference which logic demands for discourse *in divinis*. Genuinely learning how to respect these differences, however, is more than just a matter for logic. That task requires the disciplines traditionally associated with religious living and practice. For attending to differences we must call upon the metaphorical resources of analogical terms. And the form of

apt metaphors is a matter for sensitivity, not for science. At this point, rules other than grammatical rules are needed. Of these Aquinas has nothing to say. He exhibits his adherence to them, however, by his manner of pursuing the questions he raises, and especially by not raising certain others. Aquinas displays his religious discernment most clearly by the ease with which he is able to endure so unknown a God.[46]

As A. M. Sertillanges, O.P., wrote of Thomas's refusal to contemplate a demonstration of God's Providence: "He respected the mystery."[47]

There is a great deal more, of course, to Thomas's theology than this. He is a theologian of revelation, of God's free, personal self-communication in history, not simply of creation, of what the structures of finite being tell us of their source and goal. Thomas's *Summa theologiae* ranges through all the major themes of the Christian gospel: the triune God, the God-Man Jesus Christ, his atonement and its sacramental participation by human beings, human beings who through the virtues, above all through faith, hope, and charity, as well as through the gifts of the Holy Spirit, are ever more closely assimilated to their Lord. But this, the story of redemption, can be rationally explored by Thomas not simply because the God who is the *prima veritas* is its source. This process of recreation is itself, as God's way of saving humankind, grafted onto a humanity intrinsically open to this second gift. If finite being is essentially dependent being, being open to its Creator, then it must be open to fresh influxes of being, to grace and to glory. This new being, poured forth by the redeeming and transfiguring God, will not destroy the spontaneity of creatures in their multitudinous activities but, on the contrary, elevate and enhance it. To return to Mascall: "A created universe—and there can be no other—is necessarily not only a finite but also an open one. Nature has, simply as nature, a *potentia oboedientalis* for the supernatural."[48] This is most clearly the case in the human being, who

> as a rational and personal being is capable of actualising his openness to a rational and personal God in a way that is impossible to beings devoid of rational personality. [More accurately] . . . he is capable of having it actualised for him. By the nature of the case the initiative must come from God by whose will and power man's very openness to him is conferred and maintained. Man, unlike (so far as we know) any other inhabitant of the material world, is made in the image of God . . . The personal creature is open to the personal Creator.[49]

Thus the distance between the personal temperaments and philosophical starting points of Thomas and Newman, noted at the outset of this chapter, is not so radical as at first sight may appear. Indeed, Mascall concludes his exposition of Thomas's thought by invoking the personalism of the words that Newman adopted as the motto of his cardinalate: *Cor ad cor loquitur*, "one heart speaks to another."[50]

Thomas's thought begins in the most publicly available of domains. It begins by scanning the stuff of the world and asking about its why and wherefore. But it concludes in the most private realm, in the interpersonal discourse of creature and Creator, of engraced humankind and gracious God, in the secret of the heart. There is a simpler word for this area of experience, although it is a much abused one: *mysticism*. May not the human experience of the wholly other, our direct experiential grasp of that other, be itself an encouragement to theistic assent? To consider this possibility, we may usefully move on from the Middle Ages to the world of renaissance and reformation in the sixteenth century, a century that historians of ideas like to identify with the moment of *die anthropocentrische Wende*, the "turning" from a sense of humankind as globally contained in nature to a sense of the uniqueness and primacy of the human subject. Here we would do worse than to take for our paradigm the wonderful efflorescence of mystical life in the church in Spain, against a background of humanist and biblical revival, and among its figures the "mystical doctor" par excellence, St. John of the Cross.

6

JOHN OF THE CROSS AND MYSTICAL EXPERIENCE

The concept of God has a double parentage. In part it is derived from reflection on the world and on human beings; but it is also derived from within religious experience itself. This chapter will attempt to concentrate on that experience in its purest and richest form, the mystical experience, and will do so through the classical representative figure of St. John of the Cross (1542–1591), the supreme "doctor" of mystical theology in the Catholic tradition.

THE EVIDENTIAL VALUE OF MYSTICISM

In a sense, this approach to a wider existence within which our everyday experience is set needs no special commending nowadays. Owing to a lapse of confidence in natural theology, concern with religious experience has largely overtaken the place that an earlier age allotted to a knowledge of God "through the things that are made." The accent now is on an awareness of God, we might say, "through the things that are suffered," undergone (*pati divina* being a traditional description of mystical encounter), in personal experience.[1] But the notion of experience, more especially of inner experience, and most especially of allegedly religious inner experience, is not by any means as straightforward as it sounds. A number of recent writers have raised the question whether that notion is not so problematic that it signals a cul-de-sac by the mystics' promising highway towards an affirmation of the reality of God. I shall try to show in this chapter that while we must take these objections seriously there may still be a way of seeing in the testimony of the mystics, represented here by

John of the Cross, a validation of religious belief, another of the voices of a grammar of consent. As the late Bernard Lonergan put it, at the root of religious experience may be the gift of God's grace, "a dynamic state that fulfills the basic thrust of the human spirit to self-transcendence."[2] An unrestricted, unconditional being in love, he would argue, lies at the heart of all religious awareness; a fortiori, it must constitute the inner energy of mystical awareness, which is religious awareness at its most intense; and since such a being in love is open to all men and women, it is, he concludes, common to both the philosopher's and the theologian's reflection.

It has been held, however, that talk about so-called experiences is part of a general category mistake that consists in treating mental events as fully equivalent to physical events save in that they can be known only by introspection. Such was the view taken by the late Gilbert Ryle in his essay *The Concept of Mind*, which enjoyed something of a *succès de scandale* at least in England.[3] To this thesis Keith Ward has replied that while it offers a salutary reminder that experiences "do not come upon us unexpectedly, with clear definite outlines, as physical objects often do," yet "on the other hand, it seems altogether too severe to say that there are no inner mental events at all."[4] His account of consciousness is very much that taken by Timothy Sprigge in "The Importance of Subjectivity." Consciousness is the answer to the question, "What is it like, being he, she, or it?" A state of experiencing, Sprigge maintains, is "that reality whose being is one with its own non-discursive knowing of itself," and he argues, *contra* the shade of Ryle, that "the intellectually disciplined study of subjective experience as such, by introspection and imagining oneself in the other person's place, is an important complement to the study of human nature by more external and observational means."[5] The practice of spiritual direction, *pace* John of the Cross, would appear to be a slayer of behaviorism, for, in Ward's words, "anyone who has helped another in the pursuit of the spiritual life will know how little behaviour may betray of a man's true feelings and attitudes to his life."[6] This leads us in to a consideration of specifically religious subjectivity.

Peter Donovan, in his recent study, *Interpreting Religious Experience*, has pointed out that the question, When is an experience religious? can only be answered in terms of the systems of belief and behavior that we call religions. There is no independent route to the identification of a religious experience that bypasses this. Similarly, a sound becomes a musical note only when it features in a wider setting, a context of tunes, rhythms, harmonies. So the fact of contemporary life I alluded to at the start of this chapter, namely, that religious experience arouses more public interest than does theology or doctrine, is in a sense based upon a confusion of thought. Moreover, Donovan's essay (and others in a similar vein) underlines the difficulties in establishing the coherence of the deliverances of the mystics one with another and the claims to correspondence of their experiences with a transcendent reality. On the first problem, there are well-intentioned, ecumenical souls who, looking for common ground among the various philosophies and religions of this planet, have seized on mystical experience, the direct apprehension of the sacred, as their most promising treasure island. Yet as Donovan says, it is hard to see how different experiences can be compared in the ways these people would wish (for instance, in order to show that there is a single, universal mystical experience appearing under different descriptions in different religions), for the way each experience is described and reacted to enters into the quality of the experience itself. On the second problem, in the post-Wittgenstein era in philosophy, with its stress on the shared character of our language and ways of verification, there will always be a nagging doubt about knowledge-claims based on experiences that by their very nature are closed off from public inspection, whatever subjective sense of certitude they may produce. We have here a formidable battery of problems: in a nutshell, those of experience and its presuppositions, on the one hand, and those of language and the ineffable on the other.[7]

How can mystical experience, summed up, say, in the life of John of the Cross, be evidence for the reality of God, if the reality of God, as believed in by John before the event, is a constitutive part of the experience we are talking about? We might perhaps respond to this question by trying to peel off what may be called layers of interpretation detectable in John's writings. Such would be, for example, the imagery of the Scriptures, the theology of Spanish Scholasticism, the vocabulary of Spain's literary golden age. Left on the platter, we might hopefully predict, would be a neutral core experience. And yet

it becomes very difficult to say how experiences could be individuated [marked off from one another] at all, at some uninterpreted level. Someone once defined a tennis net as "holes joined together by string." The search for completely uninterpreted experiences is a little like the search for a "pure" hole, one without any surroundings at all. What would make such a pure hole the hole it is, rather than some other pure hole? Similarly, no means for identifying or individuating experiences seem to remain, once all interpretations (actual and possible) are left out of the picture, for it is largely they which make an experience the experience it is.[8]

And again, if we cannot permit the most important religious experiences to be incarnate in words, if the mystical is strictly the ineffable, what reason is there to suppose that the source of these experiences is adorable and precious beyond all else? At most, it would be an unknown quantity. Fortunately, the mystics themselves are rich in words, even though they may use these words at various crucial points to say that words fall short of their experience.

> When it is said that God (or some other ultimate reality) is inexpressible, this must be taken to mean not that one can say absolutely nothing about God, but rather that one can say nothing absolutely about God. For God would not be an ultimate reality if any words or descriptions could fully comprehend or be "the last word" on the subject.[9]

We must trust to language when meeting the mystics, even if it be language stretched to breaking point; and so we shall try to do with John.

The approach adopted in this chapter will be to incorporate a response to these questions in Donovan's study in, through, and alongside a brief portrait of John of the Cross. Donovan insists that where the varieties of religious experience are concerned, the truth or falsity of an interpretation is not to be found by looking merely at the experience involved: we must examine the whole of the theological system, or vision, within which that interpretation is offered. A few pages will not, of course, succeed in assessing the truth-claims of Christianity as a whole, nor even those of the Christianity of a sixteenth-century Spanish Carmelite friar, nor will they aim at doing so. Instead, two moves will be made. In the first, it will be suggested that John's mystical experiences do have a limited, but real, autonomy vis-à-vis the wider religious tradition from which they came and on which, for the overwhelmingly greater part, they must be indeed allowed to depend. Those experiences can be seen as a creative rupture within the traditional religious system to which he belonged. Of John's account of aridity in prayer Ruth Burrows has remarked, and the remark is more significant than might appear at first sight: "Other writers were aware of this phenomenon and saw it as a trial and testing of the soul, but he saw further. He saw that it was the effect of the mystic touch."[10] It has reasonably been claimed for the mystics at large, and for John of the Cross in particular, that their "greatest gift is that of fixing on essentials, as if the mystical encounter had arranged *or re-arranged* the basic conceptions and principles bearing on man's destiny and God's nature."[11] But if the claim staked out here in the words italicized is indeed justified, then the mystics do enjoy a certain autonomy vis-à-vis the religious tradition to which they belong; in which case, the truth-claims of their particular experience, if conceded, will have a degree of independent value in verifying the truth-claims of the religion in which that experience was lived out. The belief-bound character of mystical experience need not wholly rule out the possibility that certain experiences help to establish the truth of the beliefs through which they found their interpretation. I agree, fundamentally, with Donovan when he writes that such experiences matter, "not because by themselves they guarantee the rightness of the interpretations given by those who experience them, but because they are the kinds of experience which would be explained if those interpretations were correct."[12] But a slightly more generous criterion may be suggested that still remains within the bounds of critical sense. Mystical experiences of the kind that, as with John of the Cross, generate a creative rupture in a tradition, are important because, although they could not have been predicted beforehand, once they take place they are seen to be "the kinds of experience which would be explained if " the interpretation of the world by their tradition were correct.[13] Such experiences extend the meaning of, say, Christian theism, but the way in which they do so can be recognized retrospectively as in the profoundest harmony with that theistic tradition's most characteristic intuitions. In the case of John of the Cross we would then ask ourselves, first, whether his experiences were predictable for a man who believed as he did (I do not think they altogether were); and second, how we might explain the fact that nevertheless in time they were seen to be as likely as anything in the world, should Christianity be true.

the religious world-view, then, not only brings out patterns . . . but gives possible significance to the patterns themselves, in a systematic, comprehensive way. And in doing so it triggers off further experiences, themselves open to interpretation within the system. All this is enough to put the believer in a quite different position from the unbeliever, not merely as to his feelings, but as to additional experiences which for him are further relevant facts to be taken account of, in support of his belief about the reality of God.[14]

We shall shortly investigate, in a second move, whether these "additional experiences" may, in certain cases, elicit a response to their meaning and truth even for those who are themselves not (yet) believers.

The Sanjuanist Way: Purgatory and Transfiguration

St. John of the Cross was born into an expansionist and religiously confident, not to say complacent, society, the Spain of the early sixteenth century, a people recently victorious over Moorish invasion, the vanguard of the Catholic reform, newly united under its "most Catholic" kings, the launching pad of a vast missionary enterprise in the Indies. It is against this background that Gerald Brenan, in his sensitive study of John of the Cross, would see not the manner of realization of John's aspirations but their scope and their style.

> Perhaps we can see these Carmelites best in their historical perspective if we regard them as a new sort of Conquistadors. The age of geographic explorations had been followed by an age of interior ones that plumbed the individual self. Montaigne in France and more indirectly Shakespeare and Donne in England provide examples of this. Yet it was not an intellectual enterprise that these friars and nuns were engaged on, but an active and spiritual one: they believed, and in this the authority of the Church supported them, that, if grace were given to them, they could carry the whole mind with its will and affections to union with the source of that mind, which is God. Since love was the motive, Eros the engine in the hull, this course took the form and is explained in the language of a love affair. . . . Such was the venture, *la dichosa ventura*, to which Fray Juan was committed.[15]

The biography in which this love affair—itself the "extreme of sublimation" of the historic movement of love for the absent, which runs from the Provençal poets, through Dante to Petrarch[16]—was embedded is an appalling story to anyone with a residual optimism about human nature. The opposition that St. Teresa's coworker in the reform of Carmel encountered, not only from those who were hostile to the reform but also from its erstwhile supporters, raised a memorable edifice of human malice, conceived on the grand scale but like all malice petty and sordid in execution. As Rowan Williams has emphasized in his portrait of John, "The Secret Stair," the young man born in 1542 into a family of silk weavers in Old Castile, between Salamanca and Avila, who at the age of twenty-one had sought entrance into the contemplative, indeed semi-eremitical, Order of Carmel, there to love God, was engaged throughout his life in an essentially practical struggle: "All of John's work is grounded in the practical—and political—struggle to create within his order a style of life authentically reflecting the poverty, the detachment and disponibilité, which for him were the central characteristics of Christian 'interior' life."[17] The "desert" John found was, in the first place, a desert of perfectly nonmysterious human suffering of a sort that it is no trivialization of language to call a kind of hell. From the lice and dysentery of a prison cell ten feet by six and the threats of liquidation on the part of his brother friars John would make a dramatic escape on 14 August 1578, the vigil of the Assumption, the feast of the mystery of hope. Letting himself down from his barred cell, with a drop of many feet into the engulfing night of Toledo beneath him, he managed to keep hold of a notebook containing some lines he had just written. They were the most crucial stanzas of his poetic and mystical masterpiece, the *Spiritual Canticle*.

In terms of the perspective on mystical experience sketched a little earlier, what most merits our attention about John's career is the way in which the personal experience of God that he claimed broke the bounds of what in the tradition had been taken for granted as the normal shape of the mystical experience. John's mystical experience was of God's reality and presence apprehended precisely through circumstances, both outer and inner, that appeared to imply his unreality or absence. These circumstances were, on the one hand, betrayal and unspeakable physical humiliation and, on the other, the sense of dereliction, of the loss of the customary consolations of the life of piety. It is sometimes suggested that the religious sense, with its claims to veridical experience of reality, is in fact constituted by a displacement of the aesthetic sense. Religiously minded people are really having warmly aesthetic feelings at the Liturgy, say, or in their musings on the metaphors of the Scriptures. But they are constantly mistaking these for an experience of the divine. John of the Cross gives the lie to this suggestion in the most complete way imaginable. Aesthetically sensitive and gifted as he was, both as artist and poet, he learned to discern the presence of God in a situation that was utterly formless and uncomely. Where the imagination admits its defeat as one symbol of God after another proves inadequate to the human experience of loss, waste, inner anguish of spirit, one would have expected to find the confession of reason that in such situations all faith is blind faith in the popular sense of those words. In such a human wasteland, faith must surely be a gritting of the teeth, a hoping against hope that out of this darkness will emerge something more conformable to Christian beliefs about reality's ultimate nature being personal Love. Instead, however, John found in just this formlessness, this absence of God, the supreme invitation of the divine Love. Within the absence there unfolded a presence, which appealed for a person's response, a response to consist of the sheerest naked clinging to God in the darkness and the dryness, for, to return to words I have cited already, this *is* "the effect of the mystic touch."

John's life and teaching are a kind of experiment into God. In this experiment we begin with the assumption that reality as we know it is often barely compatible with belief in an all-powerful, all-wise, and all-loving Providence. Nevertheless, the hypothesis of that Providence can be tested in the laboratory of the human spirit. Let us take the most repellent human situations and see what comes of them if we approach them as the hidden presence and invitation of the love of God. John's experiment in living tested the reality of God and came to a particular result. The triumphant survival of his humanity through a personal holocaust produced in his poetry and prose an extension of the awareness of Catholic Christianity which was, at the same time, a rediscovery of its "central revelation-bearing moment," Christ on the Cross. What else save these two things can be meant by proclaiming him the mystical doctor of the community of Jesus of Nazareth? On the relation of John's personal experience to his writings, Edith Stein, herself a philosopher, Carmelite, and victim of Auschwitz, has this to say:

> If we speak of a Science of the Cross this is not to be understood in the ordinary meaning of science [*Wissenschaft*]: it is no mere theory, that is, no combination of—really or supposedly—true axioms, no ideal structure of thought. It is, indeed, known truth, a theology of the Cross, but it is living, actual and active truth: it is placed in the soul like a seed, strikes root and grows, giving the soul a certain character and forming it in all it does or leaves undone, so that its own being shines forth and is recognised in it. In this sense we speak of a science of sanctity and this is how we understand the science of the Cross. This form and force living in the depths of

the soul nourish the philosophy of this man and the way in which God and the world present themselves to him, and thus they can be expressed in a theory. In the doctrine of St. John of the Cross we have such an expression.[18]

John's experience had been that the abandonment of the familiar and the secure, including in that our familiar and secure images of God, is the costly way in which God brings human beings into union with himself. Two unfinished prose commentaries, the *Ascent of Mount Carmel* and the *Dark Night of the Soul*, give us John's reflections on this demanding process of purification and self-stripping, and in the latter work the accents of his period of imprisonment are unmistakable. In II. 6 John evokes for us the felt absence of consolation and the sense of God as distant, even, in the words of one student, "rejecting and hostile." John speaks of pain and suffering as the vehicles of a meeting between "the two extremes" of God's refining action and its object, the human being.

> The divine extreme is the purgative contemplation and the human extreme is the soul, the receiver of this contemplation. Since the divine extreme strikes it in order to renew the soul and divinize it (by stripping it of the habitual affection and properties of the old man to which it is strongly united, attached and conformed), it so disentangles and dissolves the spiritual substance—absorbing it in a profound darkness—that the soul at the sight of its miseries feels that it is melting away and being undone by a cruel spiritual death; it feels as if it were swallowed by a beast and being digested in the dark belly, and it suffers an anguish comparable to Jonas's when in the belly of the whale. It is fitting that the soul be in this sepulchre of dark death in order that it attain the spiritual resurrection for which it hopes.[19]

This is what John calls the "passive night," the aspect of growth in mystical awareness that is out of our hands, mediated as it is by events in a public order not controlled by us and by events in the private order of the soul not chosen by us: indeed, if we consulted our religious instinct we would flee from the horror of this testing. But this terrible purgatory on earth proves to be illumination, the start of a new quality of insight into God and the self.

> Loneliness, illimitable and terrifying is that in man which awaits that presence which alone fulfills his infinite capacity. This presence seems to oppress the spirit almost to destruction, yet it is opening the spirit to itself,

to its own dimensions. It is only by facing one's loneliness fully and continuously that one discovers God within it, the presence which has all the time been calling us onward.[20]

This night is "lovelier than the dawn" in the controlling metaphor of John's poetic crystallization of this experience, the "Noche oscura."

> Upon a gloomy night,
> With all my cares to loving ardours flushed,
> (O venture of delight!)
> With nobody in sight
> I went abroad when all my house was hushed.
>
> In safety, in disguise,
> In darkness up the secret stair I crept,
> (O happy enterprise)
> concealed from other eyes,
> When all my house at length in silence slept.
>
> Upon that lucky night
> In secrecy, inscrutable to sight,
> I went without discerning
> And with no other light
> Except for that which in my heart was burning.
>
> It lit and led me through
> More certain than the light of noonday clear
> To where One waited near
> Whose presence well I knew,
> There where no other presence might appear.
>
> O night that was my guide!
> O darkness dearer than the morning's pride,
> To the beloved bride,
> Transfiguring them each into the other.[21]

At this point the poem moves into a lyrical celebration of the mutual love of God and the soul in images drawn from the Old Testament Song of Songs. Here it returns to the theme of the stanzas that John wrote in the ghastly circumstances of the Carmel of Toledo, the *Cántico espiritual*, with its glorious effusion of delicate, sensuous images. In that poem, the delight in God and God's world is utterly palpable and, in context, well-nigh incredible. The bride, the human soul, in seeking her divine lover, questions the world of nature:

> O woods and thickets
> Planted by the hand of the Beloved!
> O meadow of verdure,
> Enamelled with flowers,
> Say if he has passed by you.

And the creatures reply:

> Scattering a thousand graces,
> He passed through these groves in haste,
> And, looking upon them as he went,
> Left them, by his glance alone,
> Clothed with beauty.[22]

Well might the Hispanic scholar Allison Peers remark in amazement of the *Spiritual Canticle*:

> From the swiftness of the poem's movement, the vigour of its language, its skillful alternation of contrasting moods and the richness of its nature images, some drawn from sacred or profane literature, others perhaps from the poet's own experience, one would deduce a youth full of life and energy, writing placidly in some country retreat, and deriving inspiration from the sights and sounds before his eyes. Never would one suspect a friar in his thirty-sixth year, prematurely aged by his ascetic life, bleeding, half-starved, deprived for months of the sight of even a square of blue heaven and writing in close confinement and in all but total darkness.[23]

The existence of that poem, written in that place, is itself theistic evidence. No willed cultivation of sensibility here, "love consists not in feeling great things, but in having great detachment and in suffering for the Beloved."[24]

I have tried to render here something of the mystical experience of John of the Cross as it comes across in his own biography and in his teaching. But can all this be of interest to the philosopher, or to the good pagan considering the truth-claims of the theistic tradition in its Christian form? Jean Baruzi ended his classic study of John by noting the "tragic difficulty" that the nonmystic, and indeed the nonbeliever, finds in seeking to understand the final secret of the mystic—"for such a solitude, and such a silence, are not open to him who has not explored them in his own life." He also added, in a slightly enigmatic aside, that perhaps, despite this, it may not be forbidden to "transpose this bitter purification of the spirit into the different key of the metaphysical enterprise."[25] The philosopher cannot follow his hero, but he can in his own way live out something of the mystical adventure. The invitation was accepted by M. Georges Morel in his monumental study, *Le Sens de l'existence selon s. Jean de la Croix*. Morel writes that while the philosopher can trace in thought the relationship of the human being, that animal conditioned and limited in so many ways, to the unconditioned and unlimited Ground of being, the Absolute, this relationship could never be for the philosopher one of actual encounter. He or she cannot admit, while speaking as a philosopher, the possibility of a meeting with the absolute God in a moment of self-transcendence that shatters in that instant the present confines of human interiority.[26] Morel points out that the philosopher's objection has to do with the legitimate limits of claims to knowledge. How could we ever *know* the mystic was telling us right? Ever since Kant awoke philosophy from its dogmatic slumbers, philosophers have insisted that the mind should come to a sense of its own intrinsic limitations before it actually gets involved in knowing. But this Morel rejects, at least in this context:

> There are some who imagine that doubt—in whose absence there can be no passage from naive to critical awareness—would be a more radical thing if one seriously put the Absolute between parentheses. But that is a profound illusion, albeit a tenacious one. On the contrary, St. John of the Cross shows us that the presence of God in a human being can create upheavals so radical that the most lucid mind would have been powerless to foresee them: doubt stretching as far as agony, as a "reduction to nothingness." God alone has the power to offer us the test of these. Our questions about human understanding are only a distant (if necessary) prelude in comparison with the "anguish" of the divine love.[27]

On this view, there is such a thing as an acute critical sense, a testing of the limits of understanding, that does not, however, consist in doubting God's existence in a formal, schoolroom manner (Morel has in mind, evidently, the practitioners of Cartesian methodical doubt). Instead, this other critical method consists in *not* doubting God in a manner that itself "makes existence tremble on its foundations." Critical philosophy is not worthy of the name if in reducing experience to the measure of a formal theory of knowledge it leaves on one side the true "crisis" ("judgment"), "that burning flame which the Absolute sustains in the heart of man by its mere presence."[28]

> Religious experience is not a pure *a priori* affair; but neither is it purely constructed *a posteriori*. No, it has its source in a kind of reality which

transcends both of these aspects and grants them their meaning as it grants them their existence.[29]

In other words, it grants the de facto experience while simultaneously creating its conditions of possibility. But what is this experience that carries with it a sense of the real as grounding both our own subjectivity and the objective world we live in? It is, in Morel's words, the experience of finitude-self-aware, and he characterizes this as a kind of dying—not the experience of the biological limit we call physical death, but a death nevertheless, and one of which biological dying is at best a metaphor. The life story of John of the Cross is the story of a man dying daily to his own particularity, exhausting and passing beyond all the finite forms, images, and metaphors of the really real, the Absolute, that make up the content of our outer and inner worlds. Now, as Morel notes, atheistic phenomenologists like Maurice Merleau-Ponty would rise up in horror at the notion that the philosopher could allow this to be so. For them the very introduction of God, "the absolute thinker of the world" for whom its ambiguities are all rationally apprehended in advance, is the suffocation and the destruction of the concrete human world.[30]

The experience of the Absolute described by John does not, however, suppress the finite but, on the contrary, gives the subject access to the truest heart of things in all their concreteness and singularity. The evidence that this actually took place in John's own life lies in the torrent of images, astonishing in their exuberance, that poured forth from him in the midst of his sufferings. The metaphors of his poetic art take up the images that he delighted to find in nature. Alonso de la Madre de Dios, in a contemporary account, describes John in the years at Calvario, after the escape from prison, seated at the window of his cell, whence he could look out over the Castilian countryside and "delectate in the whole variety of things, and enrich his spirit."[31] And in the commentary on the Spiritual Canticle, when he reaches the words of the bride, "Rejoice, my love, with me And in your beauty see us both reflected By mountain-slope and lea,"[32] John says that the soul asks God to "inform her with the beauty of this other lesser wisdom, contained in his creatures and other mysterious works. This wisdom is also the beauty of the Son of God by which the soul desires to be illumined."[33]

Yet we must not exaggerate the degree of difference between John's experience and our own. In nonmystical, religiously relevant experience, the divine presents itself through some aspect of experience, yet does so obscurely and obliquely. There is always a sense of God's difference, distance, separation. The presence manifests itself as a kind of absence. Mystical experience does not differ from this in being unmediated, a raw contact with transcendence (the very phrase is doubtless a contradiction in terms),[34] but in being a mediation of God in the mode of communion. To claim anything other than this is to make the mystic superhuman rather than one in whom the life of faith comes to its natural flowering. Von Hügel, rejecting the notion that there is "strictly speaking, such a thing as a specifically distinct, self-sufficing, purely mystical mode of apprehending reality," went on to say that only when safeguarded by such a denial does mysticism attain "its full dignity which consists precisely in being not everything in any one soul, but something in every soul of man; and in presenting at its fullest the amplest development, among certain special natures, with the help of certain special graces and heroisms, of what in some degree and form, is present in every truly human soul, and in such a soul's every, at all genuine and complete grace-stimulated religious act and state."[35] What this might be is surely not far to seek. William Johnston, S. J., speaking of the inner eye of the mystic which, when opened "sees the real glory and beauty and meaning of the universe," writes: "Love is the motivation and driving force behind the mystical journey – it is precisely love that leads one beyond thoughts and images and concepts into the world of silence. The inner eye is now the eye of love."[36] However, we must add: Love may be wonderful, yet it cannot be all. Human experience, however transfigured, retains its own complexity and internal differentiation – which is why scholastic theologians regarded charity as the form of all the virtues rather than as their displacement. The element of direct communion with God will be recognized by the believer as the most important duty and privilege of life; but even the most devout cannot make it ubiquitous without becoming a pious fool. Human beings have other sides to their subjectivity, and, if we would say with the poet and Scholastic Gerard Manley Hopkins that "the mind has mountains," we must agree that it will also have troughs and depressions and, most commonly of all, great areas of plateau. In any attempt to produce a balanced portrait of humanity, the name of Blaise Pascal is likely to be mentioned; and it is to his writings that we may look for confirmation of the mystic's experience in the experience of all human beings, in their greatness and their littleness, too.

7

BLAISE PASCAL AND THE METHOD OF IMMANENCE

In the previous chapter it was shown via John of the Cross that mystical experience is a surd, an inexplicable quantity, on any naturalistic reading of the world. But it was also accepted that a philosophy, even a theistic philosophy, cannot do justice to a kind of experience where (it is claimed) the Absolute itself is encountered in the mode of communion, not of otherness, by the human mind. Only a *theology*, which can allow God himself to speak of God as one of its own methodological postulates, can cope with an Absolute that empties itself in order to draw close to man. If reason alone could describe this supernatural purgation and elevation of human life, then the supernatural would itself be part of nature. Yet if the supernatural is a reality, it is bound to have effects within the order of nature. It may be, therefore, that philosophy, when applied to the structures of human existence, can disclose that human beings aspire naturally to an end beyond nature. By a sympathetic analysis of the nature of human subjectivity it may be possible for the philosopher to show that the existence of God is somehow implicated in human aspirations. This was in fact the peculiar achievement of Blaise Pascal (1623–1662).

The concern with human subjectivity appears and reappears at a number of points in the history of religious philosophy. In late antiquity, we meet it in Plotinus and Augustine; in the early Middle Ages, in Bernard and medieval humanism; in the modern period, among the existentialists such as Gabriel Marcel. The seventeenth century is also a period when the starting point of theistic argumentation is found in the nature and peculiar exigencies of the thinking and acting subject. This becomes clear if we reflect that the period binds together two writers as diverse as Pascal and René Descartes, whose philosophical methods (but, arguably, not aims) were written off by Pascal in the *Pensées* with the words "useless and uncertain."[1]

THE CARTESIAN COGITO: GOD AND SELF

For the ordinary person, Descartes's celebrated *cogito ergo sum*, "I think, therefore I am," has become a caricature of the uselessness and triviality of philosophy. At the other extreme, in the hands of later philosophers, the idealists, it became a barricade against the openness of human experience to the divine. In these writers the mind does not open onto the mystery of being, for the creative powers of the knowing human subject are seen as all important, and reality beyond them, whether humble or sublime, as literally inconceivable. But what Descartes saw as his great discovery may well have been read too much through the distorting spectacles of detractors and admirers. The *cogito* is not so much a logical starting point as an existential one. That is, the question that exercised Pascal's elder contemporary was not the trivial query, Am I? but the question that has at all times linked the humanist and metaphysical traditions: namely, What am I? If we consider the repercussions of Descartes's *cogito* on the philosophy of spirit in France down to our own century, it is plausible to argue that Descartes provided a philosophical expression for a truth divined by the mystics: God as, in the Augustinian maxim, *intimius intimo meo*, a reality "more interior to me than I am to myself." As Cathal Daly has suggested, there is negative corroboration for this thesis in the tendency of much modern philosophy to find both God and self meaningless constructs of the idling metaphysical mind.[2] The historical credibility of Daly's version appears to be confirmed by what is known of Descartes's relations with the Oratory of Cardinal de Bérulle, with its enthusiasm for patristic studies and its mystically oriented spirituality.[3]

The *cogito* on this view is an act of reflection that reveals the nature of the human being and of his or her situation in the world:[4] "I know that I exist precisely in my knowing that I think about and seek to understand the world; and that I demand certitude but encounter error and feel doubt; that I think beyond the limits of my knowledge and grasp the idea of perfection in and with my recognition of my own imperfection."[5] In terms of the "Third Meditation" thus summarized, the *cogito* is not a bare, formal act but the carrier of a rich content that can be unpacked and laid out by subsequent reflection. On this basis, Descartes goes on to consider "the circumstance that I doubted and that, consequently, my being was not wholly perfect," its grasp of truth fleeting and vulnerable. He asks himself, therefore, "whence I had learned to think of something more perfect than myself": "How could I know that I doubt, desire or that something is wanting to me and that I am not wholly perfect, if I possessed no idea of a being more perfect than myself, by confession of which I knew the deficiencies of my own nature?"[6] So in his own lack of being, his desire and need for being, an aspiration after the perfection of being, Descartes finds himself obliged to affirm a dependence for being on the perfect being that all human beings call "God." This is already *in nuce* the "method of immanence"[7] that relates the truth-claims of religion to their "affinity with the internal exigencies of human subjectivity."[8]

PASCAL AND THE "PENSÉES"

What Pascal did was to render a fundamentally similar approach to God very much more dramatically powerful. This greater dramatic force derives from recontextualizing the *cogito* within the entire schema of human existence, as that could only be done by a great imaginative writer. Pascal's imaginative gifts were little recognized in his own lifetime. His first major theological production, the *Provincial Letters*, a polemic against the moral theology of the influential Society of Jesus, was an anonymous work. His projected study of Christian apologetics was left incomplete at his death at the age of thirty-nine: the *Pensées* are its debris. Pascal's contemporary celebrity was of a different character. As Alban Krailsheimer has written in one of his Pascalian studies, few today "would suspect that the author of the *Pensées* was the same M. Pascal whom the general public of his own day knew as a transport pioneer (he invented a system of free public travel for the poor of Blois), the salons as a witty conversationalist and the learned world as an internationally respected scientist."[9]

Pascal's family, despite his mother's early death, was close knit. He received his education from his mathematically gifted lawyer father and from the company of his father's international medley of learned friends. Hence it is not surprising that he was deeply marked in his early twenties by the elder Pascal's discovery of the spirituality of the

Abbé Saint-Cyran that was practiced by those shortly to be called *Jansenists*.[10] The Jansenist movement, which took its name from the Flemish bishop of Ypres, an Augustinian scholar, Cornelius Jansen, was, in Krailsheimer's somewhat loaded phrase, "an attempt to counteract Protestantism without betraying Christ." A movement of internal reform within the Catholic church, Jansenism closely identified with the parochial and hierarchical patterns of that church but looked to the Bible and the Fathers—especially Augustine—for a rigorous statement of evangelical values. Theologically, its most characteristic doctrine, expressed in a way eventually to be found incompatible with Catholic orthodoxy, was the absolute primacy of God's grace vis-à-vis human freedom.[11] Spiritually, it taught a rejection of worldly values,[12] in sharp contrast to the Jesuit tendency to tailor the suit of religious practice according to the cloth provided by the modish nobility of the Bourbon court. In extreme cases, Jansenist austerity led to a kind of solitary life with vows (the gentlemen of Port-Royal), but more usually it contented itself with an interiorized form of such separation. It was within this context that Pascal's apologetic writing was to be pursued.

However, insofar as Pascal's writing can be placed autobiographically, it does not seem that his portrait of human life came to him on the sole basis of this general background of Saint-Cyranist affiliation, a background whose adoption is sometimes referred to as his "first conversion." The uniquely personal force of the *Pensées* argues a uniquely personal experience, and this can only be the moment of real assent to God in the night of 23 November 1654 of which an exact record survives in the shape of the "Memorial," two scraps in Pascal's handwriting found accidentally after his death, sewn into the lining of his clothes.

> Fire.
> "God of Abraham, God of Isaac, God of Jacob," not of philosophers
>   and scholars.
> Certainty, certainty, heartfelt joy, peace. God of Jesus Christ.[13]

In the *Pensées* he would write, obliquely, of this conversion in terms of a transposition from the order of reason to the order of charity, or the order of the heart.[14]

> The heart has its order, the mind has its own, which uses principles and demonstrations. The heart has a different one. We do not prove that we ought to be loved by setting out the causes of love. That would be absurd.

Jesus Christ and St. Paul possess the order of charity, not of the mind, for they wished to humble, not to teach.

The same with St. Augustine.

This order consists mainly in digressions upon each point which relates to the end, so that this [end] shall be kept always in sight.[15]

What this somewhat gnomic statement means can only be determined by looking at the *Pensées* as a whole.[16]

Pascal had discovered, through the reception given the *Provincial Letters*, that he could write about religious questions in a way that was convincing to nonbelievers as well as to Christians. In the early months of 1657, therefore, he turned his mind to a project apparently long stored up in his mind. This was an apologia, a defense of religious faith, more specifically, of Christian faith. In addition to his main source, Scripture, and to various devotional and apologetic tracts of the time, he returned to his favorite author: the Stoic philosophers, Montaigne, and Augustine. At first he wrote nothing. But as his illness became more acute (he suffered poor health from 1658 until his death in 1662), he found it necessary to jot down notes, some so cryptic as to be almost unintelligible. Nevertheless, the main lines of what we now know as the *Pensées* are clear enough. Pascal saw these fragments as a deliberate challenge to Cartesian thought. But as I have suggested, it is the form, not the substance, of Cartesianism that Pascal found so offputting. From the instinctive viewpoint of a philosopher who was at once a scientific empiricist, an imaginative artist, and a Christian evangelist, the writings of Descartes seemed impotent to touch the lives of thousands living effectively as atheists amid the glories of the *grand siècle* of French Catholicism. The theater of Moliére, the pulpit oratory of Bossuet, the *Maxims* of La Rochefoucauld depict the kind of skeptical *honnêtes hommes* for whom Pascal wrote, refined in manners but morally without any definite foundation of principle to their lives. For those who could make the sophisticated mental moves of Cartesian philosophy, there was a way to affirm the indigence of the Godless self and its radical need of a gift of perfection. Pascal considered that there was a simpler way to unmask the fundamental orientation of the self towards or away from the perfection of which the Cartesian *Meditations* had spoken. It is here that the best-known fragment, *Pensée* 423, belongs: "The heart has its reasons of which the reason knows nothing."

This sentence, which is almost as familiar as the *cogito* itself, has been almost equally misunderstood. It is not a recipe for sentimentalism, for the indulging of feeling-states without questioning their basis and value. The reasons of the heart for Pascal are in different respects (causal) motives for action and (justificatory) reasons. In the first respect, Pascal is saying that frequently our actions are determined not by grounds that we could explicitly assign to them but by a fundamental attraction to, or love of, either God or the self. This overall orientation can be discovered, but it has to be uncovered; it is not necessarily something present to our conscious mind at any given moment. In the second respect, the heart is that whereby we grasp the basic principles of our self-understanding. As he writes:

> We know that we are awake. However, we may be unable to prove this by reason. This inability of ours only shows the weakness of our reason, not (as the sceptics assert) the uncertainty of all our knowledge. . . . It is as useless and ridiculous for reason to demand that the heart shall prove its first principles before it will accept them as for the heart to demand of reason a direct perception of all the propositions that it discovers before it will admit them.[17]

Human rationality, in other words, works at different levels and possesses different orders. Because of this differentiation within rationality, what counts as reasonable evidence will differ in differing areas of experience and reflection. Because of this, Pascal's anthropology, though embedded in the disjointed and unfinished form of the *Pensées*, is a properly philosophical one. E. S. Brightman once defined philosophy as "thinking that aims at maximum concreteness, or thinking that seeks to discover connected truth about all available experience."[18] This is Pascalian, so long as "experience" here is taken to be experience relevant to the fundamental Cartesian question, What am I? Inspired by Montaigne's presentation of the vagaries of human life and sharing his vividness of expression, Pascal tries to demonstrate the fundamental contradictions implicit in human experience once the orientation to transcendence is left out.

THE PASCALIAN PICTURE OF HUMAN BEINGS

Pascal begins by comparing human beings with the rest of nature and at once comes across a staggering disproportion. Human beings cannot regard themselves as simply the product of nature, for nature returns no answer as to how they have come to be here, what they should do, and what will happen to them when they die. Whereas the world consists of things, man and man alone is a "subject." But then, if we turn our attention from external nature and try to narrate man's inside story, we find a creature pitiably riddled with contradiction, uncertainty, folly, and misery.

Man's condition: inconstancy, boredom, anxiety.[19]

Anyone who does not see the vanity of the world is very vain himself. So who does not see it, apart from young people whose lives are all noise, diversions and thoughts for the future? But take away their diversion and you will see them bored to extinction. Then they feel their nullity without recognizing it for nothing could be more wretched than to be intolerably depressed as soon as one is reduced to introspection with no means of diversion.[20]

A trifle consoles us because a trifle upsets us.[21]

Even worse, human reason is constantly invaded by self-deception. In the crucial matter of self-knowledge, reason is at the mercy of custom, of fantasy, and of the power of choice.

Truly it is an evil to be full of faults; but it is a still greater evil . . . to be unwilling to recognise them. . . . [Yet] is it not true that we hate truth and those who tell it to us, and we like them to be deceived in our favour, and prefer to be esteemed by them as being other than we are? Human life is thus only a perpetual illusion. . . . No one speaks of us in our presence as he does of us in our absence. . . . Man is, then, only disguise, falsehood and hypocrisy, both in himself and in regard to others.[22]

Everyone looks for security; yet none can reach security without self-knowledge; but self-knowledge is what everyone seeks to avoid. Nevertheless, these miseries are symptomatic of our greatness. They spring from our capacity for thought, for freedom, for imagination.

Man is but a reed, the most feeble thing in nature, but he is a thinking reed. The entire universe need not arm itself to crush him. A vapour, a drop of water, suffices to kill him. But if the universe were to crush him, man would still be nobler than that which the universe has over him; the universe knows nothing of this.[23]

Pascal's portrait of humankind uses contrasts of light and dark in a manner worthy of Titian. It is the simultaneous greatness and misery of humanity which is its mystery: on the one hand, great aspirations, hopes, and ideals; on the other, wretched performance. "What sort of freak then is man! How novel, how monstrous, how chaotic, how paradoxical, how prodigious! Judge of all things, feeble earthworm, repository of truth, sink of doubt and error, glory and refuse of the universe."[24] The contrast is designed to shock us but not to present us with pure paradox, a surd or element of the sheerly unintelligible. The anthropological contraries are not admitted as final, nor do they imply that a coherent account of human existence is unattainable. They can be compared to pistons moving the machinery of Pascal's thinking: from their motion he drew the impetus to move forward on an intellectual adventure. On closer inspection, the miseries are intimately connected with the greatness, for they are "those of a *grand seigneur*, a displaced king."[25] Even the apparent desire for nothingness, the will to suicide, seemingly the most abject of all expressions of our wretchedness, has behind it the positive demand for the resolution of the anthropological contradiction in a beatitude that lies beyond it.[26] And so we are not merely a riddle; we are a tragedy.

PASCAL'S WAGER

In the situation of apparent stalemate to which consideration of human greatness and misery brings us, some fresh initiative is called for; here Pascal's "wager" comes into play.[27] A need has disclosed itself for resources beyond our present economy. To resolve the human tragedy both practically and intellectually, a way must be found across the current boundaries of mind and will: "Let us then conceive that man's condition is dual. Let us conceive that man infinitely transcends man, and that without the aid of faith he would remain inconceivable to himself."[28] The wager, which serves just this purpose, is not simply, however, the "passional" decision that William James defended in *The Will to Believe*.[29] In the title essay of that collection, James used the *Pensées* as a stick to belabor the kind of rationalism which holds that on questions that reason cannot determine decisively, the only honest and courageous course is to face the blank. Against this rationalistic veto, James wished to vindicate our right to such beliefs as help us to live our lives happily and well: basing his defense on the contention that when confronted with a "genuine option," it is no more truly rational to decide against than to decide in favor. James was caustic about the element of "mechanical calculation" in the wager—eternity a bigger prize than time. Were we ourselves in the place of the Deity, he thought, we should take particular pleasure in cutting off believers of this type from their eternal reward. Nevertheless, he endorsed what he took to be Pascal's central thesis:

> Our passional nature not only lawfully may, but must, decide an option between propositions whenever it is a genuine option that cannot from its nature be decided on intellectual grounds; for to say, under such circumstances, "Do not decide, but leave the question open," is itself a passional decision—just like deciding yes or no—and is attended with the same risk of losing the truth.[30]

However, it is doubtful whether anyone has ever permanently founded their ideas on moral expediency alone, and this was not in fact Pascal's meaning. He wanted his readers, rather, to reach that point where, looking to reason for guidance, they would find themselves staring into the yawning hole of its failure. The wager then enters not as a permanent philosophy (or antiphilosophy) but as a decisive step that must now be taken. It symbolizes a crisis, but the resolution of the crisis for Pascal is not blind faith (or passional self-determination) but intellectual day. As the moment when our passions are indeed transcended, the resolution is also the moment of restoration of clear vision.

> Your chief maladies are your pride that withdraws you from God and the concupiscence that binds you to the earth. If they gave you God for object it was only to exercise your pride; they made you think that you were like him and of a similar nature. And those who saw the vanity of such a pretention cast you into the other abyss, by giving you to understand that your nature was like that of the beasts, and they induced you to seek your good in concupiscence, which is the lot of the animals.
> This is not the way to cure you of the unrighteousness which these men failed to recognise in you. Only I can make you understand what you are.[31]

Pascal's suggestion is that if we venture ourselves in action, that kind of action that may be called "trying for ourselves" certain gestures of faith,[32] we shall come not only to a practical resolution of our suspended animation between greatness and misery but also at the same time to an intellectual apprehension of the supernatural dimension to which our essential paradox, or tragedy, testifies.

In any case, and here James is perfectly correct, we must find a way to act. Personal subjectivity for Pascal is expressed primarily through the engagements of the will, not through the entertaining of notions. When Pascal writes in *Pensée* 113, "through space, the universe seizes me and swallows me up like a speck; but through thought it is I who seize the universe," he has in mind primarily self-awareness rather than speculation. It is through the self- directing engagements of the will that we take up the stuff of the universe and make of it what we choose. In the Pascalian scheme, the concept of will (or, as Pascal's disciple Maurice Blondel preferred, *action*)[33] is central to the postulation of the supernatural domain.

WILL AND TRANSCENDENCE

According to Pascal, the will always imparts to our actions an overall character and direction corresponding to its own secret aim and motive. This direction may be quite diverse in outwardly indistinguishable actions on the part of different human subjects. Fundamentally, however, the will can move us in one of only two such directions, since its hidden aim and motive can only be one of two: charity, or self-love. Either the will can seek its own transcendent liberation in charity, using phenomena to that end and resituating the temporal in the eternal; or actuated by self-love and taking the finite self as its end, it can impart to the finite the false infinity of endless egoistic action, in which case, secretly desiring that the transitory shall be the eternal, the will locates the eternal in the temporal. Either way, the will is master of its own fate: "The will of man is divided between two principles: cupidity and charity. . . . Cupidity makes use of God and delights in the world, while charity does just the opposite."[34]

This Augustinian commonplace is transformed by the sense of urgency that suffuses the *Pensées*. Dithering as we do before the probabilities of experience we are in peril. To withhold our assent to the transcendent resolution of our own self-contradicting nature is an act in a drama larger than this life. When life has ended, the curtain rises upon eternity. With death, desire's passing objects are swept away.

But the will itself persists. It cannot will its own annihilation and its impulse is eternal, it remains throughout eternity, infinite will without desire, impulse without aim. A state of anomaly so terrible is best represented by the image of consuming fire. To escape from this destiny we must make an act of self-surrender: "The will itself will never bring satisfaction, even if it had power over everything it wanted, but we are satisfied the moment we give it up. Without it we can never be discontented, with it we can never be content."[35] Human greatness reveals its true colors only when the human being is regarded as made for fellowship with God. Only if this is man's destiny can we make sense of his intrinsic ambiguity and tell why "his restlessness cannot be remedied until he finds his way back to the infinite and eternal which is his only true good."[36]

The way of immanence is not theological reductionism but anthropological expansionism: it explores humanity's metaphysical expansiveness towards God. *Avant la lettre*, it offers its own nuanced criticism of Feuerbach's critique of religion: "Those who claim that God is a projection of man's needs and desires are so far right, that it is from within the unrealised infinites of his being that man opens to God."[37]

THE ACCEPTABILITY OF PASCAL'S WAY TO GOD

The later nineteenth century saw the nadir of Pascal's reputation.[38] Victorian optimism and scientism were equally inimical to his reading of the world. The dark side of human life, depicted so uncompromisingly in the *Pensées*, was explained away as a dreary distortion by Jansenism, aided and abetted by the skepticism of Montaigne. The move to affirm the existence, and grace, of God in the face of the anthropological contraries was an irrational cry for help in the dark: the *sacrificium intellectus* demanded by Catholic doctrine in its extreme Augustinian form. Similarly, the scientific rationalism of the last century was outraged by Pascal's inversion of its own cognitive ideal: an exhaustive, objective knowledge of an impersonal law-governed universe.

Science, in its effort to attain the absolute, to embrace the whole, pursued what may be called a centrifugal method, tending in the direction of ever greater generality and abstraction, or, as it appeared later, the unity of a blank. But the thought of Pascal, on the contrary, is essentially centripetal, fixing as it were on one point in the whole of space and time, singling out one personality as . . . "the object of all things, the centre towards which all things tend," the one clear truth in a world of illusion, a light in darkness to such a degree that . . . "whoever knows him, knows the reason for everything."[39]

The insurrection of personality that overthrew the reign of science as the unquestioned paradigm of what counts as reality played a major part in the revival of interest in Pascal. Around the turn of the century, the sense of the real shifted dramatically in Western European culture.[40] The sense of privileged moments in the experience of the real moved away from the quantifiable, settling instead on personal consciousness and inner life. Henri Bergson's studies of the relation of human beings to nature symptomize the change and, among the philosophically minded, helped to precipitate it. The inwardness of things escapes the net of scientific method, which of its nature must prescind from consciousness. More than this, a host of movements in literature, history, and psychology that were included under the umbrella term *modernism* conspired to demand that the mind must admit more things than scientific rationalism had dreamt of. It is characteristic of cultural modernism that it is unhappy with either deductive or strictly inductive accounts of reality. Deduction admits at the end only what is already implicit in the beginning. Induction, when strictly applied, ignores the fact that not all aspects of existence offer themselves evidentially in the same fashion. To achieve a satisfactory mental contact with the complexity of the real we must grasp simultaneously a number of divergent principles, as various as reality itself. In rediscovering a sense of the many-orderedness of the real, people rediscovered the world of the *Pensées*. For the nub of Pascal's thought is found in just such an awareness of the contrasts in existence, above all the contrast between human greatness and human misery, presented by Pascal as the most important of all antinomies. The paradox of reality is not incapable of resolution: but its resolution is found only by moving into another order of investigation, the order of charity, or of the reasons of the heart. It is in this new order, which reconciles the conflicting elements of our experience in transcending them, that Pascal locates God. To a world composed of a bewildering variety of worldviews, it is not an objection to the *Pensées* but rather the opposite to say that they make a virtue out of contradiction: "a system of contradictions rather than the contradictions of a system."[41]

For Pascal, while the choice between the two most fundamental orientations of life (towards charity, towards egoism) is central to an account of man, that choice cannot be prosecuted for charity unless divine grace exists.[42] Pascal does not bring out the point that the very insistence, or authority, with which that choice can present itself (the voice of conscience) may be itself an epiphany of the divine. That is, the phenomenon of conscience is itself a pointer to the existence of God. The experience of moral obligation provides another opening for the illative sense to find its way to transcendence. To follow up this possibility, we may look to the German Enlightenment of the succeeding century and in particular to Immanuel Kant.

8

IMMANUEL KANT AND THE POSTULATES OF PRACTICAL REASON

THE APPEAL OF VALUE

The approach to divine transcendence that the writings of Immanuel Kant (1724–1804) offer us is bound up with our experience of moral values. More precisely, it turns on our sense of value as obliging us, weighing upon us, arresting us, binding us with what we call the force of duty. On any showing, the moral realm is of great significance whenever we try to seize what is distinctively human about human life. But this dimension of ethical evaluation, and the words that evaluation has at its command, can be variously assessed. In many styles of philosophizing, ethics are seen as in every sense a human creation. This may be done by treating ethical language as simply the expression of emotional attitudes—whether my own or those I wish others to take up—on emotional grounds. Alternatively, ethics may be regarded as conventions adopted by society to oil the wheels of social exchange. Again, as in the writings of Iris Murdoch, ethics may be seen as a genuinely cognitive enquiry, though one giving us access, simply, to our own human mystery. (Of course, if the intelligibility of human life is seen as itself the fruit of God's creative activity, this view will itself yield us a knowledge of God.) Christian ethics has indeed taken up what is fundamentally Murdoch's view, as she herself recognizes, but it has tried to bring out more fully the peculiar character of the insistence with which values present themselves in our experience. It is this character that, as we shall see, Kant's religious philosophy sets out to explore.[1] After a long trail whose more tortuous patches are compared by one commentator to the hardships of a trek across the Great Arabian desert, Kant will come to the claim, expressed in unfinished essays found after his death, that "in

125

recognising the [moral] law we find ourselves in God's presence; and the language of personal intercourse is no longer forbidden us as involving an inadmissible severance of God from his law; for the law itself *is* the revelation of his personality."[2]

I have stressed here the way values seem to impose themselves because this is, I think, an experiential presupposition of what Kant has to say, without which his philosophy of God cannot get off the ground. We do not feel happy with the idea that values can be changed at will, although were we purely their creators we could in principle change them quite as legitimately and as often as we change our clothes. On the contrary, it is false to much human experience of morality to see human beings as creating value *ex nihilo*. Instead, we should speak of their "welcoming" or "recognizing" value, rather as did the French philosophers of value-uncovered-in-action, René Le Senne and Maurice Blondel: they coined for this the term *l'agnition*, an activity of acknowledgement. The point of this term is to indicate the peculiar halfway house that value seems to inhabit between the fully objective and the utterly subjective. Our consciousness does not have a purely passive relationship to the moral law, as though values were infused into our awareness without any demand for reflection, integrity, insight into human situations, and control of the fantasy life of the subconscious mind. In one sense, then, mind can be said to be constitutive of value. But it is hard to see how this originating power could bring forth products carrying the note of obligatoriness, pressing upon us in a way that we would describe in metaphors drawn from external objects, and calling upon us for our dutiful response – unless it were itself originated and so always sent us back to God as its final and absolute foundation.[3] On this view divine transcendence lies at the heart of our moral awareness, grounds our sense of obligation, and justifies that sense before the bar of reason, preventing it from being a mere unintelligibility in experience, a pure surd. No doubt a naturalistic explanation of our moral consciousness, once accepted, can suppress the sense of sin, the sentiment of remorse. But it can rarely destroy the sense of obligation in some particular area of experience close to our hearts, the obligation, for instance, to be truthful at all costs. And so we have left on our hands

> a quite unresolved contradiction . . . between an apparently self-evidencing authority and an intellectual assent to a theory which in inconsistent with that authority. This unresolved contradiction is after all a greater

scandal to philosophy than is involved in a frank acknowledgement of the authority of the moral law speaking in our conscience – along with a frank recognition of the mystery which is involved both in the inability of man to fulfill the obligation thus laid upon him, and also in the difficulty of finding in the world satisfying evidence of a government in accordance with demands suggested by the moral consciousness.[4]

These words were written à propos de Pascal, but they were evidently inspired by Immanuel Kant.

KANT'S SITUATION: CHRISTIANITY AND ENLIGHTENMENT

Kant was born in the city of Königsberg, now the Soviet Kaliningrad, on the old ducal demesne of the house of Brandenburg, the heartland of the original Prussia.[5] In the first two-thirds of the eighteenth century, the intellectual and literary center of Germany lay at Leipzig, some hundreds of miles to the south and west, across Poland. Königsberg could be described, therefore, by unfriendly critics as ein Gelehrtes Sibirien, "a scholar's Siberia." Kant himself felt this isolation from the world of letters, but he was evidently determined to make the best of his situation. He wrote of his home city:

A large town, the centre of a kingdom, in which are situated the ministries of the local government, which has a university (for the culture of the sciences), and which, moreover, possesses a site suitable for maritime trade with . . . lands of different languages and customs, such a town . . . may be taken as a suitable spot for extending not merely a knowledge of men, but even a knowledge of the world, so far as it is possible to acquire the latter without travelling.[6]

Königsberg had its salons, and remote as it was from the atmosphere of the court, it possessed, like many frontier towns, a certain spiritual republicanism, the air of a commonwealth where man meets man on the universal field of intelligent human interests. Kant's forbears for two generations had been skilled artisans in a tight-knit urban economy, strap makers in their traditional quarter of the city, Sadler Street, where Kant himself was born and reared. He was to live in Königsberg for the rest of his life, with the exception of two brief periods as a tutor, first in the family of the Lutheran pastor at nearby Judschen, and then at Gross Arnsdorf, the seat of a family of the Prussian aristocracy in a hilly and lake-studded tract of country which gave the young Kant ample opportunity to develop his love of nature. His own family belonged to the Pietist movement within the Lutheran church, practicing a type of spirituality that placed its stress on ethical rectitude and purity of heart.[7] At university, the teacher whose influence on Kant's mind seems to have been greatest, Martin Knutzen, combined just this Pietist Lutheranism with the rationalist philosophical method of Christian Wolff.[8] Knutzen argued that a supernatural revelation is necessary to humankind because unaided human reason cannot find an adequate means of atoning for human guilt. A putative divine revelation may be judged authentic, Knutzen thought, if it discloses the holiness of God, brings home to human beings the facts of their state of disobedience, and provides for their salvation. Much later, in defending the essay on *Religion within the Limits of Reason Alone*, Kant would insist that he had served the Christian faith by showing how the failure of natural religion to account for the origin of evil leaves room for divine revelation.

In 1755 Kant returned to his old university as *Privatdozent*, a licensed but unsalaried lecturer, paying his way by means of a modest sublibrarian's stipend at the castle library. Around 1763 the young J. G. Herder, later to lead the poetic movement of the German Enlightenment as well as to advocate an approach to the Bible as literature, came to hear Kant's philosophy course and was excited enough to render the content of his lectures in verse. In 1770 Kant was given the chair of logic and metaphysics at Königsberg, and from then on the rhythm of solitary reflection and social affability (he held a small dinner party every night of his life) would continue until his death in 1804. In 1795 Kant ceased to give more than a single daily lecture, eager, as he said, *sarcinas colligere*, to pack up for the long last journey. He divided his mental energy between ruminations on the late revolution in France and final thoughts on the interrelation of theology and the human sciences. In the *Quarrel of the Faculties*, published in 1798, he would grant "the proud claim of the theological faculty to call philosophy her maid," adding, characteristically, that "we still ask whether the maid carries the torch before her lady-mistress, or carries her train behind."[9] The inherent difficulty and abstraction of the first Critique, the *Critique of Pure Reason*, in particular, and the contemporary pen portraits of the aging Kant of the years of celebrity that have come down to us, can conspire to produce an unattractive picture: "a little old man, bent forward as he sits, in a brown coat with yellow buttons, with wig and hair-bag to boot."[10] But this is to miss the wide human sympathies of Kant, the sensitivity to natural beauty so amply demonstrated in the *Critique of Judgement*, and the profound religiosity of spirit, his penetration by the concepts of "regeneration and redemption, the idea of divine grace and wisdom, which accepts the totality of a soul's good disposition in lieu of that soul's ever defective single good works, the belief in a providence which strengthens the good throughout the world against evil, and adoring awe in face of the majesty of the Supersensible."[11]

In the philosophical writings of his maturity, above all in the *Critique of Practical Reason* and the treatise on *Religion within the Limits of Reason Alone*, Kant was concerned with showing that the practice of ethics points us towards God. God, for Kant, is postulated within our awareness of moral value and moral striving. It was, surely, the influence of Kant's particular kind of Christian childhood that encouraged him to look to such experience for the grounds of our assent to what he calls "the only holy one." But equally his own driving passion for rationality urged him on to explore the intelligible structure of ethical behavior and to search out to the very last its metaphysical implications: "morality for Kant is reason in action; hence the critical examination of practical reason is at the same time a search for the supreme principle of morality."[12] It is the peculiar fascination of Kant's work that he tried, with some success, to hold together two concerns stemming from the dominant motifs in his culture: the Christian insistence on each human being as possessing an infinite spiritual destiny and a unique and incommensurable importance in his or her own right; and the rationalist Enlightenment's longing for coherence, unity, universality and necessity.[13]

KNOWING AND ITS CONDITIONS

Let us try to situate Kant's religious philosophy within the overall picture of humanity and the world he entertained. The so-called Copernican revolution in philosophy, more especially in the theory of knowledge, with which Kant is accredited was not perhaps so radical as is sometimes made out. This is so both if one thinks of some of his predecessors in the great tradition (for instance, the scholastic philosophers of the high Middle Ages with their dictum that knowledge "is received according to the capacity of the receiver"); and also if one looks at Kant's own supposed pessimism about our power to know the world "as it really is," at the pattern, then, of his own thinking. The distinction he made between *noumenon*, the thing as it really and intrinsically is, and *phenomenon*, the things as it appears to us, can be made into a schism yet need not be.[14] But Kant did insist with a peculiar forcefulness on the fact that for an object to be known it must somehow conform to the structure of the human mind. This is the burden of the first Critique, written when acquaintance with the empiricist tradition of British philosophy had woke him from the "dogmatic slumbers" of an epistemologically naive metaphysics. Things cannot become objects of knowledge unless they yield themselves to certain conditions imposed by the cognitive capacities of the human mind. Briefly, Kant held that while the content of our knowledge is derived from sense experience, its form is imposed by our understanding, which makes certain claims on reality prior to any particular experience of reality. There are, he thought, patterns or forms of intellectual organization that come into play whenever impressions are presented to our minds. Preference may be given neither to the receptive power of the mind to take in impressions, nor to its active power to organize those impressions into the shape of a common world: "Thoughts without content are empty; intuitions without concepts are blind. . . . The understanding can intuit nothing, the senses can think nothing. Only through their union can knowledge arise."[15] Because the mind is not just sensing but is thinking, it can go beyond the stimuli of momentary sensations to find a world of permanent substances engaged in interaction one with another. But the world of which it is thus aware is itself a world transformed in perception by the necessary conditions and limitations of our finite experience. In appearances things-in-themselves are indeed present to us, immediately so; but their ultimate character as sheer realities is finally baffling.[16]

For Kant, our minds exhibit in various ways a tendency to seek unity and completeness in knowing. This urge, he thought, tends to precede us in all our commerce with the world about us. At one level, the level of the "understanding" (*Verstand*), which makes sense of sense experience, this tendency of the mind is simply concerned with apprehending the many shifting images and sensations of our sense-experience as a discriminated world of objects, chairs, trees, persons, rather than a "buzzing, blooming confusion." Kant calls this, rather grandiloquently, the "necessary unity of apperception" and holds that it works by means of the "transcendental synthesis of imagination," "transcendental" because this belongs to the very structure of the knowing mind, the creativity of finite spirit. This is not the imposition of order on what is, so far as we can tell, absolute chaos; rather, it is the rendering in a human idiom of an order that must, in fact, be given in the nature of things.

> The fundamental demand of thought is that reality should be thinkable. . . . Thought, we may say, manifests itself in the synthesis of concepts; and if truth is to be possible at all, there must be a corresponding synthesis or combination in the manifold which is assumed to be given to sense. . . . Without such combination in the manifold, there can be no truth at all, no knowledge of objects and no objects for us.[17]

But mind's drive to unify exists also at a second level, which Kant calls the level of "reason" (*Vernunft*). We have just witnessed it in action in the quotation above: pure reason is concerned with the conditions that render the interplay of sensation and understanding possible and intelligible. The most important idea with which reason works is that of the Unconditioned, the Absolute, which, when we consider it as legitimately eliciting a response of religious awe and reverence, people call God. This is, in Kant's words,

> the ideal of the supreme and complete material condition of the possibility of all that exists — the condition to which all thought of objects, so far as their content is concerned, has to be traced back. . . . All possibility of things (that is, of the synthesis of the manifold, in respect of its contents) must therefore be regarded as derivative, with only one exception, namely, the possibility of that which includes in itself all reality.[18]

The idea of God entertained by pure reason is therefore described by Kant as the idea of "primordial being, . . . highest being, . . . the being of all beings,"[19] the supreme reality that conditions the possibility of things, not as their sum but as their ground. Unfortunately for the traditional theologians, however, the whole point of this "idea of reason" is that it remains precisely that: an idea that pure reason needs in order to think through by contrast the content of concepts of the finite; or, as Kant has it, "These terms . . . are not to be taken as signifying the objective relation of an actual object to other things, but of an idea to concepts. We are left entirely without knowledge as to the existence of a being of such outstanding pre-eminence."[20] While the claims of speculative reason that one can move from the apprehension of phenomena to the divine ground of those phenomena were, Kant thought, hubristic and mistaken, reason's delineation of the image of God could come into its own if only some more secure way of establishing God's existence could be found. Towards the close of the *Critique of Pure Reason* Kant allows us a first glimpse of what this way may be: "One other line of enquiry remains open to us: namely, whether pure reason may not also be met with in the practical sphere, and whether it may not there conduct us to ideas which reach to those highest ends of pure reason that we have just stated, and whether, therefore, reason may not be able to supply to us from the standpoint of its practical interest what it altogether refuses to supply in respect of its speculative interest."[21]

THE ANALYSIS OF MORAL EXPERIENCE

The *Critique of Practical Reason* is Kant's exploration of this second "line of enquiry." In it he gave a theological interpretation of his analysis of moral experience, itself lapidarily expressed in the brief *Groundwork of the Metaphysic of Morals*. Kant there focuses our attention on the authoritative aspect of values, touched on at the start of this chapter. The pressure of our obligations upon us is not a peculiar instance of the pressure of our interests, for "the expression *I ought* represents an experience which is ultimate and self-explanatory; and in any attempt to get, so to speak, behind it, the true nature of it is let slip, and it becomes a mere illusion, in which appetite or self-interest masquerade as something quite different."[22] As Professor Donald MacKinnon has written in his sensitive essay on Kant, *A Study of Ethical Theory*, here, in moral experience, we find that about which the metaphysician has been trying incompetently to speak: "For Kant the absolute for human beings is always realised as a *Sollen* [an 'ought'] . . . What is ultimate is what engages the allegiance of our will without possibility of question and cavil."[23] Kant is pointing to a type of situation distinctive enough to constitute the operating theater of a distinctive type of human rationality. He will go on, in the *Critique of Practical Reason*, the later essay *Religion within the Limits of Reason Alone*, and certain minor works issued after his death, to find within this rationality a disclosure of God in human life.[24] The situation Kant has in mind is one where we find ourselves called on to obey a moral imperative for its own sake and for that alone. We lay aside such considerations as whether some course of action will lead to our happiness or self-realization or to the commonweal. We see at once that time spent on thoughts such as those is wasted time. The experience has an irruptive quality about it: it breaks in on us as from without. As Arthur Koestler in the Spanish prison described in his political autobiography, *The God That Failed*, "listening to the ceaseless butcherings of Franco's murder squads, we are made vividly and dramatically aware of the unconditional authority over us of a universe in which due regard is paid to the dignity of human nature, in which respect and not contempt has sway."[25] In this experience of the "categorical imperative" we are confronted by the question of our validity as human beings, "pitch-forked, willy-nilly, from the level of the conditioned to that of the unconditioned."[26] But "man feels in himself a powerful counterweight to all the commands of duty presented to him by reason as so worthy of esteem—the counterweight of his needs and inclinations. . . . On this account wisdom itself—which in any case consists more in doing and not doing than in knowing—does require science as well, not in order to learn from it, but in order to win acceptance and durability for its own prescriptions."[27] The role of moral and religious philosophy must be, therefore, to preserve the experience of the unconditioned from denaturing by any kind of reductionist analysis that would remove the note of sovereignty from the accents of duty. Thus "Kant's confidence of the transcendent import of moral experience . . . is grounded in a rationally achieved comprehension of the powerlessness of theoretical activity to impugn its inescapable uniqueness."[28] At the same time, philosophy's task is to unfold the implications of the experience practical reason finds astride its path. The moral realm, as we trace its contours in reflection, proves to open out onto a transcendent realm, a wider ambience of freedom, immortality and the divine, within which our lives are set.[29] The metaphysical is not patient of theoretical description, for it lies beyond the frontiers of intelligible descriptive discourse, yet it presses on us in moral experience with "a directness and immediacy which requires no argument to convince us of its reality."[30]

KANT'S PATH TO GOD

At the close of the *Critique of Practical Reason*, Kant indicates two possible sources of the sense of God: "Two things fill the mind with ever new and increasing admiration and awe, the oftener and the more steadily we reflect on them: the starry heavens above and the moral law within."[31] Yet despite his own personal susceptibility to the impression of design that nature makes on the mind, Kant held that that impression would not be turned into an argument.[32] But to the other set of experiential cues, those given in reason's instinctive reverence for the moral law, a different situation applied.[33] The categorical imperative binds the finite spirit, possessed as it is of rational freedom, to certain policies of action in this world. In Kantian studies in the British Isles it has long been supposed that the relation of these policies to the formal expression of the imperative ("Act only on that maxim whereby thou canst at the same time will that it should become a universal law") is a purely logical one (so that only such actions are obligatory the contradictories of which are logically self-contradictory). More recently, it has become clear that this will not do: "Against this traditional view, it is correct to say that Kant had a much wider, teleological notion of consistency in mind, for which what is important is not logical consistency and inconsistency, but the contribution to or frustration of a universal harmony of purposes, the constitutive purposes of which are to be freely and creatively set and pursued."[34] And Keith Ward continues his exposition of Kantian ethics by noting: "If Kant's ethics is formalistic, it is a formalism which means to take full account of all natural and human purposes, and of the essential ends of humanity, perfection and happiness."[35] Our response to the sovereign appeal of value cannot be made in terms of the contribution of moral action to our own well-being; the goodness of the good will is not dependent on the goodness of anything else (such as our happiness) to which it may be the means. Nevertheless, the good will is not for Kant the whole good. It may be, he says, the *summum bonum*; it is not *bonum perfectissimum*, for that resides in human virtue when crowned with happiness, when issuing in the flourishing of the free and personal spirit.[36] Our duty is to produce the best state of the world, and our will to perform our duty is frustrated if the desire for happiness remains unfulfilled even though we deserve what we desire. I may accept my own exclusion from that perfect good as fair and just, yet I cannot refrain from demanding the inclusion within it of those who are worthy. Morality is centrally concerned with human fulfillment, and yet this fulfillment Kant concedes to be impossible in this life.

The resolution of this paradox, for Kant, is only possible through the affirmation of God. Our moral awareness postulates a power able to bring into being a state of things where the rational purposes of free spirits are perfected and made harmonious. Either God is, or we must dismiss the call to total ethical righteousness, the sense of the sovereignty of the good, as a joke played on us by an unwitting cosmos: "The moral law ordains that man ought to be perfectly virtuous, and what is thus required must somehow be possible, else the moral order, by demanding the impossible of man, proves itself fundamentally unreasonable and non-moral."[37] The rationality of morals is saved only if there is an agency that has power both over the empirical order, the order of our present humanity in all its concrete struggles with the materials of an intractable environment, and over the transcendent order, the order of the endless duration of our personal will in its striving for holiness.[38]

The process involved may be illustrated from materials for the life of an English novelist whose passion for human truth led her to a close study of the German philosophical tradition. In the gardens of Trinity College, Cambridge, George Eliot talked "with terrible earnestness" of God, duty, and immortality: "How inconceivable the first, how unbelievable the third, and yet how peremptory and absolute the second!"[39] Her position, held as it was with intense sincerity, seems nevertheless pervasively unsatisfactory. It discomforts itself, urging anyone who finds her- or himself in it to advance to faith in God by way of justifying such recognition of the authority of the moral law. This is not because that authority stands in need of any external sanction to secure it, but because without faith in God it must seem "a voice crying in the wilderness of an alien world, its presence wherein must remain an inexplicable and baffling mystery," and because this impression, "while it does not take away from us our inexpugnable consciousness of the urgency of the claim made by that law upon us, can hardly but tend to discourage us in our moral endeavours and to sap our moral energies, which seem destined to perpetual disappointment in a system of things wholly indifferent to our moral purposes." It is from these internal demands of moral experience, then, that Kant proceeds to give his assent to the reality of a God of whom pure reason alone can only furnish the barest concept. This God Kant affirms as "the only holy one, the only blessed one, the only wise one."[42]

In *Religion within the Limits of Reason Alone* Kant will take this discovery a good deal further. He finds in the possibility of a sheer "no" to the categorical imperative evidence for a "radical evil" in human beings. There may be any amount of empirical goodness in the world, in the way men and women deport themselves towards their fellows;

but where they decide to follow the moral law not for its own sake but as a means to their own long-term self-interest (either in secular or religious guise) they reverse the ethical order of incentives and draw moral evil into being. Here, in clean contradiction to the spirit of the *Aufklärung* Kant summons up the shade of the doctrine of original sin—not as revealed dogma but as an implication of our moral experience. For this reversal of the proper order of "maxims," of the subjective springs of action, is what it means to be radically evil. When we consider this propensity within us we accept responsibility for it as moral agents, and yet at the same time we are quite baffled when seeking out its origin in our own lives. We are confronted with an insoluble, and terrible, mystery. But "better, Kant thinks, to confess to something in the situation which baffles our understanding than to tamper with our moral consciousness (which is to him the primary certainty in our experience) by denying our responsibility as free agents, or to give the lie to patent facts by disputing the existence of a propensity to evil in man to which all history and all experience testify."[43] The story of Adam and Eve, then, is our personal story. As Kant remarks, citing a phrase of Horace's *Satires*, "Only the names are changed: it is of you that the legend is recited."[44] Only the hope for a conversion of self in the ultimate ground of our willing, which must mean a hope for God's grace, can save our situation. For despite our propensity to evil the moral law continues to make its absolute demands upon us. Religion defined within the limits of reason alone cannot, indeed, affirm the reality of supernatural grace in particular personal histories. It will revolt against any attempt to incorporate grace into the nexus of empirical cause and effect in this world, since the laws whereby phenomena affect each other do not necessarily express the laws of the interaction of noumena. The realm that houses the freedom of finite spirit in its interplay with infinite spirit is not the realm of measurement and mechanics. Yet reason lays herself open to this possibility of grace, even while renouncing forever the claim to describe and define its inner reality.

Reason does not dispute the possibility or "the reality of the objects of these ideas. She simply cannot adopt them into her maxims of thought and action. She even holds that if in the inscrutable realm of the supernatural there is something more than she can explain to herself, which may yet be necessary as a complement to her moral insufficiency, this will be, even though unknown, available to her good will."[45]

In later sections of *Religion within the Limits of Reason Alone*, Kant will go on to reexpress Christian doctrines – incarnation, atonement, sanctification – as symbols of the conflict of good and evil principles, expressed in our choice of grounds for action. By his refusal to move beyond the methodology of philosophy, Kant, quite properly in the context of the terms he has set, cannot regard the grace of God in history as "entering constitutively into the moral life."[46] Seen as dogmatic theology, therefore, these passages are an utter disaster; read as meditations on how reason, at her own level, can find the symbols of faith illuminating for her own activity, they are profoundly instructive. To what extent these reflections modified Kant's understanding of the implication of divinity in moral experience will probably remain in dispute so long as interest in his memory survives. For after his death were found a series of short writings, scarcely more than fragments, sometimes nothing more than jottings, in which whatever answer is possible to this question lies. Many students of these writings hold that in them Kant had come to see God as not simply logically implicated in our moral beliefs as the condition of intelligibility of those beliefs; rather for him God is now *personally* implicated in our moral experience.[47] The consciousness of the moral law, on this view, is now identified by Kant with a consciousness of being in the presence of the personal God. If this is so, then in the moment of divine encounter and judgment that awareness of the sovereignty of the good brings, Kant would be saying, with his hero Job, "I have heard thy voice now; nay, more, I have had sight of thee; now I am all remorse, I do penance in dust and ashes" (Job 42:6). Here we may find the final outcome of our initial puzzlement at the quality of what we call moral "claims" upon us. We experience their pressure and constraint, yet, enigmatically, taken in themselves they are impersonal. As Professor H. P. Owen has written, "In order to perceive this ontological incongruity it is enough to consider ordinary language. The words 'obligation,' 'duty,' 'claim' always imply a *personal* constraint whenever they refer to an object within the finite world. . . . The task of theism is to show how morality, when it is most true to itself, raises questions to which the Christian concept of God is the only answer."[48]

Life without ethics would be life deprived of the exercise of all discriminating intelligence on our outer and inner actions. Kant's way to God, then, must be of rather general appeal, so long as human beings are human beings. Yet the moral life can be lived out impeccably by people who are as personalities confused, neurotic, and "untogether."

Not all human growth can be subsumed under moral growth for this very fact. Is there not an activity at least as fundamental as ethical activity (and sometimes overlapping with it) that we may call the activity of self-making, of becoming a self? In our own age with its stress, at least in the Western world, on problems of personal identity and selfhood this is, perhaps, our primary reading of the cast and lie of human experience. In one sense we are all existentialists now. If there is a way to God here too, then it will be pointed to by the prophet of the existentialist vision, Søren Kierkegaard.

9

SØREN KIERKEGAARD AND THE STRUGGLE WITH SELF-ESTRANGEMENT

Nineteenth-century Denmark figures in the history books of other western European countries chiefly through that most prolix of diplomatic controversies, the Schleswig- (Slesvig-) Holstein (Holsten) question. Some years before the crisis over those border dutchies had poisoned relations between the Danish kingdom and a renascent Prussia, a very different Dano-German struggle was enacted in the life story of Søren Kierkegaard (1813–1855).[1]

The Man and the Mission

Kierkegaard was the product of a Copenhagen merchant family who had been peasants a generation back. As a theological student in his twenties he visited Prussia so as to investigate and, as it would turn out, reject the prestigious intellectual establishment of the new university of Berlin, then presided over by the philosophical disciples of G. F. W. Hegel. He had already presented his thesis for the degree of master of arts at Copenhagen. A puzzle to his examiners, who considered its style an outrage, it could be read as the work of the most brilliant Hegelian to date — or as a vigorous rebuttal of all Hegel's work. In *The Concept of Irony* Kierkegaard shared Hegel's dislike of romantic irony: they both despised its ethical noncommitment for which, as in the characters of the novels of Thomas Mann, the unconditional longings of human beings are locked in eternal conflict with the infinite smallness of the everyday world.[2] Yet Kierkegaard, unlike Hegel, had a positive view of irony at another level. Transformed by resignation into self-mastery, irony marks the beginning of subjectivity, the birth of the personal life. The question, "How may I achieve the personal life?" stands at the center of Kierkegaard's philosophical enterprise. It explains why the stream of largely pseudonymous writings that, on his return from Germany to Denmark, he set flowing is, above all, a critical response to the claims of a speculative, universal Hegelianism to be a Christian philosophy.[3] Kierkegaard's death at the age of forty-two found his own writings unreceived except among a small circle of readers in the Danish capital. But the isolation, mistrust, and ridicule he endured—and which he thought proper, given his vocation as a witness to truth and to Christ, to draw upon his own head—gave way in the twentieth century to admiration and acceptance in a variety of intellectual milieux.

Chiefly through the school of dialectical theology associated with Karl Barth, Kierkegaard has become, in fact, a major figure of the Christian tradition, though he has not lacked Catholic students also.[4] He has been accorded an honored place in the philosophical tradition as well, by way of the existentialist movement. Indeed, Kierkegaard's thought is generally recognized as the fountainhead of modern existentialism; but a note of warning will be timely before we bestow here praise or blame. In violent disagreement with each other over the direction in which human existence points, the existentialists can hardly be described as simple purveyors of footnotes to Kierkegaard's work. The most that can be said is that he bequeathed to them his central philosophical concern. Yet the human existence that occupies the center of the Kierkegaardian universe is, for him a "specifically religious category . . . the single, finite, responsible, simple, suffering and guilty creature, who has to make a decision in favour of God and who, consequently, is more interested in ethical questions and in salvation than in abstract speculations."[5] After Kierkegaard's lifetime, these religious terms would suffer translation into secular equivalents. Heidegger arrived at a kind of reverent agnosticism before the mystery of being; Camus and Sartre were openly atheistic. Other writers indebted to the original Kierkegaardian impulse reintroduced the Judaeo-Christian element so prominent in Kierkegaard's own work; thus Marcel, Berdyaev, Buber, and, towards the end of his life, Jaspers. There are, then, many existentialisms, but at least one attempt to enumerate them, that of Emmanuel Mounier in his *Introduction aux existentialismes*, argues that every type of existentialism presents a "dialectic of conversion." Whether believing or not, it swings backwards and forwards between the two poles of existence lost and existence regained. Christian or atheistic, existentialism marks, in this way, the return of the religious question to contemporary culture.[6] This is, perhaps, overstated. Yet for many, the way of existentialism has indeed led from religion through agnosticism and atheism back to religion once more.

Kierkegaard's autobiographical essay, entitled *The Point of View for My Work as an Author*, offers an overview of his life by drawing attention to three crucial moments in his development.[7] First, he describes his childhood formation. His father, Michael, combined rationalist philosophy in the manner of Christian Wolff with a Lutheran Christianity whose twin axes were the radical sinfulness of human beings and the gracious mercy of God in the Cross of Christ. The elder Kierkegaard, who had the misfortune to lose his wife and five of his children within a period of two years, conveyed the ethos of the first, rather than the second, of those Lutheran tenets. Søren grew up in a household dominated by dark feelings of melancholy and guilt. Oppressed by the sense of a flawed inheritance amounting almost to a family curse, Kierkegaard's *The Sickness unto Death* would later ask, How can one emerge again into freedom, if the burden of the past forecloses what should be the possibilities of the future?[8]

Reconciled, at the age of twenty-five, with the formidable father through whose unwitting agency he had suffered so much, Kierkegaard discovered an efficacious belief in the fatherly goodness of God and dedicated himself to exploring the problem of religious existence with all the powers of his being. But no sooner was this commitment made than he plunged into the second crisis of his life, which turns on his unhappy love affair with Regina Olsen. He considered himself to be, spiritually, "an eternity too old" for the girl he would have married and, in any case, unable to inhabit the common categories of ordinary living. But what he called, in retrospect, his inability to "realise the universal" served to disclose the quite particular fate that in the concrete was to be individually his. He came to believe that "he was asked to forego the security and consolation of the ordinary ways of life, in order to further the positive ends of Providence. He had received sealed orders, and those orders read, 'Go further!' "[9]

The future was to carry a third, and this time more public, crisis: conflict with the Danish state church. The prelude to this battle was a wrangle with the Danish press, which had given a rough reception to Kierkegaard's first major study in religious philosophy: *Either/Or : A Fragment of Life*.[10] He interpreted the nonsupport of Copenhagen society and, especially, the deafening silence of the Lutheran church in his defense as symptomatic of a widespread indifference to the individual—to actually existing, nameable men and women—that had been induced by Hegelianism and its theological disciples. From now on, Kierkegaard would take the typical posture of the Christian to be a responsible witnessing to the truth on the part of an individual person, exposing him or her to suffering at the hands of a majority. The Christian message, he will now assume, is in scandalous contrast to the position of Christendom.

THE MASKS AND THE MESSAGE

The content of Kierkegaard's mature presentation of that message is, however, elusive, chiefly because of the strange literary forms that he used as its vehicles. Unable to find direct expression for what he had to say, he chose the way of indirect communication, writing pseudonymously as Johannes de Silentio, Constantine Constantinus, Johannes Climacus, Nikolaus Notabene, Hilarius Bookbinder, and Victor Eremita—the last presented as merely the editor of two authors' posthumously discovered papers which turned up accidentally in the secret compartment of a desk bought from an antique shop! How can we explain this "sometimes amusing, and sometimes exasperating game of hide-and-seek"?[11]

Two considerations throw light on Kierkegaard's decision to adopt such a variety of masks. First, he had the artist's observant eye for human types, and the penetrating insight of the born psychologist. What could have been more natural than that he should create a range of pseudonymous figures to embody the diverse solutions to life's problems on offer around him? The masks enabled him to develop the leitmotifs of these various solutions in a consistent and plausible way. Second, Kierkegaard regarded his writings as so many essays in "Socratic deceit."[12] Like Socrates with his pupils, Kierkegaard worked under the sign of "Either/Or": the decision about the truth is a personal matter, left to the reader's discretion as he or she seeks enlightenment amid the melee of ideas and ideals jostling for attention.

> If anyone should be so polite as to attribute a point of view to me, if he should even stretch his gallantry to the limit and accept this point of view because it is mine, I regret his politeness, for he shows it to one who is unworthy. I also regret his point of view, if indeed he has no other point

of view than mine. My life I can risk; my life in all seriousness I can wager; but not that of another.[13]

The combination of factors made the early Kierkegaard elusive. The *vox ipsissima* is hard to catch amid the cacophony of assumed voices, the authorial viewpoint disappears behind the single-minded passion to set the reader free to achieve his or her own existence. In his later years, however, faced with what he considered the deteriorating circumstances of society and church in Denmark, Kierkegaard came to see it as a human and spiritual duty to witness to truth in as direct and unequivocal a way as possible.

Through the mediation of these various literary forms, Kierkegaard hoped to work a philosophical revolution. In his view, his writing represented a deliberate rupture in the philosophical tradition that reached from Descartes to Hegel. In the polemic against Descartes's disciples, found among his papers under the title *Johannes Climacus: Or, De omnibus est disputandum*, he rejected the Cartesian *cogito ergo sum* and replaced it with his own *sum, ergo cogito*.[14] That is, for the primacy of formal consciousness and formal thought he substituted a countervailing primacy of the concrete, spiritual individual, the bearer of interiority and subjectivity. For this alone matches human need.

How so? Every human being is self-estranged. Ensnared in the toils of a speculation uprooted from the concrete and leveled down by the tyranny of public opinion, we have lost ourselves in a spurious objectivity. Each person's ability to be a true, functioning subject in his or her own right has withered from nonuse.[15] Human selfhood is not a quantity to be taken for granted. Rather are we, in an important sense, our own creators. As *The Concept of Dread* sets out to show, we have a hand in our own making.[16] Poised between nothingness and God, we can use freedom to negate as well as to affirm. The endemic *angest*, "anxiety," of the modern world derives from a sense of fright at the possible loss of the proper human power to form the self. In its sharpest form, such anxiety becomes despair. And despair, for Kierkegaard, is itself a major clue to deciphering the mystery of our existence, is an important signpost in reading the map of being.

The point of despair, as of anxiety, is that it has no point, that is, no definite object. No animal in the universe save the human being alone suffers such an emotion. But no other animal is confronted by so giddy a range of possibilities of being. In Kierkegaard's analysis, despair is a failure in relation to these possibilities. It is a sickness of

selfhood; a disturbance in the process of becoming a self; a disproportion in the relation of the self to itself; an illness of the human being
as a spiritual being. Despair arises from the fact that we neglect what
is eternal in us—our relation to the Infinite. For, according to
Kierkegaard, the proper selfhood of the human being is a finite-infinite
relationship. If this relationship is denied or sorely neglected, then
our very being, our concrete existence and felt subjectivity, is imper-
iled. Such despair at not being a self is, Kierkegaard surmises, inevitable wherever there is no adequate lived realization of the
theological self—his term for the individual human being in his or her
plenary perfection, as a man or woman of God.[17]

In this particular, yet crucial, aspect of Kierkegaard's thinking, a
medieval inheritance is at work. Despite its contemporary ring, there
is here, transmitted presumably via Luther, a new version of the piety
of the fourteenth-century German Dominican, Johann Tauler. The
contemporary Tauler scholar Alois Haas, following up a cue given by
the Swiss dogmatician Hans Urs von Balthasar,[18] speaks of Taulerian
humanity as suspended between eternity and time, occupying an inter-
mediate space that separates the "most sublime union" from the "utmost
deprivation of God."[19] As Haas points out, the experience arising
from such a state is one of anguish. Suspended between heaven and
earth, the typical man or woman of Tauler's sermons is familiar at
once with "sublimity and humility, knowledge and non-knowledge,
security and insecurity, peace in spirit but not in nature, imageless-
ness and the world of images."[20]

What is new in Kierkegaard is above all the attempt to stake out
rational grounds for this estimate of the human situation by a form of
suasion that works through confronting us with various interpretations of existence and requiring us to choose. Kierkegaard identified
three spheres of existence—the aesthetic, the ethical and the religious—
as the fundamental possible forms of existence among which every
human being has to make his or her choice. The basic condition of
the aesthetic individual is sensual immediacy, summed up in the figure of Don Juan and given its finest artistic expression in Mozart's
Don Giovanni.

> The sensuality of which Don Juan is an incarnation is a kind of counter-
> kingdom of the flesh, in counter-distinction to (and, ultimately, in oppo-
> sition to) the kingdom of the spirit. . . . Don Juan has all the exuberance
> and primitive drive which are present in a man before reflection sets in.

His is the first phase of aesthetic life, which begins innocently enough in isolation from, but not deliberate revolt against, motives which might regulate and discipline sensuous desire.[21]

Don Juan's aim is to experience anew in each fresh experience of love all the immediacy of first love. His fear is that, failing this, love will acquire continuity and so a history and thus obligations stemming from outside the individual and careless of his satisfaction. In *Either/Or*, Kierkegaard shows how, when passion is thus divorced from moral will, the individual eventually loses all power over her- or himself and becomes a slave in search of the pleasurable moment. Since that moment can never become eternal, aesthetic existence is marked by ennui and restlessness.

The figure of Faust embodies an intellectual version of the same phenomenon: man driven hither and thither by the play of demonic genius. And in a third legendary character, Ahasuerus, the "Wandering Jew," Kierkegaard found his supreme symbol for the aesthetic life as a movement within a closed circle. In the *Journals* he depicts Ahasuerus wandering endlessly through the world in dull indifference and utter absence of hope.[22] Confronted with such a prospect, he points out, the aesthetic mind turns in despair to romantic irony: the force that reduces all values to a common ground, finding all contrasts, and not least among them that between good and evil, to be, at bottom, delusion.

Such despair is only provisionally neutralized when the aesthetic stage passes into the second sphere of existence, the ethical. Over against Don Juan's defense of promiscuity, the moralist stresses the significance of time, which gives to love, in the form of marriage, the very history and continuity that Don Juan deplored.

Recollection and hope merge, so that the high point does not lie *behind* the lovers as a past event, the way it does for the aesthetic representative of "first love," but instead always lies before them as a possibility perpetually renewed. In marriage, true love lives on the possibility of repetition — in other words, on just what the aesthete fears so terribly. The moral philosopher . . . can say that he too preserves the aesthetic element, because the important thing is not to *represent* what is aesthetically beautiful but to *live* an aesthetically beautiful life.[23]

Here at last there can be purpose and direction in life. Mere whim yields to the governing of a personal project by a moral standard, itself hailed as binding on all men and women. Through the free commitment of the will to the ideal of moral perfection, that succession of moments, on whose multiplicity the aesthete came to grief, can be bound together into the lifetime's work of creating a self. Only the moral person solves the great riddle of living in eternity and yet hearing the hall-clock strike. Obligation is not external to us: it arises as a need to express what is universally human in the particularities of our lives.[24]

Yet this cannot be the whole story, as Kierkegaard's own disastrous attempt at forging a marriage bond had shown. One always meets this universal demand of ethics within the context of individual fate. Failure to follow the commands of conscience is not just a matter of defects in practical reasoning. Here be dragons: malice; the passions; and, above all, the fascinated, Hamlet-like impotence of the individual at the prospect of exercising his or her own freedom. And so the ethical stage, like the aesthetic, engenders its characteristic despair. It holds the individual responsible for things that he or she cannot help. Cruelly, it treats us as though in truth we were masters of our own destiny. From within this second variety of despair, Kierkegaard reaches his conclusion that "the finite, derived spirit cannot extricate itself from despair or disequilibrium in existence, solely through its own power. It must not only relate itself to God but receive from God the conditions of liberation and balance."[25] In the light of this conviction, it is not hard to understand Kierkegaard's prediction that the journey to God for modern people may be routed by way of the experience of despair: "I believe the time is not far off when one will experience perhaps dearly enough that one has to start, if one wants to find the Absolute, not with doubt but with despair."[26]

SUBJECTIVITY AND TRUTH

What, in these circumstances, should philosophy be? It will waste no time on any putative knowledge that is unrelated to human existence in its inward heart. Rather, it must assist the existing subject to enter into its own subjectivity. Any knowledge that cannot be personally appropriated is inessential. Subjectivity "becomes the truth," since "the passion of the infinite is precisely subjectivity."[27] The constant striving that is the lot of the "child born of the infinite and the finite" an allusion to Plato's description of erōs in the *Symposium*) belongs not only to the human subject as such but also to the thinking in which that subject is engaged. As Stephen Crites points out, when Kierkegaard says that truth is subjectivity he is reserving the word *truth* for the self-reflexive relationship; the individual's appropriation of the grounds of his or her ethical and religious existence. It is chiefly a human being, not a proposition, that is true or false.[28]

Here we must remember that Kierkegaard's writing is deliberately couched in a rhetorical mode. True, a philosophy can never rely simply on feeling or imagination; a philosophy that did not care for rationality would be a queer fish indeed: at best poetry, at worst propaganda. But rationality is not such a straightforward notion as it may at first appear. It can include a number of diverse argumentative textures, both "hard" and "soft." Part of intelligence, as Aristotle surmised, is to know just when just which degree of rigor should be applied. The major philosophical tradition of the West, stemming as it does from Kierkegaard's hero Socrates, has always united dialectic and rhetoric. It has realized that to produce personal conviction one must first have understanding, in the sense of imaginative and affective identification. Kierkegaard is perhaps the most extreme representative of this thesis: at times, its walking caricature. He once described himself as "a peculiar kind of poet and thinker who would read the fundamental doctrine of the individual human existence-relationship, the old well-known, handed down from the fathers."[29] Louis Mackey, in taking up the phrase "a kind of poet" into the title of his study of Kierkegaard's thought, insists that there the philosophical (and theological) elements are "sacramentally transmitted in, with, and under the poetry."

> His argument, like the argument of the poet, cannot be taken as the ground of a merely theoretical assent. It must be imaginatively re-lived by the reader and, to have its full effect, must be met with a personal response, an existential "duplication" or an equally existential refusal.[38]

Because Kierkegaard's vision of the human is disturbing, such refusal, including a refusal to be seduced into understanding itself, would not be surprising. If the human being is "a synthesis of the infinite and the finite,"[31] of temporal and eternal, human life will always be an incongruous affair. It is mirrored both in tragedy and comedy. Should we think of our longing for the eternal, our incongruity is tragic; of the perpetual inadequacy of our means of expressing our own inwardness, it is comic. The *aporia* (of existence, not of intellection alone) is resolved, for Kierkegaard, only by moving onto another level, that of faith. For to this same humanity, compounded of finite and infinite, temporal with eternal, there comes the God-man Jesus Christ, the Absolute Paradox who is, in his own person, the union of these antinomies.[32]

In this perspective, the claims of Hegelianism to offer a speculative resolution of the difference between the finite and the infinite were necessarily unconvincing. For whatever Hegel's intentions may have been, the essence of his philosophy lay in an attempt to find a space for the human thinker between orthodox theism and pantheism. Hegelian thought regards all finite things as genuine, but not ultimate, realities. And yet it sees the character of their reality as deriving from their status as necessary moments in the life of the self-expressing, and thus self-constituting, God. To assert in this way that the world exists within the divine life seems to involve God inextricably in its finitude and temporality, introducing them into him.[33] While Hegel rejected an outright pantheism of the kind represented by Spinoza, for whom all beings are modes of a single reality that may be termed indifferently God or nature, his fear of making God a "false infinite,"[34] defined over against the finite beings of the world and thus separated from them, led him into turns and twists of language and thought that invite a quasi-pantheistic interpretation. Wolfhart Pannenberg, despite his spirited defense of Hegel in this and related matters, concedes that he seriously underplayed the elements of risk, decision, and undeterminedness in human life and, especially, in the human being's relation to God: "In Hegel's concept of the freedom both of God and man, the element which fails to achieve adequate expression is its contingency, in the sense of something that happens on the basis of the future alone, and the impossibility of deriving it from anything that already exists, even from what the person who makes the act of will already is in himself."[35] Pannenberg's concern here with the future as the "indispensable horizon for the understanding of present reality" is a peculiar preoccupation of his own, but the gravamen of his criticism is much the same as Kierkegaard's. Though Kierkegaard feared for Hegel's christological faith ("That the human race is or should be akin to God is ancient paganism; but that an individual man is God is Christianity"),[36] the sharpest cuts were reserved for his philosophy's ethical implications. If the individual is simply a manifestation of the universal Spirit, then the nerve of moral effort has effectively been severed. The disciple of Hegel, so Kierkegaard thought, cannot but become one of a crowd, conforming to the world-process, reflecting the spirit of the age. Hegelianism's remedy for the agonies of the finite being—its anxiety, indeed despair, at not being a self—is the prospective consciousness of being spirit in the divine Spirit. But such a solution is dissolution: it swallows up finite being till nothing uniquely individual remains. The patient disappears along with the illness. Though criticism in so radical a form may touch Hegel's disciples and interpreters more woundingly than himself,[37] his system is foreign to the order of true novelty in the mode of individual human existing. While in his *Phenomenology of Spirit* Hegel tries to represent the stages through which consciousness progresses by way of protracted dialogue with itself, his consciousness is as much universal as Kierkegaard's is individual.[38] Yet if the ambitiousness and many of the categories of Hegel's philosophy never ceased to haunt Kierkegaard, he could not forget the lesson that he had learned from Plato's Socrates: to unsettle the unthinking appropriation of social norms, the individual must be raised from out of "immediate existence" by a decisive differentiation of self and society.[39] For the Danish writer, to speak of the human being as spiritual (*geistlig*) can only be to speak of him or her as constituted by a relation to God that is mediated through the sheer contingencies of individual autobiography—which is why his philosophy has been described as an extended *Bildungsroman* in which the individual, as Everyman, comes to himself through a variety of educative experiences.[40] By contrast, the speculative philosopher has "forgotten, in a sort of world-historical absentmindedness, what it means to be a human being."[41]

Kierkegaard spent his life in trying to answer better than Hegel the question of human self-estrangement that Hegel had raised. The facts to which the term *self-estrangement* or *alienation* refers are, objectively, different kinds of rupture or disassociation between the human subject and his or her object, be the latter another human person, or the natural world, or humanity's own creations in art, science, and society. Subjectively, alienation refers to corresponding states of disequilibrium, inner disturbance, and anxiety. Hegel had pointed to what one may call creative alienation: in every act of creation an element of estrangement, positing something other than oneself, must be implied. Karl Marx took Hegel to mean that the essence of creativity lies in the labor of the task, so that the human being in the concrete would be the result of the laboring of the generations at the work of intellectual activity. Turning the Hegelian system on to its head, Marx would replace creative thinking, in this sense, by the labor of material production. Hegel thus found himself translated into the language of political economy. On the basis of these premises Marx set out to interpret the history of his time, and in a broader sense the history of capitalist enterprise, as a history of the self-alienation of humanity that could only be overcome by proletarian revolution. Marx and Kierkegaard lived blissfully unconscious of each other's existence. But contemporary existentialism had recourse to this Dane whose living and dying were so obscure in European terms partly because the solutions of Hegel and Marx to the fact of humanity's self-estrangement only aggravated the disease they were to cure.[42] Hegel's all-embracing World-Mind of a God seemed to absorb the individual personality. Marx's proletarian revolution brought about the dictatorship of the proletariat by proxy of the party, only to succeed in crushing the liberty and integrity of the person in the machinery of a totalitarian state. All three philosophies, Hegel's, Marx's, Kierkegaard's, wish to liberate us from our self-estrangement; but only the last focuses centrally on that alienation itself. The despairing anxiety at not being a self is at root: "a separation phobia, a dread of separation from the foundation of existence, the meaning of life, what is worthy of trust." It escapes the analyses of Hegel or Marx, instructive as these are in certain respects, because it is, in the last resort, not subject to analysis, being a fear of fear: "a heightened and diffused anxiety which spreads, takes on independent existence and robs men and women of their self-confidence and their very identity."[44] Some minutes before his death, Kierkegaard was heard to pray that despair might not attack him at the last but that he might come through to a place where he could sing Alleluia with the angels of God. He was asked by the priest whether this hope rested on the grace of God through Christ. "Yes of course," he replied. "What else?"[45] God is posited in the very act of posing the problem of humanity's self-estrangement; but God's free initiative in our regard belongs not to philosophy but to revelation, which is the divine therapy for the human sickness. Our ascent to God via the materials of human experience at large leaves us inevitably with a question mark that can be removed only by the fresh resources of Scripture and tradition, for they are the rustling of the hem of the Infinite in his personal descent and self-communication to us.

The further reaches of self-making, then, take us ineluctably to that infinite pole of the self which is God. It is for this reason that we expect the saints to be whole and radiant as persons, as selves; and for this reason too we are tempted to ascribe a kind of natural holiness to all those men and women we meet who are able to give of self because they have found self and are at home with self. But to suppose that most human life is lived at a level of existential attainment and actualization of this sort, would be jolly. For most of us, this picture of the self constantly transcending self because inwardly selved by the divine incarnate Selfhood is more a portrait of what we should like to be than of what we are. Which is why it may be useful to turn for our penultimate witness to a philosopher whose master theme is that of hope: not surprisingly, he will be the first of our twentieth-century voices, the century in which the optimistic expectations of the Victorian world took on, through holocaust, that chastened, and more realistic, temper.

10

GABRIEL MARCEL AND THE
DIMENSION OF HOPE

Gabriel Marcel (1889–1973) was one of the seminal minds of Catholicism in the mid-twentieth century. It follows from the nature of Catholic tradition, as an organically developing communion of Christ and his Spirit, that no such mind ever becomes irrelevant, that is, out of relation to other spirits that follow it in history. The difficulty with introducing Marcel's religious philosophy, however, lies not so much in any seeming obsolescence as in the character of that center to which, again and again, Marcel returned. He was a philosopher of mystery.

Notoriously, he disliked philosophical systems, which he regarded as an affront to the Socratic spirit of continuous questioning in the search for truth. As a result, Marcel nowhere offers a systematic exposition of his own philosophy of religion. He preferred to present many of his reflections in the deliberately unsystematic form of a journal, a diary, or an occasional article. At times, his meditations sprang from crucial events of his own lifetime. But undergirding everything he wrote lies a constant concern to highlight the unchanging and ultimate issues of existence. He wanted to restore to words a power of signifying of which, he felt, they had been denuded. In so doing, he would help give back to language its power to reveal *le poids ontologique*, the "ontological weight," of human experience. This weight produces a bias — *pondus meus, amor meus*, inverting Augustine's adage about how love carries one away — and this bias, if we follow where it tends, directs us towards the reality of God. In this essay I shall try to retrace the Marcellian path to transcendence, whose crucial steps are three: the mystery of human personhood, the mystery of intersubjectivity, and the mystery of hope. But let us begin with a few words about the man and his setting.

F. H. Heinemann, the chronicler of twentieth-century existentialisms, has described the conversations in Marcel's home in the 1920s
where and when, in discussion with Nicholas Berdyaev, Louis Lavelle,
and René La Senne, Marcel worked out many of the basic themes of
his writing. It is characteristic of the Christian existentialism of Marcel
that it should derive in this way from dialogue—or, rather, polylogue—
with Orthodox and Catholic thinkers in a setting that can be called,
therefore, corporate and ecclesial. Heinemann summed up the man as
"a complex and polyphonic nature."[1] Dramatist and critic, composer
as well as lover of music, if primarily philosopher, Marcel could scarcely
have been less than many faceted. In his autobiographical essay "Regard
en arrière" he sketched what he himself took to be significant in his
personal background.[2] Born in December 1889 in a privileged section
of French society, his father a diplomat and later administrator in the
arts, Marcel suffered a tense and unhappy childhood. His mother, a
Jew, died when he was four, and his father, an agnostic of Catholic
background, married his deceased wife's sister. A silence fell on his
mother's memory, due to fastidiousness or perhaps despair (he claimed
he did not know which). Against the foil of this experience, the two
other principal features of his boyhood stood out the sharper: the
dominativeness of his aunt-stepmother and the total impersonality of
his schooling. He wrote later: "A mind is metaphysical insofar as its
position within reality appears to it essentially unacceptable. . . . It is
in a false position. The problem is to correct this or to bring about an
easing of the tension. Metaphysics is just this correction or this
relief."[3] Roger Troisfontaines, whose massive study of Marcel's thought
is based, like Heinemann's essay, on personal conversation as well as
published texts, stresses the role of the First World War in bringing
home to Marcel the full force of this bereavement and so providing
him with the departure point of his philosophy.[4] Because of his indifferent health, he was not conscripted when war broke out but spent
the war years in the service of the French Red Cross. His work was to
trace missing soldiers, and it often brought him into contact with
bereaved families and their anguish. The reactions of his clients drew
out of depths of memory his own childhood question: "What becomes
of the dead?"[5] He called these encounters "a first apprenticeship in
inter-subjectivity."[6] Biological extinction was undeniable; yet the sense
of intersubjective communion seemed often to rise above it. Once

again, the "false position," the apparent antinomy that engenders meta-physics, lay round about him.

An outstanding contemporary interpreter of Marcel summed up the departure point of his philosophy in this way:

> For Marcel, philosophising begins in dissatisfaction with the situations in which we find ourselves. He likens the metaphysician to a sick person who is tossing and turning to find a comfortable position. If there is no discomfort, that is, if there are no antinomies in our experience, there is no need and in fact no sense or possible meaning in trying to make the antinomic intelligible by philosophical reflection.[7]

In 1929 the resources of meaning that Marcel could bring to these seeming contradictions in experience were to be enlarged. Under the influence of the novelist François Mauriac, Marcel presented himself for baptism in the Catholic church. His Christian faith appears to have come to him through a sense of the imaginative power of the Gospel to interpret existence. He ascribed the occasion of the dawn-ing of his faith to the cantatas of J. S. Bach. The orientation to Cath-olic, rather than Protestant, Christendom was by no means a foregone conclusion. But in the end he felt he divined in Catholicism a stron-ger echo of his own sense of intersubjectivity, *communio sanctorum*.[8] His faith was to be not so much the object of his philosophical explo-ration as its energy. He was not in any classic sense a Christian apol-ogist, but he discovered in faith *le point de rajeunissement absolu*, "the absolute point at which youth is renewed."[9]

THE MYSTERY OF HUMAN PERSONHOOD

Marcel's most characteristic writing, so far as style reveals the man, is his *Journal métaphysique*, a diary filled with day-to-day reflections on philosophical problems, scattered seeds of thought cracking open in germination, drafts of prospective metaphysical essays. Philosophy was never likely to be brought to a satisfactory conclusion, a line neatly ruled across the page, since its central questions are not so much problems as mysteries. Fragments, not treatises, are therefore the proper literary form of the philosophical enterprise. It is not too much to say that for Marcel the central philosophical questions are mysteries because they are all aspects of the single concrete mystery of humankind itself.[10] To convey his understanding of the human situation, Marcel often invokes the symbol of a traveler or pilgrim. *Homo viator* is en route to a destination that he or she will not reach during his or her temporal existence but towards which the traveler is inexorably drawn. For the moment, however, we should concentrate not on the antinomy traveling/arriving but on the mysteriousness of human personhood that requires that mystery to be thought in terms of a symbol, not a concept.

So little does Western society cherish the human person, according to Marcel, that the very idea of personhood is becoming ever harder to grasp. The mastery over nature that technology has brought tends not to enhance and liberate human beings but to debase them into units or objects. Persons are treated as though their reality could be expressed in terms of the functions they perform: "The present age seems to me to be characterised by the misplacement of the idea of function. . . . The individual tends to appear to himself and to others as a simple bundle of functions . . . an aggregate of functions whose inner order is bafflingly problematic."[11] At the root of the abuse of science Marcel identified what he called the "spirit of abstraction" in philosophy. This spirit is present whenever there is an exclusive emphasis on one particular aspect of reality, coupled with a deliberate policy of refusing even to raise questions about adjacent regions of existence thereby excluded. The inevitable outcome is a distorted and truncated philosophy of the person. To come to terms with personhood, the partiality and myopia of current ideology must be overcome by a process Marcel termed "recollection," *recueillement*. Through this process a person can regain his or her self-possession in the most fundamental sense of the word. But here the questioner, the man or woman who wants to know what personhood is, finds himself or herself inextricably involved in his or her own question.[12] There is no possibility of a detached stance. Instead, we are faced not with a problem but with a mystery. This is the classic instance of a Marcellian mystery, defined as "a problem that encroaches upon the intrinsic conditions of its own possibility (and not upon its data)."[13]

No doubt many people would say that to make the human person into a metaphysical mystery, bathed in some transfiguring light, is evidence of a good heart rather than of a strong mind. Marcel disagrees, and he goes to some lengths to show that the "recuperative" thinking that he recommends is no less solidly based than more analytic or systematic styles of philosophizing. He begins by making a distinction between *primary* and *secondary* reflection. A first level of reflection by which we distance ourselves from lived experience separates us from the objects of our experience—albeit often for desirable, even necessary, purposes. Analysis makes it possible for us to recognize those objects as other than ourselves, and to recognize ourselves as subjects, distinct from the objects of our experience. But the clarity we achieve in this way is bought at a price. It does not really belong to our lived experience: it is a mediation of that experience through deciding to don thinking caps. Within this modification of experience empirical science and common sense are rightly monarchs of all they survey. But we must reserve the right to ask how it was possible for us to make this useful distinction of subject and object in the first place. And in putting this question, a secondary level of reflection opens up. We discover that the distinction and separation of subject and object rest upon a more fundamental belonging together, a *commercium* in lived experience. In this way thought can become recuperative, a therapy helping us to recover from the ruptures in our account of experience that primary reflection generates.[14]

Marcel was perfectly well aware that other philosophical options available in contemporary France resembled his in rejecting an uncommitted, neutral stance towards these questions of personal identity but, unlike his, returned to the most pessimistic of answers. Above all, there was the formidably influential figure of J.-P. Sartre. At the root of Sartre's nihilism lies a vivid experience of existence as contingent, absurd, superfluous, a distorted version of Heideggerian philosophical sensibility. On this nihilism Gerald Hanratty has written:

> Marcel does not doubt that this initial experience is genuine. Rather his objection is that Sartre succumbs completely to it and makes no attempt to question its validity and finality. The initial experience is buttressed by a refusal to be consoled, by a rejection of all possible sources of light and hope.[15]

Marcel responds to the Sartrian challenge by pointing out that such stark despair itself witnesses to an urgent need for deliverance and fulfillment in the depths of the person. The denial of intelligibility, in which the core of nihilism consists, is conditional on an awareness of the possibility of affirmation. To experience the void is only within our powers if at the same time we have a notion of what fulfillment might be. In this way, Marcel coaxes us into adverting to a thirst for meaning within us, termed by him a "demand," "exigence," "appeal," or "need" for being.[16] Seen in this light, the metaphysician has what amounts to a quasi-salvific role via-à-vis humanity. Metaphysics is "the exorcising of despair," a despair characterized as "total submission to [the] void, in such a way as to allow oneself to be dissolved interiorly by it. The closed time of despair is a sort of counter-eternity, an eternity forced back on itself, the eternity of hell."[17]

But what reasons are there to suppose that to our "desire for being," or thirst for meaning, there corresponds some appropriate depth and reliability in reality itself? Marcel refuses to give this question an answer that is independent and free-floating from the person who posed it. He will not claim to show that this depth in being exists "out there" in a way that brackets off the questioner himself or herself (thus confining the mystery to the limits of a problem). But he is not simply saying that psychologically we are so structured that we must act *as if* being had such a character. Deeper than our conscious experience, though pointed to by it, our ontological structure testifies to the fact that this is what the wider reality in which we are placed is genuinely like. First of all, our ability to raise the question of personhood itself indicates our spiritual nature. We are involved in the world of things, but we also transcend that world and are aware of doing so. Secondly and more profoundly, when I put the question, "What am I?" I give voice to an appeal for meaning that stems from the depths of the self: but this appeal does not make sense unless an answer could be simultaneously certain and yet rooted in my own inner being.

> I can only refer myself without contradiction to a judgment which is absolute, but which is at the same time more within me than my own judgment. . . . Perhaps in proportion as I take cognizance of this appeal *qua* appeal, I am led to recognise that the appeal is possible only because, deep down in me, there is something other than me, something further within me than I am myself—and at once the appeal changes its index.[18]

But this highly Augustinian approach to transcendence through personal interiority is hedged about with a number of "perhaps"-es in Marcel's text, and it is not in fact his distinctive account of the relation between personhood and transcendence.

The Mystery of Intersubjectivity

Marcel's principal reason for regarding humankind's thirst for meaning as ontologically informative is more characteristically his own. He points out that our language is full of verbs of promising, engaging, committing, vowing faithfulness, and the like. We have a capacity to bind self with a promise, to commit self so unconditionally that the remit of commitment can extend to the sacrifice of life itself. Marcel takes this as evidence for what he calls the "supratemporal identity of the subject." Our picture of the universe must take into account the fact that it has nurtured a finite being who yet transcends time. The account of interiority just cited from Marcel's *Being and Having* does not do justice to what is most intimately constitutive of our existence as persons. Marcel deliberately displaces the Cartesian *cogito* and replaces it with his own *sumus*: "we are."

> A complete concrete knowledge of oneself cannot be self-centred; however paradoxical it may seem, I should prefer to say that it must be centred on others. We can understand ourselves by starting from the other, or from others, and only by starting from them. . . . Fundamentally I have no reason to set any particular store by myself, except insofar as I know that I am loved by other beings who are loved by me. . . . [19]
> In its own intrinsic structure subjectivity is already, and in the most profound sense, genuinely inter-subjective. [20]

To live a personal existence is to live in communion with others. In his search for transcendence, Marcel relies much more on experiences of interpersonal communion than on analysis of pure interiority. He concentrates on the experiences of faithfulness, love, and — above all — hope as crucial and complementary features of intersubjective relationship. Reflection on these experiences at their highest and most creative testifies that they are grounded in fidelity to, love for, and hope in the eternal and absolute Being without whom they remain destined to ultimate frustration.

The approach to transcendence by way of fidelity proceeds by a meditation on the nature of promising. As Nietzsche had recognized, the human being is the only being in nature who is capable of making a promise. This power to bind self by a promise gives human beings a certain transcendence over the flux of time. But fidelity cannot be defined in terms of the individual. It resists identification with such limited virtues of the agent as resoluteness, constancy, reliance on one's own resources. Fidelity is always a gift of self to another who is at once present to the self and accepted by it as a unique person — in Marcel's favorite word, a *thou*. But in all such faithful relationships there is always a tiny seed of deception and betrayal. No one can be absolutely sure that such a relationship will not perish from within. In addition, there is the external threat of death, the gravest of all threats to communion. Fidelity is vindicated only if it triumphs over these hostile powers. If fidelity is really to be a total, irrevocable commitment of self, then it has to be grounded in a Presence that cannot fail: "It is in this way that fidelity reveals its true nature, which is to be an evidence, a testimony. It is in this way too that a code of ethics centred on fidelity is irresistibly led to become attached to what is more than human, to a desire for the unconditional which is the requirement and the very mark of the Absolute in us."[21] In its highest reaches, then, fidelity is a sharing in the infinite faithfulness of an absolute Presence or Thou. And Marcel hazards that there may be a kind of negative confirmation between loss of belief in God on the one hand and an increasing incidence of lack of fidelity between persons on the other. By contrast, the contours of fidelity are seen at their sharpest in the case of the martyr who witnesses on behalf of others to his total confidence in God.

The theme of fidelity leads on naturally to that of love. For Marcel our earliest tutoring in love takes the form of hospitality. In receiving a guest we ask no precise information about his status, nor do we expect anything in the objective order from his coming. Instead, we convey to him the sense that we welcome him without conditions, freely and entirely: "To receive a guest is, no doubt to enrich him, but it is also to enrich oneself—not on the plane of the immediately useful but on that of the communion of 'I' and 'thou.' Hospitality reaches out to that in man which goes beyond the domain of having, it reaches the realm of being and so it is the beginning of love."[22] As human love grows, its affirmations change their inflection. They become charged with an unconditionality that is the mark of absolute copresence. Love says, under many metaphors and turns of phrase: "Thou, thou at least shalt never die." Thus love leads of its nature to a proclamation of the indestructibility of communion. In this sense, Marcel unforgettably remarks "metaphysics *is* our neighbour." Belief in immortality is, therefore, the most common symptom of the existence of genuine love, for love refuses all objectification of the beloved (including an objectification in terms of "mortal organism") in favor of the act of pure presence.

The dead person can no longer show himself, not because he has fallen back into nothingness but because his mode of presence implies precisely that he cannot descend to the level of the inventory-list [*l'inventoriable*]. The caricature of love sketched in terms of "having" is situated entirely in the register of the "him," but "mystery" plunges us into the world of the "thou."[23]

THE MYSTERY OF HOPE

From here we move effortlessly to Marcel's motif of hope, and so we return to the content, rather than the mode, of the symbol of the wayfarer, *homo viator*. Thinking perhaps of his wartime work among the relatives of captured or fallen French soldiers, he wrote:

> If it is true that man's trial is infinite in its varieties and can assume the innumerable forms under which we can know privation, exile or captivity, it is no less certain that, by a symmetrical but inverted process, each one of us can rise by his own special path from the humblest forms of communion which experience offers the most despised to a communion which is both more intimate and more abundant, of which hope can be regarded equally well as the foreshadowing or the outcome.[24]

To clarify the specific qualities of hoping, Marcel is at pains to distinguish it from desire. Whereas desire is always geared to definable objectives, hope is not concerned with particular states of affairs. Desire is the anticipation that we will acquire a given object, whereas hope does not predict, or even try to imagine, outcomes. Far from basing itself on calculation of what is possible in this or that situation, hope consists in a refusal to be bound by the limits that calculation would set. As such, it is for Marcel our most direct means of apprehending the meaning of the word *transcendent*.

> For hope is a spring; it is the leaping of a gulf. It implies a kind of radical refusal to reckon possibilities, and this is enormously important. It is as though it carried with it, as postulate, the assertion that reality overflows all possible reckonings; as though it claimed in virtue unknown secret affinity, to touch a principle hidden in the heart of things, or rather in the heart of events, which mocks such reckonings.[25]

Hope is a "piercing through of time," a river flowing through and beyond the empirically accessible and having "estuaries" that "do not lie entirely within the bounds of the visible world."[26] To hope, in the pregnant Marcellian sense, is to have an absolute, not a calculating, confidence.

> We can . . . conceive, at least theoretically, of the inner disposition of one
> who, setting no condition or limit or abandoning himself in absolute con-
> fidence, would thus transcend all possible disappointment and would expe-
> rience a security of his being, or in his being, which is contrary to the
> radical insecurity of *having*. This is what determines the ontological posi-
> tion of hope — absolute hope, inseparable from a faith which is likewise
> absolute.[27]

Such absolute hope, though statistically unusual, cannot be deemed humanly abnormal. Human hope has always exerted itself most force-fully in the face of experiences that appear to spell utter defeat. Marcel bids us ask how such hope can arise, and what are the conditions that render intelligible hope's refusal to be overcome by circumstances. He holds that such features of the human landscape only make sense if they are contextualized within a wider whole. What he says in this regard of fidelity is equally pertinent to a discussion of hope: "In order for my limited acts of fidelity to be meaningful they must find their place in an order of reality in which it is already given that fidelity is preferable to infidelity. It is this givenness of fidelity, in which my fidelity partakes, which is the unconditional basis for my finite fideli-ties, and which is ultimately the 'place of being.' "[28] In the language of John Henry Newman in the *Grammar of Assent*, we have here an exer-cise of the illative sense, apprehending through the particularities of experience a transcendent ground of hope and fidelity. Here our onto-logical exigency, or thirst for meaning, comes into contact with its own satisfaction. All attempts to demystify such absolute and uncon-ditional fidelity, with a view to undermining the move to transcen-dence that they trigger off, are reductionist: they reduce to something less than itself the reality of experience. Yet the reality of experience, when critically tested and explored, is also the experience of reality.

The preservation of our humanity has certain transcendental con-ditions. The artist striving to complete a creative act against all odds and in failing health; the person who risks life and limb to defend innocent victims of oppression; the man or woman who sacrifices his or her own interests to come to the aid of afflicted fellows: all of these are practicing a hope-filled courage that is a pointer to an ultimate Providence. Peter Berger, in a Marcellian moment in his *A Rumour of Angels*, echoes through such examples the interconnected themes we have been considering: the mysteries of personhood, intersubjectivity, and hope:

> Man's "no!" to death—be it in the frantic fear of his own annihilation, in moral outrage at the death of a loved one, or in death-defying acts of courage and self-sacrifice—appears to be an intrinsic constituent of his being. There seems to be a death-refusing hope at the very core of our *humanitas*. . . . In a world where man is surrounded by death on all sides, he continues to be a being who says "no!" to death—and through this "no!" is brought to faith in another world, the reality of which would vindicate his hope as something other than illusion.[29]

The theologian who has done most in the century to refresh this theme among confessing Christians, Jürgen Moltmann, tells us in an autobiographical fragment that he himself came to faith precisely through the loss of all meaningful personal communion in the prisoner-of-war camps of postwar Europe. And he writes: "By the foundation of hope I do not mean well-weighed arguments in favour of hope. I mean the living source from which this power springs. The living source of hope lies in a future from which new time, new potentiality and new freedom continually advance to meet us."[30] And Moltmann connects this with the paschal salutation of the church in its Easter liturgy: Christ is risen: he is risen indeed![31]

Within the theme of hope, then, there opens up that of joy. A human world in which the only rational disposition is hope is still, by that very fact, a hopeful world; and the gift of a hopeful world is a source of joy. If there is an implicit affirmation of God in the experience of hope, we may expect to find something similar in that most liberating of all human experiences, the response of joy. In taking G. K. Chesterton as the last of our theistic witnesses, we are isolating a theme that is at once the keynote of the good news that the Word has become flesh ("Rejoice, full of grace!") and a feature of all human living worth the name, all meaningful life, all life with the *Logos*. So long as joy is around, there is no need to fear that the human species will be denatured, or that the language of faith will die on the lips of human beings.

11

G. K. CHESTERTON AND
THE FACT OF JOY

Gilbert Keith Chesterton was born in London on 29 May 1874 and was brought up in the Church of England. After his schoolboy years at London's cathedral school, St. Paul's, he studied at the Slade School of Art. Though he continued to draw and remained enduringly interested in visual art (he would write a book about the Victorian "baroque" painter G. F. Watts), his developing mastery of both image and word made William Blake a more suitable patron. Abandoning art school, Chesterton entered the world of publishing and soon began to write with an astonishing originality of style and approach, utilizing the panoply of modernistic literary techniques for the commending of traditional verities. After his marriage in 1901, he immersed himself at once in the worlds of journalism and politics, violently opposing, as *The Dictionary of Catholic Biography* would put it in a splendid concatenation of objects, "imperialism, the Boer War, Kipling, Shaw and Wells." By 1901 he had completed twenty books, of which *Orthodoxy* was both the best known and the clearest indication of his own movement, partly under the influence of his wife, Frances, to a more full-blooded Christian (and notably Anglo-Catholic) commitment. The great variety of his talent was deployed in biographies, fantasies, works of literary criticism, detective stories, and verse, both epic and comic. In 1922 he entered the Catholic church, and after his conversion he produced a major essay in Christian apologetics, *The Everlasting Man*, as well as delightful evocations of his medieval masters, St. Francis, St. Thomas Aquinas, and Chaucer. Chesterton died at his home in Beaconsfield, now preserved in his honor by the Chesterton Society, on 14 June 1936.

Although the last twenty years have seen a marked recrudescence of interest in Chesterton, stimulated in part by the admiration for his work by the influential English poet W. H. Auden and sustained by the Canadian *Chesterton Review*, it does not often seem to have been noted that Chesterton's writings contain what appears to be a novel argument for the existence of God. This argument may be termed the *argument from joy*. According to Chesterton, joy as a response to being is the principal signal of transcendence that human experience offers, the most persistent and eloquent of what the sociologist of religion, Peter Berger, has called "rumours of angels."[1]

Joy as Experience

In the *Ballad of the White Horse*, Chesterton suggests that the theme of joy, pervasive in his writings, indicates a kind of aperture in experience: via this aperture we are open to the transcendent realm that is God. Chesterton speaks of it as a kind of rupture in the chain of cause and effect that governs the finite universe. The passage in question consists of some lines placed in the mouth of the mother of Jesus and spoken to King Alfred the Great at the darkest point of his struggle with the Danes:

> I tell you naught for your comfort.
> Yea, naught for your desire,
> Save that the sky grows darker yet
> And the sea rises higher.
>
> Night shall be thrice night over you,
> And heaven an iron cope.
> Do you have joy without a cause,
> Yea, faith without a hope.[2]

The phrase "joy without a cause" is the phrase that I should like to explore further in this chapter.

It may be said at once that by calling joy uncaused, Chesterton did not mean that it was a random or chance occurrence, ontologically rootless. On the contrary, precisely because, for him, joy is neither empirically bounded nor ethically relevant, its foundation must be sought at a deeper level, where the finite opens onto the infinite. Were joy a reaction to empirically specific states or situations, it could be regarded as determined by those states and situations. Were it ethical in content, it could be seen as a reflection of a self-constituted human meaning. But since, as Chesterton indicates at numerous points in his oeuvre, it is neither of these things, its raison d'être must be sought at a point which may be called metaphysical: on the finite-infinite frontier. Joy, he argued, lies deeper than happiness or unhappiness, pleasure or pain. All of these are reactions to particular conditions or events within existence, whereas joy is the reaction to the fact that there should be such a thing as existence as such. Intimately related to wonder, *admiratio*, before the fact of being, it is, according to Chesterton, an implicit affirmation of the doctrine of creation, and hence of the truth of theism.

Sheer wondering joy before the face of existence is claimed by Chesterton in the *Autobiography* as a characteristic feature of childhood. The child, he held, sees the world in the light of an "eternal morning" that "had a sort of wonder in it as if the world were as new as" itself.[3] Childhood figures prominently in Chesterton's writings for reasons almost directly opposed to those that operate in the tradition of autobiographical writing at large. Chesterton is virtually uninterested in childhood as the foundation stage of the individual's psychological development. Childhood is not significant for its contribution to the making of an individual self, but for its role in the disclosure of a shared cosmos. In this sense he sees it retrospectively as "real life; the real beginnings of what should have been a more real life; a lost experience in the land of the living."[4] Far from continuously happy himself as a child, he maintained that nevertheless, whatever unhappiness and pain there might have been were "of a different texture or held on a different tenure": "What was wonderful about childhood is that anything in it was a wonder. It was not merely a world full of miracles; it was a miraculous world. What gives me this shock is almost anything I recall; not the things I should think most worth recalling."[5] Yet Chesterton does not regard childhood as a lost fairyland from which adult life is merely an ever-accelerating descent into reality. On the contrary, it is reality itself in its own utterly nonnecessary yet glorious being has the qualities that we normally ascribe to the realm of faëry. For this reason, childhood remains the proper criterion for adult sensibility. The child's response to existence as sheer gift, through wondering joy, is the key to ontology, and, by a supreme irony, far from being a piece of knowledge acquired through the ratiocination of the mature man or woman, it is a gift received with the dawn of consciousness itself. However, the role of philosophizing is to unpack this gift, what elsewhere Chesterton calls the "birthday present" of birth itself, and so uncover its further implications which lead, in fact, to the postulation of a divine Source for the world.

A PHILOSOPHY FOR JOY

At the same time, philosophical reflection is also needed to sustain the gift of joy since, as the young Chesterton discovered, the experience of living in a flawed human environment quickly obscures the sense of joy. Autobiographically, Chesterton identified the causes of this as first, an extreme skepticism, partly brought on by his immersion in the currently fashionable impressionism, a painterly equivalent of epiphenomenalism, and second, a growing sense of the perverse attractiveness of evil, which he associates with his dabblings in spiritualism. He seems to have realized at this point that the gift of joy is only of enduring value if, by means of it, the mind can get a sustained hold on the truth of things, *natura rerum*. The rest of his life, in this perspective, is the attempt to work out a philosophy of joy.

Although, at its most conventionally expressed, Chesterton found this philosophy in the concept of *pulchrum*, the beautiful, as a transcendental in Thomism, this was no more than a confirmatory check from the history of Christian philosophy of something that he had been working out more personally in a wide variety of writings. As Marshall McLuhan pointed out, Chesterton did not seek out ideas in the philosophical tradition. Without the apparatus of formal philosophizing, he "seems never to have reached any position by dialectic or doctrine, but to have enjoyed a kind of connaturality with every kind of reasonableness."[6] This connatural philosophizing, insofar as it touches the subject of joy, can be seen in three of Chesterton's widely separated works. In his study of Dickens, Chesterton introduces the topic of the gratuitously joy-provoking character of existence by describing Dickens as a man who, if he had learnt to whitewash the universe, had done so in a blacking factory:

> Charles Dickens, who was most miserable at the receptive age when most people are most happy, is afterwards happy when all men weep. Circumstances break man's bones; it has never been shown that they break men's optimism. . . . When those who starve or suffer speak for a moment, they do not profess merely an optimism; they are too poor to afford a dear one. They cannot indulge in any detailed or merely logical defence of life; that

would be to delay the enjoyment of it. These higher optimists, of whom Dickens was one, do not approve of the universe, they do not even admire the universe; they fall in love with it. They embrace life too close to criticise or even to see it. Existence to such men has the wild beauty of a woman, and those love her with most intensity who love her with least cause.[7]

Again, in his apologetic masterpiece, *Orthodoxy*, Chesterton speaks of the Christian belief in a God who creates by the communication of his own goodness as the crucial factor in showing the consonance of Christianity with an experientially based ontology: "The mass of men have been forced to be gay about the little things, but sad about the big ones. Nevertheless . . . it is not native to man to be so. Man is more himself, man is more manlike, when joy is the fundamental thing in him and grief the superficial. Melancholy should be an innocent interlude, a tender and fugitive frame of mind; praise should be the permanent pulsation of the soul."[8] And yet, Chesterton continues:

according to the estate of man, as seen by the pagan or the agnostic, this primary need of human nature can never be fulfilled. Joy ought to be expansive; but for the agnostic it must be concentrated, it must cling to one corner of the world. Grief ought to be a concentration; but for the agnostic its desolation is spread through an unthinkable eternity. . . . Christianity satisfies suddenly and perfectly man's ancestral instinct for being the right way up; satisfies it supremely in this: that by its creed joy becomes something gigantic and sadness becomes something special and small.[9]

Finally, in his life of Francis of Assisi, Chesterton refers to joy in the face of existence, ontologically significant joy, as a sign of our relation to the divine creative act. It brings about a kind of contemporaneity with the original creation from nothing: "In a fashion" Francis "endures and answers even the earthquake irony of the Book of Job; in some sense he is there when the foundations of the world are laid, with the morning stars singing together and the sons of God shouting for joy."[10]

Chesterton was well aware that not every reader could immediately echo this allegedly universal element in the tissue of living. From his earliest writings, Chesterton considered human beings to be in need of a kind of therapy of perception. As he put it in *The Defendant*, "his eyes have changed."[11] P. N. Furbank was right in identifying Chesterton's "central belief" in these words: "at the back of our brains . . . there was a forgotten blaze or burst of astonishment at our

own existence. The object of the artistic and spiritual life was to dig
for this submerged sunrise of wonder."[12] What Chesterton admires in
an artist or writer is, often enough, the ability to cleanse the inner eye
from the filming effects of excessive familiarity or of cultural distortion so that our perceptual limits may approximate more fully to those
of integral nature. This is essentially the basis for his veneration of
Blake: admitting that the sentimental classicism of Blake's rival,
Thomas Stothard, was sometimes more finely executed in strict painterly terms than Blake's own work, Chesterton adds that this argument reflects "the duel between the artist who wishes only to be an
artist and the artist who has the higher and harder ambition to be a
man—that is, an archangel."[13] Chesterton belongs, in fact, to the
tradition of philosophy stretching from Plato to Kierkegaard which
regards rhetoric as a necessary concomitant of argument, precisely
because rhetoric can begin to shift certain mental blocks to insight,
blocks that may yield to imagination's power to unsettle and reshape
consciousness while they might well stay where they are if left to pure
ratiocination alone.[14]

If the poet or artist, sage or saint can elicit this primordial response
to being which is joy, then the philosopher can analyze its content.
Insofar as Chesterton came in later life to understand and accept
Thomism, he seems to have been happy with the Thomist account of
beauty as a "transcendental determination of being."[15] Found more
systematically in some later Thomists rather than in Aquinas himself,
this concept proposes that a feature of all existent things is their power
to arouse our sense of beauty. Finite being as such in its manifold
diversity is, in the words of Yves Denis, "apte à satisfaire notre registre
entier de jouissance."[16] We encounter this deliciousness or radiance
in such a variety of beings that the concept that covers it, *pulchrum*,
the beautiful, may be termed "transcendental," that is, belonging to
participation in being at large rather than to a limited set of kinds of
being. But because all finite being is received or participated being,
because it is not self-explanatory or self-sufficient, the concept of the
pulchrum becomes one of the ways whereby we may speak of the infinite Source from which the finite realm of being comes forth.[17] More
characteristically Chestertonian, however, is the suggestion that joy
may be explained by reference to its conceptual correlative of gift.
The conceptual link is formed by the notion of surprise. Joy is not
delight in a settled possession (as in "The Marquis of Lothian enjoys
possession of twenty thousand acres"), but delight in what was in

itself wholly unexpected, namely, that there should be something at all rather than simply nothing. It is, therefore, intimately associated with the concept of gift, as a passage in Chesterton's novel, *The Poet and the Lunatics*, well illustrates:

> Man is a creature; all his happiness consists in being a creature; or, as the Great Voice commanded us, in being a child. All his fun is in having a gift or present; which the child, with profound understanding, values because it is a "surprise." But surprise implies that a thing came from outside ourselves; and gratitude that it comes from someone other than ourselves. It is thrust through the letter-box; it is thrown in at the window; it is thrown over the wall. Those limits are the lines of the very plan of human pleasure.[18]

It is in this way that Chesterton's *argumentum e gaudio* proceeds from a certain recurrent feature of human experience, rendered intelligible by reflection about the existence of God. No doubt such an argument needs contextualization in a setting where other types of theistically suggestive experience are also included and appraised. Nevertheless, it seems as worthy of attention by philosophers as, for instance, the argument from desire, *erōs*, found in Gregory of Nyssa, or the argument from hope in Gabriel Marcel, or even the argument *e contingentia mundi* in Aquinas to which, indeed, it might be usefully related.

If an argument for God's existence can be based on the phenomenon of joy then we are in the presence of one of Chesterton's celebrated paradoxes. Because it would certainly be paradoxical if a problem that has aroused the conceptual and argumentative intricacies of, say, the argument from a First Mover, or the argument from design, were in some sense soluble by reference to what is, on Chesterton's own showing, an essentially infantile emotion. Tiresome as Chesterton's exploitation of paradox can sometimes be, it was for him justifiable by considerations based on ontology rather than on style. In *Orthodoxy*, Chesterton declared a hatred for pure paradox, and a love for truth which has, he argued, an objectively extravagant aspect.[19] As Denis has written, "Pour lui, le paradoxe n'est pas un masque, main un révélateur."[20] That the point of insertion of God into the human continuum should be something as simple as joy is a serious suggestion, though made in a playful way. Here as elsewhere, Chesterton's imagination is formidably intellectual. The paradox is not a game, but the sense of play is a pleasure arising simultaneously with the paradox from the perceived truth: "The humour is inseparable from the argument. It is . . . the 'bloom' on dialectic itself."[21]

In this connection, it is worth returning by way of conclusion to Berger's *A Rumour of Angels*, an essay that Chesterton would undoubtedly have found highly sympathetic. Berger points out that ludic, or playful, elements can be found in virtually every sector of human culture. This is so to such a degree that it can be argued that culture as such would be impossible without play. And here reference is made to the Dutch historian, Jan Huizinga's *Homo Ludens* where these ludic elements can be connected to the theme of joy.[22] Berger writes:

> Joy is play's intention. When this intention is actually realised, in joyful play, the time structure of the playful universe takes on a very specific quality — namely, it becomes eternity. . . . Even as one remains conscious of the poignant reality of that other "serious" time in which one is moving towards death, one apprehends joy as being, in some barely conceivable way, a joy forever. Joyful play appears to suspend, or bracket, the reality of our "living towards death" (as Heidegger aptly described our serious condition).[23]

And, from an astonishing concentration of the insights of Chesterton's writings, Berger infers that it is the human being's ludic constitution that enables us to regain and realize the deathless joy of our childhood. Thus play becomes the anthropological key to joy; and joy, the ontological key to truth. Can one echo the words of a French Chestertonian scholar and agree that "he has found the gateway to the land of marvels"?[24]

ENVOI

A book with the aim, and offering the materials, of this one can have no conclusion. At best, it can have an envoi that sends the reader back over the preceding chapters and forward to the making of his or her own response to their various claims. The author cannot substitute for the actual exercise of the illative sense by the reader. It is you who must assess the significance of the pieces that now one, now another, thinker has exhibited for your attention. Are these the fragments of a mosaic, the bits of a jigsaw? Are they to be (re)assembled in theistic assent? Will the mind, by taking such a step, become a wise mind—not only loving wisdom (philo-sophical) but actually reflecting that divine Wisdom which, in the natural theology of the Scriptures, is portrayed as the final source of illumination? The psyche in open-ended desiring; the spirit in its transparence to truth; the *zōon logikon* or "speech-using animal" who finds the language of perfection on his or her lips; the sense of the fragility of beings; the witness of mystical encounter; the inner contradictions of the human being that call for a resolution from beyond themselves; the imperiousness of conscience; the existential demands of becoming a self; the phenomenon of hope; the surprise of joy: Are these merely facts about the human condition, or are they significant facts, facts which, when interpreted in terms of each other, become signs of, pointers to, the reality of God? Dear reader, only you can judge.

NOTES

PREFACE

1. A. Nichols, O.P., *The Art of God Incarnate: Theology and Image in Christian Tradition* (London, 1980).

2. Ortega y Gasset, *Ideas y creancias* (Madrid, 1940); cited and translated in F. C. Copleston, S.J., *Religion and Philosophy* (Dublin, 1974), p. 19.

3. A. Nichols, O.P., *The Shape of Catholic Theology: An Introduction to Its Sources, Principles, and History* (Collegeville, Minn., 1991).

4. See R. G. Collingwood, *The Idea of History* (London, 1946).

5. A. Nichols, O.P., *Yves Congar* (London, 1989).

6. A. Nichols, O.P., *The Theology of Joseph Ratzinger: An Introductory Study* (Edinburgh, 1988).

7. Y. Congar, O.P., *Je crois en l'Esprit-Saint* (Paris, 1979), vol. 1, p. 7.

8. Nichols, *Yves Congar*.

9. N. D. O'Donoghue, O.C.D., *Heaven in Ordinarie* (Edinburgh, 1980), p. 112.

10. F. von Hügel, *The Mystical Element in Religion as Studied in Saint Catherine of Genoa and Her Friends*, 2d ed. (London, 1923), vol. 1, p. xxvii.

INTRODUCTION

1. J. H. Newman, *An Essay in Aid of a Grammar of Assent* (London, 1870); 2d ed. (London, 1895); critical ed., edited by Ian T. Ker (Oxford, 1985). Page references are to the 2d ed. (1895).

2. D. Nicholl, *Recent Thought in Focus* (London, 1952), pp. 66–67.

3. K. Ward, *The Concept of God* (Oxford, 1974); 2d ed. (London, 1977), p. 54.

4. Ibid. Cf. H. Küng, *Does God Exist?* English trans. (London, 1980), pp. 124–125.

5. On Dilthey's concept of experience, see H.-G. Gadamer, *Truth and Method*, English trans. (London, 1975), pp. 56–61; W. Pannenberg, *Basic Question in Theology*, vol. 1, English trans. (London, 1970), p. 107.

6. L. Wittgenstein, *Philosophical Investigations* (Oxford, 1953); one may note the citation from Augustine at the head of this work.

175

7. T. S. Eliot, "The Dry Salvages," in *Four Quartets* (London, 1944); 2d ed. (London, 1959), p. 39.

8. W. Pannenberg, *Basic Questions in Theology*, vol. 2, English trans. (London, 1971), pp. 222–223.

9. Newman, *Grammar of Assent*, p. 353.

10. Ibid., p. 359.

11. Ibid., p. 321.

12. Ibid., p. 390.

13. Ibid., p. 464.

14. Ward, *Concept of God*, pp. 48–49.

15. Newman, *Grammar of Assent*, p. 411.

16. J. J. Shepherd, *Experience, Inference, and God* (London, 1975), p. 163. Cf. p. 32, where Shepherd affirms that emphasis must be placed both on experience and argument and writes that (in the specific context of cosmology, but the implications are broader than this): "if emphasis is laid on the apprehension of an effect *implying* a cause, or a transcendent cause . . . , then there exists the possibility of rationally assessing the nature and strength of the implication and of developing it in the form of an argument without begging the question." For a lucid analysis of the sense in which experience may, in these matters, furnish argument, see C. Franks Davies, *Evidential Force of Religious Experience* (Oxford, 1989).

17. J. Coulson, "Philosopher's English: A Protest," *Downside Review* 74.237 (Summer, 1956), p. 213. The reference to Plato is to *Republic* 539.

18. G. Daly, O.S.A., *Transcendence and Immanence: A Study in Catholic Modernism and Integralism* (Oxford, 1980), p. 216. A sustained case for a view of theistically relevant experience as something wider than "religious experience" *tout court* is offered in N. Lash, *Easter in Ordinary: Reflections on Human Experience and the Knowledge of God* (London, 1988; Notre Dame, Ind., 1990).

19. R. Jolivet, *The God of Reason*, English trans. (London, 1958), pp. 116–117.

20. Ibid., p. 113.

21. H. Denzinger and A. Schönmetzer, eds., *Enchiridion Symbolorum Definitionum et Declarationem de Rebus Fidei et Morum* (Freiburg, 1965), n. 3004. An English translation may be found in K. Rahner, ed., *The Teaching of the Catholic Church*, English trans. (Cork, 1966), pp. 31–32.

22. M. Blondel in *Bulletin de la Société française de philosophie* for 1928, p. 55, as cited in Jolivet, *God of Reason*, p. 9. The article was written in response to a lecture by E. Bréhier that sparked a three-year debate in France. This debate, which led, inter alia, to the writing of E. Gilson's Gifford Lectures, *The Spirit of Mediaeval Philosophy* (New York, 1940), is described in A. Renard, *La Querelle sur la possibilité de la philosophie chrétienne*

(Paris, 1941), itself usefully summarized in M. Nédoncelle, *Is There a Christian Philosophy?* English trans. (New York, 1960).

23. For a statement of the case that revelation actually postulates philosophy as grace does nature, see A. Léonard, *Pensées des hommes et foi en Jésus Christ* (Paris, 1980), pp. 23–31. Philosophy is here taken to be the autonomous self-reflection of the human subject as one capable of welcoming revelation.

24. J. Pelikan, *Historical Theology: Continuity and Change in Christian Doctrine* (London, 1971), p. 157.

25. K. Barth, *Protestant Theology in the Nineteenth Century: Its Background and History*, English trans. (London, 1972), p. 17.

26. P. Berger, *A Rumour of Angels: Modern Society and the Rediscovery of the Supernatural* (Harmondsworth, 1970), p. 94.

27. Ibid., p. 65.

28. F. C. Copleston, S.J., *Religion and Philosophy* (Dublin, 1974), p. 42.

29. Cf. I. Trethowan, O.S.B., *The Basis of Belief* (London, 1961), p. 112; and the same author, more fully, *Absolute Value* (London, 1970), pp. 124–128.

30. E. L. Mascall, *The Openness of Being: Natural Theology Today* (London, 1971), p. 36.

31. Ward, *Concept of God*, p. 81.

32. Cf. H. Küng, *On Being a Christian*, English trans. (London, 1977), for a cognate account of how reason should be used in affirming the existence of God: "a meditative reflection, accompanying, opening up, elucidating the concrete experience of reality" (p. 69). One might compare also A. N. Whitehead's suggestion that the philosopher should begin with an "imaginative generalisation" insinuated by one area of experience and seek to apply it in all areas in order to test its adequacy as an interpretation of reality as a whole (*Process and Reality* [Cambridge, 1929], pp. 5–8). On the whole issue, see further R. La Senne, *Obstacle et valeur* (Paris, 1934), chapter 1, "Expérience et philosophie."

1. JOHN HENRY NEWMAN AND THE ILLATIVE SENSE

1. E. Gilson, *The Spirit of Mediaeval Philosophy* (New York, 1940), p. 12.

2. There are of course exceptions: see especially A. J. Boekraad, *The Personal Conquest of Truth According to J. H. Newman* (Louvain, 1955); and, by the same author, *The Argument from Conscience to the Existence of God According to J. H. Newman* (Louvain, 1961); also D. Pailin, *The Way to Faith: An Examination of Newman's "Grammar of Assent" as a Response to the Search for Certainty in Faith* (London, 1969).

3. J. H. Newman, *An Essay on the Development of Christian Doctrine* (London, 1845); 2d ed. (London, 1878); reprint of 1888 imprint of 2d ed. (Notre Dame, Ind.), p. 445.

4. C. S. Dessain, *John Henry Newman* (London, 1966), p. xii.

5. A writer with a strong conviction of the integrity and distinctiveness of divine revelation may have the more courage to treat philosophy generously in a religious context: see B. Gunderson, *Cardinal Newman and Apologetics* (Oslo, 1952), p. 38.

6. J. H. Newman, *Fifteen Sermons Preached before the University of Oxford* (London, 1871); 2d ed. (London, 1909); Facsimile ed. (London, 1970); cited hereafter as *University Sermons*. A series of extracts, arranged under thematic heads, may be found in O. Chadwick, *The Mind of the Oxford Movement* (London, 1960), pp. 71–102.

7. Newman, *University Sermons*, p. 183.

8. Ibid., p. 187.

9. Ibid., p. 193.

10. Ibid., p. 257.

11. Ibid., pp. 257–258.

12. Ibid., p. 200.

13. Ibid., p. 187.

14. For the biographical background to the *Essay in Aid of a Grammar of Assent*, see M. Trevor, *Newman: Light in Winter* (London, 1962), p. 457. And see now the critical edition by I. T. Ker (Oxford, 1985). It was after the collapse of the scheme for an Oxford Oratory in 1867 that Newman turned once more to writing. He was nearing seventy and without any idea that twenty years of life still remained to him.

15. The lifelong concern with apologetics that this implies may be related not only to the contemporary situation of the Anglican and Catholic churches, but also to the chief sources of Newman's theology: the Alexandrian church fathers and the Anglican divines of the seventeenth and eighteenth centuries, as a glance at the writings of the representative figures of Clement of Alexandria and Joseph Butler will show.

16. J. H. Newman, *Autobiographical Writings*, edited by H. Tristram (London, 1956), pp. 272–273.

17. A. Huxley, *Proper Studies*, 3d ed. (London, 1939), p. xix.

18. Cited in Dessain, *John Henry Newman*, p. 148.

19. J. H. Newman, *An Essay in Aid of a Grammar of Assent* (London, 1870); 2d ed. (London, 1895), pp. 31–32.

20. Ibid., p. 34.

21. Ibid., p. 83.

22. See S. Prickett, *Romanticism and Religion: The Tradition of Coleridge and Wordsworth in the Victorian Church* (Cambridge, 1976), pp. 199–200.

23. S. T. Coleridge, *The Statesman's Manual*, in *Lay Sermons*, edited by R. J. White (London, 1972), p. 30. Prickett's *Romanticism and Religion* contains a full discussion of Newman's increasing correspondence to Coleridge. On the general issue of Newman and imagination, a diffuse, but suggestive, account

is available in J. Coulson, *Religion and Imagination "in Aid of a Grammar of Assent"* (Oxford, 1981).

24. Newman, *Grammar of Assent*, p. 89.

25. Ibid., p. 119.

26. Ibid., p. 121.

27. Ibid., p. 120.

28. Ibid., p. 489.

29. Ibid., p. 121. Here Newman is engaged in a gesture of *faire ses adieux* to the Pietists and Evangelicals of his early years as well as to the Liberals and Broad Churchmen he had known at Oxford. Both of these houses set little store by dogmatic formularies. Nevertheless, it is important to realize that Newman remained a child of the Oxford movement in always seeing dogma "in relation to worship, to the numinous, to the movement of the heart, to the conscience and the moral need, to the immediate experience of the hidden hand of God—so that without this attention to worship of the moral need, dogma could not be apprehended rightly" (Chadwick, *Mind of the Oxford Movement*, pp. 11–12). In this way Newman carried much of an earlier Anglican inheritance with him, especially Evangelicalism.

30. Newman, *Grammar of Assent*, p. 81.

31. G. H. Harper, *Cardinal Newman and William Froude: A Correspondence* (Baltimore, 1933).

32. Newman, *Grammar of Assent*, p. 159.

33. Ibid., p. 160.

34. Ibid., p. 176.

35. Newman, *University Sermons*, pp. 222–250.

36. W. G. Ward, *The Philosophy of Theism* (London, 1884), vol. 2, p. 215.

37. Newman, *Grammar of Assent*, p. 177.

38. Ibid., p. 288.

39. Ibid.

40. Ibid., p. 301.

41. Ibid., p. 321.

42. John Henry Newman, *Letters and Diaries*, C. S. Dessain et al., eds., vol. 24 (Oxford, 1973), p. 375. See also C. S. Dessain, "Cardinal Newman on the Theory and Practice of Knowledge: The Purpose of the *Grammar of Assent*," *Downside Review* (January 1957), pp. 1–23.

43. Cited in Dessain, *John Henry Newman*, p. 157.

44. W. Ward, *The Life of John Henry Cardinal Newman, Based on His Private Journals and Correspondence* (London, 1912), vol. 2, p. 43. For the complete passage that Ward summarizes, see Newman, *Letters and Diaries*, vol. 21 (London, 1971), p. 146.

45. J. H. Newman, *Loss and Gain: The Story of a Convert* (London, 1848); 11th ed. (London, 1893), p. 379.

46. Ibid., p. 383.

47. Ibid., pp. 384–385.

48. C. F. Harrold, *John Henry Newman: An Expository and Critical Study of His Mind, Thought, and Art* (New York, 1945), p. 157.

49. Chadwick, *Mind of the Oxford Movement*, p. 18.

50. G. Herbert, "Teach Me, My God and King," *The Temple*.

51. J. H. Walgrave, *Newman the Theologian*, English trans. (London, 1960), p. 18. In the light of the "discovery" of the common Coleridgean tradition behind Newman in recent years, it would also be possible to explain this phenomenon in terms of Coleridgean epistemology. For Coleridge, right response to reality is an organically unified sensibility comprising aesthetic (immediacy) and ontological (depth) elements: see Prickett, *Romanticism and Religion*, especially pp. 174–210. On the place of Newman in the development of specifically English theology, see V. F. Storr, *The Development of English Theology in the Nineteenth Century, 1800–1860* (London, 1913); and B. M. G. Reardon, *From Coleridge to Gore* (London, 1971).

52. Newman, *Grammar of Assent*, p. 346.

53. Ibid., p. 488.

54. Ibid., pp. 397–398.

55. A. Flew, *God and Philosophy* (London, 1966), p. 63.

56. R. Swinburne, *The Existence of God* (Oxford, 1979), pp. 13–14.

57. F. D. Maurice, "Review of Dr. Newman's *Grammar of Assent*," *The Contemporary Review* 14 (1870). The closest that a near-contemporary writer came to identifying the source of this unsatisfactoriness is W. Ward, "Newman's Philosophy," *Last Lectures* (London, 1918), pp. 72–101. Here Ward points out that the corporate, communitarian account of the acquisition of truth in the *Essay on the Development of Christian Doctrine* is needed to correct the individualism of the *Grammar of Assent*.

58. See, e.g., H. P. Owen, *The Moral Argument for the Existence of God* (London, 1967).

59. J. J. Shepherd, *Experience, Inference, and God* (London, 1979), p. 163.

2. GREGORY OF NYSSA AND THE MOVEMENT OF ERŌS

1. W. Jaeger, *Early Christianity and Greek Paideia* (Cambridge, Mass., 1961), pp. 92–93.

2. Ibid., p. 86.

3. See L. W. Bernard, *Justin Martyr, His Life and Thought* (Cambridge, 1967).

4. R. A. Markus, *Christianity in the Roman World* (London, 1974), pp. 42–43.

5. Ibid., pp. 128–129.

6. Thomas Aquinas, *Summa theologiae*, IIa–IIae. 184, 7 ad 3.

7. H. von Campenhausen, *The Fathers of the Greek Church*, English translation (London, 1963), p. 115.

8. V. M. Callahan, *The Ascetical Treatises of Gregory of Nyssa* (Washington, 1967), p. xiii.

9. On the patristic use of the Platonist tradition, see E. von Ivanka, *Plato Christianus: Übernahme und Umgestaltung des Platonismus durch die Väter* (Einsiedeln, 1964); on Gregory, see especially pp. 151–188, where the related themes of creation and grace are seen as the transformative element in Gregory's use of Plato.

10. A. J. Festugière, O.P., *Antioche païenne et chrétienne* (Paris, 1959).

11. Gregory of Nyssa, *The Life of Moses*, translated by A. J. Malherbe and E. Ferguson (New York, 1978), p. 4. Other estimates of Gregory's debt to philosophical culture may be found in H. F. Cherniss, *The Platonism of Gregory of Nyssa* (Berkeley, Cal., 1930); H. Merki, *Homoiōsis Theō: Von der platonischen Angleichung an Gott zur Gottähnlichkeit bei Gregor von Nyssa* (Fribourg, 1952); and H. Dörrie, "Gregors Theologie auf dem Hintergrunde der neuplatonischen Metaphysik," in H. Dörrie et al., eds., *Gregor von Nyssa und die Philosophie* (Leiden, 1976), pp. 21–39.

12. H. von Campenhausen, *Fathers of the Greek Church*, p. 117.

13. Gregory of Nyssa, *De virginitate* 3.

14. *Grégoire de Nysse: La Vie de sainte Macrine*, edited by P. Maraval (Paris, 1971), p. 23.

15. W. Jaeger, *Two Rediscovered Works of Ancient Christian Literature: Gregory of Nyssa and Macarius* (Leiden, 1954), p. 18.

16. *Grégoire de Nysse: La Vie de sainte Macrine*, p. 95.

17. Cf. S. T. Coleridge's definition: "Love is a desire of the whole being to be united to something or some being felt necessary to its completeness by the most perfect means that nature permits and reason dictates" (cited in M. D'Arcy, S.J., *The Mind and Heart of Love* [London, 1945], p. 54).

18. I. P. Sheldon-Williams, "The Greek Christian Platonist Tradition from the Cappadocians to Maximus and Eriugena," in A. H. Armstrong, ed., *The Cambridge History of Later Greek and Early Mediaeval Philosophy* (Cambridge, 1967), pp. 425–426.

19. Basil, *Ad adolescentes*, PG 31, 563–590.

20. Gregory Nazianzen, *Orationes* IV, 100; XI, 1; XIII, 11.

21. Gregory of Nyssa, *De vita Moysis*, PG 44, 360B.

22. For the concept of the "links" (*syndesmoi*) in the chain of being, see W. Jaeger, *Nemesios von Emesa* (Berlin, 1914), II. 2.

23. Gregory of Nyssa, *Oratio catechetica magna* VI, PG 45, 25C–28A.

24. Gregory of Nyssa, *De opificio hominis* VIII, PG 44, 144B–150A.

25. Gregory of Nyssa, *Dialogus de anima et resurrectione*, PG 46, 28B; *De opificio hominis*, passim. See here E. Corsini, "L'Harmonie du monde et l'homme

microcosme," in C. Kannengiesser, ed., *Epektasis: Mélanges patristiques offerts au cardinal Jean Daniélou* (Paris, 1972), pp. 455–462.

26. See D. S. Wallace-Hadrill, *The Greek Patristic View of Nature* (Manchester, 1968), p. 19.

27. Gregory of Nyssa, *De opificio hominis* I, PG 44, 128A–132C.

28. On Gregory's account of the creation and fall of humankind, see J. Daniélou, S. J., *From Glory to Glory: Texts from Gregory of Nyssa's Mystical Writings*, English translation (London, 1962), pp. 10–16.

29. Gregory of Nyssa, *De opificio hominis* XVI, PG 44, 184C.

30. Ibid. XXI–XXVII, where Gregory, without any sense of rupture, goes on to deal with the resurrection.

31. Sheldon-Williams, "Greek Christian Platonist Tradition," pp. 451–452. However, while this exceptionally clear threefold scheme is found (following Origen) at *In Canticum Canticorum homilia* 1, PG 44, 768A, a more complex progression is suggested in the homilies *In inscriptione psalmorum*, PG 44, 468A. The late Cardinal Daniélou pointed out Gregory's (not necessarily deplorable) lack of rigor in schematizing experience (*Platonisme et théologie mystique: Doctrine spirituelle de saint Grégoire de Nysse* [Paris, 1944]; 2d ed. [Paris, 1953], p. 22).

32. *Grégoire de Nysse: La Vie de sainte Macrine*, p. 95.

33. Gregory of Nyssa, *In Canticum Canticorum homilia* 1, PG 44, 768C.

34. Gregory of Nyssa, *De virginitate* XI, PG 46, 365B.

35. Plato, Symposium 211. On the background here, see A. J. Festugière, O.P., *Contemplation et vie contemplative selon Platon* (Paris, 1936); 2d ed. (Paris, 1950). See also J. Rist, *Eros and Psyche: Studies in Plato, Plotinus, and Origen* (Toronto, 1964).

36. Gregory of Nyssa, *De virginitate* XI, PG 46, 364B–C.

37. Ibid. VI.

38. Ibid. XI.

39. Gregory of Nyssa, *In Canticum Canticorum homilia* VI, PG 44, 893A–B.

40. Gregory of Nyssa, *De vita Moysis*, PG 44, 377A.

41. Gregory of Nyssa, *Dialogus de anima et resurrectione*, PG 46, 97A. See also J. Maréchal, S. J., *Essai sur la psychologie des mystiques* (Brussels and Paris, 1937–1938), vol. 2, pp. 105–111.

42. Gregory of Nyssa, *In Canticum Canticorum*, PG 44, 1037C.

43. Daniélou, *From Glory to Glory*, p. 26.

44. In the ascetical works, Gregory frequently alludes to this "co-fighting," *summachia*.

45. Gregory of Nyssa, *Oratio catechetica magna* 30, PG 45, 77A.

46. Gregory of Nyssa, *De virginitate*, PG 46, 364B–C.

47. *Grégoire de Nysse: La Vie de sainte Macrine*, pp. 22, 37.

48. Ibid., p. 97. Cf. *De institutione christiana* 40, 7, where the soul's *erōs* for the good is said to be *sunousiomenos*, part of the essence of human nature.

49. The attempt of this chapter to disengage Gregory's natural theology from his entire Christian vision of things suggests that he might well have accepted, had he been shown it, T. F. Torrance's view of their interrelation. Torrance sets aside an *independent* natural theology, arguing that it is unscientific not to allow every preconceived framework to be "called in question by what is actually disclosed in the process of inquiry" (i.e., Christian revelation); nevertheless, natural theology can be transposed into "the material content of theology where in a changed form it constitutes the epistemological structure of our knowledge of God" (*Space, Time, and Resurrection* [Edinburgh, 1976], p. x).

50. R. Williams, *The Wound of Knowledge: Christian Spirituality from the New Testament to St. John of the Cross* (London, 1979), p. 55.

51. The Swedish theologican Anders Nygren, in his study *Agape and Eros* (English translation, London, 1939) denied that this view of humankind as naturally "erotic" for God could find a rightful place in Christianity; for him, the latter was concerned solely with the divine agape or self-giving. But as Martin D'Arcy wrote, if God is agape, then "we should naturally expect someone to be the beneficiary of that love, and as beneficiary to respond. But if this theory is taken literally, there is no one to respond. . . . In the elimination of eros, man is eliminated" (D'Arcy, *Mind and Heart of Love*, p. 71).

52. On *epektasis*, see Daniélou, *Platonisme et théologie mystique*, pp. 291–307.

53. Gregory of Nyssa, *De perfectione et qualem oporteat esse christianum*, PG 46, 285B–C.

54. Ibid.

55. E. Mühlenberg, *Die Unendlichkeit Gottes bei Gregor von Nyssa* (Göttingen, 1966), p. 204.

56. Gregory of Nyssa, *De opificio hominis* XXI, PG 44, 201B.

57. Mühlenberg, *Unendlichkeit Gottes*, pp. 100–147.

58. Ibid., p. 204.

59. F. C. Copleston, S.J., *Religion and Philosophy* (Dublin, 1974), p. 12.

60. Ibid., pp. 12–13.

61. Ibid., p. 141.

62. C. S. Lewis, *Surprised by Joy* (London, 1935; 1959), p. 20.

63. Ibid.

64. Lewis was also influenced by conversation with Owen Barfield, the Coleridgean anthroposophical writer and an Oxford contemporary. See H. Carpenter, *The Inklings: C. S. Lewis, J. R. R. Tolkien, Charles Williams, and Their Friends* (London, 1978); 2d ed. (London, 1981), p. 37.

65. Lewis, *Surprised by Joy*, p. 174.

66. Ibid.

3. Augustine of Hippo and the Life of Spirit

1. For Augustine's life, see G. Bonner, *St. Augustine: Life and Controversies* (London, 1963); P. Brown, *Augustine of Hippo: A Biography* (London, 1967).

2. Given lapidary expression in the *Confessions*, whose structure is best seen as a *peregrinatio animae*, "pilgrimage of the soul." The soul has wandered away from God, but God himself, by his interior attracting of the soul and by the manifold concrete events that his providence puts before it, gradually brings it back to him. This return of the soul to God is expressed in its anticipation of the eternal Sabbath, with which book 13 closes. This interpretation has the advantage of doing justice to both the biblical and the Platonist elements in Augustine's thought; others are possible and perhaps were meant to be. See on this R. J. O'Connell, *St. Augustine's Confessions: The Odyssey of the Soul* (Cambridge, Mass., 1969).

3. F. Cayré, A.A., *Dieu présent dans la vie de l'esprit* (Bruges, 1951), p. 12.

4. On the world of Augustine's childhood, see Brown, *Augustine*, pp. 19–39; and for an evocation of the African background, see W. H. C. Frend, *The Donatist Church: A Movement of Protest in Roman North Africa* (London, 1952), pp. 25–75.

5. Augustine, *Confessiones* V. 8, 15.

6. Ibid. III. 12, 21.

7. Brown, *Augustine*, p. 32.

8. Ibid., p. 35.

9. Augustine, *Confessiones* I. 16, 26.

10. Augustine tells us in the *Confessions* that from the time of reading *Hortensius* he had been filled with a *magnum incendium*, a "burning desire" to devote himself to the search for wisdom. In ancient philosophy this search might be identified at once with a quest for transcendence, for it was axiomatic that only an object capable of filling the human mind with "bliss" (*beatitudo*), and so fulfilling it, was worthy of the name of "wisdom" (*sapientia*). See R. Holte, *Béatitude et sagesse: S. Augustin et le fin de l'homme dans la philosophie ancienne* (Paris, 1962). Compare Augustine, *De beata vita* IV. 34.

11. Bonner, *St. Augustine*, pp. 157–192; for a more general account, see H. C. Puech, *La manichéisme: Son fondateur, sa doctrine* (Paris, 1949).

12. The post included responsibility for writing official imperial speeches (see Brown, *Augustine*, p. 69).

13. F. Holmes-Dudden, *The Life and Times of St. Ambrose* (London, 1935).

14. "He had made up his mind, even before he accepted Christ, to live a life of philosophy in community. . . . The pattern of Augustine's later life was set even before he was converted; there was afterwards no sudden, unexpected or incomprehensible change" (J. J. O'Meara, *The Young Augustine:*

The Growth of St. Augustine's Mind up to His Conversion [London, 1954; 1980], p. 160).

15. On Plotinus, see A. H. Armstrong, *Cambridge History of Later Greek and Early Mediaeval Philosophy* (Cambridge, 1967), pp. 195–268; see also A. H. Armstrong, "Salvation, Plotinian and Christian," *Downside Review* 1957, pp. 126–139. Augustine may also have known certain passages of the slightly later Neoplatonist, Porphyry, who was Plotinus's biographer (see W. Theiler, *Porphyrios und Augustin* [Halle, 1933], discussed in E. TeSelle, *Augustine the Theologian* [London, 1970], pp. 49–55). On Porphyry and on Neoplatonism in general, see R. T. Wallis, *Neo-platonism* (London, 1972). On the general issue of Augustine's Platonism, see J. J. O'Meara, "Augustine and Neo-Platonism," *Revue des étude Augustiniennes* 1 (1958), pp. 91–111; J. J. O'Meara, "The Neoplatonism of St. Augustine," in D. O'Meara, ed., *Neoplatonism and Christian Thought* (Norfolk, Va., 1982), pp. 34–41; A. H. Armstrong, *St. Augustine and Christian Platonism* (Villanova, Pa., 1967).

16. Augustine, *Confessiones* VII. 20.

17. E.g., Augustine, *Sermones*, serm. 141, 2.

18. Augustine, *Tractatus in Evangelium Johannis* 106, 4.

19. Augustine, *Confessiones* V. 6, 9–10.

20. On his influence on the tradition, see H. I. Marrou, *St. Augustine and His Influence through the Ages* (New York and London, 1957), pp. 147–179.

21. Cayré, *Dieu présent*.

22. Cf. Brown's judgment that the *Confessions* "are a manifesto of the inner world" (*Augustine*, p. 168).

23. See J. Burnaby, *Amor Dei: A Study of the Religion of St. Augustine* (London, 1938).

24. These terms are used in their modern sense, an inevitable accommodation to changing usage (cf. TeSelle, *Augustine the Theologian*, p. 20). For Augustine's own usage, see *Contra Julianum* IV. 14, 72.

25. The celebrated controversy initiated by P. Alfaric in *L'Evolution intellectuelle de s. Augustin: I. Du manichéisme au néo-platonisme* (Paris, 1918).

26. The most substantial contributions are P. Courcelle, *Recherches sur les Confessions de saint Augustin* (Paris, 1950); J.-M. Le Blond, *Les Conversions de saint Augustin* (Paris, 1950); J. J. O'Meara, *The Young Augustine*.

27. For the affinities between Augustine and Hegel, see E. Booth, O.P., "Hegel's Conception of Self-knowledge Seen in Conjunction with Augustine's," *Augustiniana* 30 (1980), pp. 221–250. Although Hegel's writings contain remarkably few references to Augustine, their common debt to the Aristotelian notion of *nous*, "self-thinking thought," and to the Johannine *Logos* produced certain similarities in their work. While for Augustine, self-knowledge is a condition of all-knowledge, union with truth is union with a fully transcendent principle ultimately beyond knowledge, a position radically unacceptable to Hegel.

28. A way of referring to Augustine consequent on the emergence of his symbol of the flaming heart in the baroque period (see "Agostino Aurelio," in *Enciclopedia cattolica*, vol. 1 (Rome, 1948), p. 567.

29. Thus, after showing, with Augustine, that there are "psychic" experiences on our part that lack the properties found in bodies (and so that the soul is incorporeal), the realist phenomonologist philosopher Ludwig Hölscher considers the soul's "rational spirituality" as Augustine presents it. Here the starting point is not simply human acts that could not be performed by a (sheerly) bodily being, but those that "show their underlying subject to possess specifically 'rational' abilities. These acts will be those of imagination, recollection and *distentio animi*, of knowledge in the sense of both sense-perception and intellectual cognition, and free will" (cited from L. Hölscher, *The Reality of the Mind: St. Augustine's Philosophical Arguments for the Human Soul as a Spiritual Substance* [London and New York, 1986], p. 9).

30. TeSelle, *Augustine the Theologian*, p. 60.

31. Augustine, *De ordine* I. 3. 6.

32. Augustine, *Contra Academicos* III. 19. 43.

33. Augustine, *Retractationes* I. 1–9.

34. A. Mandouze, *Saint Augustin: L'Aventure de la raison et de la grâce* (Paris, 1968), p. 251.

35. Augustine, *Soliloquia* I. 1. 3.

36. Ibid.

37. TeSelle, *Augustine the Theologian*, p. 88.

38. Augustine, *De gratia et libero arbitrio* II. 2. 5.

39. Ibid. II. 12. 33.

40. Ibid. II. 13. 34.

41. Cf., for instance, Plotinus, *Enneads* VI. 5. 10.

42. Augustine, *De gratia et libero arbitrio* II. 13. 35.

43. Ibid. II. 14. 48.

44. Augustine, *De vera religione* 39, 73.

45. See above, note 26.

46. For a modern restatement of this argument to God's existence, see I. Trethowan, O.S.B., *The Basis of Belief* (London, 1961), p. 41; and the same author's *Mysticism and Theology* (London, 1979), p. 124.

47. N. D. O'Donoghue, *Heaven in Ordinarie* (Edinburgh, 1980), p. 14.

48. Cayré, *Dieu présent*, p. 220.

49. G. Bonner, "The Christian Humanism of Augustine," in D. Baker, ed., *Renaissance and Renewal in Church History* (Oxford, 1977), p. 12. On Augustine's milieu as pastor, see F. van der Meer, *Augustine the Bishop*, English trans. (London, 1961). Bonner might also have mentioned in this connection Augustine's religious life in the communities that he founded at Thagaste and Hippo, for Augustinian monasticism is a biblical and ecclesial monasticism. The monk, by his increasingly deepened appropriation of Scripture,

becomes, as preacher and teacher and spiritual father, the servant of the Church, herself founded on the Bible. See T. J. van Bavel, "The Evangelical Inspiration of the Rule of St. Augustine," *Downside Review* 93 (April 1975), pp. 83–99; and G. Lawless, O.S.A., *Augustine of Hippo and His Monastic Rule* (Oxford, 1987), pp. 155–161 (stressing, however, the "congruity of vocation" that joined the philosopher with the monk).

50. Brown, *Augustine*, p. 324.

51. The position is not greatly altered should it turn out that Augustine's principal source is Porphyry rather than Plotinus, as some would argue in the wake of Theiler, *Porphyrios und Augustin*.

52. Thus our enquiry confirms the intuition found in Christian iconography, where Augustine's distinctive symbols are the open book (symbol of knowledge) and the flaming heart (symbol of love); cf. Marrou, *St. Augustine and His Influence*, p. 69.

53. R. D. Williams, *The Wound of Knowledge: Christian Spirituality from the New Testament to St. John of the Cross* (London, 1979), pp. 68–69.

4. ANSELM AND THE LANGUAGE OF PERFECTION

1. B. Ward, ed., *The Prayers and Meditations of St. Anselm* (Harmondsworth, 1973).

2. R. W. Southern, in Ward, *Prayers and Meditations*, p. 12.

3. See R. W. Southern, *St. Anselm and His Biographer* (Cambridge, 1962).

4. N. F. Cantor, *Church, Kingship, and Lay Investiture in England, 1089–1135* (Princeton, 1958), p. 39.

5. Eadmer, *De vita et conversatione Anselmi archiepiscopi Cantuarensis* I, 19. See R. W. Southern, ed. and trans., *The Life of St. Anselm, Archbishop of Canterbury, by Eadmer* (London [1962]).

6. See G. R. Evans, *Old Arts and New Theology: The Beginnings of Theology as an Academic Discipline* (Oxford, 1980).

7. M. J. Charlesworth, "St. Anselm: Life and Times," in *St. Anselm's Proslogion* (Oxford, 1965), pp. 9–10.

8. A. Wilmart, O.S.B., *Auteurs spirituels et textes dévotes du moyen âge* (Paris, 1932), pp. 147–216.

9. For the problems of dating Anselm's writings, see F. S. Schmitt, O.S.B., "Zur Chronologie des hl. Anselm von Canterbury," *Revue Bénédictine* 44 (1932), pp. 332–350.

10. A. J. MacDonald, *Lanfranc: A Study of His Life, Work, and Writing* (Oxford, 1926).

11. D. P. Henry, *The Logic of St. Anselm* (Oxford, 1967).

12. Anselm, *Monologion* 1; cf. F. J. Thonnard, "Caractères augustiniens de la méthode philosophique de saint Anselm," in *Spicilegium Beccense: Congrès*

international de IXe centenaire de l'arrivée d'Anselme au Bec (Paris, 1959), pp. 171–184.

13. Charlesworth, *St. Anselm's Proslogion*, p. 25. See also A. J. MacDonald, *Authority and Reason in the Middle Ages* (London, 1933).

14. J. F. A. Mason, "Saint Anselm's Relations with Laymen: Selected Letters," in *Spicilegium Beccense*, pp. 547–560.

15. D. Knowles, O.S.B., *The Monastic Order in England* (London, 1940), chapter 26.

16. Anselm, *Proslogion*, preface.

17. Ibid.

18. Southern, *The Life of Anselm*, pp. 28–31.

19. Southern, in Ward, *Prayers and Meditation*, p. 9.

20. See Gaunilo, *A Reply on Behalf of the Fool*, in Charlesworth, *St. Anselm's Proslogion*, pp. 156–167.

21. R. W. Southern, "St. Anselm and Gilbert Crispin, Abbot of Westminster," *Mediaeval and Renaissance Studies* 3 (1954), pp. 78–115.

22. Charlesworth, *St. Anselm's Proslogion*, p. 3.

23. Ibid., pp. 6–7.

24. *Spicilegium Beccense: Congrès international du IXe centenaire de l'arrivée d'Anselme au Bec* (Paris, 1959).

25. A. Stolz, O.S.B., "Anselm's Theology in the Proslogion," in J. Hick and A. McGill, eds., *The Many-Faced Argument* (London, 1968), pp. 183–208.

26. E. L. Mascall, *The Openness of Being: Natural Theology Today* (London, 1971), p. 40.

27. Cf. Charlesworth, *St. Anselm's Proslogion*, p. 37.

28. Anselm, *Soliloquies* II, 271, 5–8.

29. Anselm, *Proslogion* I; cf. Augustine, *De gratia et libero arbitrio* II, 2.

30. Anselm, *Cur Deus homo* II. 15; cf. *Proslogion* XXVI.

31. J. Hopkins, *A Companion to the Study of Saint Anselm* (Minneapolis, 1972), p. 43.

32. Cf. G. R. Evans, *Anselm and a New Generation* (Oxford, 1980), pp. 63–68.

33. That the *Proslogion* was really meant to be a philosophy rules out Karl Barth's claim, in *Fides Quaerens Intellectum* (London, 1960), that there is no natural theology anywhere present in Anselm's work. Were Barth's claim correct, Anselm would have been at odds with the whole Augustinian tradition of his time. On the questionableness of Barth's proposal, see J. McIntyre, *St. Anselm and His Critics* (Edinburgh, 1954), where reference is made particularly to the *Cur Deus homo*. The significance of the latter work for Anselm's theological project as a whole is, in this context, its recurrence to the phrase *rationes necessariae*, which suggests a rationalism equally far from Anselm's intention. The phrase in his use denotes sometimes logical demonstration, but at other times, as in Cassiodorus, it means any argument attaining to

truth about a thing or event by whatever means. See on this A. M. Jacquin, "Les 'rationes necessariae' de s. Anselme," in *Mélanges Mandonnet* (Paris, 1930), vol. 2, pp. 67–78.

34. See R. Campbell, *From Belief to Understanding* (Canberra, 1976), to which my treatment of the *Prologion* is much indebted.

35. Anselm, *Proslogion* XV.

36. Campbell, *From Belief to Understanding*, p. 27.

37. Stolz, "Anselm's Theology in the Proslogion."

38. Anselm, *Proslogion* II.

39. Campbell, *From Belief to Understanding*, p. 37.

40. Ibid., p. 203.

41. See P. Michaud-Quentin, "Notes sur le vocabulaire psychologique de saint Anselme," in *Spicilegium Beccense*, pp. 23–30.

42. Anselm, *Proslogion* II.

43. I. Kant, *Critique of Pure Reason* B 628/9. Alternatively, one may espouse Charlesworth's formulation: "To function as a subject of predication in a real realm of discourse is greater than to function as a subject of predication in a functional or imaginary or conceptual realm of discourse" (*St. Anselm's Proslogion*, p. 67). This translation makes it clear that *exists* is not being used as a predicate in the ordinary sense, but that nevertheless some distinction and some comparison is being made between real and conceptual existence.

44. Anselm, *Proslogion* II.

45. Ibid. III.

46. Campbell, *From Belief to Understanding*, pp. 177–178; cf. L. Wittgenstein, *Philosophical Investigations* (Oxford, 1953), especially pp. 243–370.

47. J. Coulson, *Newman and the Common Tradition: A Study in the Language of Church and Society* (Oxford, 1970), pp. 3–13.

48. G. R. Evans, *Anselm and Talking about God* (Oxford, 1978), p. 49.

49. Evans, *Anselm and a New Generation*, p. 86.

50. See N. Fruman, *Coleridge, the Damaged Archangel* (London, 1971).

51. S. T. Coleridge, *Aids to Reflection* (London, 1825; Edinburgh, 1905), p. xvii

52. S. T. Coleridge, *The Statesman's Manual* (London, 1816), in W. G. T. Shedd, *The Works of S. T. Coleridge* (New York, 1853), vol. 1, p. 436.

53. The ground for this has been located in Coleridge's debts to German romantic idealism. As G. Hough wrote, "The aim of all Coleridge's religious writing is to show that all the central doctrines of Christianity . . . are deducible, with the aid of revelation, from the structure of the human mind itself" ("Coleridge and the Victorians," *The English Mind* [Cambridge, 1964]). It is difficult not to see in this a fundamental affinity with the later philosophy of Schelling, or even with Hegel's *Phenomenology*.

54. For Coleridge's account of the relation between mind and extramental reality, see S. Prickett, *Coleridge and Wordsworth: The Poetry of Growth* (Cambridge, 1970).

55. G. Steiner, "The House of Being," *Times Literary Supplement* (9 October 1981), p. 1143.

56. M. Heidegger, *Unterwegs zur Sprache* (Tübingen, 1959).

57. Ibid., pp. 14–15.

58. Ibid., pp. 85–155. Heidegger had already spoken in similar tones in the *Brief über den Humanismus* (Frankfurt am Main, 1949), p. 5.

59. Heidegger, *Unterwegs zur Sprache*, p. 30.

60. One might consult further here the article, "Language," by F. Mayr, in *Sacramentum Mundi* (London, 1968); for the period between the early Middle Ages and the romantics, see K. O. Apel, *Die Idee der Sprache in der Tradition des Humanismus von Dante bis Vico* (Bonn, 1963).

5. THOMAS AQUINAS AND THE FRAGILITY OF BEINGS

1. Thomas, *Summa contra gentiles* IV. 11.

2. For Thomas's biography, see K. Foster, O.P., *The Life of St. Thomas Aquinas: Biographical Documents* (London, 1959); J. A. Weisheipl, *Friar Thomas d'Aquino: His Life, Thought, and Works* (Garden City, N. Y., 1974), reprint ed., with corrections and additions (Washington, D.C., 1983). There is a useful brief portrait in A. Kenny, *Aquinas* (Oxford, 1980), chapter 1.

3. For an attempt to disengage these interests, see E. Gilson, *The Christian Philosophy of St. Thomas Aquinas*, English trans. (London, 1957).

4. E. L. Mascall, *The Openness of Being: Natural Theology Today* (London, 1971), p. 109.

5. Cf. Louis de Raeymaeker: "It is this reality which possesses an unshakeable solidity, an absolutely definitive consistency, an absolute validity. This also holds for all existence; whatever its nature and its duration, it etches into reality its indelible traits and it forces itself for ever and ever on the mind. Being exists, and by its own peculiar power, its *virtus essendi*, it excludes radically and without condition or any restriction all that would be opposed to it" (*The Philosophy of Being* [St. Louis, Mo., and London, 1964], p. 24, with reference to Thomas's *In De divinis nominibus* 5, 1; *De malo* 16, 9, 5; *Summa contra gentiles* I. 28).

6. N. Malcolm, *Ludwig Wittgenstein: A Memoir* (London, 1958), p. 70.

7. Thomas, *Summa theologiae* Ia. 2, 3. In the *Summa contra gentiles*, Thomas gives another version of the first, second, fourth, and fifth ways, the first mentioned of these being developed there at somewhat greater length than in the *Summa theologiae*.

8. E. L. Mascall, *Words and Images: A Study in Theological Discourse* (London, 1957), p. 85. The concept of *contuitus* is taken by Mascall from Thomas's Franciscan contemporary, Bonaventure.

9. Mascall, *Openness of Being*, p. 112.

10. On Heidegger's possible debt to Thomism and related medieval systems, see F. Kerr, O.P., "Metaphysics after Heidegger: For His Eighty-fifth Birthday," *New Blackfriars* 55.651 (1974), pp. 344–358, and especially pp. 345–346. For the theme of the forgetfulness of being, see "Der Ursprung des Kunstwerkes," in M. Heidegger, *Holzwege* (Frankfurt am Main, 1950), 6th ed. (Frankfurt am Main, 1980), pp. 1–72; English trans., "The Origin of the Work of Art," in M. Heidegger, *Poetry, Language, Thought* (New York, 1971), pp. 15–88. See also "Das Ding," in M. Heidegger, *Vorträge und Aufsätze* (Pfullingen, 1954), pp. 45 ff; English trans., "The Thing," in *Poetry, Language, Thought*, pp. 163–186. And *Was heisst Denken?* (Tübingen, 1964); English trans., *What Is Called Thinking?* (New York, 1968).

11. See M. Heidegger, *Was ist Metaphysik?* (Frankfurt am Main, 1955); English trans., "What is Metaphysics?" in *Existence and Being* (London, 1949; 1956), pp. 355–392.

12. D. E. Roberts, *Existentialism and Religious Belief* (New York, 1957), p. 177.

13. Ibid.

14. M. Heidegger, *Einführung in die Metaphysik* (Tübingen, 1953), p. 1; English trans., *Introduction to Metaphysics* (New Haven, 1959). See also V. Vycinas, *Earth and Gods: An Introduction to the Philosophy of Martin Heidegger* (The Hague, 1969), pp. 103–106.

15. D. B. J. Hawkins, *Being and Becoming* (London, 1954), p. 54.

16. Not that a thing only partially exists, but that, rather, it has a share in being: it receives, and plays a part. See Thomas's commentary *In libros Boethii De hebdomadibus* lect. 2; *In libros De caelo et mundo* II. lect. 8; *In epistolam Hebraeos* ch. VI, lect. 1. On the great theme of participation, see, above all, L. B. Geiger, O.P., *La Participation dans la philosophie de s. Thomas d'Aquin*, 2d ed. (Paris, 1953).

17. E. L. Mascall, *Existence and Analogy: A Sequel to "He Who Is"* (London, 1966), pp. 143–148. Cf. G. K. Chesterton, *St. Thomas Aquinas* (London, 1943), p. 70.

18. F. D. Wilhelmsen, "Meditation on Nothing," *Downside Review* 72.228 (Spring 1954), pp. 135–145.

19. As Thomas points out in his *Quaestiones De anima* 6, ad. ii: "*Esse* is the last act that is participable by all; it itself, however, does not participate in anything."

20. V. Turner, "Preliminaries to Theism," *Dublin Review* 225 (1951), pp. 12–27. Cf. P. Cornelio Fabro: "In fact, rather than insisting on being, rather than opening itself to the presence of being as the foundation of its own truth, philosophical thought has been carried off, dispersed along the length of the many branches of appearance [*l'apparaître*], and in the disappearing of 'philosophy,' 'philosophies' have pullulated. The dispersed forms have pushed

being into oblivion" ("La Retour au fondement de l'être," in J. Y. Jolif, O.P., et al., *Saint Thomas d'Aquin aujourd'hui* [Paris, 1963], p. 177).

21. A. Léonard, *Pensées des hommes et foi en Jésus Christ: Pour un discernement intellectuel chrétien* (Paris, 1980), p. 265.

22. N. D. O'Donoghue, *Heaven in Ordinarie* (Edinburgh, 1980), p. 48.

23. Cf. Chesterton's remark: "Until we realize that things might not be, we cannot realize that things are. It is one of the million wild jests of truth that we know nothing until we know nothing" (*Heretics*, 3d ed. [London, 1906], p. 65).

24. Alcuin, "O mea cella," in E. Dümmler, *Poetae Latini Aevi Carolini*, vol. 1 (Berlin, 1881), pp. 243–244 (= Alcuin, poem 23).

25. H. Waddell, *Mediaeval Latin Lyrics* (London, 1929), 5th ed. (London, 1948), pp. 97–99; though the poem is in Alcuin's manner, Waddell inclined to the view that, given its subject matter, Alcuin's empty cell, it is more likely the work of his disciple Fredugis (p. 305).

26. Thomas, *Summa theologiae* Ia. 2, 2. Cf. Josef Pieper's comment that "the language of St. Thomas does not have the quality of beauty proper to a work of art as we find it, for instance, in Augustine; it is beautiful as a perfect instrument is beautiful" (*The Silence of St. Thomas*, English trans. [London, n.d.], pp. 34–35).

27. Thomas, *Summa theologiae* II–IIae. 85, 1.

28. Ibid. Ia. prologue.

29. Ibid. Ia. 1, 1. See on this P. E. Persson, *Sacra Doctrina: Reason and Revelation in Aquinas* (Oxford, 1970).

30. V. White, O.P., "Prelude to the Five Ways," in *God the Unknown and Other Essays* (London, 1956), p. 41.

31. Ibid.

32. Ibid.

33. W. Paley, *View of the Evidences of Christianity* (London, 1794).

34. T. McDermott, O.P., *Thomas Aquinas, "Summa Theologiae," Volume 2 (Ia. 2–11): The Existence and Nature of God* (London, 1964).

35. J. H. Newman, *Fifteen Sermons Preached before the University of Oxford* (London, 1871); 2d ed. (London, 1909); facsimile ed. (London, 1970), p. 275.

36. Keith Ward has written appositely: "The Thomist proofs of God's existence . . . locate areas of experience which remain permanently baffling and mysterious for human understanding. . . . These areas of experience give an index of what is meant by 'God.' While the mystery remains, reflection on these facts enables one to characterize God as the transcendent cause of all being, the creator who discloses his being in one's apprehension of the radical contingency and limitedness of all finite beings, including, of course, oneself" (*The Concept of God* [Oxford, 1974], 2d ed. [London, 1977], pp. 152–153).

37. J. Maritain, *Approches de Dieu* (Paris, 1952); = *Oeuvres complètes*, vol. 10 (Fribourg, 1985), p. 27.

38. A. Farrer, *Faith and Speculation* (London, 1967), pp. 116–117.

39. D. H. Burrell, *Aquinas: God and Action* (London, 1979).

40. Cf. Thomas, *Summa theologiae* Ia. 13, 5: "The word *God* signifies the divine nature: it is used to mean something that is above all that is, and that is the source of all things and is distinct from them all. This is how those who use it mean it to be used."

41. Burrell, *Aquinas*, pp. 16–17.

42. Cf. Gilson's comment: "If he is pure Existing . . . in itself, and without any addition whatsoever, since all that could be added to it would limit it by defining it . . . God is by that very fact the absolute plenitude of Being" (*History of Christian Philosophy in the Middle Ages*, English trans. [London, 1955], p. 372). The same point is made by Mascall in *He Who Is: A Study in Traditional Theism* (London, 1943; 1966), p. 13. This "metaphysic of Exodus," which appealed to the revelation of the divine Name in Exodus 3:14, saturated patristic and medieval thinking on God (J. Pelikan, *The Christian Tradition: A History of the Development of Doctrine. I. The Emergence of the Catholic Tradition 100–600* [Chicago, 1971], p. 54).

43. Burrell, *Aquinas*, p. 62.

44. See, from a vast literature, H. Lyttkens, *The Analogy between God and the World: An Investigation of Its Use by Thomas Aquinas* (Uppsala, 1952).

45. T. Gilby, O.P., "Style of the *Summa*," in T. Gilby, O.P., ed., *Thomas Aquinas, "Summa theologiae," Volume 1 (Ia. 1, 1), Theology* (London, 1964), p. 52.

46. Burrell, *Aquinas*, p. 67.

47. A. M. Sertillanges, O.P., *St. Thomas Aquinas and His Work*, English trans. (London, 1932), p. 105.

48. Mascall, *Openness of Being*, p. 146. Cf. N. D. O'Donoghue: "Man as we know him is 'at home' in the finite; it is from the centre of his finitude that he opens himself to the infinite. But precisely because he is responsive to the infinite, we can envisage a transformation of man by which, while remaining finite, he would yet find his centre in the infinite pole of his being" (*Heaven in Ordinarie*, p. 15).

49. Mascall, *Openness of Being*, p. 46.

50. For a detailed discussion of texts relevant to the points made in this chapter, see F. van Steenberghen, *Le Problème de l'existence de Dieu dans les écrits de s. Thomas d'Aquin* (Louvain-la-Neuve, 1980).

6. John of the Cross and Mystical Experience

1. With considerable sobriety, Paul Murray, O.P., writes: "The tendency to consider Christian truth exclusively in terms of religious experience is relatively recent" (*The Mysticism Debate* [Chicago, 1977], p. 14).

2. B. Lonergan, S.J., *Philosophy of God and Theology* (London, 1973), pp. 9–10.

3. G. Ryle, *The Concept of Mind* (London, 1949).

4. K. Ward, *The Concept of God* (London, 1974), 2d ed. (London, 1977), p. 20.

5. T. Sprigge, "The Importance of Subjectivity," synopsis of inaugural lecture, chair of logic and metaphysics, University of Edinburgh, 27 November 1980. See now his *The Vindication of Absolute Idealism* (Edinburgh, 1983), for a full account.

6. Ward, *Concept of God*, 20.

7. P. Donovan, *Interpreting Religious Experience* (London, 1979), pp. 3–8; see also S. T. Katz, "Language, Epistemology, and Mysticism," in S. T. Katz, ed., *Mysticism and Philosophical Analysis* (London, 1978), pp. 22–74.

8. Donovan, *Interpreting Religious Experience*, p. 29.

9. Ibid., p. 33.

10. R. Burrows, *Guidelines for Mystical Prayer* (London, 1976), p. 46.

11. N. D. O'Donoghue, *Heaven in Ordinarie* (Edinburgh, 1980), p. 154 (emphasis added).

12. Donovan, *Interpreting Religious Experience*, p. 72.

13. One thinks of Michel de Certeau's idea of *une rupture sans cesse instauratrice*, "A rupture that proves endlessly constructive." See F. Kerr, O.P., "The 'Essence' of Christianity: Notes after Certeau," *New Blackfriars* (December 1973), p. 554.

14. Donovan, *Interpreting Religious Experience*, p. 82.

15. G. Brenan, *St. John of the Cross: His Life and Poetry* (Cambridge, 1973), pp. 12–13.

16. Ibid.

17. R. Williams, *The Wound of Knowledge: Christian Spirituality from the New Testament to St. John of the Cross* (London, 1979), p. 16.

18. E. Stein, *The Science of the Cross*, English trans. (London, 1960), p. 1.

19. John of the Cross, *The Dark Night of the Soul* II. 6; translated by K. Kavanaugh, O.C.D., and O. Rodriguez, O.C.D., *The Collected Works of St. John of the Cross* (London, 1966), p. 337.

20. O'Donoghue, *Heaven in Ordinarie*, p. 67.

21. John of the Cross, *Poems*, translated by R. Campbell (London, 1951), 2d ed. (London, 1979), pp. 11–13.

22. Ibid., 15.

23. E. A. Peers, *Spirit of Flame: A Study of St. John of the Cross* (London, 1943), p. 43.

24. John of the Cross, *Points of Love*, in E. A. Peers, *The Collected Works of St. John of the Cross* (London, 1935), 2d ed. (London, 1953), vol. 3, p. 253.

25. J. Baruzi, *S. Jean de la Croix et le problème de l'expérience mystique*, 2d ed. (Paris, 1931), pp. 685–686.

26. G. Morel, *Le Sens de l'existence selon s. Jean de la Croix* (Paris, 1960), vol. 1, p. 16.

27. Ibid., vol. 1, pp. 18–19.

28. Ibid., vol. 1, p. 19.

29. Ibid.

30. M. Merleau-Ponty, "La Métaphysique dans l'homme," in *Sens et Non-Sens*, 5th ed. (Paris, 1965), pp. 145–172.

31. A. de la Madre de Dios Asturicense, *Vida, virtitudes y milagros del santo padre fray Juan de la Cruz*, I. 37, National Library of Madrid, MS 13460; cited in M. Florisoone, *Esthétique et mystique d'après sainte Therese d'Avila et saint Jean de la Croix* (Paris, 1956), p. 27.

32. John of the Cross, *Poems*, translated by Campbell.

33. John of the Cross, *The Spiritual Canticle*, on stanza 36, 7; translated by Kavanaugh and Rodriguez, *Collected Works*, p. 548.

34. A. Nichols, O.P., *The Art of God Incarnate: Theology and Image in Christian Tradition* (London, 1980), p. 116.

35. F. von Hügel, *The Mystical Element of Religion as Studied in Saint Catherine of Genoa and Her Friends*, 2d ed. (London, 1923), vol. 2, pp. 283–284.

36. W. Johnston, S.J., *The Inner Eye of Love* (London, 1978), p. 19. This emphasis on love as the proper modality of contemplative awareness and its means is itself sanjuanist (see "Ascent of Mount Carmel," ch. xiii and xv; see also *Dark Night* II, xviii). See too, here, M. de la Taille, S.J., "Theories mystiques," *Recherches de science religieuse* 18 (1929), pp. 298–300 ("One is overtaken by the experience of a sustained love"). It is noteworthy that Karl Rahner could suggest that "monistic" mysticism, the chief contender with theistic, may be based upon a misinterpretation of loving communion with the divine: "Possibly . . . the elimination of egotistical, particularist individualism in a mystically experienced radical love for the self-communicating God simply leads in subsequent reflection to a mistaken belief in absolute cessation of the finite subject" ("Mystical Experience and Mystical Theology," in *Theological Investigations* 17, English trans. [London, 1981], p. 92).

7. Blaise Pascal and the Method of Immanence

1. B. Pascal, *Pensées*, translated by A. J. Krailsheimer (Harmondsworth, 1966), no. 84.

2. C. B. Daly, "Metaphysics and the Limits of Language," in I. Ramsey, ed., *Prospect for Metaphysics: Essays of Metaphysical Exploration* (London, 1961), p. 185. On the metaphysical and religious character of Descartes's view of the philosophical enterprise, see H. Gouhier, *La Pensée métaphysique de Descartes* (Paris, 1962).

3. See F. C. Copleston, S.J., *A History of Philosophy*, vol. 4 (London, 1965), p. 103.

4. For an understanding of the *cogito* from within a tradition marked by ontological realism, see L. de Raeymaker, *The Philosophy of Being: A Synthesis of Metaphysics* (London, 1954), pp. 6–23.

5. Daly, "Metaphysics and the Limits of Language," p. 184.

6. R. Descartes, "Third Meditation"; original in R. Descartes, *Meditationes de prima philosophia*, edited and translated by the duke of Luynes, introduction and notes by G. Lewis, 2d edition (Paris, 1946; 1960).

7. J. Chevalier, in his influential edition of the *Pensées* (Paris, 1922), called Pascal's approach to God's existence the "method of immanence" because it seeks an inner *Anknüpfungspunkt* (point of contact, starting point) in humanity. But taking up a distinction of M. Blondel's, Chevalier rightly stressed the difference between the method of immanence and the doctrine of immanence, the religious immanentism condemned by the magisterium of the Roman church during the modernist crisis. The difference turns on the fact that the method of immanence accepts both continuity and discontinuity between the *ordre des esprits*, which is human and natural, and the *ordre de la charité*, which is divine and beyond nature (Pascal, *Pensées*, edited by J. Chevalier [Paris, 1922], pp. 203–204). Blondel's distinction is found in his "Lettre sur les exigences de la pensée contemporaine en matière de apologétique et sur la méthode de la philosophie dans l'étude des problèmes religieux," *Annales de philosophie chrétienne* (1896); English trans. by A. Dru and I. Trethowan, *Maurice Blondel: The Letter on Apologetics and History and Dogma* (London, 1964).

8. A. Léonard, *Pensées des hommes et foi en Jésus Christ: Pour un discernement intellectuel chrétien* (Paris, 198), p. 160.

9. A. J. Krailsheimer, "Pascal," in A. J. Krailsheimer, *Conversion* (London, 1980), p. 59.

10. See J. Orcibal, *Saint-Cyran et le jansénisme* (Paris, 1961).

11. On the theological aspect, see N. J. Abercrombie, *The Origins of Jansenism* (London, 1936).

12. See A. Adam, *Du mysticisme à la révolte: Les Jansénistes du dix-septième siècle* (Paris, 1968).

13. Pascal, *Pensées*, no. 913. This is now the customary place at which to insert the "Memorial."

14. The notion of orders Pascal took from mathematics: lines, squares, and cubes, though related, cannot be summated. Cf. Pascal, *Pensées*, trans. by Krailsheimer, p. 22.

15. Pascal, *Pensées*, no. 298.

16. On the origins and plan of the *Pensées*, see A. J. Krailsheimer, *Pascal* (Oxford, 1980), pp. 41–49.

17. Pascal, *Pensées*, no. 110; cf. no. 131.

18. E. S. Brightman, *An Introduction to Philosophy* (New York, 1963), p. 7.

19. Pascal, *Pensées*, no. 24.

20. Ibid., no. 36.

21. Ibid., no. 43.

22. Ibid., no. 978.

23. Ibid., no. 220; cf. no. 759.

24. Ibid., no. 131.

25. Ibid., no. 122.

26. Cf. M. Blondel, *L'Action* (Paris, 1893), pp. 30–31; and Pascal, *Pensées*, no. 148.

27. Pascal, *Pensées*, no. 418.

28. Ibid., no. 131.

29. W. James, *The Will to Believe* (New York, 1897).

30. Ibid., p. 11.

31. Pascal, *Pensées*, no. 149.

32. The "gestures" that Pascal suggests are those of the Western Catholic liturgical tradition known to him (assisting at Mass, blessing oneself with holy water); but manifestly these stand here for an entire religious "form of life."

33. For an account of this philosopher who attempted to systematize Pascal's vision, see B. Reardon, "Maurice Blondel and the Philosophy of Action," in B. Reardon, ed., *Liberalism and Tradition: Aspects of Catholic Thought in Nineteenth-Century France* (Cambridge, 1975). On the revolutionary nature of the Blondelian attempt to "introduce the Pascalian vision into the mainstream of Catholic theology," see G. Daly, O.S.A., *Transcendence and Immanence: A Study in Catholic Modernism and Integralism* (Oxford, 1980), pp. 22–25. The question turns on the need of a subjective apologetics to complement, not (*pace* Daly) replace, an objective one.

34. Pascal, *Pensées*, n. 148.

35. Ibid., no. 362. Here Pascal's thought presses onward to that of Maurice Blondel, in whose terms I have ventured to restate it. See Blondel, *L'Action*; English trans., *Action: Essay on a Critique of Life and a Science of Practice* (Notre Dame, Ind., 1984), part 4: "The Necessary Being of Action: How the Terms of the Problem of Human Destiny Are Inevitably and Voluntarily Posited," pp. 300–357.

36. D. L. Roberts, *Existentialism and Religious Belief* (New York, 1957; 1959), p. 41.

37. N. D. O'Donoghue, *Heaven in Ordinarie* (Edinburgh, 1980), p. 88.

38. On the decline and renaissance of interest in Pascal, see D. Eastwood, *The Revival of Pascal: A Study of His Relation to Modern French Thought* (Oxford, 1936).

39. Ibid., pp. 15–16, citing Pascal, *Pensées*, no. 449.

40. See H. S. Hughes, *Consciousness and Society: The Reorientation of European Social Thought 1890–1920* (London, 1959).

41. E. Droz, *Etude sur le scepticisme de Pascal* (Paris, 1886), cited by Eastwood, *The Revival of Pascal.*

42. It was not for nothing that the subtitle of Jansen's *Augustinus* was *The Doctrine of St. Augustine on the Health, Sickness, and Healing of Human Nature* by grace (C. Jansenius, *Augustinus seu doctrina sancti Augustini de humanae naturae sanitate, aegritudine, medicina adversus Pelagianos et Massilienses* (Louvain, 1640).

8. Immanuel Kant and the Postulates of Practical Reason

1. K. Ward, in the fullest modern survey in English of Kantian ethics and while setting out to stress the teleological character of Kant's view of morals, concedes that Kant stressed "as no one hand previously" the categorical nature of moral obligation (*The Development of Kant's View of Ethics* [Oxford, 1972], p. 1).

2. C. C. J. Webb, *Kant's Philosophy of Religion* (Oxford, 1926), p. 192.

3. P. Nasset, "Le Problème de Dieu dans la philosophie française contemporaine," *Nouvelle revue théologique* (November 1974).

4. C. C. J. Webb, *Pascal's Philosophy of Religion* (Oxford, 1922), pp. 71–72.

5. For Kant's biography, see especially J. H. W. Stuckenberg, *Life of Immanuel Kant* (London, 1882).

6. Cited in W. Wallace, *Kant* (London, 1902), p. 6.

7. On the significance of Pietism for Kant's thought, see Webb, *Development of Kant's View of Ethics*, p. 3.

8. T. M. Greene, "The Historical Context and Religious Significance of Kant's *Religion*," in I. Kant, *Religion within the Limits of Reason Alone*, English trans., introduction, and notes by T. M. Greene and H. H. Hudson, 2d ed. (New York, 1960), pp. xxvi–xxvii. Wolff was a Christian rationalist of the school of Leibniz.

9. I. Kant, "Der Streit der Fakultäten," in *Werke*, edited by W. Weischedl, vol. 6, p. 291.

10. Cited in Wallace, *Kant*, p. 38.

11. E. Troeltsch, "Das Kritische in Kants Religionsphilosophie," *Kant Studien* (1904), pp. 43–44; cited in F. von Hügel, *The Mystical Element in Religion*, 2d ed. (London, 1923), vol. 2, pp. 261–263.

12. J. Kemp, *The Philosophy of Kant* (Oxford, 1968), p. 156.

13. Ward, *Development of Kant's View of Ethics*, pp. 13–14.

14. H. J. Paton, *Kant's Metaphysics of Experience* (London, 1936), vol. 1, p. 61; R. Scruton, *Kant* (Oxford, 1982), pp. 23–24.

15. I. Kant, *Critique of Pure Reason* A51 (=B75), English trans. by N. K. Smith (London, 1929), 2d ed. (London, 1933; 1973), p. 92.

16. Paton, *Kant's Metaphysics of Experience*, vol. 1, pp. 62–63; 70.

17. Cf. ibid., vol. 2, p. 428.

18. Kant, *Critique of Pure Reason* A576 (=B604), A578 (=B606), English trans. by Smith, pp. 491–492.

19. Ibid. A579 (=B607), English trans. by Smith, p. 492.

20. Ibid.

21. Ibid. A804 (=832), English trans. by Smith, p. 635.

22. Webb, *Kant's Philosophy of Religion*, p. 57.

23. D. M. MacKinnon, *A Study of Ethical Theory* (London, 1957), p. 81.

24. Ward has spoken of the "continuing centrality for Kant's ethics of certain metaphysical or religious concerns and a continuous development in his treatment of them" (*Development of Kant's Views of Ethics*, p. 3).

25. A. Koestler, *The God That Failed* (London, 1950); cited in MacKinnon, *Study in Ethical Theory*, p. 75.

26. MacKinnon, *Study in Ethical Theory*, p. 72.

27. I. Kant, *Groundwork of the Metaphysics of Morals* 26–27.

28. MacKinnon, *Study in Ethical Theory*, p. 74.

29. I. Kant, *Critique of Practical Reason*, English trans. by T. K. Abbott (London, 1879), pp. 333–336.

30. D. M. MacKinnon, *The Problem of Metaphysics* (London, 1974), p. 55.

31. Kant, *Critique of Practical Reason*, trans. by Abbott, p. 376.

32. G. F. Thomas, *Religious Philosophies of the West* (New York, 1965), p. 247. In the *Critique of Judgment*, Kant's concern with purposiveness in nature led him, however, to within an ace of the kind of argument from design that he had earlier repudiated in the *Critique of Pure Reason*.

33. In the second edition of the *Critique of Pure Reason*, Kant remarked in the preface: "We are convinced that there is an absolutely necessary practical employment of pure reason—the *moral*—in which it inevitably goes beyond the limits of sensibility. . . . Speculative reason has . . . at least made room for such an extension (by thinking the transcendent concept of the unconditioned); and if it must at the same time leave it empty, yet none the less we are at liberty, indeed we are summoned, to take occupation of it if we can by practical data of reason" (English trans. by Smith, pp. 26–27).

34. Ward, *Development of Kant's View of Ethics*, p. 126.

35. Ibid., p. 129.

36. Kant, *Critique of Practical Reason*, English trans. by Abbott, pp. 298–303.

37. Greene, "Historical Context and Religious Significance of Kant's *Religion*," pp. lviii–lix.

38. Kant, *Critique of Practical Reason*.

39. The anecdote is related by M. Laski in her *George Eliot and Her World* (London, 1973), p. 99. Laski calls George Eliot's words "portentous"—but they have something of the tender gravity that critics have ascribed to her prose (and her person).

40. Webb, *Kant's Philosophy of Religion*, p. 86.

41. Ibid.

42. Kant, *Critique of Practical Reason*, English trans. by Abbott, p. 331.

43. Webb, *Kant's Philosophy of Religion*, p. 102.

44. I. Kant, *Religion within the Limits of Reason Alone* (LaSalle, Ill., 1934; New York, 1960), p. 37, citing Horace, *Satire* I. 1, 69–70.

45. Kant, *Religion within the Limits of Reason Alone*, p. 48.

46. Ward, *Development of Kant's View of Ethics*, p. 149.

47. E. Adickes, *Kants Opus Posthumum* (Berlin, 1920).

48. H. P. Owen, *The Moral Argument for Christian Theism* (London, 1965), pp. 49, 34.

9. Søren Kierkegaard and the Struggle with Self-estrangement

1. For Kierkegaard's biography, see W. Lowrie, *Kierkegaard* (New York, 1938).

2. S. Kierkegaard, *The Concept of Irony*, English trans. (London, 1966); R. Poole, "Kierkegaard on Irony," *New Blackfriars* 48.601 (1967), pp. 243–247.

3. Cf. K. Löwith, *From Hegel to Nietzsche: The Revolution in Nineteenth-Century Thought*, English trans. (New York, 1964).

4. In the latter respect, three major studies appeared within a little over a decade: R. Jolivet, *Introduction to Kierkegaard*, English trans. (New York, 1951); J. Collins, *The Mind of Kierkegaard* (Chicago, 1953; London, 1954); L. Dupré, *Kierkegaard's Theologie* (Antwerp and Utrecht, 1958), English trans. (London, 1964).

5. F. H. Heinemann, *Existentialism and the Modern Predicament*, 2d ed. (New York, 1958), p. 2.

6. E. Mounier, *Introduction aux existentialismes* (Paris, 1947) = *Oeuvres complètes* (Paris, 1962), vol. 3, pp. 69–178.

7. S. Kierkegaard, *The Point of View for My Work as an Author*, English trans. (Oxford, 1939).

8. S. Kierkegaard, *The Sickness unto Death*, English trans. (Princeton, 1941), 2d ed. (Princeton, 1970).

9. Collins, *Mind of Kierkegaard*, p. 11.

10. S. Kierkegaard, *Either/Or: A Fragment of Life*, English trans. (Princeton and London, 1944).

11. Heinemann, *Existentialism and the Modern Predicament*, pp. 30–31.

12. Kierkegaard, *Point of View for My Work as an Author*, p. 39.

13. From S. Kierkegaard, *Philosophical Fragments, or a Fragment of Philosophy*, English trans. (Princeton, 1936), p. 3.

14. P. A. Heiberg and V. Kuhr, eds., *Søren Kierkegaards Papirer* (Copenhagen, 1912), vol. 4, pp. 103–150.

15. Cf. S. Kierkegaard, *The Present Age, and Two Minor Ethico-Religious Treatises*, English trans. (New York, 1940).

16. S. Kierkegaard, *The Concept of Dread*, English trans. (Princeton, 1944).

17. Kierkegaard, *Sickness unto Death*, p. 127.

18. H. U. von Balthasar, *Herrlichkeit*, vol. 3 (Einsiedeln, 1965), pp. 411–416.

19. A. Haas, preface, in M. Shrady, ed. and trans., *Johannes Tauler: Sermons* (Mahwah, N.J., 1985), pp. xiii–xvi.

20. Ibid., p. xv, a comment on Tauler's statement that "this poor man feels as if he were suspended between two walls, as if there were no room for him, neither here nor there" (F. Vetter, ed., *Die Predigten Taulers* [Berlin, 1910; Dublin and Zurich, 1968], vol. 5, p. 152).

21. Collins, *Mind of Kierkegaard*, p. 53.

22. S. Kierkegaard, *The Journals*, English trans. (New York, 1938), p. 21.

23. H. Diem, *Kierkegaard: An Introduction*, English trans. (Richmond, Va., 1966), p. 26.

24. Kierkegaard, *Either/Or*, vol. 2, pp. 214–222.

25. Collins, *Mind of Kierkegaard*, p. 206.

26. Cited in Heinemann, *Existentialism and the Modern Predicament*, p. 37; cf. Kierkegaard, *Either/Or*, pp. 178–179.

27. S. Kierkegaard, *Concluding Unscientific Postscript*, English trans. (Princeton, 1941), p. 181.

28. S. Crites, *In the Twilight of Christendom: Hegel versus Kierkegaard on Faith and History* (Chambersberg, Pa., 1972), pp. 24–25.

29. Cited in L. Mackey, *Kierkegaard: A Kind of Poet* (Philadelphia, 1971), pp. xi–xii.

30. Ibid.

31. Kierkegaard, *Sickness unto Death*, p. 17.

32. The issue for Kierkegaard is "that of human apotheosis versus Incarnation." In the *Philosophical Fragments*, the Absolute Paradox, the God in time, "causes offence to the Reason. 'Reason' is broadly construed to include feeling and imagination as human capacities that may all be merely immediate or objective. The Absolute Paradox challenges this Reason, the claims of feeling, imagination, or cognition to have the truth 'within themselves'; even the inwardness of religion [when not based on this *scandalon*] falters, and 'subjectivity becomes untruth.' The Absolute Paradox charges that the dreams of likeness with the divine and of the immediate recognition of the divine are illusory. Christ as the Absolute Paradox asserts the unlikeliness of God and persons, and proposes to do away with the unlikeness not in immediate recognition, but by faith in the God who is incognito in Jesus Christ. The Absolute Paradox is absurd, not as a logical contradiction or as the doctrine of Christ's two natures, but as an 'existential contradiction' to human reliance" (D. J. Gouwens, "Kierkegaard's Understanding of Doctrine," *Modern Theology* 5.1 [October 1988], p. 16).

33. Hegel's thought does indeed recognize the existence of difference and opposition, but it "minimizes and relativizes them. Continuity and unity are discovered everywhere and all differences are reconciled in the whole" (G. F. Thomas, *Religious Philosophies of the West* [New York, 1965], p. 293).

34. See G. F. W. Hegel, *The Philosophy of Religion*, English trans. (London, 1895), vol. 1, p. 183. E. S. Schmidt, in his study of Hegel's teaching on God regards the "concept of the true infinite" as "the fundamental principle of Hegel's philosophy" (*Hegel's Lehre von Gott* [Gütersloh, 1952], p. 153).

35. W. Pannenberg, "The Significance of Christianity in the Philosophy of Hegel," *Basic Questions in Theology* 3, English trans. (London, 1973), pp. 144–177.

36. S. Kierkegaard, *Training in Christianity*, English trans. (Princeton, 1941), p. 84; cited in C. Gunton, *Yesterday and Today: A Study of Continuities in Christology* (London, 1983), p. 17.

37. Cf. J. N. Findlay: "It is as essential . . . for Spirit to be wedded to particular finite contents and to determinate places in the world, as it is for it to be freely ranging and 'infinite,' since it is only by being the former that it can be the latter" (*Hegel: A Re-examination* [London, 1958], p. 43).

38. A Kojève, *Introduction to the Reading of Hegel*, English trans. (New York, 1969), p. 171.

39. S. Kierkegaard, *The Concept of Irony*, English trans. (Bloomington, Ind., 1968), p. 85.

40. A. Henriksen, *Kierkegaards Romaner* (Copenhagen, 1969), takes this as its central idea.

41. Kierkegaard, *Concluding Unscientific Postscript*, p. 109. M. C. Taylor, however, holds that they simply develop "alternative phenomenologies of spirit that are designed to lead the reader from inauthentic to authentic selfhood" (*Journeys to Selfhood: Hegel and Kierkegaard* [Berkeley and London, 1980], p. 13).

42. For these affinities and contrasts, see R. Heiss, *Die grossen Dialektiker des 19. Jahrhunderts: Hegel, Kierkegaard, Marx* (Cologne and Berlin, 1963).

43. Or, as L. Kolakowski has written: "The self-deification of mankind to which Marxism gave philosophical expression has ended in the same way as all such attempts, whether individual or collective; it has revealed itself as the farcical aspect of human bondage" (*Main Currents of Marxism* [Oxford, 1981], vol. 3, p. 530).

44. J. Moltmann, *Experiences of God*, English trans. (London, 1980), p. 54.

45. Transcribed in Kierkegaard, *Journals*, p. 551.

10. GABRIEL MARCEL AND THE DIMENSION OF HOPE

1. F. H. Heinemann, *Existentialism and the Modern Predicament*, 2d ed. (New York, 1958), p. 135.

2. G. Marcel, "Regard en arrière," in E. Gilson et al., *Existentialisme chrétien: Gabriel Marcel* (Paris, 1947).

3. G. Marcel, *Journal métaphysique* (Paris, 1927), p. 279.

4. R. Troisfontaines, *De l'existence a l'être: La Philosophie de Gabriel Marcel* (Louvain, 1953), vol. 1, pp. 22–23.

5. C. Moeller, "Gabriel Marcel et le mystère de l'espérance," *Littérature du XXe siècle et christianisme*, vol. 4 (Tournai, 1965), pp. 149–157.

6. G. Marcel, *En chemin, vers quel éveil?* (Paris, 1971).

7. C. Pax, "Marcel's Way of Creative Fidelity," *Philosophy Today* (Spring 1975), pp. 12–21; cf. G. Marcel, *The Mystery of Being*, vol. 1, English trans. (London, 1950), pp. 42–43.

8. Troisfontaines, *De l'existence a l'être*, vol. 2, pp. 304–305.

9. G. Marcel, *Being and Having*, English trans. (London, 1965), p. 29.

10. The nature and destiny of human persons is taken by Marcel to be the integrating focus of philosophical investigation. See J. B. O'Malley, *The Fellowship of Being: An Essay on the Concept of Person in the Philosophy of Gabriel Marcel* (The Hague, 1966).

11. G. Marcel, *Le Monde cassé* (Bruges and Paris, 1933), pp. 256–257.

12. Marcel, *Being and Having*, p. 127.

13. Ibid., p. 137.

14. Pax, "Marcel's Way of Creative Fidelity."

15. G. Hanratty, "The Religious Philosophy of Gabriel Marcel," *Heythrop Journal* 17.4 (October 1976), p. 399.

16. See especially G. Marcel, *The Mystery of Being*, vol. 2, English trans. (London, 1960), pp. 37–57.

17. G. Marcel, *Structure de l'espérance* (Paris, 1951), p. 76.

18. Marcel, *Being and Having*, p. 135–136.

19. Marcel, *Mystery of Being*, vol. 2, p. 8.

20. Ibid., vol. 1, pp. 182–183.

21. G. Marcel, *Homo Viator*, English trans. (London, 1951), p. 134.

22. Moeller, "Gabriel Marcel et le mystère de l'espérance," *Littérature du XXe siècle et le christianisme*, vol. 4, p. 224.

23. Ibid., vol. 4, p. 211.

24. Marcel, *Homo viator*, p. 60.

25. Marcel, *Being and Having*, pp. 86–87.

26. Ibid., p. 84.

27. Marcel, *Homo Viator*, p. 36. The essay, "Sketch of a Phenomenology and a Metaphysic of Hope," in this collection (pp. 29–67), is Marcel's most important text on this subject.

28. Pax, "Marcel's Way of Creative Fidelity," p. 19; cf. Marcel, *Being and Having*, p. 19.

29. P. Berger, *A Rumour of Angels: Society and the Rediscovery of the Supernatural* (London 1970; Harmondsworth, 1971), p. 83.

30. J. Moltmann, *Experiences of God*, English trans. (London, 1980), p. 28. I refer to Moltmann's study, *The Theology of Hope*, English trans. (London, 1967).

31. Moltmann, *Experiences of God*, p. 36.

11. G. K. CHESTERTON AND THE FACT OF JOY

1. P. Berger, *A Rumour of Angels: Modern Society and the Rediscovery of the Supernatural* (London, 1970; Harmondsworth 1971).

2. G. K. Chesterton, *The Ballad of the White Horse* (London, 1911), p. 1.

3. M. Ward, *Gilbert Keith Chesterton* (London, 1944; Harmondsworth, 1958), p. 15.

4. Ward, *Gilbert Keith Chesterton*, p. 14. Cited from Chesterton's unpublished notebooks.

5. G. K. Chesterton, *Autobiography* (London, 1936; 1969), p. 38.

6. M. McLuhan, introduction to Hugh Kenner, *Paradox in Chesterton* (London, 1948), p. xix.

7. G. K. Chesterton, *Charles Dickens* (London, 1906), pp. 41–42.

8. G. K. Chesterton, *Orthodoxy* (London, 1908; 1961), pp. 158–159.

9. Chesterton, *Orthodoxy*, pp. 158–159.

10. G. K. Chesterton, *St. Francis of Assisi* (London, 1923), p. 87.

11. G. K. Chesterton, *The Defendant* (London, 1901), p. 3.

12. P. N. Furbank, "Chesterton the Edwardian," in J. Sullivan, ed., *G. K. Chesterton: A Centenary Appraisal* (London, 1974), pp. 21–22.

13. G. K. Chesterton, *William Blake* (London, 1911), p. 56. It seems likely that Blake's *Songs of Innocence* played a part in confirming Chesterton's view of the significance of joy (see K. Raine, *William Blake* [London, 1970], p. 50).

14. See L. Mackey, *Kierkegaard: A Kind of Poet* (Philadelphia, 1971), pp. xi–xii.

15. G. K. Chesterton, *St. Thomas Aquinas* (London, 1933), pp. 175–195.

16. Yves Denis, *G. K. Chesterton: Paradoxe et catholicisme* (Paris, 1978), p. 37.

17. See Jacques Maritain, *Creative Intuition in Art and Poetry*, English trans. (New York, 1954), pp. 160–167.

18. G. K. Chesterton, *The Poet and the Lunatics: Episodes in the Life of Gabriel Gale* (London, 1929), p. 129.

19. Cf. Chesterton, *Orthodoxy*, p. 11.

20. Denis, *G. K. Chesterton*, p. 17.

21. C. S. Lewis, *Surprised by Joy* (London, 1935; 1959), p. 143.

22. See J. Huizinga, *Homo Ludens: A Study of the Play Element in Culture* (Boston, 1955).

23. Berger, *Rumour of Angels*, pp. 76–77.

24. Denis, *G. K. Chesterton*, p. 38.

SELECT BIBLIOGRAPHY

GENERAL WORKS

Charlesworth, M. J. *Philosophy of Religion: The Historical Approaches.* London, 1972.
Copleston, F. C., S. J. *A History of Philosophy.* 9 vols. London, 1946–1975.
———. *Religion and Philosophy.* Dublin, 1974.
Davies, B., O. P. *An Introduction to the Philosophy of Religion.* Oxford, 1982.
———. *Thinking about God.* London, 1985.
Davies, C. F. *The Evidential Force of Religious Experience.* Oxford, 1989.
Gilson, E. *God and Philosophy.* New Haven, 1941.
Lewis, H. D. *Philosophy of Religion.* London, 1965.
Nédoncelle, M. *Is There a Christian Philosophy?* English trans. New York, 1960.
O'Donoghue, N. D. *Heaven in Ordinarie.* Edinburgh, 1979.
Roberts, D. E. *Existentialism and Religious Belief.* Oxford and New York, 1957. 2d ed. Oxford and New York, 1960.
Swinburne, R. *The Existence of God.* Oxford, 1979.
Thomas, G. F. *Religious Philosophies of the West.* New York, 1965.

1. JOHN HENRY NEWMAN

Boekraad, A. J. *The Argument from Conscience to the Existence of God According to J. H. Newman.* Louvain, 1961.
———. *The Personal Conquest of Truth According to J. H. Newman.* Louvain, 1955.
Coulson, J. *Newman and the Common Tradition.* Oxford, 1970.
———. *Religion and Imagination "in Aid of a Grammar of Assent."* Oxford, 1981.
Dessain, C. S. *John Henry Newman.* London, 1966.
———. *Newman's Spiritual Themes.* Dublin, 1977.

Flanagan, P. *Newman, Faith, and the Believer.* London, 1946.

Harrold, C. F. J. H. *Newman: An Expository and Critical Study of His Mind, Thought, and Art.* London, 1945.

Ker, I. *John Henry Newman: A Biography.* Oxford, 1988.

Newman, J. H. *Autobiographical Writings.* Edited by H. Tristram. London,

——. *An Essay in Aid of a Grammar of Assent.* London, 1870. 2d ed. London, 1895. Edited by I. Ker. Oxford, 1985.

——. *Fifteen Sermons Preached before the University of Oxford.* London, 1843. 2d ed. London, 1872.

Pailin, D. *The Way to Faith: An Examination of Newman's "Grammar of Assent" as a Response to the Search for Certainty in Faith.* London, 1969.

Ward. W. *The Life of John Henry Cardinal Newman.* London, 1912.

2. Gregory of Nyssa

Balthasar, H. U. von. *Présence et pensée: Essai sur la philosophie religieuse de Grégoire de Nysse.* Paris, 1942.

Daniélou, J., S. J. *Platonisme et théologie mystique.* 2d ed. Paris, 1953.

Gregory of Nyssa. *The Life of Moses.* English trans. London, 1979.

——. *From Glory to Glory.* Texts edited and translated by H. Musurillo. London, 1962.

Mühlenberg, H. *Die Unendlichkeit Gottes bei Gregor von Nyssa.* Göttingen, 1966.

3. Augustine of Hippo

Augustine. *On Free Choice of the Will (De gratia et de libero arbitrio).* Translated by A. S. Benjamin and L. H. Hackstaff. Indianapolis, Ind., 1964.

——. *Writings of Saint Augustine.* Edited by L. Schopp. Vol. 1: *The Happy Life (De beata vita); Answer to Skeptics (Contra Academicos); Divine Providence and the Problem of Evil (De ordine); Soliloquies (Soliloquia).* New York, 1948.

Bonner, G. *St. Augustine of Hippo: His Life and Controversies.* London, 1973.

Brown, P. *Augustine of Hippo: A Biography.* London, 1967.

Cayré, A. *Dieu présent dans la vie de l'esprit.* Bruges, 1951.

Gilson, E. *The Christian Philosophy of St. Augustine.* English trans. London,

Kirwan, S. *Augustine* London, 1988.

Marrou, H. I. *St. Augustine and His Influence through the Ages.* English trans. London, 1957.

4. Anselm of Canterbury

Anselm. *The Prayers and Meditations of St. Anselm.* Translated by Benedicta Ward, S.L.G. Harmondsworth, 1973.

——. *St. Anselm's Proslogion.* Translated by M. J. Charlesworth. Oxford, 1965. Notre Dame, Ind., 1979.

——. *Sancti Anselmi Cantauriensis Archiepiscopi Opera Omnia.* 4 vols. Edited by F. S. Schmitt. Rome and Edinburgh, 1938–1968.

Campbell, R. *From Belief to Understanding.* Canberra, 1976.

Evans, G. R. *Anselm and Talking about God.* Oxford, 1978.

Hick, J., and A. McGill, eds. *The Many-Faced Argument.* London, 1968.

Hopkins, J. *A Companion to the Study of Saint Anselm.* Minneapolis, Minn., 1972.

Southern, R. W. *St. Anselm and His Biographer.* Cambridge, 1963.

5. Thomas Aquinas

Aquinas, Thomas. *Philosophical Texts.* Translated by T. Gilby, O. P. Oxford, 1951.

——. *Summa contra gentiles.* Translated by A. C. Pegis et al., under the title *On the Truth of the Catholic Faith.* New York, 1955.

——. *Summa theologiae.* English trans. 61 vols. London, 1964–1981.

Burrell, D. B. *Aquinas, God, and Action.* London and Henley, 1979.

Chenu, M. D., O. P. *Toward Understanding Saint Thomas.* English trans. Chicago, 1964.

Chesterton, G. K. *St. Thomas Aquinas.* London, 1933.

Copleston, F. C., S. J. *Aquinas.* London, 1955.

Gilson, E. *The Christian Philosophy of St. Thomas Aquinas.* English trans. London, 1957.

Kenny, A. *Aquinas.* Oxford, 1980.

Knowles, David. "The Historical Context of the Philosophical Work of St. Thomas Aquinas." In *Aquinas: A Collection of Critical Essays,* edited by A. Kenny. New York, 1969.

van Steenberghen, F. *Le Problème de L'existence de Dieu dans les éscrits de s. Thomas d'Aquin.* Louvain, 1980.

Weisheipl, J., O. P. *Friar Thomas d'Aquina: His Life, Thought, and Works.* Oxford, 1974. 2d ed., with corrections and additions. Washington, D. C. 1983.

6. John of the Cross

Baruzi, J. *S. Jean de la Croix et le problème de l'expérience mystique.* 2d ed. Paris, 1931.

Bruno de Jésus-Marie, P., O.C.D. *St. John of the Cross.* English trans. London, 1932.

Donovan, P. *Interpreting Religious Experience.* London, 1979.

Hook, S., ed. *Religious Experience and Truth.* New York, 1961.

John of the Cross. *The Complete Works of Saint John of the Cross.* Edited and translated by E. A. Peers. London, 1935. 2d ed. London, 1953.

——. *The Poems of St. John of the Cross.* Translated by R. Campbell, with and introduction by M. D'Arcy, S. J. London, 1951.

Katz, S. T., ed. *Mysticism and Philosophical Analysis.* London, 1978.

Miles, T. R. *Religious Experience.* London, 1972.

Morel, G. *Le Sens de l'existence selon s. Jean de la Croix.* 3 vols. Paris, 1960.

Peers, E. A. *Spirit of Flame.* London, 1943.

Stein, E. *The Science of the Cross.* English trans. London, 1960.

7. Blaise Pascal

Fletcher, F. T. H. *Pascal and the Mystical Tradition.* Oxford, 1954.

Krailsheimer, A. J. *Pascal.* Oxford, 1980.

Magnard, P. *Nature et histoire dans l'apologétique de Pascal.* Paris, 1975.

Mesnard, J. *Pascal: His Life and Works.* English trans. New York, 1952.

Miel, J. *Pascal and Theology.* Baltimore, 1969.

Pascal, B. *Oeuvres complètes.* Paris, 1963.

——. *Pensées.* Translated by A. J. Krailsheimer. Harmondsworth, 1966.

Webb, C. C. J. *Pascal's Philosophy of Religion.* Oxford, 1929.

8. Immanuel Kant

Kant, I. *Critique of Practical Reason.* Translated by T. K. Abbott. London, 1879.

——. *Critique of Pure Reason.* Translated by N. K. Smith. Edinburgh, 1929.

——. *Theorie-Werkausgabe.* Edited by W. Weischedl. Frankfort am Main, 1968–.

Kemp, J. *The Philosophy of Kant.* Oxford, 1968.

Paton, H. J. *The Categorical Imperative.* London, 1947.

——. *Kant's Metaphysics of Experience.* London, 1936.

Paulsen, F. *Immanuel Kant: His Life and Doctrine.* London, 1902.

Scruton, R. *Kant.* Oxford, 1982.

Stuckenberg, J. W. H. *The Life of Immanuel Kant.* London, 1882.

Ward, K. *The Development of Kant's View of Ethics.* London, 1972.

Webb, C. C. F. *Kant's Philosophy of Religion.* Oxford, 1926.

Wood, A. W. *Kant's Moral Religion.* Ithaca, N.Y., 1970.

9. Søren Kierkegaard

Auden, W. H. *The Living Thought of Kierkegaard*. New York, 1952.
Bretall, R. *A Kierkegaard Anthology*. Princeton, 1946.
Collins, J. *The Mind of Kierkegaard*. London, 1954.
Dupré, L. *Kierkegaard as Theologian*. English trans. London. 1964.
Kierkegaard, S. *Samlede vaerker*. 14 vols. Copenhagen, 1920–1936.
———. *Papirer*. 16 vols. Copenhagen, 1909–1948; 1968–1970; 1975–1985.
Lowrie, W. *A Short Life of Kierkegaard*. Princeton, 1942.

10. Gabriel Marcel

Gallagher, K. T. *The Philosophy of Gabriel Marcel*. New York, 1962.
Gilson, E., et al. *Existentialisme chrétien: Gabriel Marcel*. Paris, 1947.
Marcel, G. *Being and Having*. English trans. London, 1965.
———. *Homo Viator*. English trans. London, 1951.
———. *Metaphysical Journal*. English trans. Chicago 1952.
———. *The Mystery of Being*. English trans. London, 1960.
Micelli, V. *Ascent to Being: Gabriel Marcel's Philosophy of Communion*. New York, 1965.
O'Malley, J. B. *The Fellowship of Being: An Essay on the Concept of Personhood in Gabriel Marcel*. The Hague, 1966.
Schilpp, P. A., and A. E. Hahn. *The Philosophy of Gabriel Marcel*. Library of Living Philosophers 17. LaSalle, Ill., 1984.
Troisfontaines, R. *De l'existence à l'être: La Philosophie de Gabriel Marcel*. Louvain and Paris, 1953.

11. G. K. Chesterton

Chesterton, G. K. *Autobiography*. London, 1936.
———. *Orthodoxy*. London, 1908; 1961.
Dale, A. *The Outline of Sanity: A Biography of G. K. Chesterton*. Grand Rapids, Mich., 1982.
Denis Y. *G. K. Chesterton: Paradoxe et catholicisme*. Paris, 1979.
Kenner, H. *Paradox in Chesterton*. London, 1948.
Ward, M. *Gilbert Keith Chesterton*. London, 1944. 2d ed. Harmondsworth, 1958.
———. *Return to Chesterton*. London, 1952.

INDEX OF NAMES

211

Popol Wuj
Sam Colop

Sam Colop
(traducción al español y notas)

POPOL WUJ

Popol Wuj
Sam Colop
(traducción al español y notas)

Segunda edición
Primera reimpresión, julio 2019

© Sam Colop
© Esta edición: F&G Editores

Diseño de colección: F&G Editores
Diseño de portada: Estuardo Diéguez
Foto de portada: Elio Morales
Edición al cuidado de José Luis Perdomo Orellana y Raúl Figueroa Sarti

Impreso en Guatemala
Printed in Guatemala

F&G Editores
31 avenida "C" 5-54, zona 7
Colonia Centro América
Guatemala, Guatemala
Teléfonos: (502) 2292 3792 y (502) 5406 0909
informacion@fygeditores.com
www.fygeditores.com

ISBN: 978-9929-552-31-9
Biblioteca Guatemala, 1

Guatemala, julio de 2019

Sam Colop

Luis Enrique Sam Colop es k'iche' de Cantel, Quetzaltenango. Abogado y notario por la universidad Rafael Landívar (1983), su tesis Hacia una propuesta de ley de educación bilingüe obtuvo el primer premio en la Facultad de Derecho ese año. Tiene una maestría en Lingüística por la Universidad de Iowa City y un doctorado por el Departamento de Inglés de la Universidad Estatal de Nueva York en Buffalo, donde escribió la disertación Maya Poetics.

Entre sus publicaciones están: "Bosquejo de algunos temas de la gramática k'iche'" en Lecturas sobre la lingüística maya (Cirma, Guatemala, 1990); Cinco siglos de encubrimiento: a propósito de 1991 (Editorial Cholsamaj, Guatemala, 1991) texto que fue traducido al italiano (Bonnano Editore, Catania, Italia 1992) y publicado en español por la revista Global Justice de la Universidad de Denver Colorado y en inglés en Maya Cultural Activism in Guatemala (editorial de la Universidad de Texas, Austin); "Xajoj Tun vs. Quiché Vinak", revista Encuentro del Instituto Guatemalteco de Cultura Hispánica (1993); Popol Wuj: versión poética kíche´ (Editorial Cholsamaj, 1999).

Ha participado en congresos de Latin American Studies Association, American Anthropological Association, Congreso Internacional de Americanistas y dictado conferencias sobre lingüística, literatura maya y temas jurídicos mayas en universidades de Estados Unidos y Ecuador.

Ha sido becario del Instituto Interamericano de Derechos Humanos de Costa Rica, de la Fundación Guggenheim de Nueva York, de Plumsock Mesoamerican Foundation, de la American Philosophical Society de Filadelfia. Obtuvo dos veces la beca Fulbright, y la Newberry Library de Chicago le otorgó una beca para edición.

Sus columnas periodísticas aparecen dos veces a la semana en Prensa Libre.

A la memoria de mi madre,
Marina Isidora

Contenido

Ro'

PRÓLOGO

La idea de traducir este libro tuvo dos fases.

La primera fue la transcripción del mismo en el idioma k'iche', con el alfabeto contemporáneo, para que los k'iche'es hablantes tuvieran acceso a leerlo en ese idioma. De ahí derivó la inquietud de traducirlo al idioma español, no porque las anteriores traducciones tuvieran grandes equivocaciones, aunque algunas versiones sí contienen errores, y otras, presentan muchas imprecisiones, que espero haber superado con esta versión. En segundo lugar, dichas traducciones, en general, han pasado por alto el lenguaje poético en que fue escrito el manuscrito original y cuya única copia que nos queda es la versión de fray Francisco Ximénez, escrita entre 1701-1703.

Realizar este trabajo tuvo varias fases.

La primera comenzó con la traducción basada en la versión poética del manuscrito, de la cual es autor quien éste suscribe. En el proceso hubo de hacerse varias correcciones a aquella versión k'iche', en lo relativo a la versificación y clarificación de términos. Para el efecto hubo de volverse a las transcripciones k'iche'es de Schultze Jena (1944), Edmonson (1971), a la copia facsimilar de Estrada Monroy (1973) y Adrián Chávez (1978), que posteriormente confronté con el manuscrito de Ximénez.

La segunda etapa consistió en leer en k'iche' palabra por palabra y frase por frase para compararlas con la versión en español con mi señor padre, Mateo Sam Pocol. Él conocía partes del texto conforme la tradición oral k'iche'; pero no lo había leído, ni escuchado en su versión escrita, y no dejó de impresionarle la parte relacionada con Tojil. Luego el texto se fue mejorando, con observaciones y revisiones posteriores.

Este libro no habría sido posible sin el apoyo de la Fundación John Simon Guggenheim de Nueva York, de Plumsock Mesoamerican Studies de Vermont y de la Newberry Library en Chicago, Illinois. La fundación Guggenheim y la Plumsock Mesoamerican Studies financiaron el estudio y traducción que se presenta en este libro.

La Newberry Library de Chicago, donde se encuentra el manuscrito de Ximénez (que llamamos "original" porque la versión escrita por los tres autores k'iche'es en el siglo XVI ha desaparecido), colaboró financiando el cotejo de notas con aquel manuscrito. Tuve la oportunidad de tener a mi disposición aquel documento de principios del siglo XVIII durante los meses de octubre de 2004 y 2005 a través de la beca Lester J. Cappon, que me permitió volver a comparar las correcciones a mi versión k'iche' para estar conforme con esta traducción. Aquel proceso fue estimulante, no sólo por haber tenido en mis manos el manuscrito de hace más de 300 años, sino porque además tuve acceso a copias de otros documentos y diccionarios del siglo XVI y siguientes.

Al inicio de este trabajo conté con el apoyo para retornar un mes a la biblioteca de la Universidad Estatal de New York en Buffalo a través de una beca de la McNulty Chair del programa de poética de la facultad de inglés donde, de hecho, comencé a estudiar estos temas.

Agradezco la colaboración de mi señor padre, las observaciones puntuales, sobre todo a las notas a pie de página; a Dennis Tedlock, a Robert Carmack y a Christopher Lutz, cuyos cuestionamientos me hicieron revisar detalles.

Agradezco además a Robert Karrow, conservador de las colecciones especiales de la Newberry, así como al personal de la biblioteca, que me facilitaron el acceso a aquellos materiales, así como a amigos que resolvieron algunos de mis problemas técnicos de computación. Ninguno de ellos, por supuesto, es responsable de los errores que contenga este libro. La introducción, traducción e interpretaciones en las notas son de mi responsabilidad.

Qastzij wi chi kamul k'amo
           oxmul k'amo rumal nabe wujil
                      ojer tz'ibam puch.
Are ketal
      kina'tabal nabe qachuch,
            nabe qajaw.

INTRODUCCIÓN

QUÉ ES EL *POPOL WUJ*

El *Popol Wuj* es el libro que contiene la mitología y la historia del pueblo k'iche', hasta la llegada de los españoles en el siglo XVI, cuando se cuenta la ejecución de los Señores principales Oxib Kej y Belejeb Tz'i'. Este libro fue transcrito en símbolos latinos, conforme a Recinos, entre los años 1554-58.

El antecedente de este manuscrito sólo pudo ser un texto jeroglífico que la segunda generación de los Señores llegó a adquirir a la "orilla del mar", es decir, Chichén Itzá, donde el Señor Nakxit les otorgó toda la parafernalia de poder, incluida "la escritura de Tulán". Seguramente no era el texto completo del *Popol Wuj*, porque la parte histórica todavía estaba ocurriendo, pero sí la parte mitológica que para esa época ya existía o estaba siendo dibujada en vasos y otros artefactos como algunos pasajes que se encuentran escritos en aquel libro. Uno de los ejemplos es el ataque en contra de Wuqub Kak'ix, quien es derribado del árbol de nance o "árbol del mundo" en otra versión pintada en un vaso del período clásico.

La versión original del *Popol Wuj* debió de tener una forma como los libros "antiguos", es decir, jeroglífica o pictográfica y esto lo reconocen algunos de los traductores y estudiosos de aquel manuscrito.

Recinos menciona, entre otros autores, a Ximénez y a Brasseur de Bourbourg. Aquí habría que agregar al mismo Recinos, a Girard,

Edmonson, Carmack, Tedlock, etcétera. Y es que en el *Popol Wuj* se habla de la constelación Orión, de una manifestación de la Osa Mayor y la Osa Menor, las Pléyades, como también se nombra a la estrella que se anticipa al Sol (Venus) y en una invocación se hace referencia a aquel astro como el de los cinco días —que conforme al calendario de Venus contenido en el *Códice de Dresde*, comienza cada uno de sus ciclos como estrella de la mañana, en cinco distintos días de los veinte que tiene el calendario maya—. También se llama a la deidad del amanecer, Wuch', para que tiznara el horizonte y cuatro veces lo hizo para dar tiempo a la reconstrucción de la cabeza de Junajpu. Este "tiznador" del Cielo, a quien se le puede ver antes de cada amanecer, conforme al *Códice de Dresde*, lleva en sus espaldas a uno de los cuatro cargadores del tiempo, que asociado al Mito del Winal del *Chilam Balam de Chumayel*, coincide con las cuatro mujeres, "madres" que crearon el tiempo.

Lo más revelador es cuando los Señores prodigiosos, Q'ukumatz y K'otuja, así como los Señores portentosos, K'ikab y Kawisimaj: "Sabían si había que hacer guerra, / todo estaba claro para ellos. / Podían ver si habría mortandad, / si habría hambre, / si habría que pelear. / Lo sabían muy bien, / porque tenían dónde verlo, / había un libro / *Popol Wuj*, llamado por ellos".

Ese texto fue transcrito a los símbolos latinos por quienes ocultaron su identidad en las primeras páginas y con un dejo de tristeza dicen que el texto no se puede ver y que lo escriben en medio de la cristiandad.

Esto ha sido tomado por otros como muestra de influencia cristiana,[*] cuando lo que están diciendo estos autores es que entre la adversidad de la persecución cristiana, tuvieron el valor de transcribir aquel documento y en la parte final del texto se identifican

---

[*] Esto es semejante a pensar que el *Antiguo testamento* de los hebreos tiene una influencia o un origen babilónico por Utnapishtim, el equivalente a Noé que antecedió a ese mito bíblico. Véase el paralelismo entre la historia épica de Gilgamesh y el *Antiguo testamento* de Heidel (1949).

como "madres de la palabra", "padres de la palabra" y luego se va identificando cada quien como: "Gran maestro de la palabra ante los Kaweq, era el primero, / gran maestro de la palabra ante los Nija'ib era el segundo, / gran maestro de la palabra era el tercer Señor ante los Ajaw K'iche'. / Eran, pues, tres maestros de la palabra, / cada uno representando un linaje". Sin estos autores, el *Popol Wuj* probablemente habría quedado como texto jeroglífico que en el mejor de los casos, se estaría descifrando; si no es que hubiera terminado en la hoguera de la Inquisición.

La versión de Ximénez que se encuentra ahora en la Newberry Library de Chicago no puede ser la traducción original del texto k'iche', que tuvo a su disposición o quién sabe si no se lo apropió, entre 1701-03. Si se los devolvió a los que guardaban el texto, éste no estaría en buen estado como sucede con el *Título C'oyoi* —texto más o menos contemporáneo— que bajo las más estrictas medidas climáticas de una biblioteca, como la propia Newberry, ha sufrido las inclemencias del tiempo antes de llegar a ese centro de estudio.

Decía, sin embargo, que esa copia no puede ser original o la primera transcripción al k'iche' del texto de 1554-58 y su primera traducción, entre otras razones: la más trivial, ¿cómo habría calculado Ximénez el espacio entre cada línea k'iche' con el espacio de traducción en español, para que cada página quedara en armonía? Lo más significativo, sin embargo, está en el folio 8r. Allí hay diez y media líneas tachadas del texto k'iche' cuya traducción al español está en blanco y la razón es que en el folio 9r, es decir, la hoja siguiente, aparece el mismo texto k'iche' aunque ya traducido al español. En el folio 8r se está hablando de la muerte de Wuqub Kak'ix y lo tachado en ese folio se refiere a la muerte de Sipakna, lo cual está contenido en el folio 9r.

¿Qué significado tiene esto?

En términos muy mundanos, a mi manera de ver, es que Ximénez transcribía y traducía el folio 8r de un "borrador" o copia preliminar, cuando el viento volteó aquella hoja y él siguió con el texto que ahora está en la Newberry Library. Al darse cuenta del equívoco, simplemente tachó lo que no correspondía a aquel pasaje, tampoco lo tradujo y continuó con el texto.

Pero ¿qué pasó con la versión de los autores k'iche'es de 1554-58? Se ha dicho que probablemente Ximénez se la devolvió a las autoridades cívico-religiosas de Chichicastenango y que ellos la guardan celosamente. Si esto fuese así, me parecería que alrededor de 450 años después, con las condiciones climáticas locales, no se encontraría en buen estado, considerando que el *Título C'oyoi*, que está resguardado de esos cambios, e incluso el manuscrito de Ximénez escrito 150 años después, tienen marcas del paso del tiempo. El *Título C'oyoi* tiene orillas y partes internas desaparecidas.

Es repetitivo contar la historia del manuscrito de Ximénez, de cómo pasó de la orden de los dominicos a la biblioteca de la Universidad de San Carlos de Guatemala —esto puede leerse en otras versiones—; baste decir que Brasseur de Bourbourg se lo apropió de aquella biblioteca en 1855.

Mas no hay mal que por bien no venga: porque si no se lo hubiera llevado a Europa, aquel manuscrito habría terminado en alguna biblioteca particular. Lo mismo puede decirse de otros manuscritos que se encuentran en bibliotecas extranjeras como el *Memorial de Sololá*, *Título C'oyoi*, el *Título Real de Don Francisco Izquin Nehaib*, etcétera. Mariano Gálvez incluso donó obras de la misma naturaleza a la Sociedad Filosófica Americana de Filadelfia. En el caso del *Popol Wuj*, el manuscrito fue devuelto a este continente en 1911, a la Biblioteca Newberry de Chicago, Illinois.

CONTENIDO

El *Popol Wuj* es un texto que contiene mitología e historia, pero también una transición entre mitología e historia, una regresión literaria que lo hace más interesante. Es decir, no es lineal. Porque ésta es la esencia del documento, hago un resumen que puede leerse con más extensión en otras versiones y en la propia traducción.

El texto comienza con una descripción de las dificultades para escribir y de la existencia de un libro antiguo; luego se habla del silencio primigenio, de cómo surgió la Tierra de entre las aguas. La preocupación inicial de los creadores eran los seres que los invocarían y de ahí su primera creación fueron los animales y las aves que poblaron montañas y barrancos. Éstos no pudieron decir el nombre de sus creadores y por eso su naturaleza fue cambiada y se constituirían en alimento de otros seres. Luego fue creado un único ser de tierra y lodo que se desmoronaba y humedecía con el agua. Esta segunda creación también fue desechada. De ahí vienen los seres de madera que conversaban y se reproducían como la gente; pero no tenían espíritu ni pensamiento. Por eso fueron aniquilados y atacados por sus propios animales y utensilios de cocina. En una transición narrativa aparece Wuqub Kak'ix, quien se asumía como el Sol y la Luna de los hombres de madera. Este personaje, que en una de sus manifestaciones es la Osa Mayor y Chimalmat, su esposa, la Osa Menor, efectivamente alumbran el cielo pero de manera muy tenue; por eso, el *Popol Wuj* dice literalmente: "su vista nada más cubría su alrededor / no se extendía a todo el espacio debajo del cielo". Wuqub Kak'ix, que literalmente quiere decir "Siete Guacamaya", fue eliminado por los héroes gemelos, Junajpu y Xbalamke. Enseguida viene la muerte de Sipakna, primer hijo de Wuqub Kak'ix, quien a su vez había matado a los 400 muchachos que después se volverían estrellas del cielo. Aquí, de nuevo, la bóveda celeste se sigue "sembrando" de luz. Sipakna termina petrificado debajo de un cerro. Luego viene la derrota del segundo hijo de Wuqub Kak'ix, llamado Kabraqan, que literalmente significa "temblor o terremoto". Lo interesante en este episodio es que no dice explícitamente que Kabraqan haya muerto, sino que, estando incapacitado de actuar, lo entierran y por eso, en una interpretación contemporánea, temblores y terremotos siguen ocurriendo sobre la faz de la Tierra.

A partir de aquí, "retrocedemos" a episodios anteriores. Se ha hablado de los héroes gemelos, sin saber su procedencia. En esta parte se aclara que son hermanos menores de Jun Batz' y de Jun Chowen, quienes junto a sus padres jugaban pelota de dos en dos. Se narra el viaje de Jun Junajpu y Wuqub Junajpu a Xibalba y su derrota en aquel lugar. Luego viene la fecundación de Ixkik', el rechazo de su padre y la orden de sacrificio por parte de los Señores de Xibalba. Los hijos de Ixkik' sufren el desprecio de Jun Batz' y Jun Chowen, pero aquellos cobrarían venganza y convierten a sus hermanos mayores en lo que sus propios nombres anticipan. Jun Batz' y Jun Chowen en otro aspecto son los dioses de la palabra, no uno solo; aunque García Márquez al hablar del poder de la palabra dijo en 1997: "Ahora sabemos, además, que los mayas lo sabían desde los tiempos de Cristo, y con tanto rigor que tenían un dios especial para las palabras". (Primer Congreso Internacional de la Lengua Española, Zacatecas).

Los héroes gemelos quieren ser agricultores y cortadores de leña pero reciben mensaje de que ésa no es su misión en la vida y, por jugar pelota como sus padres y hermanos mayores, son llamados a Xibalba. Allá pasan las pruebas de los Señores del inframundo, pero, contrario a sus propios padres, no son vencidos y terminan derrotando a Jun Kame y a Wuqub Kame y demás Señores de la muerte. Aquí ocurre una de las ironías más finas: los gemelos, antes de matar a los Señores de la muerte, preguntan: "¿Acaso hay muerte para ustedes?". Habiéndolos ajusticiado reivindican el nombre de sus padres, a quienes tratan de revivir. A todo esto, su abuela Ixmukane quema copal frente a las plantas de maíz que ellos dejaron sembradas y luego ascienden al Cielo donde uno se vuelve el Sol y el otro la Luna.

De ahí en adelante empieza lo que se conoce como parte "histórica"; pero de nuevo, hay una transición porque la parte mitológica continúa y se va diluyendo entre la creación humana y sucesos posteriores. Así cuatro animales descubren el maíz que será esencia de la humanidad, son cuatro los primeros varones creados cuya visión cubría la faz de la Tierra y por eso se les tuvo que nublar la vista para que sólo vieran lo que estaba cercano. Fueron también cuatro las mujeres creadas y de ellas se originaron pueblos y casas reales. Hasta aquí, el Sol no había aparecido y por eso invocaban por el amanecer.

La primera generación fue al Oriente para recibir sus deidades y ahí se menciona que eso está contenido en un antiguo texto. Viene la creación del fuego y el sometimiento de otros pueblos. Por fin llega el amanecer con el aparecimiento del lucero de la mañana, el Sol, la Luna y las estrellas. La peregrinación por distintos lugares continúa, así como el ataque de que son objeto los padres primigenios k'iche'es. Luego viene la desaparición de las personas que caminaban solas o de dos en dos. Cuando los pueblos afectados buscaban huellas de los responsables, sólo encontraban huellas de animales o algún fenómeno natural les obstruía la misión. Como alternativa desesperada, envían a dos de sus hijas, aunque en *El Título de Totonicapán* se habla de tres de ellas, al "baño de Tojil", el río donde las deidades k'iche'es transformadas en materia humana se bañaban. La intención era una alianza política, pero no fructificó. Una vez asegurado el poderío k'iche', los cuatro padres primigenios desaparecen no sin antes dejar recuerdo de su presencia, el Pisom Q'aq'al o "Envoltorio Sagrado"; se despiden de sus esposas y de sus hijos a quienes también dejan instrucciones.

La segunda generación va al Oriente, aunque esta vez a la "orilla del mar" para recibir la parafernalia del poder de parte de Nakxit, nombre asociado con Quetzalcóatl. Este peregrinaje los lleva a atravesar las costas del océano Atlántico en las orillas de Yucatán hasta llegar a Chichén Itzá. Entre lo más valioso, reciben copia de lo que habría sido el original del *Popol Wuj*, seguramente no con toda la parte histórica final que ahora conocemos, pero sí con la parte esencial del libro que también era conocida en fragmentos en aquellas tierras, por lo que aún se puede ver en vasijas, murales, templos, etcétera. De lo escrito en aquel documento se infiere que sabían interpretarlo correctamente y para eso debían conocer el movimiento de los astros. De esa cuenta se hace referencia a Orión, a la Osa Mayor, a la Osa Menor, a la deidad que oscurece cuatro veces el amanecer, a los ciclos de la Luna, Venus, el Sol, lo que implicaba un conocimiento matemático del tiempo.

Se hace un recuento de su establecimiento en Q'umaraq Aj, las casas reales, las generaciones hasta la llegada de los españoles y de manera muy escueta la tortura de Oxib Kej y Belejeb Tz'i' por parte de Pedro de Alvarado.

Por último, los transcriptores de aquel texto que una vez tuvo que ser jeroglífico o pictográfico, revelan su origen y el linaje al que pertenecen: uno de los Kaweq, otro de los Nija'ib y el tercero de los Ajaw K'iche'. En una metáfora se identifican como "madres de la palabra", "padres de la palabra". Pero para que no todo quede oscuro, terminan escribiendo que "Esto es, entonces, la esencia de los k'iche'es..." Reiteran, además, que antes había un libro donde podía leerse esto y eso fue lo que terminó de ocurrir en lo que llegó a llamarse Santa Cruz del Quiché.

DE OTRAS VERSIONES

Aquí no se trata de menospreciar.

Yo agradezco las demás traducciones, desde la de Ximénez a las otras versiones publicadas a la fecha. Las traducciones efectuadas desde el texto k'iche' merecen respeto especial, sea en el idioma que se haya traducido. No es fácil traducir metonimias, metáforas y otras figuras literarias. Podremos estar o no de acuerdo pero en líneas generales hay un hilo conductor.

Baste mencionar que no se habla de un caos inicial sino de la existencia de un Cielo y de la Tierra existente debajo de las aguas; no se habla "del otro lado del mar" sino de la orilla del mar. No se habla de leones y tigres, sino de pumas y jaguares; se habla de un chilacayote en la reconstrucción de la cabeza de Junajpu y no de una tortuga. El supuesto llamado de paz: "que todos se levanten, que nadie se quede atrás..." es en realidad un llamado a la guerra. Los héroes gemelos no son uno, son dos como gramatical y textualmente dice el manuscrito.

DEL NOMBRE *POPOL WUJ*

En los folios 1r y 54r de la copia que hizo Francisco Ximénez se lee *popo vuh* y *popol vuh* respectivamente, esto hizo proponer a don Adrián Inés Chávez, uno de los traductores de origen k'iche', que en la primera mención la segunda vocal estaba de más. El error del copista fue omitir la letra –*l*, como consta en el folio 54r y otras páginas del mismo texto donde aparece la palabra *popol* como en *popol winaq* (cuatro veces), *ajpopol* (dos veces). En la *Primera parte del Tesoro de las lenguas Cakchiquel, Quiché y Zutuhil* (sic) del mismo Ximénez encontramos las palabras *popol*, "cabildo"; *popolij*, "consultar en cabildo". En el *Título Yax* se encuentra la palabra *popol*, como en *El Título de Totonicapán* se encuentran las palabras *ajpopol*. En el *Vocabulario en lengua quiché* de Basseta (ca. 1698) encontramos las palabras *popol ech, popol tzij,* que traduce como "cosa común"; *popol ja,* "cabildo, casa de consejo"; *popol ulew,* "baldío"; *popol k'ayij,* "almoneda". En el diccionario kaqchikel de Coto encontramos las palabras *popol tzij,* "acuerdo, consejo"; *popol ulew,* "heredad"; *popol ajawa',* "principales", también están las frases *popol wa'im, popol samaj, popolij,* etcétera. Nótese aquí que la copia del manuscrito del *Título de Totonicapán* es contemporánea a la transcripción del *Popol Wuj* que Ximénez traduciría siglo y medio después; asimismo que los trabajos de Basseta y Coto antecedieron la traducción de Ximénez y, en el caso de Coto, es claro que se basó en fuentes anteriores.

En el diccionario maya-yucateco también están las palabras *popol, popol na,* "edificio municipal en tiempos coloniales". En el diccionario "cakchiquel-español" de Sáenz de Santamaría (1940), encontramos *popol, popol wa'im,* que traduce como "comida popular" y concretamente: *Popol Wuj,* "el libro del común; el libro del pueblo; el libro del consejo". En el diccionario q'eqchi' de Haeserijn encontramos *poopol,* como "cabildo, juzgado, autoridades civiles". Es decir que la palabra *popol* siempre ha existido, como el término *pop.*

A mediados del siglo pasado, cuando Adrián Recinos publicó su traducción en México, la tituló *Popol Vuh* pero hizo notar que la h debe pronunciarse "como la j española" y que "el sonido de la v es igual al de la u, gu o w en palabras como vach, que tiene el mismo sonido de guach o wach; Popol Vuh, que suena como Popol Uuj o Wuj". En 1955, Dora Burgess y Patricio Xec publicaron otra versión del mismo documento bajo el título *Popol Wuj,* como se hace en esta ocasión y como se hizo en una versión k'iche' del mismo manuscrito.

EL LENGUAJE DEL *POPOL WUJ*

En la mayoría de traducciones se ha obviado el lenguaje en el que fue escrito el *Popol Wuj.* Se han enfocado más en su contenido. El lenguaje en que fue escrito este libro, combina verso y prosa. El verso paralelo que lo caracteriza, sin embargo, no son dos líneas contiguas únicamente. Existen versos de tres y cuatro líneas. En los tercetos, la última generalmente rompe el paradigma para dar fluidez al discurso como en los cuartetos que si no es la tercera línea es la cuarta la que cambia. En el verso pareado podemos ver estos ejemplos:

> *Madre y*
> *Padre de la vida.*
> *de la existencia...*

o como se dice en la última página del manuscrito:

> *las que son madres de la palabra,*
> *los que son padres de la palabra.*

Un ejemplo de terceto es el siguiente:

> *Todo está en suspenso,*
> *todo está en reposo,*
> *en sosiego.*

La tercera línea cambia el paradigma como en un verso pareado donde el segundo modifica a la primera. En el siguiente ejemplo de cuarteto es la cuarta línea la que cambia:

> *un recipiente de pétalos rojos,*
> *un recipiente de pétalos blancos,*
> *un recipiente de pétalos amarillos*
> *un recipiente de [pétalos] grandes*

Aquí puede verse que la última línea rompe el paradigma porque era de esperarse que se dijera de "pétalos negros"; en cambio, se habla de pétalos grandes.

NOTA FINAL

En este libro se escribe la letra *b* sin apóstrofo, no como se establece en el alfabeto oficial; el autor es de la opinión que los diacríticos, si son obvios, hay que evitarlos. Si hablamos en k'iche' y sabemos que la *b* es implosiva y por ley se le agrega otro símbolo, sólo dificulta la lectoescritura.

Por último, hay que hacer notar que en k'iche' existe un trato formal para hablar con los mayores y con los dioses como la manera en que Ixkik' se dirige a Ixmukane al decirle *in alib la*, "yo soy nuera de usted"; aquí traducido como "yo soy su nuera", o como cuando los héroes gemelos se dirigen a Uk'u'x Kaj, "Corazón del Cielo", antes de ir a vencer a Kabraqan y dicen:

¿Acaso no está usted,

   usted su excelencia

   usted Uk'u'x Kaj?, dijeron los muchachos al acatar

      [la palabra

de Jun Raqan.

NABE
CAPÍTULO PRIMERO

Éste es el origen de la antigua historia de este lugar llamado K'iche'.
Aquí escribiremos
        estableceremos la palabra antigua;
el origen
el comienzo de todo lo acontecido en el pueblo k'iche',
                                nación de la gente k'iche'.
Aquí iniciamos la enseñanza,
                la aclaración y
                la relación de lo oculto y
                lo revelado por Tz'aqol
                        Bitol;[1]
                        Alom,
                        K'ajolom[2] nombres de Junajpu Wuch',
                                        Junajpu Utiw;[3]
                                        Saqi Nim Aq
                                                Sis;[4]
                                        Tepew
                                        [Q'ukumatz;[5]
                                        Corazón del
                                                [lago
                                        Corazón del
                                                [mar.
Los de la superficie plana,

los de la bóveda azul,[6] como se dice,
se nombra,
se menciona a la comadrona
al abuelo,[7] Xpiyakok
Ixmukane,[8]

así llamados los protectores,
amparadores,
dos veces comadrona,
dos veces abuelo, como se les dice en la historia
[k'iche'

cuando lo narraron todo,
junto con lo que hicieron en la claridad de la existencia
claridad de la palabra.
Esto lo escribiremos ya adentro de la prédica de dios,
en el cristianismo.

Vamos a sacarlo a luz porque ya no hay dónde ver el *Popol Wuj*,[9]
instrumento de claridad venido de la orilla del mar[10]
donde se cuenta nuestra oscuridad[11]
instrumento de claridad sobre el origen de la vida, como se le
[dice.[12]

Había un libro original,
que fue escrito antiguamente,
sólo que están ocultos quienes lo leen
quienes lo interpretan.

Es grande su descripción
y el relato de cómo se terminó de crear todo el Cielo y
la Tierra:

sus cuatro esquinas
sus cuatro lados,
su medición
sus cuatro ángulos;[13]
doblez de la cuerda para medir[14]
extensión total de esa cuerda en el Cielo,
en la Tierra;

en las cuatro esquinas
en los cuatro lados, como se dice por parte de Tz'aqol,
                                        Bitol;
Madre y
Padre de la vida
        de la existencia;
dador de la respiración,
dador del corazón;
Creador y
Pálpito de la luz,
        de la eternidad;
        de las hijas nacidas en claridad
        de los hijos nacidos en claridad.
El que medita,
el que conoce de todo lo que existe en el Cielo y en la Tierra
                en lagos y mares.[15]

Ésta es, pues, su narración:
todo está en suspenso,
todo está en reposo,
        en sosiego,
todo está en silencio;
todo es murmullo y
        está vacía la bóveda del Cielo.[16]
Ésta es, pues, la primera palabra
                la primera expresión:
cuando todavía no existía una persona
                        ni animal,
                        pájaro,
                        pez,
                        cangrejo,
                        árbol,
                        piedra,
                        cueva,
                        barranco,

pajón,
bosque,
sólo el Cielo existía.
Todavía no había aparecido la faz de la Tierra,
sólo estaba el mar en calma
            al igual que toda la extensión del Cielo.
Todavía no había nada que estuviera junto
                    que hiciera ruido,
                    que se moviera por su obra.
No había movimiento,
nada ocurría en el Cielo.
No había nada que estuviera levantado
sólo agua reposada,
sólo el mar apacible,
sólo reposaba la soledad.
Y es que no había nada todavía,
sólo había quietud
y sosiego en la oscuridad
            en la noche.
Sólo estaban Tz'aqol,
            Bitol,
            Tepew Q'ukumatz,
            Alom,
            K'ajolom en el agua.[17]
Dimanaban luz
estando envueltos en plumas de quetzal
                    en plumas azules;[18]
de ahí la nominación de "Serpiente Emplumada".[19]
De grandes sabios,
de grandes pensadores es su esencia.
Asimismo estaba sólo el Cielo
y también Uk'u'x Kaj
que es el nombre de dios, como se le dice.

Vino entonces aquí su palabra
llegó donde estaba Tepew Q'ukumatz en la oscuridad,
                                en la aurora.
Habló con Tepew Q'ukumatz,[20]
dijeron entonces cuando pensaron,
                cuando meditaron.
Se encontraron y
    juntaron sus palabras y
            sus pensamientos.
Estaba claro,
se pusieron de acuerdo bajo la luz;
se manifestó la humanidad y
se dispuso el surgimiento,
                la generación de árboles,
                        de bejucos y
            el origen de la vida,
                    de la existencia en la oscuridad
                            en la aurora, por parte de
Uk'u'x Kaj llamado Jun Raqan.
Kaqulja Jun Raqan, el primero,
el segundo es Ch'ipi Kaqulja y
el tercero Raxa Kaqulja.[21]
Eran tres, pues, las manifestaciones de Uk'u'x Kaj[22]
cuando vinieron a hablar con Tepew Q'ukumatz,
cuando se concibió el origen de la vida:
—¿Cuándo tendrá que ser la siembra y
                el amanecer?[23]
¿Quiénes serán los proveedores,
                los cuidadores?
¡Que se haga realidad!
¡Las aguas que se aparten,
            que se vacíe!
Porque debe surgir la Tierra
                su superficie debe verse.
Luego que venga la siembra
        que nazcan Cielo y Tierra,

¿No es acaso el lugar de veneración
de invocación de nuestros seres formados
de nuestros seres creados?
¡Que se origine la gente formada
la gente construida!, dijeron entonces.
Luego surgió la Tierra por su obra,
sus palabras fueron suficientes para que esto ocurriera,
para que la Tierra apareciera:
—¡Tierra!, dijeron y de inmediato emergió como si fuera sólo nube,
como si fuera neblina
empezó a
[aparecer
empezó a crecer.

Del agua empezaron a salir los cerros y
de inmediato en grandes montañas se convirtieron.
Sólo por su prodigio
sólo por su poder se consiguió la concepción de las montañas y valles;²⁴
que de inmediato rebosaron de cipreses y
de pinos.
Así, pues, se puso contenta la Serpiente Emplumada:
—Estuvo bien que hayas venido tú Uk'u'x Kaj,
tú Jun Raqan y
tú Ch'ipi Kaqulja
Raxa Kaqulja.²⁵
Salió bien nuestra obra
nuestra construcción, dijeron entonces.
Primero, pues, se originó la Tierra
las montañas y valles;
se dispuso el camino de las aguas
los arroyos empezaron a caminar entre los cerros;
ya se sabía el lugar de las aguas cuando aparecieron
las grandes montañas.
Así fue, pues, el origen de la Tierra
cuando fue formada por Uk'u'x Kaj

Uk'u'x Ulew,²⁶ así llamados porque ellos
[fueron los primeros en pensarlo.

El Cielo fue separado y
la Tierra fue apartada de las aguas.
Así fue, entonces, lo ejecutado cuando pensaron
cuando meditaron concluir,
terminar su obra.

Luego se pensó en los animales del monte,
cuidadores de cerros;
en todas la criaturas del bosque:
venados;
pájaros;
pumas;
jaguares;
serpientes
cascabel,
barbamarilla;
guardianes de los bejucos.
Luego dijeron Alom
K'ajolom:
—¿Es sólo silencio
o murmullo lo que ha de haber debajo de los árboles y
de los bejucos?
Es mejor que tengan sus guardianes, dijeron.
Fue entonces cuando pensaron
cuando decidieron
y fueron creados de una vez los venados y
los pájaros;²⁷
luego les repartieron sus moradas a los venados y
a los pájaros.
—Tú, venado, en las orillas de los ríos
en los barrancos has de dormir;
aquí has de habitar: en el pajón

entre la hierba;
en el bosque se han de multiplicar.

En cuatro patas han de andar y
sostenerse, les fue dicho.
Luego establecieron morada a los pequeños pájaros
a los grandes pájaros:
—Ustedes, aves, sobre los árboles
sobre los bejucos han de anidar
han de habitar,
aquí se han de reproducir
se han de multiplicar,
en las ramas de los árboles
en las ramas de los bejucos, les fue dicho a los venados
a los pájaros.

Cuando hicieron
lo que había que hacer;
todos tomaron sus habitaciones y
lugar de estancia.

Fue así, pues, como les fue dado sus nidos a los animales por
la Concebidora,
el Engendrador;
y estando terminada la creación de los cuadrúpedos y
las aves,
les fue dicho a los cuadrúpedos y
aves por el Creador
Formador;
Alom,
K'ajolom:
—¡Hablen
invoquen,
que no sólo sean gorjeos
deben invocar!
Que hable cada quien
según su especie
según su grupo, les fue dicho a los venados,

                              a las aves,
                              a los pumas,
                              a los jaguares,
                              a las serpientes.
—¡Digan nuestros nombres,
alábennos, a nosotros su madre creadora
                a nosotros su padre creador!
Digan entonces:
Jun Raqan,
Ch'ipi Kaqulja,
Raxa Kaqulja;
Uk'u'x Kaj,
Uk'u'x Ulew;
Tz'aqol,
Bitol;
Alom,
K'ajolom;
¡Hablen,
invóquennos,
adórennos!, les fue dicho.
Pero no pudieron hablar,
        no como la gente;
sólo chillaban,
sólo cacareaban,
sólo aullaban.
Su lenguaje no se manifestó claramente
cada quien gritó diferente.
Cuando escucharon esto el Creador y
                        el Formador,
—No resultó bien,
no hablaron, se dijeron entre sí.
—No ha sido posible que digan nuestros nombres,
el de nosotros sus creadores
                sus formadores.
—No está bien, dijeron entre sí Alom,
                              K'ajolom.

Entonces les dijeron:
—Serán cambiados, porque no resultaron bien
                            no hablaron.
Hemos cambiado nuestro parecer:
su comida,
sus porciones;
sus habitaciones,
su lugar de reproducción.
Lo de ustedes serán los barrancos
                    los bosques porque no lograron adorarnos
                                no lograron invocarnos.
Todavía hay quien mire hacia nosotros,
seres que adoren
seres que respeten, habremos de hacer.
Sólo acepten su destino,[28]
sus cuerpos serán masticados.
¡Que así sea!
Ese es su destino, les fue dicho,
cuando hicieron saber su voluntad a los animales pequeños
                            animales grandes que hay
                                    [sobre la Tierra.

Entonces probaron de nuevo
            intentaron otra vez,
            probaron crear a los que los invocaran,
porque no escucharon su habla para llamarlos;
no fue claro y
no resultó.
De esta manera sus carnes fueron destinadas a ser comidas
se decidió su oficio: ser comidos
                    ser muertos los animales que hay sobre la Tierra.
Fue así como se intentó de nuevo con gente creada
                        gente formada por
                            [el Creador
                            el Formador;
                            la Concebidora
                            el Engendrador.

—Intentémoslo de nuevo
¿Acaso no se acerca la época de la siembra y
                              el amanecer?
Construyamos quien nos sustente
                    quien nos guarde.
Si no, ¿cómo habremos de ser nombrados
                         ser recordados sobre la Tierra?
Ya probamos con nuestras primeras obras
                    nuestras primeras criaturas.
Pero no se logró que fuésemos adorados ni
                              honrados por ellos.
Así pues probemos hacer seres obedientes
                         respetuosos
                         que nos sustenten
                         que nos cuiden, dijeron.

Luego fue la construcción,
          la creación; con tierra
                    con lodo hicieron el cuerpo.
Pero no lo vieron bien,
no estaba bien construido;
nada más estaba blando,
nada más estaba aguado
se deshacía
se desmoronaba y
se humedecía.
Su cabeza no se sostenía
su cara estaba para un lado
su cara estaba inmóvil
no podía voltear su mirada.
Habló al principio pero sin sentido.
Rápidamente se humedecía en el agua.[29]
—¡Todavía no!, se dijeron entre sí el Creador y
                              el Formador.
—Consultémoslo.

¡Que así sea!
Se ve que no va a caminar
        que no se va a multiplicar.
¡Que así sea!
Hay que pensarlo de nuevo, dijeron.
Y luego deshicieron
        desbarataron su obra
                su creación.
Dijeron entonces:
—¿Qué habremos de hacer?
Que se realice,
que aparezcan
nuestros adoradores
quienes nos invoquen, dijeron cuando lo pensaron de nuevo.
—Mejor digámosle a Xpiyakok
                Ixmukane;
                Deidad del amanecer
                Deidad del anochecer,
que consulten la cuenta de los días
        la división de las semillas,[30] se
                        [dijeron a sí mismos el Creador
                                el Formador.
Luego hablaron con Xpiyakok
                Ixmukane.
Esto es, pues, lo que les dijeron a los adivinos
Abuela del Sol
Abuela de la claridad, como son llamados por el Creador
                                el Formador.
Éstos son los nombres de Xpiyakok
                Ixmukane.

Dijo entonces Jun Raqan junto con la Majestuosa Serpiente
                                [Emplumada
cuando dijeron a los sacerdotes[31]
        a los constructores

                    a los adivinos:
—Encuentren,
revelen cómo habremos de formar la gente creada
                              la gente formada
                                   [para que nos mantenga
                                      que nos guarde.

Que nos llame y
que nos recuerde.
Que venga pues tu palabra comadrona
                              anciano guía,
                              nuestra abuela
                              nuestro abuelo, Xpiyakok
                                        Ixmukane.

Que lleguen la siembra y
          el amanecer
para ser invocados
para ser adorados
para ser recordados por gente creada
                         gente formada;
                         la gente de madera
                         la gente hecha.
¡Que así sea!
Hagan honor a su nombre Deidad del amanecer
                         Deidad del anochecer;
                         dos veces Concebidora,
                         dos veces Engendrador;
                         anciana madre
                         anciano padre;
                         los de las piedras preciosas[32]
                         los de las joyas;
                         los talladores,
                         los escultores;
                         los de la superficie verde
                         los de la bóveda azul;
                         maestros del incienso
                         maestros artesanos[33]

                              abuela del Sol
                              abuela de la claridad. —Así llamados por
                                 nuestro
                                    [Creador y
                                 nuestro
                                    [Formador—.
Pasen sus manos sobre el maíz
                    sobre el tz'ite',[34]
para que se haga
para que se aclare si hemos de escarbar y
                    si hemos de esculpir su boca,
                              su cara en madera,
                                    [les fue dicho
a los sacerdotes.
De ahí entonces se echó
               se adivinó sobre el maíz
                    sobre el tz'ite' la cuenta de los días,
                              de la formación.
Dijeron entonces aquella abuela,
               aquel abuelo;
el abuelo era el del tz'ite', Xpiyakok por nombre;
la abuela sacerdotisa,
            creadora asistente,[35] Ixmukane por nombre.
Así dijeron entonces cuando comenzaron la cuenta de los días:
—¡Que se encuentre,
y que se revele!
Díganlo que nuestros oídos escuchan.
Que hable
que se pronuncie.
Solamente que se encuentre la madera precisa,
                    la que deber ser
                              [esculpida por el Creador
                              por el Formador.

Si son los que sustenten
        los que guarden
¡Que se haga la siembra y

el amanecer!
Tú maíz
tú tz'ite'
tú cuenta de los días
        de la formación, has de trabajar
                has de mandar, le dijeron al maíz,
                        al tz'ite';
                        al conteo de los
                              [días;
                        a la formación.
—Ten vergüenza, tú Uk'u'x Kaj,
no decepciones la boca
        la cara de la Majestuosa Serpiente Emplumada,
                                [dijeron.
Luego respondieron en forma directa:
—Buenos saldrán los muñecos de madera
            gente de madera que hable
                      que converse sobre la faz de
                          [la Tierra.
¡Que así sea!
Dijeron entonces.

Al momento que hablaron, fueron hechos los muñecos,
                        la gente de madera;
parecían humanos en su hablado
parecían humanos en su conversación;
fue la gente que pobló la Tierra,
se reprodujeron
tuvieron hijas
tuvieron hijos los muñecos
        la gente de madera.
Pero no tenían espíritu[36] y
    no tenían pensamiento;
        no se acordaban de sus Creadores
                de sus Formadores.

Solamente caminaron
        gatearon.
Ya no se acordaban de Uk'u'x Kaj.
Así, pues, fueron juzgados:
sólo fue un intento
sólo fue una demostración de gente.
Hablaron al principio; pero sus caras eran secas,
no tenían consistencia sus piernas ni
                sus brazos;
no tenían sangre ni
        color;[37]
todavía no tenían sudor ni
        grasa.
Sus mejillas estaban secas
parecían máscaras;
tiesas estaban sus piernas
        sus manos;
hacían ruido, sus cuerpos.
Así, pues, no supieron comportarse ante el Creador
                el Formador;
                el Dador de vida
                el Dador del corazón.
Al principio fue mucha la gente que estuvo sobre la Tierra.

He aquí, pues, su aniquilación
        su desaparición;
        su destrucción.
Fueron muertos los muñecos
        la gente de madera.
Se pensó inundarlos por parte de Uk'u'x Kaj,
una gran inundación se hizo
que cayó sobre los muñecos
        la gente de madera.
De tz'ite' era el cuerpo del hombre que labraron el Creador
                el Formador;

de sibaque[38] fue el cuerpo de la mujer que quisieron
[hacer el Creador
el Formador.

Pero no fueron competentes
y tampoco hablaron ante sus creadores
sus formadores;
quienes los habían hecho,
quienes les dieron vida.
Por eso fueron aniquilados
inundados.
Cayó una gran trementina del Cielo,
vino el Escarbador[39] como se llama al que les escarbó los ojos
vinieron los murciélagos decapitadores[40] que les cortaban sus cabezas,
vino el jaguar masticador[41] que comió sus carnes,
vino el jaguar batidor que revolvió
desparramó sus huesos
sus nervios.
Fueron quebrados,
fueron astillados sus huesos.
Fueron escarmentados por incompetencia ante su madre creadora y
ante su padre creador,
ante Uk'u'x Kaj, llamado
Jun Raqan.
Por ello se oscureció la faz de la Tierra,
comenzó un temporal;[42]
llovía de día,
llovía de noche.
Entraron entonces los animales pequeños
los animales grandes;
sus caras fueron cortadas con palos y
piedras.
Hablaron todas sus tinajas,
sus comales;
sus platos;
sus ollas;
su nixtamal,[43]

sus piedras de moler.
Todo lo disponible se hizo presente.
—Nos provocaste mucho daño,
nos mordiste
ahora serán ustedes los mordidos, les dijeron sus perros y
sus chompipes.[44]
Sus piedras de moler dijeron:
—En nuestra cara ustedes molían todos los días
día tras día;
al anochecer
al amanecer;
siempre joli
joli
juk'i
juk'i[45] sobre nuestras caras.
Éste era nuestro oficio ante ustedes,
cuando aún eran gente,
ahora probarán nuestras fuerzas
los moleremos
y haremos polvo con sus cuerpos, les dijeron sus piedras de moler.
Luego sus perros les dijeron, cuando hablaron:
—¿Por qué no nos daban de comer?
Sólo nos echaban
nos sacaban;
tenían un palo para echarnos cuando comían;
siempre les teníamos miedo
porque no hablábamos.
Por poco moríamos de hambre por su causa.
Pero ¿cómo iban a saberlo?
Si son incompetentes
con ustedes habríamos perecido.
Ahora probarán los dientes que tenemos en la boca:
¡Los morderemos!, les dijeron los perros cuando les destrozaron
[sus caras.
Luego sus comales
sus ollas les dijeron:

—Mucho dolor nos causaste;
nuestras bocas están tiznadas
nuestras caras están tiznadas;
siempre estábamos sobre el fuego
ustedes nos quemaban
porque no sentíamos dolor.
Pruébenlo ahora: ¡Los quemaremos!, dijeron sus ollas.
Y todos les destrozaron sus caras.

Las piedras
los tenamastes[46] que estaban en el fuego se lanzaron con ímpetu a
sus cabezas.
Les hicieron daño:
desesperados,
corrían apresurados,
querían subir sobre las casas;
        pero las casas se desmoronaban y ellos caían;
querían subir sobre los árboles y
        los árboles los rechazaban,
querían entrar en las cuevas y
        las cuevas se cerraban ante ellos.
Así fue, pues, la destrucción de esa gente
        la gente formada,
la gente desperdiciable
    cambiable;
fueron desaparecidos
se les destrozó sus bocas
        sus caras a todos.
Se dice ahora que sus descendientes son los micos que habitan los
bosques;
son su señal porque sólo madera se empleó para sus
        [cuerpos por el Creador,
        por el Formador.

Son los micos que parecen gente
señal de una generación de gente creada
        de gente formada;

que sólo eran muñecos y
  sólo gente de madera.

Cuando apenas había poca claridad sobre la faz de la Tierra y aún
[no había Sol,
había un ser que se enorgullecía de sí mismo,
Wuqub Kak'ix[47] era su nombre.
Ya estaban el Cielo y
la Tierra,
pero todavía era tenue la luz del Sol y
de la Luna.
Decía éste entonces,
cuando él era como la luz de la gente que había sido inundada
cual si fuera prodigioso en su esencia[48]
—Yo soy grandioso sobre la gente creada
la gente formada.
Soy su Sol y
soy su claridad;
ellos además a mí es al que miran.
¡Que así sea!
Es grande mi esplendor
soy camino y
andar seguro para la gente porque de plata son mis ojos que brillan
cual piedras preciosas
cual gemas verdes.[49]
Asimismo mis dientes resplandecen de piedras como la faz del Cielo.[50]
En cuanto a mi nariz, resplandece tan lejos como si fuera la Luna.

Es de plata mi trono
que ilumina la faz de la Tierra cada vez que salgo de ese trono.
Así, pues, soy el Sol
        soy la Luna para las nacidas en claridad
                los nacidos en claridad.
¡Que así sea!
Porque mi mirada llega muy lejos, decía Wuqub Kak'ix.

Pero no era cierto que Wuqub Kak'ix fuera el Sol,
nada más se vanagloriaba
de sus plumas y
de sus joyas preciosas.
Su vista nada más cubría su alrededor
no se extendía a todo el espacio debajo del Cielo.
Y es que, todavía, no se veía la cara del Sol,
                ni de la Luna,
                ni de las estrellas.
Aún no había amanecido.
Por esta razón se envanecía Wuqub Kak'ix como si fuera el Sol
                        como si fuera la Luna.
Aún no se había mostrado
      no se había manifestado la luz del Sol
              ni de la Luna.
Sólo ambicionaba grandeza y
              ventaja
cuando ocurrió la inundación de los muñecos
              de la gente de madera.

Ahora vamos a contar cómo murió Wuqub Kak'ix,
            cómo fue derrotado
            cómo fue hecha la gente por
                      [parte del Creador,
                      del Formador.

Éste es el principio de su derrota

la caída del día de Wuqub Kak'ix por parte de dos
[muchachos, Junajpu,⁵¹ llamado uno
Xbalamke,⁵² el nombre del segundo.
Éstos eran dioses.
Como vieron mal la soberbia que quiso hacer ante Uk'u'x Kaj,
se dijeron los muchachos:
—No está bien que esto sea así.
Todavía no hay gente sobre la faz de la Tierra.
Así, pues, probemos tirarle con nuestras cerbatanas cuando esté
[comiendo.
¡Tirémosle aquí,
ocasionémosle una enfermedad!
Que se acabe su riqueza
su jade,
su plata,
sus joyas,
sus gemas que lo envanecen.
Si no, así lo hará toda la gente,
que no se origine poder sólo de riqueza.
¡Que así sea!
Dijeron los muchachos y cada quien cargó su cerbatana.

Wuqub Kak'ix tenía dos hijos: el primero era Sipakna⁵³
el segundo era Kabraqan.⁵⁴
Chimalmat⁵⁵ era el nombre de la madre de los dos,
la esposa de Wuqub Kak'ix.

Mientras tanto, Sipakna nada más jugaba con las grandes montañas
con el volcán de Fuego,
el volcán de Acatenango,
el Pekul,
el Ya' xkanul,
el Makamob,
el Julisnab⁵⁶ como se llamaba a esas montañas cuando amaneció.
Sólo una noche necesitaba Sipakna para hacer surgir estas montañas.
En cuanto a Kabraqan, éste movía las montañas

meneaba pequeñas montañas
grandes montañas.
Y así era como se envanecían los hijos de Wuqub Kak'ix.
—¡Yo soy el Sol!, decía Wuqub Kak'ix.
—¡Yo soy el que hace la Tierra!, decía Sipakna.
—¡Yo soy el que sacude el Cielo,
el que derriba toda la Tierra!, decía Kabraqan.
Pero solamente eran hijos de Wuqub Kak'ix,
solamente de ahí tomaron su grandeza,
siguiendo el ejemplo de su padre.

Esto lo vieron mal los muchachos.
Aún no había sido creada nuestra primera madre
nuestro primer padre.
De ahí que se planificó su muerte
su desaparición por parte de los muchachos.

Esto es, pues, el tiro de cerbatana contra Wuqub Kak'ix
por parte de los dos muchachos.
Contaremos ahora la derrota de cada uno de aquellos que se habían
ensoberbecido.

Wuqub Kak'ix tenía un gran árbol de nance
era la comida de Wuqub Kak'ix,
se alimentaba de la fruta de nance.
Subía al árbol todos los días
esta manera de alimentarse había sido vista por Junajpu y
Xbalamke.
Aguardando debajo del árbol de Wuqub Kak'ix
escondidos entre las hojas del árbol estaban los dos muchachos
cuando llegó Wuqub Kak'ix y de una vez sobre su comida, el nance.
Cuando fue herido de un tiro de cerbatana por parte de Junajpu,[57]
el tiro de cerbatana dio precisamente en su quijada,
gritó cuando se vino del árbol y
cayó al suelo.

Corriendo se fue Junajpu
de verdad que fue rápido para apoderarse de él;
pero Wuqub Kak'ix le arrancó el brazo a Junajpu
de una vez lo perdió
        se lo arrancó desde el hombro;
y sólo así Junajpu soltó a Wuqub Kak'ix.
Pero estuvo bien
al principio no fueron derrotados por Wuqub Kak'ix.
Llevó pues el brazo de Junajpu, Wuqub Kak'ix cuando se fue para su
casa; sólo que llegó sosteniendo con cuidado su quijada.
—¿Qué le ha sucedido a usted?, dijo Chimalmat, esposa de Wuqub
Kak'ix
—¿Qué ha de ser?
Los dos malvados me tiraron con cerbatana
        me dislocaron la quijada por eso tengo flojos
                         [los dientes;
me duele demasiado; pero antes que todo traje algo:
sobre el fuego debe estar
sobre el fuego debemos colgarlo.
Para cuando vengan a traerlo veremos si de verdad son tan
                        [malvados, dijo
Wuqub Kak'ix y colgó el brazo de Junajpu.
Por su lado meditaban Junajpu y
            Xbalamke.
Le hablaron entonces a un abuelo
de verdad era blanco el cabello del abuelo,
junto a una abuela
de verdad, era muy humilde la abuela;
ambos encorvados ya, por su ancianidad,
Saqi nim aq era el nombre del abuelo
Saqi nim sis era el nombre de la abuela.[58]
Dijeron entonces los muchachos a la abuela
           al abuelo:
—Permitan acompañarlos
vamos a traer nuestro brazo donde Wuqub Kak'ix
nosotros sólo los seguiremos.

"Éstos son nietos que acompañamos, ya están muertos su madre y
su padre.
Así, pues, nos siguen y
van detrás de nosotros,
tal vez los regalemos porque nosotros sólo sabemos sacar gusanos
[de las muelas".
Han de decir para que parezcamos niños ante Wuqub Kak'ix.
[De todas maneras,
nosotros estaremos para aconsejarlos, dijeron los dos muchachos.
—Está bien, respondieron.

Entonces se pusieron en camino,
Wuqub Kak'ix se encontraba recostado ante su trono
cuando pasaron la abuela
el abuelo, los dos muchachos jugaban detrás de ellos
Cuando pasaron al pie de la casa del Señor,
Wuqub Kak'ix estaba gritando por el dolor de muelas.
Al ver Wuqub Kak'ix al abuelo
a la abuela que iban acompañados:
—¿De dónde vienen, abuelo nuestro?, preguntó el Señor.
—Nada más buscamos nuestro alimento, Señor, contestaron.
—¿Qué es su comida? ¿No son sus hijos los que los acompañan?
—De ninguna manera, Señor, son nuestros nietos a quienes tenemos
[lástima;
que cada porción de comida
cada pedazo lo compartimos con ellos, Señor, dijeron la abuela
el abuelo.
Mientras tanto, el Señor se moría por el dolor de los dientes y
apenas podía hablar:
—Yo les ruego a ustedes,
les pido que tengan lástima de mí.
¿Qué es lo que pueden hacer?
¿Qué es lo que curan?, dijo entonces el Señor.
—Solamente sacamos gusanos de los dientes
solamente curamos ojos,

solamente volvemos a su lugar los huesos, Señor, respondieron
[entonces.
—Está muy bien. Cúrenme los dientes
que de verdad me hacen sufrir cada día
ya no se aguanta.
Ya no puedo dormir por eso y de mis ojos.
Dos malvados me tiraron con su cerbatana y desde entonces no he
[podido comer,
así, pues, tengan piedad de mí,
mis dientes deben estar flojos.
—Está bien, Señor,
son gusanos los que causan dolor
sólo hay que cambiarle sus dientes.
—Tal vez no está bien que me saquen los dientes porque soy Señor,
mi ornamento son mis dientes
junto con mis ojos.
—Pondremos otros en su lugar
hechos de hueso molido.
Pero esto del hueso molido era únicamente maíz blanco.
—Está bien pues que los saquen. Denme socorro, replicó.
Le sacaron entonces los dientes a Wuqub Kak'ix
solamente fueron granos de maíz blanco los que pusieron en su lugar
y sólo estos granos de maíz blanco eran los que resplandecían en
[su boca.
De inmediato decayeron sus facciones,
ya no parecía ser un gran Señor.
Terminaron de sacarle los dientes con jade que brillaban en su boca.
De inmediato le curaron[59] los ojos a Wuqub Kak'ix
le desollaron los ojos,
acabaron sacándole sus joyas sin que lo sintiera,
estaba con la miraba perdida
cuando terminaron de despojarlo de lo que se enorgullecía.
Esto era idea de Junajpu y
Xbalamke.
Así fue, la muerte de Wuqub Kak'ix
y así recuperó su brazo Junajpu.[60]

Luego murió Chimalmat
la esposa de Wuqub Kak'ix.

Así, se perdió la riqueza de Wuqub Kak'ix,
fue un médico quien tomó sus joyas y
sus gemas;
con las cuales se ensoberbecía aquí sobre la Tierra.[61]
El genio de la abuela
el genio del abuelo lo lograron,
luego recuperaron su brazo
lo volvieron a implantar en su lugar
y quedó bien otra vez.
Sólo para lograr la muerte de Wuqub Kak'ix obraron de esta manera,
porque les pareció mal que éste fuera soberbio.
Enseguida se fueron los dos muchachos y lo que habían hecho
[era nada
más la voluntad de Uk'u'x Kaj.

He aquí entonces los hechos de Sipakna, primer hijo de Wuqub Kak'ix.
—Yo soy el creador de las montañas, decía Sipakna.
Sipakna se estaba bañando a la orilla de un río cuando pasaron
cuatrocientos[62] muchachos arrastrando un tronco,
puntal de su cabaña.
Eran cuatrocientos los que arrastraban
los que cortaron un gran árbol para cumbrera
[de su cabaña.
Entonces se fue Sipakna,
llegó donde estaban los cuatrocientos muchachos:
—¿Qué es lo que están haciendo, muchachos?
—Sólo estamos tratando de levantar este tronco, y llevarlo
[en hombros.
—Yo lo levantaré. ¿Adónde hay que llevarlo? ¿Para qué quieren
[este tronco?
—Es la cumbrera de nuestra cabaña.
—¡Está bien!, dijo.

Luego arrastró y
        lo llevó en hombros hasta la puerta de la cabaña de los
cuatrocientos muchachos.
—Mejor quédate con nosotros, muchacho.
¿Tienes madre o
        padre?
—No tengo, contestó.
—Te pedimos que mañana nos ayudes a levantar
                        [otro tronco
                                puntal de nuestra cabaña.
—¡Bueno!, contestó.
Enseguida los cuatrocientos muchachos empezaron a deliberar:
—A este muchacho ¿qué le habremos de hacer?
Debemos matarlo, porque no está bien lo que hace. Sólo él levanta
                                [un tronco.
Escarbemos un gran hoyo y
allí lo echaremos a ese hoyo:
¡Anda a sacar la tierra del hoyo!, le diremos.
Cuando esté agachado en el hoyo le arrojaremos encima el
                                [gran tronco.
Allí, pues, que muera en el hoyo, dijeron los cuatrocientos muchachos.

Luego empezaron a escarbar un gran hoyo,
grande en profundidad.
Entonces mandaron a Sipakna:
—Te rogamos por favor
anda a escarbar la tierra porque nosotros ya no llegamos, le dijeron.
—Está muy bien, dijo entonces cuando bajó al hoyo.
—Nos avisas cuando esté escarbada la tierra
debes bajar muy profundo, le dijeron.
—Sí, contestó.
Luego empezó a escarbar el hoyo;
pero sólo fue un hoyo
donde él podía resguardarse porque sabía que lo querían matar.
De ahí que escarbó un gran hoyo al lado
hizo una segunda excavación para salvarse.

—¿Hasta dónde vas?, le fue preguntado por los cuatrocientos
[muchachos.
—¡Todavía estoy escarbando!, los llamaré cuando termine de
[escarbar, contestó
Sipakna desde el hoyo. Pero no estaba escarbando un hoyo para su
sepultura, sino que estaba escarbando otro para resguardarse.
Luego, Sipakna gritó a los muchachos.
Ya estaba a salvo dentro del hoyo, cuando llamó Sipakna:
—Vengan,
llévense el asiento de la tierra que he escarbado.
De verdad muy profundo he ahondado.
¿Pueden oír mi llamado?
En cuanto al llamado de ustedes sólo se escuchan ecos,
es como si ustedes estuvieran a un nivel
dos niveles, así se oye, dijo
[Sipakna desde
el hoyo.
Allí estaba escondido,
cuando llamaba desde el fondo del hoyo.
Mientras tanto los muchachos arrastraron el gran tronco
y de una vez lo arrojaron con fuerza hacia el fondo del hoyo.
—No está.
No habla.
¡Escuchemos su grito cuando muera!, se dijeron entre sí,
hablando en secreto,
cada quien se tapó la cara
mientras caía el tronco.
De ahí se escuchó un grito,
sólo se le escuchó una llamada cuando cayó el tronco al fondo.
—¡Qué bien! Ya estuvo.
Hemos hecho muy bien con él,
está muerto.
¿Quién lo mandó a hacer lo que hace
lo que trabaja?
¡Que así sea!
En primer lugar, se metió con nosotros,

en medio de nosotros, los cuatrocientos muchachos,

[dijeron entonces,
estaban contentos.

—Ahora vamos a fabricar nuestra bebida,[63]
han de pasar tres días, y
en tres días brindaremos por nuestra construcción,

nuestra cabaña, nosotros los
[cuatrocientos muchachos, dijeron.

—Mañana habremos de verlo,
pasado mañana también,
Veremos si no vienen las hormigas entre la tierra cuando hieda

cuando se pudra.

Hasta entonces se contentará nuestro corazón,
entonces tomaremos nuestra bebida, dijeron.
Todo esto lo escuchaba Sipakna desde el hoyo,
todo lo que decían los muchachos.
Al día siguiente, se alborotaron las hormigas: caminaban,

se arremolinaban,
se amontonaron debajo del tronco;

unas traían cabellos
otras pedazos de uñas de Sipakna.
Cuando vieron esto los muchachos, dijeron:
—¿Acaso no hemos terminado con el malvado?
Sólo miren las hormigas:
¡Salen por montón,
se arremolinan!
Unas traen cabellos,
otras pedazos de uñas.
Lo hemos derrotado, se dijeron entre sí.

Pero Sipakna estaba vivo:
se había cortado los cabellos de su cabeza
se había cortado las uñas con los dientes y se las daba a las hormigas.
De ahí que los cuatrocientos muchachos creyeran que había muerto.

Después de esto, su bebida estaba lista al tercer día

se emborracharon todos los muchachos;
estaban ebrios los cuatrocientos muchachos,
ya no sentían nada,
cuando la cabaña fue derrumbada sobre ellos por parte de Sipakna.
Todos fueron golpeados;
no hubo uno solo
            ni dos que sobrevivieran de los cuatrocientos muchachos;
fueron muertos por Sipakna,
hijo de Wuqub Kak'ix.

Así, pues, fue la muerte de los cuatrocientos muchachos.
Se dice que se convirtieron en estrellas,
las Pléyades así llamadas;
aunque esto sólo puede ser un juego de palabras.
Ahora contaremos la derrota de Sipakna por los dos
                                    [muchachos Junajpu y
                                        Xbalamke.

He aquí la derrota,
        la muerte de Sipakna;
cuando fue vencido por los dos muchachos Junajpu y
                                        Xbalamke.
Lo que hería el corazón de estos jóvenes
era la muerte de los cuatrocientos muchachos por parte de Sipakna.

Éste sólo pescados
sólo cangrejos buscaba en las orillas de los ríos;
esto era lo que comía todos los días.
Durante el día se paseaba buscando su comida y
durante la noche cargaba montañas.

Enseguida se falsificó un gran cangrejo por parte de Junajpu y
                                        Xbalamke:
le pusieron patas de gallo[64]
la flor que se recolecta en los bosques;

esto sirvió como antebrazo del cangrejo
las que ya estaban abiertas sirvieron para pinzas;
una piedra con forma de concha sirvió para imitar una
[caparazón ruidosa
de cangrejo.
Luego lo fueron a poner debajo de un peñasco
debajo de una gran montaña,
Me'awan se llama la montaña[65] donde
[fue vencido.
Después se fueron los muchachos a encontrar a Sipakna a la
[orilla del río.
—¿Adónde vas, muchacho?, le fue dicho a Sipakna.
—No voy a ninguna parte, sólo busco mi comida, muchachos,
[contestó Sipakna.
—¿Qué es tu comida?
—Sólo pescados
sólo cangrejos; pero aquí no los encuentro.
Desde hace dos días que me he quedado sin comer
y ya no aguanto el hambre, dijo Sipakna a Junajpu y
Xbalamke.
—Hay un cangrejo allá en el fondo del barranco,
de verdad que es grande el cangrejo;
tal vez te apetezca comerlo.
A nosotros nos mordió cuando quisimos agarrarlo.
Por eso le tenemos miedo.
Si no se ha ido, puedes ir a atraparlo, dijeron Junajpu y
Xbalamke.
—¡Tengan lástima de mí!
Vengan a enseñármelo, muchachos, dijo Sipakna.
—No queremos, ve tú solo;
no te perderás, sólo sigue la vega del río
y llegarás al pie de una gran montaña,
cuando llegues estará haciendo ruido en el fondo del barranco,
[dijeron Junajpu y
Xbalamke.
—Les ruego que tengan lástima de mí.

Tal vez no lo encuentre, muchachos.
Vengan a enseñármelo.
Hay gran cantidad de pájaros
que pueden tirar con cerbatana y yo sé dónde se encuentran,
                                    [dijo entonces Sipakna.
Su humillación convenció a los muchachos:
—¿Y si no lo atrapas?, porque sólo por eso regresamos contigo
Nosotros ya no lo intentaremos porque muerde al instante,
nosotros entramos boca abajo y enseguida se asustó
entramos boca arriba y por poco lo alcanzamos;
por eso es mejor que tú entres boca arriba, le dijeron.
—¡Está muy bien!, dijo Sipakna.

Luego se fueron, ya iba acompañado Sipakna,
se fueron
llegaron al fondo del barranco;
allí estaba tendido de lado el cangrejo
roja y blanca era su caparazón debajo del barranco,
así se miraba la parte que no estaba encubierta.
—¡Qué bien!, exclamó Sipakna con alegría.
Habría querido tenerlo de una vez en la boca porque de verdad
                                    [se moría de hambre;
habría querido comerlo de una vez.

Quiso entrar boca abajo,
intentó entrar;
pero el cangrejo subió boca arriba.
Entonces volvió a salir.
—¿No lo has encontrado?, le preguntaron.
—Todavía no, subió boca arriba,
                por poco y lo atrapo.
Tal vez sea mejor que entre boca arriba, agregó.

Luego se fue metiendo boca arriba
entró por completo,
ya sólo sus rodillas se miraban,

como si se lo hubieran tragado
cuando se derrumba la gran montaña sobre su pecho.
Ya no pudo voltearse,
en piedra se convirtió Sipakna.

Así, pues, fue la derrota de Sipakna por parte de los muchachos
[Junajpu y
Xbalamke.
Aquel que hacía montañas, según la tradición antigua
primer hijo de Wuqub Kak'ix.
Debajo de una montaña
llamada Me'awan, fue vencido.
Sólo por prodigio fue derrotado el segundo de los soberbios.
Ahora vamos a contar otro relato.

El tercero de los soberbios,
era el segundo hijo de Wuqub Kak'ix, llamado Kabraqan.
—Yo soy el destructor de montañas, decía.
Pero fueron Junajpu y
Xbalamke quienes vencieron a Kabraqan.
Dijeron Jun Raqan
Ch'ipi Kaqulja
Raxa Kaqulja cuando hablaron con Junajpu y
Xbalamke:
—El segundo hijo de Wuqub Kak'ix, es otro,
otro al que hay que vencer.
Ésta es nuestra voluntad porque no está bien lo que hacen sobre
[la Tierra:
quieren sobrepasar al Sol en grandeza
en poder,
y esto no debe ser así.
Convénzanlo a irse hacia allá donde sale el Sol, dijo Jun Raqan
[a los dos muchachos.
—Está bien, respetable Señor.
Se tiene que ir, no está bien lo que miramos.

¿Acaso no está usted,
                usted su excelencia
                usted Uk'u'x Kaj?, dijeron los muchachos al acatar
                                [la palabra
de Jun Raqan.

Mientras tanto Kabraqan seguía sacudiendo montañas.
Al más pequeño golpe de sus pies sobre la tierra,
se derrumbaban de inmediato grandes montañas,
                        pequeñas montañas por su causa.
En eso lo encontraron los muchachos.
—¿Adónde vas, muchacho? le dijeron a Kabraqan.
—No voy a ninguna parte, sólo estoy derribando montañas,
yo soy pues quien las sacude mientras haya Sol,
                        mientras haya claridad,[66] dijo
                                [cuando habló.

A continuación preguntó Kabraqan a Junajpu y
                                Xbalamke:
—¿De dónde vienen?
No los conozco.
¿Cómo se llaman?, dijo Kabraqan.
—No tenemos nombre, sólo somos cerbataneros,
                sólo ponemos trampas para pájaros en
                                [las montañas,
                simplemente somos pobres.
No poseemos nada, muchacho;
solamente a las pequeñas montañas
solamente a las grandes montañas vamos, muchacho.
De allí que hemos visto una gran montaña
que a cada instante crece
de verdad que se yergue altísima;
que cada vez rebasa todas las montañas.
Pero de allí ni siquiera uno
                ni dos pájaros pudimos atrapar, muchacho.

Pero ¿es verdad que tú derribas todas las montañas, muchacho?,

[dijeron

Junajpu y
Xbalamke a Kabraqan.
—¿De verdad han visto esa montaña como dicen?
¿Dónde se encuentra?
Tengo que verla
tengo que derribarla.
¿En dónde la vieron?
—Allá está pues,
donde sale el Sol, contestaron Junajpu y

Xbalamke.

—¡Bien! Guíen nuestro camino, les fue dicho a los dos muchachos.
—No simplemente así. Te tienes que ir en medio

entre nosotros te tienes que ir.

Uno de nosotros irá a tu lado izquierdo

otro a tu lado derecho;

porque tenemos nuestras cerbatanas y si hay pájaros les tiraremos,

[dijeron.

Muy contentos empezaron a probar sus cerbatanas;
pero en sus tiros no había bodoques de tierra cada vez que tiraban
sólo con su soplo derribaban a los pájaros; lo cual fue muy admirado
por Kabraqan.
Enseguida frotando palillos los muchachos[67] hicieron fuego y
pusieron a asar sus pájaros sobre el fuego.
A uno de los pájaros lo untaron con tizate,[68]
lo cubrieron con tierra blanca.
—Esto le daremos.
¡Que se lo trague!
Para cuando sienta el aroma de nuestros pájaros
que se están cocinando.
Así como la tierra que cubre este pájaro por obra nuestra
en la tierra lo echaremos;
así, en la tierra lo sepultaremos.
Si es gran sabio el Creador

el Formador

¡Que se haga la siembra y
          el amanecer!,[69] dijeron los muchachos.
—Porque es un deseo del corazón comer un bocado
                   comer carne;
así también desea el corazón de Kabraqan, dijeron entre sí,
                             [Junajpu y
                             Xbalamke.

Luego asaron los pájaros,
éstos se iban dorando al cocerse:
chorreaban,
caía la grasa de los pájaros
con una fragancia apetecible.
Ante esto Kabraqan sentía ganas de comérselos,
se le hacía agua la boca,
se mantenía deglutiendo
tragaba y se le escurría la saliva,
                 la baba por la fragancia de los pájaros.
Entonces preguntó:
—¿Qué es su comida?
De verdad es delicioso el aroma que siento.
Denme un pedazo, les dijo.
Le dieron un pájaro a Kabraqan
y ésta fue su derrota.
Cuando terminó de comer al pájaro, se fueron de nuevo
llegaron al Oriente donde estaba la gran montaña.
Pero para entonces Kabraqan ya no tenía fuerzas en los pies ni
                        en las manos;
ya no pudo hacer nada por la tierra con que untaron el pájaro
                           [que se comió.
Ya no hizo nada
no le hizo nada a la montaña;
no la destruyó
no la derribó.
Enseguida fue amarrado por los muchachos
le ataron los brazos en su espalda
le fueron aseguradas las manos por parte de los muchachos;

también le amarraron los tobillos en par
y enseguida lo arrojaron al suelo y lo enterraron.
De esta manera fue vencido Kabraqan tan sólo por Junajpu y
                                          Xbalamke
son innumerables las cosas que hicieron aquí sobre la Tierra.

Ahora contaremos el nacimiento de Junajpu y
                              Xbalamke;
habiendo relatado ya, la destrucción de Wuqub Kak'ix
                                     con la de Sipakna
                                     y la de Kabraqan aquí sobre
                                         [la Tierra.

Rox
CAPÍTULO TERCERO

Ahora diremos también el nombre de los padres de Junajpu y
                                                    Xbalamke.
Brindemos por ello
brindemos porque vamos a decir
                            a relatar la concepción de Junajpu y
                                                    Xbalamke.
Pero sólo la mitad vamos a contar
sólo una parte de la historia de sus padres.

Éste es su relato:
he aquí sus nombres, Jun Junajpu y
                        Wuqub Junajpu se llamaban;[70]
y los nombres de sus padres eran Xpiyakok e
                                    Ixmukane.
En la oscuridad
al amanecer nacieron Jun Junajpu y
                        Wuqub Junajpu de Xpiyakok e
                                    Ixmukane.
Ahora bien, Jun Junajpu engendró dos hijos,
                        dos varones: Jun Batz' se llamaba
el primogénito
                                        Jun Chowen se
                                            [llamaba
el segundo.[71]

Éste era el nombre de su madre: Ixbaqiyalo[72] le decían,
esposa de Jun Junajpu.
Ahora bien, Wuqub Junajpu no tenía esposa;
sólo estaba en edad para casarse,[73]
era el segundo,
sólo era un muchacho.
Eran grandes sabios,
tenían gran conocimiento,
ellos eran adivinos aquí sobre la faz de la Tierra;
de buena índole
y buenas costumbres.
Enseñaron las artes y el trabajo a Jun Batz' y
Jun Chowen, hijos de Jun Junajpu.
En flautistas,
en cantantes,
en cerbataneros,
escritores;[74]
así mismo en escultores,
en orfebres del jade
en orfebres de la plata se constituyeron Jun Batz' y
Jun Chowen.
En cuanto a Jun Junajpu y
Wuqub Junajpu solamente jugaban a los dados,
a la pelota, todos
[los días
De dos en dos jugaban
eran cuatro por todos.

Cuando se reunían para entretenerse en el campo de juego
llegaba un halcón[75] a observarlos,
era el mensajero de Jun Raqan,
Ch'ipi Kaqulja,
Raxa Kaqulja.
Ahora bien, para este halcón no quedaba lejos la Tierra
no quedaba lejos Xibalba,
y en un instante subía al Cielo a donde Jun Raqan.

Estuvieron bastante tiempo sobre la faz de la Tierra
después de haber muerto la madre de Jun Batz' y
                                    Jun Chowen.
Como era camino a Xibalba donde jugaban,
fueron escuchados por Jun Kame[76] y
                        Wuqub Kame, Señores de Xibalba:
—¿Qué es lo que está pasando sobre la faz de la Tierra?
Están saltando y
corren haciendo bulla.
¡Que los vayan a traer!
Que vengan a jugar pelota aquí,
que habremos de derrotarlos.
Ya no nos tienen deferencia,
    no nos respetan
y tampoco tienen vergüenza.
Que los vayan a jalar de allá arriba,
dijeron todos los de Xibalba al tomar
una decisión en conjunto.
Los llamados Jun Kame y
                Wuqub Kame eran los jueces supremos.[77]
En cuanto a los otros Señores, cada quien tenía su oficio y
                                    su autoridad dados
                                                    [por
Jun Kame y
Wuqub Kame.
Así pues, Xikiri Pat y
                Kuchuma Kik'[78] los nombres de los Señores,
tenían como oficio enfermar la sangre de la gente.[79]
Por aparte, Ajal Puj y
                Ajal Q'ana,[80] nombres de los Señores
tenían el oficio de hinchar a las personas
hacerles brotar pus de sus piernas
ponerles amarillenta la cara; lo que se llama ictericia.[81]
Tal era la autoridad de Ajal Puj y
                Ajal Q'ana.

Los siguientes Señores eran Ch'amiyabaq y
                    Ch'amiyajolom,[82] alguaciles de Xibalba;
cuyas varas eran de hueso.
La ocupación de éstos era enflaquecer a la gente,
hasta que los volvían sólo huesos
                    sólo calaveras.

Cuando se morían sólo el esqueleto se recogía.
Éste era el oficio de Ch'amiyabaq y
                    Ch'amiyajolom, así llamados.
Los otros eran los Señores Ajal Mes y
                    Ajal Toq'ob,[83] así llamados.
Su oficio era encontrarse de repente con la gente
provocando enemistad
ya sea detrás de la casa,
          delante de la casa donde los encontraran,
los herían hasta caer boca abajo en el suelo
                    hasta que murieran.
Ésta era la atribución de Ajal Mes y
                    Ajal Toq'ob, así nombrados.
En cuanto a los Señores Xik y
                    Patan,[84] así llamados,
su oficio era causar la muerte de la gente en los caminos,
muerte súbita, se denomina.
Llegaba la sangre a sus bocas
y morían vomitando sangre.
Así cada quien con su oficio y
                    su responsabilidad.[85]
Sólo oprimían la garganta,
          el pecho[86] de la gente para que muriera en los caminos.
Esto podía ocurrir estuvieran caminando o
                    estuvieran sentados.
Ésta era pues la ocupación de Xik y
                    Patan.

Éstos eran los que juntaron sus pensamientos,

cuando fueron acosados
cuando fueron perseguidos Jun Junajpu y
                    Wuqub Junajpu.
Lo que deseaban los de Xibalba eran los implementos de juego de
Jun Junajpu y
Wuqub Junajpu:
sus protectores de cuero
sus cinturones[87]
sus protectores de brazos
sus penachos
sus pañuelos protectores[88]
los atavíos de Jun Junajpu y
                    Wuqub Junajpu.

Ahora contaremos su ida a Xibalba
y cómo dejaron atrás a Jun Batz' y
                    Jun Chowen, hijos de Jun Junajpu.
Su madre ya había muerto
sobre eso, habrían de ser derrotados Jun Batz' y
                    Jun Chowen por Junajpu y
                                        Xbalamke.

Enseguida vinieron los mensajeros por parte de Jun Kame y
                                        Wuqub Kame:
—Vayan ustedes guardianes de la estera
vayan a ordenarles a Jun Junajpu y
                    Wuqub Junajpu.[89]
Díganles cuando lleguen con ellos:
"¡Que vengan!", mandan a decirles los Señores.
"Aquí es donde deben jugar pelota con nosotros;
que se levante nuestro ánimo con ellos.
De verdad estamos admirados de ellos.
Así pues que vengan", dicen los Señores.
"¡Que traigan sus instrumentos de juego!
su cinturón,

sus protectores de brazo
junto con su pelota. Dicen los Señores",
deben decir cuando lleguen, les fue dicho a los
mensajeros.
Los mensajeros eran tecolotes:
Tecolote Flecha,
Tecolote de una Pierna,
Tecolote Guacamaya,
Tecolote Cabeza,⁹⁰ eran llamados los mensajeros de Xibalba.
Tecolote Flecha era veloz como una flecha disparada,
Tecolote de una Pierna, solamente tenía una pierna pero tenía alas,
Tecolote Guacamaya tenía plumas de fuego y tenía alas
en cuanto a Tecolote Cabeza era sólo una cabeza
no tenía piernas; pero sí tenía alas.
Eran cuatro los mensajeros, con rango de guardianes de la estera.

Cuando salieron de Xibalba
de inmediato llegaron al campo de juego.
Jugaban allí Jun Junajpu y
Wuqub Junajpu en ese campo de pelota,
en la gran hondonada,⁹¹ como es llamada.
Se pararon los tecolotes a la orilla del campo para emitir su mensaje,
pero sólo repitieron las palabras de Jun Kame
Wuqub Kame;
Ajal Puj
Ajal Q'ana;
Ch'amiyabaq
Ch'amiyajolom;
Xikiri Pat
Kuchuma Kik';
Ajal Mes
Ajal Toq'ob;
Xik
Patan, el nombre de todos
[los Señores.
Su mensaje fue emitido por los tecolotes.

—¿De veras han hablado así los Señores Jun Kame y
                                    Wuqub Kame?
—Es verdad —dijeron—. ¡Vamos! Nosotros habremos de
                                    [acompañarlos.
"Que traigan todos sus implementos de juego"; han dicho los Señores.
—¡Está bien!
Sólo que deben esperarnos,
tenemos que ir a despedirnos de nuestra madre, contestaron los
                                    [muchachos.
Se fueron pues para su casa,
dijeron entonces a su madre —su padre ya estaba muerto—[92]
—Tenemos que irnos, madre nuestra;
acaban de llegar,
vinieron los mensajeros de los Señores a llevarnos.
"¡Que vengan!", han dicho; según manifiestan los enviados.
Pero aquí se quedará nuestra pelota, dijeron.
Enseguida fueron a amarrarla al tapanco de la casa.

—¡Volveremos!
Y jugaremos de nuevo.
Ustedes ocúpense de tocar flauta
          ocúpense del canto;
          continúen escribiendo.
          continúen esculpiendo.
Mantengan el calor del hogar
alegren el corazón de su abuela,[93] instruyeron a Jun Batz' y
                                    Jun Chowen al
                                    [despedirse.
Mientras tanto lloraba amargamente su madre, Ixmukane.
—Vámonos. No vamos a morir.
No se pongan tristes, dijeron al partir Jun Junajpu y
                                    Wuqub Junajpu.

Enseguida se fueron Jun Junajpu y
                    Wuqub Junajpu.

Iban guiados por los mensajeros
cuando bajaron al camino de Xibalba,
descendieron por unos escalones,
bajaron y salieron por unos barrancos de aguas turbulentas,[94]
                    barranco agitado
                    barranco ruidoso, se llamaba el lugar
                                                    [por
donde pasaron.
Pasaron luego en medio de turbulentas y espinadas corrientes,
eran incontables las espinas[95] pero no sufrieron daño.

Luego arribaron a la orilla de un río
                    a la orilla del río de sangre
pasaron allí sin beber sus aguas.
Luego llegaron a otro río
donde sólo corría agua podrida,[96]
y tampoco allí fueron derrotados cuando pasaron.

Enseguida llegaron donde se encontraban cuatro caminos
y allí sí fueron vencidos, donde se entrecruzan los cuatro caminos:
un camino era rojo
los otros eran un camino negro,
                    un camino blanco;
y el otro un camino amarillo.
Eran cuatro caminos.
Entonces habló el camino negro:
—A mí deben seguirme
yo soy el camino hacia los Señores, dijo el camino.
Allí pues comenzó su derrota,
al tomar el camino de Xibalba.

Cuando llegaron a la casa de consejo de los Señores de Xibalba
fueron vencidos de nuevo.
Los primeros que estaban sentados eran un muñeco de madera y
                    un maniquí adornados por
                                            [Xibalba.

A ellos saludaron primero:
—¡Buenos días, Jun Kame!, le dijeron al muñeco de madera.
—¡Buenos días, Wuqub Kame!, le dijeron al maniquí.
Pero no lograron vencerlos,
y de ahí que se rieran a carcajadas de ellos los Señores de Xibalba,
se burlaron de ellos porque prácticamente estaban vencidos.
En sus corazones ya estaban derrotados Jun Junajpu y
                                        Wuqub Junajpu.

Se siguieron riendo.
Hasta que hablaron Jun Kame y
                    Wuqub Kame:
—Está muy bien que vinieron,
mañana pondrán en juego su cinturón y
          sus protectores de brazos, les fue dicho.
—¡Siéntense en nuestra banca!, les fue dicho enseguida.
Pero era de piedra candente el banco que les dieron,
se quemaron en esa banca de piedra;
de verdad, quisieron darse vuelta sobre la banca pero no encontraron
                                        [alivio;
de verdad se tuvieron que levantar pero ya se habían quemado sus
                                        [sentaderas.
De nuevo se rieron los de Xibalba,
se descompusieron de la risa,
se originó un calambre de risa que llegó a sus corazones,
                              a su sangre,
                              a sus huesos;
se carcajeaban todos los Señores de Xibalba.
—Mejor váyanse a esa casa donde se les entregará su antorcha[97] y
                                        sus puros;
          al lugar donde han de dormir, les dijeron.

Luego llegaron a la Casa Oscura
donde sólo reinaba la oscuridad.
Enseguida se pusieron de acuerdo los de Xibalba:
—Mañana habremos de sacrificarlos,

49

que sea pronto
que mueran rápido por sus implementos de juego
                    su juego de pelota, dijeron entre sí los de
                                        [Xibalba.

En cuanto al juego de ellos, era un chay[98] redondo
"pedernal blanco" se llamaba el juego que jugaban los de Xibalba.
Era afilado lo que jugaban que de una vez desbarataba los huesos
                                                    [por
donde pasaba este instrumento de juego de Xibalba.

Entraron entonces Jun Junajpu y
                    Wuqub Junajpu a la Casa Oscura.
Luego les fueron a dejar una raja de ocote;
pero el ocote iba ya encendido desde que salió de donde
                                            [Jun Kame y
                                            Wuqub Kame;
también les llevaron un puro a cada uno; pero ya iban encendidos
desde que salieron de la casa de los Señores cuando se los
entregaron a Jun Junajpu y
                    Wuqub Junajpu.
Estaban de cuclillas en la oscuridad cuando llegaron los
portadores del ocote y
                de los puros;
resplandecía la antorcha que llevaban sus centinelas:
—Encienda cada quien su puro,
y así deben devolverlos al amanecer.
Que no se consuman, porque así hemos de recolectarlos. Han mandado
                                                    [a decirles
los Señores, les fue dicho.
Y así fueron derrotados:
se consumió el ocote,
y se acabaron los puros que les habían llevado.

Eran numerosas las pruebas de Xibalba,
de varias maneras eran los castigos:

la primera prueba era la Casa Oscura;
donde sólo reinaba oscuridad adentro.
La segunda era la Casa de Hielo, así llamada;
donde el frío era intenso,
el viento era helado y
en los resquicios penetraba el hielo.
La tercera prueba era la llamada Casa de Jaguares,
sólo jaguares había adentro:
se revolvían,
se arremolinaban;
gruñían y
estaban furiosos, esos jaguares, de estar encerrados en esa casa.
Casa de los Murciélagos se llamaba la cuarta prueba:
sólo murciélagos habitaban el lugar
sólo murciélagos había adentro
chillaban,
chirriaban y
revoloteaban en la casa.
Estaban encerrados los murciélagos
y no había lugar por donde pudieran salir.
La quinta prueba era la Casa de los Chayes, así llamada,
sólo chayes había adentro,
se entrecruzaban los chayes;
hacían ruido y
rechinaban unos contra otros dentro de la casa.

Eran bastantes las pruebas de Xibalba
pero no entraron a todas Jun Junajpu y
                    Wuqub Junajpu;
sólo mencionamos los nombres de esas casas de castigo.

Luego se presentaron Jun Junajpu y
                    Wuqub Junajpu ante Jun Kame y
                                        Wuqub Kame.
—¿Dónde están mis puros?

¿Dónde está mi raja de ocote que les fueron a dejar anoche?,
[les preguntaron.

—Los acabamos, Señor.

—¡Está bien!

Hoy se acabaron sus días.

Van a morir;

van a desaparecer;

vamos a acabarlos,[99]

aquí quedará oculta su presencia:[100]

—¡Serán sacrificados!, dijeron Jun Kame y
Wuqub Kame.

Enseguida fueron sacrificados

fueron enterrados.

"Lugar del sacrificio"[101] se llama el lugar donde los enterraron.

Le cortaron la cabeza a Jun Junajpu,

sólo su cuerpo enterraron junto al de su hermano menor.

—Vayan a dejar su cabeza en medio del árbol

aquel que está sembrado en el camino, dijeron Jun Kame y
Wuqub Kame.

Cuando fueron a poner la cabeza entre las ramas del árbol,

al punto fructificó aquel árbol.

No daba frutos;

sino hasta que se colocó la cabeza de Jun Junajpu entre sus ramas.

Éste es el árbol de jícaro[102] que le llamamos ahora,

"cabeza de Jun Junajpu", se le dice.

Se admiraron, entonces, Jun Kame y
Wukub Kame de la fructificación del árbol.

El fruto redondo estaba en todas partes

que ya no se distinguía la cabeza de Jun Junajpu

era igual a los demás frutos de jícaro.

Esto lo miraban todos los de Xibalba cuando llegaban a observarlo.

Grande en esencia se volvió para ellos aquel árbol porque todo ocurrió en un instante,

cuando se puso la cabeza de Jun Junajpu entre sus ramas.

Dijeron entonces los de Xibalba entre sí:

—Que nadie venga a cortar estos frutos y
que nadie se ponga debajo del árbol, dijeron

[restringiéndose a sí mismos,
limitándose a sí mismos

todos los de Xibalba.
Ya no se diferenciaba, pues, la cabeza de Jun Junajpu
ya era igual al fruto del árbol que ahora se llama jícaro.
Este acontecimiento fue muy comentado,
que lo escuchó una doncella;
y ahora vamos a relatar su llegada.

Ésta es la historia de una doncella,
hija de un Señor llamado Kuchuma Kik'.
Cuando lo escuchó una doncella
hija de uno de los Señores,
Kuchuma Kik' se llamaba este Señor e
Ixkik',[103] se llamaba la doncella.
Cuando escuchó lo que se decía del fruto de aquel árbol,
cuando se lo relató su propio padre
quedó maravillada de cuanto se le contaba.
—¿Será bueno ir a ver el árbol del que hablan?
De verdad es fragante, según dicen

según escucho, dijo entonces.

Enseguida se fue ella sola,
llegó al pie donde el árbol estaba sembrado,
en Pusbal Chaaj estaba plantado.
—¡Ah! ¿Qué clase de fruto será éste?
¿Será dulce el fruto de este árbol?
No he de morir,
no he de desaparecer si corto uno de sus frutos, dijo la doncella.
De pronto habló la calavera que estaba entre las ramas del árbol:
—¿Qué es lo que deseas de lo que son sólo huesos,
los objetos redondeados en las ramas de los árboles?, dijo la

[cabeza de

Jun Junajpu cuando le habló a la doncella.

—¿Los deseas?, agregó.

—¡Sí, los deseo!, contestó la doncella.

—¡Está bien!

Extiende tu mano derecha, que yo la vea, dijo la calavera.

—¡Sí!, respondió la doncella, extendiendo su mano derecha hacia la
                                                            [calavera.

En ese instante la calavera lanzó un chisguete de saliva que vino
                                                            [a dar

directamente en la palma de la mano de la doncella.

Cuando ella vio la palma de su mano que examinó de inmediato

ya no había saliva de la calavera en su mano.

—Sólo señal te he dejado con mi saliva
                        mi baba;

Mi cabeza ya no trabaja bien,

es sólo hueso,

ya no tiene carne.

Es como la cabeza de los grandes Señores:

sólo los músculos les dan apariencia.

Pero cuando se mueren, espantan a la gente a causa de sus huesos.

Así, pues, son sus hijos, como su saliva
                        como su baba;
                        ésa es la naturaleza de
                                [los hijos de los Señores
                                    sean éstos hijos de sabios,
                                        de oradores.

Su condición no se pierde cuando se van;
                        cuando completan sus días.

No se extingue,

no desaparece la faz de los Señores,
                        de los varones,
                        de los sabios,
                        de los oradores;

sino se queda en sus hijas,
                        sus hijos.

¡Que así sea!

Esto es, pues, lo que yo he hecho contigo.

Sube a la superficie de la Tierra que no has de morir,
                              porque entras en la palabra.¹⁰⁴
—¡Que así sea!
Dijo la cabeza de Jun Junajpu
              Wuqub Junajpu
pero no sólo fue idea de ambos lo que hicieron,¹⁰⁵
era el mandato de Jun Raqan
                  Ch'ipi Kaqulja,
                  Raxa Kaqulja.
Así regresó la doncella a su casa,
después que le fueron dados muchos consejos.
De inmediato fueron concebidos los hijos en su vientre por la sola
                                          [virtud
de la saliva
y así fueron engendrados Junajpu y
                  Xbalamke.
Llegó, pues, la joven a su casa y después de haberse cumplido seis
                                          [meses,
su estado fue advertido por su padre,
Kuchuma Kik' era el nombre del padre.

Hasta entonces se acordó de la joven su Señor padre
cuando se dio cuenta de que estaba embarazada.¹⁰⁶
Luego se reunieron en consejo todos los Señores, Jun Kame
                              Wuqub Kame con
Kuchuma Kik':
—Mi hija ya lleva un hijo en el vientre, Señores;
producto de su fornicación, exclamó Kuchuma Kik', cuando llegó
con los Señores.
—¡Está bien!
¡Interrógala!
Si no dice la verdad, que se le sacrifique,
que la lleven a sacrificar lejos de aquí.
—¡Está bien!
Honorables Señores, contestó y de inmediato fue a interrogar a su
                                          [hija:

—¿De quién es el hijo que llevas en el vientre, hija mía?, preguntó.
—No tengo hijo, padre mío
no ha habido hombre a quien haya conocido,[107] contestó ella.
—¡Está bien!
De verdad que eres una mujerzuela.
¡Sacrifíquenla!, ustedes guardianes de la estera.
¡Traigan de regreso su corazón dentro de un guacal![108]
¡Que los Señores puedan tenerlo en sus manos de inmediato! les
                                                            [dijo
a los tecolotes.
Eran cuatro los que se fueron
tomaron el guacal al partir,
cargaron en sus brazos a la doncella
y también llevaron el pedernal,
                    instrumento para sacrificarla.
—Todavía no debo desaparecer,[109]
            no me maten, mensajeros, porque no he fornicado,
lo que llevo en el vientre se generó por sí mismo,
sólo fui a admirar la cabeza de Jun Junajpu que está en Pusbal Chaaj.
¡Así que deténganse!
¡Que no haya sacrificio, mensajeros!, dijo la doncella cuando les
                                                            [habló.
—Pero ¿qué pondremos en lugar de tu corazón?
¿Acaso no nos fue dicho por tu padre?
"Traigan de regreso su corazón;
que le den vueltas con sus manos los Señores,
no lo dejarán caer;
hasta que asemeje ser una construcción de ellos.[110]
Tráiganlo pronto en una jícara
guarden el corazón en el fondo de la jícara".
¿No es esto, pues, lo que nos fue indicado?
¿Qué pondríamos adentro de la jícara?
Nosotros bien quisiéramos que no murieras, contestaron los
                                                            [mensajeros.
—¡Muy bien!
Este corazón no será de ellos.

¡Que así sea!
Como tampoco debe seguir siendo aquí la morada de ustedes.
No deben forzar a la gente hacia la muerte.
Después, de verdad, serán de ustedes los verdaderos fornicantes.
Después, también para Jun Kame y
                    Wukub Kame sólo sangre,
                              sólo savia coagulada será para
                                        [ellos.¹¹¹
¡Que así sea!
Que sea esto lo que arda en su presencia.
Que no sea un corazón el que se queme ante ellos.
¡Que así sea!
Utilicen el producto de árbol, dijo entonces la doncella.
Era rojo el jugo que brotó del árbol,
lo que se asentó en el guacal.
Luego se coaguló,
se hizo redondo el sustituto de su corazón.
Cuando se exprimió de nuevo la savia del árbol rojo,
era como sangre el jugo del árbol que sustituyó a su sangre.
Cuando se guardó la savia ahí adentro
el jugo del árbol rojo formó una capa parecida a la sangre;
de un rojo resplandeciente era lo que se guardó en el guacal
cuando el árbol fue sajado por la doncella.
"Árbol rojo de grana" se le llama,¹¹²
y se le denomina sangre por su savia color roja, se dice.
—Allá serán muy bien amados,
sobre la faz de la Tierra está lo que debe ser de ustedes, dijo la joven
                                        [a los tecolotes.
—¡Está bien, doncella!
Caminemos entonces,
te guiaremos hacia arriba
tu sólo debes seguir caminando;
mientras nosotros llevamos el reemplazo de tu corazón ante los
                                        [Señores, dijeron
los mensajeros.
Cuando llegaron ante la presencia de los Señores,

todos ellos estaban ansiosos.
—¿Todavía no está?, preguntó Jun Kame.
—Ya estuvo, Señores,
he aquí su corazón en el fondo del guacal.
—¡Muy bien! Veamos, dijo entonces Jun Kame.
Y tomándolo con los dedos lo levantó,
chorreaba por encima la sangre coagulada,
era de un rojo resplandeciente por la sangre.
—Aticen bien el fuego,
pónganlo sobre el fuego, dijo Jun Kame.
Enseguida lo pusieron sobre el fuego;
lo sintieron oloroso los de Xibalba
que terminaron levantándose todos;
se inclinaron encima.
Ciertamente muy dulce sintieron el humo de la sangre.

Y mientras ellos estaban agachados, se fueron los tecolotes,
los guías de la
[doncella.
La subieron a la orilla de un hoyo sobre la faz de la Tierra,
luego regresaron para abajo los guías.
De esta manera fueron vencidos los Señores de Xibalba por la doncella
que los engañó a todos.

Estaba entonces la madre de Jun Batz' y
Jun Chowen,[113]
cuando llegó la mujer llamada Ixkik'.
Cuando llegó entonces la mujer Ixkik' donde la madre de
[Jun Batz' y
Jun Chowen
llevaba a sus hijos en el vientre,
faltaba poco para el nacimiento de Junajpu y
Xbalamke, así llamados.
Cuando llegó la mujer ante la abuela,
le dijo la mujer a la abuela

—He llegado, Señora madre,
yo soy su nuera,
yo soy su hija, Señora madre, dijo cuando entró donde estaba
[la abuela.
—¿De dónde has venido?
En cuanto a mis pequeños hijos[114]
¿no murieron acaso en Xibalba?
Estos dos que aquí quedan son su señal
su descendencia,[115] Jun Batz' y
Jun Chowen, se llaman.
A saber de dónde vienes.
¡Vete de aquí!, le fue dicho a la doncella por parte de la abuela.
—Pero es verdad que soy su nuera,
desde hace tiempo que lo soy.
Es de Jun Junajpu lo que traigo.
¡Están vivos!
No están muertos Jun Junajpu y
Wuqub Junajpu;
ésta es la evidencia clara de lo ocurrido, Señora suegra.
Ya lo verá en los rostros de lo que traigo,[116] le fue dicho a la abuela.

Entonces se enfurecieron Jun Batz' y
Jun Chowen.
Sólo tocando flauta,
sólo con el canto se entretenían.
Sólo a escribir y
sólo a esculpir se dedicaban todos los días.
Esto consolaba el corazón de la abuela.

Dijo entonces la abuela:
—No quiero que seas mi nuera.
Es fruto de tu deshonestidad lo que llevas adentro.
¡Eres una embustera!
Han muerto mis hijos de quienes hablas.
Luego agregó la abuela:
—Esto que voy a decir es cierto:

está bien, eres mi nuera, según te he oído.
Anda, pues,
anda a traer la comida para los que hay que alimentar.
Anda a tapiscar[117] y que sea una red grande la que traigas;
ya que eres mi nuera, según te he escuchado, le fue dicho a la doncella.
—¡Está bien!, contestó.

Enseguida se fue para el sembrado de milpa.
Tenían su milpa Jun Batz' y
                    Jun Chowen;
el camino hacia el lugar había sido limpiado por ellos.
Ese camino fue el que siguió la doncella,
y llegó, pues, aquí a la milpa;[118]
pero no encontró más que una mata de milpa;[119]
no había dos
        ni tres;
aunque empezaban a dar fruto esas plantas.
Se desconsoló de una vez la doncella:
—¡Ay, soy culpable,
            soy responsable!
¿De dónde voy a traer la red de comida que me han pedido?,
                                    [dijo ella.
Y de inmediato fueron invocados los guardianes de la comida,
                                        [por ella.
—Vengan para acá,
Hagan acto de presencia Ixtoj,
                    Ixq'anil,[120]
                    Ixkakaw e
                    Ixtziya'[121]
Ustedes, guardianes de la comida de
                        [Jun Batz' y
                        Jun Chowen, exclamó la doncella.
Tomó entonces unos pelos de maíz,
la flor de las mazorcas;
los arrancó para arriba,
no tapiscó las mazorcas.

Luego arregló la comida de maíz en la red,
hasta sobrecargarse la gran red.

Enseguida regresó la doncella,
pero fueron animales los que cargaron la red.
Cuando llegaron la fueron a dejar al lado de la casa
para que ante los ojos de la abuela, pareciera que ella la hubiera
[cargado.

Y cuando la abuela vio la comida que había en la gran red:
—¿De dónde has traído todo este alimento?
¿Peor si echaste a perder el lugar,
y si se acabó de una vez toda nuestra milpa?
¡Tengo que ir a ver!, dijo la abuela.

Se puso en camino,
fue a ver la milpa.
Pero estaba igual la mata de milpa,
sólo se miraban las huellas de la red al pie de la mata.[122]
A toda prisa se vino de regreso, la abuela
y al llegar a su casa
le dijo a la doncella:
—¡Ésta es una señal!
Es cierto que eres mi nuera.
He de estar atenta a lo que haces.
Esos nietos míos han demostrado su prodigio, le fue dicho a la
[doncella.

Ahora contaremos el nacimiento de Junajpu y
                    Xbalamke,
sobre su nacimiento vamos a hablar;
de cuando llegó el día de su nacimiento,
de cuando dio a luz la doncella, llamada Ixkik'.
La abuela no estuvo presente cuando nacieron,
en un instante nacieron las dos criaturas, Junajpu y

Xbalamke, así llamados.
En la montaña fueron dados a luz.

Cuando los llevaron a casa no podían dormirse.
—¡Anda a botarlos!
De verdad que hacen mucha bulla, dijo la abuela.
Enseguida los fueron a poner sobre un hormiguero
y allí su sueño fue placentero.
Los sacaron de este lugar
y los fueron a poner sobre espinas.
Lo que habrían querido Jun Batz' y
                    Jun Chowen, es que murieran sobre el
                                        [hormiguero,
                              que murieran sobre las
                                        [espinas.
Querían esto por el alboroto y
              la envidia que sentían hacia ellos Jun Batz' y
                                        Jun Chowen.
Al principio no eran bien recibidos en la casa por sus "hermanos
menores",¹²³ los ignoraban y
por eso crecieron en las montañas.

Eran grandes flautistas,
              cantantes Jun Batz' y
                    Jun Chowen.
Mientras fueron creciendo
pasaron por grandes penas y
                    sufrimientos.
Tuvieron que pasar por muchas aflicciones,
pero se volvieron grandes sabios.
También se volvieron flautistas,
                    cantantes,
                         así como escritores y
                                   escultores.
Todo lo que hacían les salía bien.
Ellos ya sabían de su nacimiento,

ya tenían poderes;
sabían que eran los sucesores de sus padres que fueron a Xibalba
y que murieron allá.
Eran grandes sabios, pues, Jun Batz' y
                            Jun Chowen;
en su corazón todo lo tenían claro.
Sin embargo, cuando nacieron sus hermanos menores
no demostraron sabiduría a causa de su envidia
y sobre ellos mismos cayó el rencor que tenían en el corazón;
Por ninguna otra razón fueron transformados por Junajpu y
                                        Xbalamke,
quienes sólo tirando con cerbatana se mantenían todos los días.
No eran amados por su abuela ni por Jun Batz' y
                            Jun Chowen.
No les daban de comer;
sino hasta terminada la comida y
cuando ya habían comido Jun Batz' y
                    Jun Chowen, entonces, entraban ellos.
Pero no se enojaban ni
            encolerizaban;
sólo se aguantaban,
ya que sabían de su condición,
así que para ellos todo estaba claro.
Traían, pues, sus pájaros cuando venían cada día
y se los comían Jun Batz' y
                Jun Chowen.
No les daban nada a ninguno de los dos, a Junajpu y
                                    Xbalamke.
Solamente tocando flauta,
y sólo cantando se la pasaban Jun Batz' y
                        Jun Chowen.
Llegaron otra vez Junajpu y
            Xbalamke;
pero no llevaban ningún pájaro cuando entraron.
Esto enfureció a la abuela:

—¿Cuál es la causa para que no traigan pájaros?,

[preguntó a Junajpu y
Xbalamke.

Y ellos contestaron:
—Lo que pasa, abuela, es que se trabaron nuestros pájaros en el árbol.
Nosotros no podemos subir sobre el árbol, abuela nuestra.
Quisiéramos que nuestros hermanos mayores fueran con nosotros,
que vayan a bajar esos pájaros, agregaron.
—¡Está bien, pues! Iremos con ustedes al amanecer, dijeron sus
[hermanos
mayores y esto significó su derrota.

Ya se habían puesto de acuerdo los dos
sobre la manera de cómo vencer a Jun Batz' y
Jun Chowen.
—Sólo vamos a cambiar su naturaleza.
Éste es el contenido de nuestras palabras.
Que se cumpla: por los grandes sufrimientos que nos han causado.
Ellos querían que muriéramos y
que desapareciéramos, nosotros,
que somos sus hermanos
[menores.
Como súbditos nos trataban[124]
de la misma manera los vamos a vencer.
Es sólo una muestra lo que vamos a hacer, se dijeron entre sí.

Así pues se fueron hacia allá, debajo del árbol
llamado q'ante'.[125]
Iban acompañando a sus hermanos mayores cuando partieron
y comenzaron a tirar con sus cerbatanas.
Era incontable la cantidad de pájaros que hacían bulla sobre los
[árboles,
que estaban admirados sus hermanos mayores de ver tanto pájaro;
pero de esos pájaros ni uno solo caía al pie del árbol.
—Nuestros pájaros de ningún modo se vienen para abajo.

Mejor vayan ustedes a bajarlos, les dijeron a sus hermanos mayores.
—¡Está bien!, contestaron éstos.

En cuanto subieron al árbol,
el árbol empezó a crecer,
su tronco se empezó a hinchar.
Quisieron bajar de inmediato;
pero ya no pudieron descender de la cima del árbol Jun Batz' y
Jun Chowen.
Enseguida exclamaron desde lo alto del árbol:
—¿Cómo nos agarramos?
¡Hermanitos nuestros, tengan piedad de nosotros!
Este árbol nos causa espanto, hermanitos nuestros, dijeron desde
[arriba del árbol.
Contestaron entonces Junajpu y
Xbalamke:
—Desaten la faja de sus pantalones,[126]
amárrense el bajo vientre dejando largas las puntas,
estírenlas como si fueran colas detrás de ustedes;
y así andarán bien, les fue dicho por parte de sus hermanos menores.
—¡Está bien!, contestaron, halándose la punta de sus fajas,
pero al instante éstas se convirtieron en colas
y ellos tomaron la apariencia de micos.
Enseguida se fueron sobre los árboles de las pequeñas montañas y
de las grandes montañas;
se internaron entre los bosques, gritando y
columpiándose entre las ramas
de los árboles.
De esa manera entonces fueron vencidos
[Jun Batz' y
Jun Chowen por Junajpu y
Xbalamke;
sólo por su prodigio lo pudieron hacer.

Cuando volvieron a su casa,
dijeron al llegar junto a su abuela y

a su madre:

—Abuela nuestra, a saber qué les habrá ocurrido a nuestros hermanos
[mayores

Ya sin ninguna vergüenza se fueron
ya son como animales ahora, dijeron.[127]
—Si ustedes les hicieron algo a sus hermanos mayores
me habrán arruinado y
me habrán desgraciado.[128]
Ojalá no hayan hecho algo así a sus hermanos mayores, nietos míos,
[dijo

la abuela a Junajpu y
       Xbalamke.
Y ellos contestaron a su abuela:
—No te pongas triste, querida abuela,
mirarás de nuevo la cara de nuestros hermanos mayores,
ellos volverán.
Eso sí, será una prueba para ti, querida abuela:
no debes reírte,
vamos a probar su suerte,[129] dijeron.

Enseguida se pusieron a tocar flauta,
ejecutaron la melodía "Junajpu k'oy".[130]
Luego cantaron,
      tocaron flauta,
      tocaron tambor.
Cuando tomaron su flauta,
           su tambor,
la abuela se fue a sentar con ellos.
Enseguida tocaron llamándolos con flauta
               con cantos;
y de ahí se denominó "Junajpu k'oy", a esa melodía.
Y entonces entraron Jun Batz' y
           Jun Chowen,
llegaron bailando;
que cuando los vio la abuela,
le parecieron feas sus caras que se echó a reír;

no pudo contener su risa la abuela.
De inmediato se marcharon,
ya no se les pudo ver, se fueron saltando hacia el bosque.
—¿Qué has hecho, querida abuela?
Sólo cuatro veces vamos a hacer esta prueba,
y ya sólo tres veces vamos a llamarlos con nuestras flautas
                                    con nuestros cantos;
por favor aguanta la risa.
Vamos a probar otra vez, dijeron Junajpu y
                              Xbalamke.
Volvieron a tocar otra vez
y entraron de nuevo,
bailando ingresaron hasta el centro del patio de la casa.
Sólo monerías hacían,
sólo incentivaban la risa de la abuela,
que de inmediato se carcajeó su abuela.
De verdad daban risa los micos con su pequeña cosa debajo
                                    [del vientre,¹³¹
                    con las colas meneando a la altura
del pecho;
que cuando entraron, hicieron carcajear a la abuela.
Por eso ellos se fueron otra vez a las montañas.
—¿Qué hacemos, querida abuela?
Porque ésta es la tercera vez que probaremos, dijeron Junajpu y
                                    Xbalamke.
Ejecutaron de nuevo la flauta,
volvieron a regresar,
y bailaban.
Esta vez, la abuela contenía la risa.
Se encaramaron sobre las paredes de la orilla de la casa.
Tenían colorados los bordes de sus caras
tenían fruncidas sus bocas,
cubiertos de pelos estaban sus hocicos
                    sus caras
como si nadie los hubiera limpiado.¹³²
Cuando llegó a ver esto la abuela

de inmediato estalló en carcajadas su abuela.
Ya no los volvieron a ver por las risas de la abuela.
—Ya sólo esta vez, querida abuela,
hemos dicho que sólo cuatro veces podíamos hacer esto.
Fueron llamados con música de nuevo,
pero ya no regresaron.
Al cuarto llamado, de una vez se fueron para el bosque.
Le dijeron entonces a su abuela:
—Lo hemos intentado, abuelita,
al principio vinieron,
y hemos intentado llamarlos otra vez.
Pero no te pongas triste:
estamos nosotros,
nosotros tus nietos.
Sólo ama a nuestra madre, querida abuela.
Nuestros hermanos mayores serán recordados.
¡Que así sea!
¿Acaso no se envanecieron?[133]
¿Acaso no se les nombró Jun Batz' y
               Jun Chowen, como serán llamados?, dijeron
               [Junajpu y
               Xbalamke.

Ellos eran invocados, pues, por los flautistas
            por los cantores y
            por la gente antigua.
También los invocaban los escritores,
            los escultores en la antigüedad;
pero se convirtieron en animales,
en micos fueron transformados por soberbios,
              por maltratar a sus hermanos
                     [menores.
Como el ánimo de subyugación que tenían en el corazón,
con la misma intensidad fueron aniquilados.
Cuando desaparecieron Jun Batz' y
            Jun Chowen,

en animales se volvieron,
y así se establecieron para siempre.
Ellos fueron flautistas y
                    cantantes;
hicieron grandes cosas mientras vivieron con su abuela y
                                con su madre.

Luego empezaron a demostrar sus capacidades,
                    a dar a conocerse ante su abuela y
                                ante su madre.
Lo primero que hicieron fue lo de la milpa.
—Vamos a ir a sembrar milpa, abuela nuestra,
                    madre nuestra, dijeron.
No estén tristes, aquí estamos nosotros,
                    sus nietos,
                    en lugar de nuestros hermanos mayores,
                                [dijeron Junajpu y
                                    Xbalamke.
Enseguida tomaron su hacha y
                    su azadón poniéndolos sobre los hombros;[134]
se fueron cada quien, además, cargando sus cerbatanas.
Al partir de su casa encargaron a su abuela ir a dejarles su almuerzo:
—A mediodía llévanos la comida, abuela nuestra, dijeron.
—Está bien, nietos míos, contestó su abuela.

Cuando llegaron al terreno donde había que sembrar,
sólo enterraron el azadón en el suelo y
sólo el azadón empezó a picar la tierra.
Pero no sólo empezó a trabajar por su cuenta el azadón
sino que también el hacha.
Sólo la clavaban en los troncos de los árboles y
por su cuenta se iba sobre las ramas de los árboles;
uno tras otro caían tendidos todos los árboles y
                                bejucos.
Apilados quedaban los árboles que cortaba una sola hacha.

En cuanto al azadón fue muchísimo lo que desyerbó
era incontable la maleza,
                    las zarzas que limpió un solo azadón,
era incontable lo que arrancaba cuando se iba por
                                        [los montes pequeños y
                                        los montes grandes.
Entonces instruyeron a un animal,
                    xmuqur es su nombre.[135]
Lo pusieron encima de un gran tronco,
luego Junajpu y
        Xbalamke, le dijeron:
—Sólo observa cuando venga nuestra abuela a dejarnos comida,
canta de inmediato cuando la veas venir,
entonces nosotros empuñaremos el azadón y
                    el hacha.
—¡Está bien!, contestó xmuqur.
Mientras tanto ellos se dedicaron a tirar con su cerbatana,
no era cierto que se pusieran a sembrar milpa.
Al poco rato cantó xmuqur,
de inmediato regresaron: uno tomó el azadón y
                    el otro tomó el hacha.
Se amarraron la cabeza,
intencionalmente uno se echó tierra en las manos,
se ensució la cara como un verdadero labrador.
En cuanto al otro,
a propósito se echó astillas sobre la cabeza como si fuera verdadero
                                        [leñador.
Así fueron vistos por la abuela y enseguida comieron.
No era cierto que sembraran maíz,
sin merecerlo les llevaron almuerzo.
Cuando se fueron a su casa:
—De verdad nos cansamos, abuela nuestra, dijeron al llegar.
Intencionalmente masajeaban,
                estiraban sus piernas y
                        sus brazos ante la abuela.
Regresaron al día siguiente y

al llegar al sembradío de milpa
ya todo estaba levantado de nuevo, árboles y
                                    bejucos;
estaba entrelazada toda la maleza y
                    las zarzas cuando llegaron.
—¿Quién nos estará tomando el pelo?,¹³⁶ se preguntaron.
Quienes hacían esto eran todos los animales pequeños,
                        los animales grandes:
                        el puma
                        el jaguar
                        el venado
                        el conejo
                        la zorra¹³⁷
                        el coyote
                        el jabalí
                        el pizote,
                    los pájaros pequeños,
                    los pájaros grandes eran quienes lo
                                    [ejecutaban,
                            en una sola
                            [noche lo hacían.
De nuevo entonces, se pusieron a sembrar la milpa,
y otra vez la tierra se cultivó a sí misma
        igual que la tala de árboles.
Luego se pusieron a discurrir allí, entre la tala de árboles y
                    sobre la tierra desyerbada.
—Es mejor que velemos nuestra milpa.
Quien sea que esté haciendo esto,
hemos de sorprenderlo, dijeron cuando se pusieron de acuerdo.
Llegaron después a la casa:
—A saber quién nos está tomando el pelo, abuela nuestra.
Era ya un gran pajonal y
era ya un gran bosque nuestra milpa cuando llegamos hace un rato,
                                    [querida
abuela, le dijeron a su abuela y
            a su madre.

—Tenemos que regresar,
vamos a velar, porque no está bien lo que nos están haciendo, dijeron.
Enseguida se arreglaron
y se fueron para el campo que habían limpiado de árboles.
Allí se escondieron,
ya estaban ocultos cuando empezaron a reunirse todos los animales,
en un solo lugar se juntaron todos los animales pequeños y
los animales grandes.
Estaba alzado el corazón de la noche[138] cuando llegaron,
venían hablando todos,
esto es lo que decían en su lenguaje:
—¡Levántense, árboles!
¡Levántense, bejucos!, decían al venir.
Se agruparon bajo los árboles
bajo los bejucos cuando aparecieron,
cuando se mostraron ante ellos.
Los primeros eran el puma y
el jaguar;
quisieron atraparlos;
pero ninguno se dejó.
Luego se acercaron el venado y
el conejo;
pero sólo por sus colas los agarraron
y sólo se las arrancaron quedando la cola del venado entre sus manos;
por esa razón la cola del venado
la cola del conejo son cortas.
Tampoco se dejaron la zorra,
el coyote,
el jabalí,
ni el pizote.
Pasaron todos los animales frente a Junajpu y
Xbalamke;
y ardían sus corazones de cólera porque no los podían atrapar.
Luego apareció otro animal
era el último;
venía dando saltos cuando llegó;

de inmediato lo detuvieron y
                    atraparon por el cuello al ratón.
Después de capturado
            lo apretaron por detrás de la nuca,
querían estrangularlo;
le quemaron la cola sobre el fuego
y por esa razón así es la cola del ratón,
que no tiene pelos en la cola;
asimismo es la razón de sus ojos saltones,
desde que intentaron estrangularlo los muchachos Junajpu y
                                            Xbalamke.
—¡No debo morir en manos de ustedes!
Y no es su oficio sembrar maíz.
¡Ahí está lo que es de ustedes!, les dijo el ratón.
—¿Dónde está lo que es nuestro?
Dilo de una vez, le dijeron los muchachos al ratón.
—¿Por qué no me sueltan?
Llevo un mensaje dentro de mí,
se los diré enseguida;
pero antes denme un poco de comida, dijo el ratón.
—Después te daremos tu comida,
habla primero, le fue dicho.
—¡Está bien!
De lo que pertenecía a sus padres, Jun Junajpu y
                        Wuqub Junajpu, así llamados,
                        los que murieron en Xibalba;
han quedado sus implementos de juego,
están colgados sobre el tapanco de la casa:
                                    [sus cinturones,
                                    sus protectores de brazos y
                                    su pelota.
Nada más no se los enseña su abuela
porque por eso murieron los padres de ustedes.
—¿De verdad lo sabes?, le dijeron los muchachos al ratón.
Grande fue la alegría de sus corazones al escuchar noticia de la pelota.
Después de haber hablado el ratón,

le asignaron su comida al ratón.
Éste es, pues, su alimento: maíz,

> pepitas de chilacayote,
> chile,
> frijol,
> pataxte,
> cacao.

—¡Esto es lo que es tuyo!
Si hay algo guardado o desperdiciado, es tuyo también.
¡Cómelo!, le fue dicho entonces al ratón por Junajpu y

> Xbalamke.

—Está bien, muchachos,
¿pero qué digo si su abuela me mira?, preguntó el ratón.
—¡No tengas pena!
Estamos nosotros,
ya sabremos qué decirle a nuestra abuela.
Cuando entremos, te vamos a poner rápido sobre un costado de la

> [casa,

y de inmediato debes llegar a donde están colgadas las cosas
allí te miraremos a través del agujero del tapanco
pero en nuestra comida te miraremos, le dijeron al ratón cuando lo

> [instruyeron.

Durante toda la noche estuvieron discurriendo Junajpu y

> Xbalamke,

ya era mediodía cuando llegaron.

No se miraba el ratón que llevaban cuando llegaron.
Uno de ellos entró directo a la casa,
el otro entró por el costado de la casa y rápido subió al ratón.
Enseguida pidieron comida a su abuela:
—Sólo muele algo para nuestra comida,
deseamos comer un chirmol,[139] abuela nuestra, dijeron.
Al momento les prepararon su comida,
una escudilla con caldo les pusieron enfrente.
Pero, para engañar a su abuela y

> a su madre,

hicieron que se evaporara el agua que había en la tinaja.
—De verdad que tenemos sed,
vayan a traernos de beber, le dijeron a su abuela.
—Está bien, contestó ella y se fue.
Ellos se quedaron comiendo;
pero no era cierto que tuvieran hambre, sólo era un engaño lo que
[hacían.

Vieron entonces al ratón reflejado en su chirmol,
el ratón estaba resguardado detrás de la pelota colgada en el techo
[de la casa.
Cuando lo vieron a través de su chirmol,
enviaron de una vez a un xan,
el animal xan es como el mosquito, y llegó al río,
éste fue el que perforó la tinaja de la abuela.
El agua recolectada empezó a salir de su tinaja,
ella intentó cerrar ese agujero de la tinaja, pero no pudo.
—¿Qué le habrá pasado a nuestra abuela?
Estamos desesperados por agua,
estamos muriendo de sed, le dijeron a su madre, cuando la mandaron
[fuera.
Después de esto, el ratón desató la pelota,
que cayó por el agujero en el techo, junto con los cinturones,
los protectores de
[brazos,
las faldillas de cuero.
De inmediato los fueron a recoger,
y los fueron a esconder en el camino,
la ruta hacia el campo de juego.
Después se encaminaron a donde su abuela al río.
Todavía estaban su abuela y
su madre, tratando de tapar el agujero de la tinaja.
Cuando ellos llegaron
cada uno llevaba su cerbatana al arribar al río.
—¿Qué les sucedió?
Nos cansamos de esperar y nos venimos, dijeron.

—Miren mi tinaja, no se puede tapar, contestó su abuela.
Al instante ellos la taparon.
Juntos regresaron,
ellos delante de su abuela.
Así fue, pues, como ellos obtuvieron la pelota.

Muy contentos se fueron al campo de juego.
Por largo tiempo estuvieron jugando solos,
limpiaron el campo de juego de sus padres.
Pero los oyeron los Señores de Xibalba:
—¿Quiénes son los que empiezan a jugar otra vez sobre nuestras
[cabezas?
¿Acaso no les da vergüenza estar saltando allá arriba?
¿Acaso no murieron Jun Junajpu y
                    Wuqub Junajpu,
que quisieron engrandecerse ante nosotros?
¡Vayan a llamarlos!, dijeron Jun Kame y
                    Wuqub Kame.
Todos los Señores los mandaron a llamar.
Les dijeron a sus mensajeros:
—Esto han de decir, cuando lleguen:
"Que vengan". Dicen los Señores.
"Aquí hemos de jugar con ellos,
dentro de siete días hemos de jugar". Dicen los Señores.
Esto han de decir, cuando lleguen,[140] les fue indicado a los mensajeros.

Éstos se vinieron por la vereda ancha,
                    el camino hacia la casa de los muchachos;
                    el que conduce directamente a su casa
y de una vez entraron los mensajeros donde estaba la abuela.
Mientras los muchachos jugaban,
habían llegado los mensajeros de Xibalba:
—"De verdad han de venir". Dicen los Señores, dijeron los
                    [mensajeros de
Xibalba y señalaron de una vez el día, esos mensajeros de Xibalba:

—En siete días se les habrá de ver jugando, le dejaron dicho a
[Ixmukane.
—Está bien, mensajeros, hay que mandarlos a llamar, dijo la abuela.

Se fueron entonces los mensajeros,
se regresaron,
pero de una vez se angustió la abuela:
—¿A quién mandaré para ir a llamar a mis nietos?
¿No es cierto que de Xibalba así vinieron los mensajeros hace tiempo,
cuando fueron a morir sus padres?, dijo la abuela, llorando afligida
a solas en casa.

De pronto cayó un piojo donde podía ser recogido,
de inmediato lo agarró,
y lo puso en la palma de su mano;
el piojo se meneaba al caminar:
—Tú, criatura, tal vez quieras que te mande,
hay que ir a llamar a mis nietos al campo de juego, le fue indicado
[al piojo.
Al irse de mandadero:
—"Acaban de venir mensajeros con su abuela". Has de decir cuando
[llegues.
"En siete días han de llegar,
dicen los mensajeros de Xibalba". Dice su abuela,
así manda a decir, le fue dicho al piojo.

Enseguida se fue el piojo,
se contoneaba cuando se fue.
En eso, estaba sentado un cachorro [de sapo] a la orilla del camino
Tamasul[141] era el nombre del sapo.
—¿Adónde vas?, le dijo el sapo al piojo.
—Llevo un mensaje adentro,[142]
voy hacia donde los muchachos, le dijo el piojo a Tamasul.
—Muy bien, pero veo que no vas muy rápido, le fue dicho al piojo
[por parte
del sapo.

—¿No quieres que te trague?
Ya verás que camino más rápido,
así llegaremos pronto.
—¡Está bien!, le dijo el piojo al sapo.
Y al instante fue tragado por el sapo.
Caminó bastante el sapo,
pero no avanzaba mucho.
En eso se encontró con una gran serpiente,
                              Saqikas es su nombre.
—¿Adónde vas, muchacho Tamasul?, le fue preguntado al sapo por
                                                    [la serpiente.
—Soy un mensajero.
Llevo un mensaje adentro, le contestó el sapo a la serpiente.
—Pero vas sin prisa, por lo que veo.
Yo llegaría más rápido, le dijo la serpiente al sapo.
—¡Entra!, le fue dicho.
Enseguida fue tragado el sapo por Saqikas.
Y así fue como las serpientes adquirieron su comida,
que se tragan a los sapos hoy en día.
Entonces se fue rápida la serpiente.
En turno, fue encontrada la serpiente por Wak,
                              un pájaro grande.
De una vez fue tragada la serpiente por parte de Wak,
Al rato llegó a la orilla del campo de juego.
Desde entonces adquirieron su alimento los halcones,
que comen serpientes en las montañas.

Y al llegar Wak
se posó en la orilla del campo de juego de pelota;
donde estaban muy felices Junajpu y
                              Xbalamke jugando.
Cuando llegó Wak,
de una vez cantó Wak:
—¡Wak k'o
wak k'o!, decía en su canto Wak[143]
—¿Quién es quien llama?[144]

Que vengan nuestras cerbatanas, dijeron.
Enseguida le dispararon a Wak,
acertándole el tiro de cerbatana en su ojo,
y éste dando vueltas se vino para abajo,
de inmediato lo fueron a agarrar,
luego le preguntaron:
—¿De dónde vienes?, le dijeron a Wak.
—Traigo un mensaje adentro,
pero primero cúrenme el ojo y de ahí se los digo, contestó Wak.
—¡Está bien!, dijeron.

Luego sacaron un poco de hule de la pelota con que jugaban,
y lo pusieron en el ojo de Wak;
"sangre de sacrificio"[145] denominaron a esto.
Inmediatamente después de haberlo curado
quedó bien otra vez la vista de Wak.
—¡Habla, pues!, le dijeron a Wak.
Enseguida éste vomitó a la gran serpiente.
—¡Habla!, le dijeron a la serpiente.
—¡Está bien!, contestó ésta y vomitó al sapo.
—¿Cuál es tu mandado?
¡Habla de una vez!, le fue dicho en turno al sapo.
—Traigo un mensaje adentro, contestó el sapo.
Luego trató de vomitar;
pero no vomitaba nada,
sólo se le llenaba la boca de baba.
Lo intentó de nuevo pero no vomitó nada.
Entonces ya le querían pegar los muchachos.
—Eres un embustero, le fue dicho.
Y le agarraron las ancas a patadas,
le quebraron de una vez el hueso de las ancas con las patadas.
Probó otra vez,
pero sólo saliva echaba de su boca.
Entonces le rasgaron la boca al sapo,
le fue rasgada por los muchachos,
buscaron adentro de la boca

y allí estaba pegado el piojo entre los dientes del sapo;
en su boca se había quedado,
no lo había tragado,
sólo pareció como si se lo hubiera tragado.
Así, entonces, fue engañado el sapo.
No está claro qué comida le fue asignada;
y como no corre, se volvió alimento de serpientes.
—¡Habla!, le fue dicho al piojo.
Entonces éste dijo su mensaje:
—Manda a decir su abuela, muchachos:
"Anda a llamarlos
han venido mensajeros a buscarlos,
vinieron de Xibalba,
son los mensajeros de Jun Kame y
                          Wuqub Kame.
En siete días han de venir para que juguemos.
Que traigan sus implementos: la pelota,
                          los cinturones,
                          los protectores de brazos y
                          las faldillas de cuero.
¡Aquí serán escarmentados! Dicen los Señores,
                          al enviar sus palabras". Dice su abuela
                                    [y por eso vine.
Sinceramente esto dice su abuela mientras llora,
                                    y los llama, por eso vine.
—¿Será esto verdad?, se preguntaron los muchachos al escucharlo.
De inmediato regresaron,
llegaron a donde su abuela,
pero sólo fueron a darle consejos a su abuela.
—Tenemos que irnos, querida abuela;
sólo venimos a darles consejo.
Ésta es la señal de nuestra palabra,
la que va a dejar cada uno de nosotros.
Vamos a sembrar unas matas de maíz[146] en medio de nuestra casa,
allí las vamos a sembrar.
Será señal de nuestra muerte si se secan.

¿Acaso han muerto? Han de decir cuando se sequen.
Pero cuando retoñen: ¡Están vivos! Han de decir. Querida abuela,
                      y tú, madre nuestra, no lloren.
Queda señal de nuestra existencia[147] con ustedes, dijeron.
Luego procedieron: sembró una mata Junajpu
               la otra fue sembrada por Xbalamke.
En la casa las sembraron,
no fue en la montaña,
tampoco fue en tierra húmeda,
sino en tierra seca;
en medio del patio de su casa las dejaron sembradas.

Se marcharon entonces,
cada quien con su cerbatana, bajaron a Xibalba.
Bajaron rápido por unos escalones,
pasaron por un barranco de aguas turbulentas,
en medio de un montón de pájaros pasaron,
estos eran los pájaros llamados molaj.[148]
Luego pasaron sobre un río de agua podrida y
              sobre un río de sangre,
lugares donde serían derrotados, pensaban los de Xibalba;
pero ni los tocaron con sus pies,
sino sobre sus cerbatanas los pasaron.
Salieron después en un lugar donde se cruzan cuatro caminos,
ellos ya sabían de los caminos de Xibalba: un camino negro,
                         un camino blanco,
                         un camino rojo,
                         un camino verde.[149]
Allí entonces enviaron a un animal
               xan es su nombre.[150]
Era quien iba a recogerles información, fue al que mandaron entonces:
—Uno a uno anda a picarlos,
primero pica al que está sentado de primero,
hasta terminar picándolos a todos;

y tuyo será chupar la sangre de la gente en los caminos, le fue dicho
[a Xan.
—¡Está bien!, dijo Xan.
Se internó por el camino negro
llegando directamente detrás de los maniquís,
de los muñecos de madera;
eran los que estaban sentados de primero y cubiertos de adornos,
picó al primero;
pero no habló.
Continuó picando
y cuando picó al segundo que estaba sentado;
tampoco habló.
Entonces picó al tercero,
el que estaba sentado de tercero era Jun Kame.
—¡Ay!, dijo éste cuando lo picaron.
—¡Ay!, dijo Jun Kame.[151]
—¿Qué sucede, Jun Kame?
—A saber qué me ha picado.
—¡Ay! ¿Quién me ha picado?, dijo el que estaba sentado de cuarto
[en la fila.
—¿Qué sucede Wuqub Kame?
—A saber qué me ha picado, dijo el que estaba sentado de quinto en
[la fila.
—¡Ay, ay!, tuvo que decir Xikiri Pat.
Entonces le preguntó Wuqub Kame:
—¿Qué te ha picado Xikiri Pat?,[152] le dijo.
Luego fue picado el sexto, que estaba sentado.
—¡Ay! ¿Qué pasa, Kuchuma Kik'?, le preguntó Xikiri Pat a éste.
—A saber quién me ha picado, contestó.
Luego fue picado el séptimo, que estaba sentado.
—¡Ay!, exclamó éste.
—¿Qué pasa, Ajal Puj?, le preguntó Kuchuma Kik'.
—A saber qué me ha picado, contestó éste.
Seguidamente fue picado el octavo que estaba sentado en fila.
—¡Ay!, dijo éste.
—¿Qué pasa, Ajal Q'ana?, le preguntó Ajal Puj.

—A saber qué me ha picado, respondió éste.

Luego fue picado el noveno sentado en fila.

—¡Ay!, exclamó.

—¿Qué sucede, Ch'amiyabaq?, le preguntó Ajal Q'ana.

—A saber qué me ha picado, respondió éste.

Enseguida fue picado el décimo sentado en fila.

—¡Ay!

—¿Qué pasa, Ch'amiyajolom?, le preguntó Ch'amiyabaq.

—A saber qué me ha picado, respondió éste.

Después fue picado el onceavo sentado en fila.

—¿Qué pasa, Xik?,[153] le preguntó Ch'amiyajolom a éste.

—A saber qué me ha picado, respondió éste.

En eso fue picado el doceavo sentado en fila.

—¡Ay!, dijo éste.

—¿Qué sucede, Patan?, le fue preguntado.

—A saber qué me ha picado, respondió éste.

Luego fue picado el treceavo sentado en fila.

—¡Ay!

—¿Qué pasa, Kik' Re?, le preguntó Patan.

—A saber qué me ha picado, respondió éste.

Enseguida fue picado el catorceavo sentado en fila.

—¡Ay!

—A saber qué me ha picado, dijo.

—¿Kik' Rixk'aq?, lo nombró Kik' Re a éste.

Así fue como revelaron sus nombres,[154]
se identificaron unos a otros.
Así lo dieron a conocer,
al nombrar sus nombres.[155]
Cada uno fue nombrado por el de rango superior,
fue dado su nombre por quien estaba sentado a la par.
Ni un solo nombre se les escapó,
todos acabaron de decir sus nombres
al ser picados por un pelo de la espinilla de Junajpu,
                    que fue lo que envió.
No fue un verdadero zancudo el que los picó,
el que fue a oír el nombre de todos para Junajpu y

Xbalamke.

Luego de esto se fueron y
                    llegaron hasta donde estaban los de Xibalba.
—Saluden a los Señores, les dijo.
—A los que están sentados, dijo quien los recibió.
—Éstos no son Señores, son sólo maniquís,
                    son sólo muñecos de madera, dijeron al
                                                      [entrar.¹⁵⁶

Enseguida dieron los buenos días:
—¡Buenos días, Señor Jun Kame!¹⁵⁷
—¡Buenos días, Señor Wuqub Kame!
—¡Buenos días, Señor Xikiri Pat!
—¡Buenos días, Señor Kuchuma Kik'!
—¡Buenos días, Señor Ajal Puj!
—¡Buenos días, Señor Ajal Q'ana!
—¡Buenos días, Señor Ch'amiyabaq!
—¡Buenos días, Señor Ch'amiyajolom!
—¡Buenos días, Señor Xik!
—¡Buenos días, Señor Patan!
—¡Buenos días, Señor Kik' Re!
—¡Buenos días, Señor Kik' Rixk'aq!, dijeron cuando llegaron.
Todos fueron identificados,
dijeron los nombres de todos,
ni un solo nombre se les escapó.
Pero lo que se esperaba de ellos,
es que no se enteraran de sus nombres.¹⁵⁸
—¡Siéntense allí!, les dijeron,
esperando que se sentaran sobre la banca;
pero no quisieron.
—¡Eso no es asiento para nosotros,
esa banca es sólo una piedra candente!, dijeron Junajpu y
                                                      Xbalamke.
No fueron vencidos.
—¡Está bien!
Vayan, pues, a aquella casa, les fue dicho.

Enseguida entraron a la Casa Oscura
y tampoco fueron vencidos allí.
Ésta era la primera prueba de Xibalba
el lugar a donde los condujeron.
Allí empezaría su derrota,
pensaban los de Xibalba.
Primero, pues, entraron a la Casa Oscura,
y enseguida les fueron a dejar una raja de ocote,
ésta iba ardiendo cuando la llevaron,
así como un puro a cada uno, por el mensajero de Jun Kame.
—Ésta es su antorcha, dice el Señor;
pero deberán devolverla al amanecer,
junto con los puros, pues vendrán a recogerlos, dice el Señor; dijo el
                                                              [mensajero
cuando llegó.
—¡Está bien!, respondieron.
Pero no dejaron encendido el ocote,
sólo sustituyeron las llamas con cola de guacamaya
y esto pareció ocote encendido a los veladores.
En cuanto a los puros,
sólo pusieron luciérnagas en la punta de esos puros
que toda una noche los hicieron resplandecer.
—¡Los hemos derrotado!, dijeron los veladores.
Pero no se consumió el ocote,
estaba como se los entregaron.
En cuanto a los puros
ni siquiera los encendieron.
estaban como se los fueron a dejar.
Así fueron devueltos a los Señores.
—¿Y éstos quiénes son?
¿De dónde han venido?
¿Quién los engendró,
quién los dio a luz?

En verdad, arden de ira nuestros corazones porque no está bien lo
[que nos hacen.
Son diferentes,
es distinta su naturaleza, se dijeron entre sí.
Luego los mandaron a llamar todos los Señores:
—Vamos a jugar, muchachos, les fue dicho.
Y a la vez fueron interrogados por Jun Kame y
Wuqub Kame.
—¿De dónde vienen?
Díganlo de una vez, muchachos, les preguntaron los de Xibalba.
—¡A saber de dónde venimos!
No lo sabemos, contestaron únicamente,
no lo revelaron.
—¡Está bien, pues!
Vamos a jugar pelota, muchachos, dijeron los de Xibalba.
—¡Está bien!, respondieron.
—Usaremos nuestra pelota, dijeron los de Xibalba.
—¡No! Usemos la nuestra, dijeron los muchachos.
—¡No es así! Usaremos la nuestra, dijeron los de Xibalba.
—¡Está bien, pues!, respondieron los muchachos.
—¡Que sea así! Ésta nada más está decorada,[159] dijeron los de Xibalba.
—¡No es eso! Digamos que es sólo una calavera,[160] respondieron los
[muchachos.
—¡No es así!, dijeron los de Xibalba.
—¡Está bien!, respondió Junajpu.
De inmediato la arrojaron los de Xibalba,
y la pelota llegó directamente al cinturón de Junajpu.
En eso vieron los de Xibalba el pedernal blanco,
que salió de la pelota y se fue haciendo ruido por el campo de juego.
—¿Qué es esto?, preguntaron Junajpu y
Xbalamke.
—Si lo que quieren es nuestra muerte,
no nos hubieran mandado a llamar.
¿Por qué entonces enviaron a sus mensajeros?
De verdad tengan lástima de nosotros,
nos vamos de regreso, dijeron los muchachos.

Lo que esperaban ellos para los muchachos
era que de una vez murieran allí por el pedernal,
que fueran vencidos.
Pero no ocurrió así.
En cambio, fueron los de Xibalba los derrotados por parte de los
[muchachos.
—¡No se vayan, muchachos!
Tenemos que jugar,
y usaremos la pelota de ustedes, les dijeron a los muchachos.
—¡Está bien!, contestaron.
Entonces usaron su pelota,
la pusieron en el campo de juego.
Enseguida decidieron sobre su trofeo.
—¿Cuál será nuestro premio?, preguntaron los de Xibalba.
—Ustedes lo han de señalar, respondieron los muchachos.
—Ganaremos cuatro recipientes de flores, dijeron los de Xibalba.
—¡Está bien!
¿Qué clase de flores?, preguntaron los muchachos a los de Xibalba.
—Un recipiente de pétalos rojos,
un recipiente de pétalos blancos,
un recipiente de pétalos amarillos,
un recipiente de [pétalos] grandes,[161] dijeron los de Xibalba.
—¡Está bien!, contestaron los muchachos.
Cuando comenzaron a jugar, ambos equipos tenían la misma fuerza;
hicieron muchas jugadas los muchachos;
pero fue con toda intención que se dejaron vencer los muchachos.
Se pusieron contentos los de Xibalba cuando aquellos fueron vencidos:
—Hemos hecho muy bien
les ganamos de primero, dijeron los de Xibalba.
—¿Adónde irán a traer las flores?, se preguntaron.
—De verdad, mañana temprano nos entregarán las flores que hemos
[ganado,
les fue dicho a los muchachos Junajpu y
Xbalamke por parte de Xibalba.
—¡Está bien!

Temprano hemos de jugar nuevamente, dijeron, emplazándose unos
[a otros.

Luego entraron los muchachos a la Casa de los Chayes,
la segunda prueba de Xibalba.
Lo que se habría querido allí
es que fueran despedazados por los chayes.
Que fuera rápido, según su deseo
que murieran, según sus corazones.
Pero no murieron.
Los muchachos hablaron con los chayes,
así los instruyeron:
—Esto es lo de ustedes: toda clase de carne de animal, le dijeron a
[los chayes.
Y éstos ya no se movieron más,
en su lugar se quedaron todos los chayes.
Allí, en la Casa de los Chayes pasaron la noche
y llamaron a todas las hormigas:
—¡Hormigas cortadoras
hormigas ganadoras! vengan[162]
entren todas.
Vayan a traernos toda clase de flores,
que han ganado los Señores.
—¡Está bien!, contestaron éstas.
Se fueron entonces las hormigas,
todas fueron a traer las flores cultivadas por Jun Kame y
Wuqub Kame.
Sin embargo, los de Xibalba ya habían instruido a los guardianes
de sus flores:
—¿Podrían ustedes cuidar nuestras flores?
No dejen que las roben porque hemos derrotado a los muchachos.
¿De qué otro lugar podría provenir lo que les hemos ganado?
¡De ningún otro lugar! Así que cuídenlas durante una noche.
—¡Está bien!, respondieron.
Pero nada sintieron esos guardianes,

nada más cantaban en las ramas de las plantas del jardín,
    saltaban de un lugar a otro;
nada más se nombraban con su canto:
—¡Xpurpuweq,
xpurpuweq!, decía uno en su canto.
—¡Pujuy
pujuy! decía en su canto el llamado pujuy.[163]
Eran dos los guardianes del jardín,
            del cultivo de Jun Kame y
                Wuqub Kame.
Pero no sintieron a las hormigas que entraron a robar lo que cuidaban;
éstas daban vueltas
se arremolinaban las acarreadoras de flores.
Las que cortaban flores sobre las plantas,
junto con las que recogían flores debajo de las plantas.
Mientras tanto los guardianes seguían cantando;
ni siquiera sintieron que les cortaban la cola
            que les cortaban las alas.
Era toda una recolección de flores,
de las que caían,
de las que recogían,
de las que cortaban.
Se llenaron rápido los cuatro recipientes de flores,
ya estaban allí listos cuando amaneció.
Luego llegaron los mensajeros,
        los mandaderos:
—"¡Que vengan!", dice el Señor.
—"Que traigan de una vez lo que hemos ganado", les fue dicho a
                        [los muchachos.
—¡Está bien!, contestaron.
Llevaron consigo las flores,
eran cuatro recipientes los que llevaron
cuando llegaron ante el Señor,
            ante los Señores,
llevaban flores muy fragantes.
Así fue como fueron vencidos los de Xibalba:

sólo fueron hormigas las que mandaron los muchachos,
sólo fue una madrugada la que emplearon las hormigas para llenar
los recipientes.
Así fue como fueron escarmentados todos los de Xibalba.
Pálidas se pusieron sus caras al ver las flores
que de inmediato mandaron a llamar a los guardianes de las flores:
—¿Por qué dejaron que nuestras flores fueran robadas?
Éstas son nuestras flores. ¡Mírenlas!, les fue dicho a los guardianes.
—No nos dimos cuenta, Señor,
ni siquiera sentimos cuando nos cortaron nuestras colas, respondieron
[éstos.
Y de una vez les rasgaron los picos,
fue su castigo por haberse dejado robar lo que cuidaban.
Así fue, pues, la derrota de Jun Kame y
                        de Wuqub Kame por parte de Junajpu y
                                     Xbalamke.

A raíz de este suceso
es que tienen el pico partido,
el pico del xpurpuweq está partido hoy en día.

Después bajaron a jugar pelota,
pero jugaron a empatar.
Al terminar el juego,
acordaron unos con otros:
—Al amanecer, otra vez, dijeron los de Xibalba.
—¡Está bien!, respondieron los muchachos cuando terminaron.

Entraron entonces a la Casa de Hielo.
Era inaguantable el frío,
era tremendo el granizo que caía adentro de esa casa,
                               la Casa del Frío.
De inmediato se derritió el hielo, por su obra,
                         por su prodigio;
se extinguió el frío por obra de los muchachos.

No murieron,
estaban vivos cuando amaneció.
Lo que querían los de Xibalba era que allí murieran.
Pero no fue así;
estaban saludables cuando amaneció.
Ya estaban allí colgados los mandaderos,[164]
pero tuvieron que irse aquellos centinelas.
—¿Por qué es que todavía no han muerto?, dijo el Señor de Xibalba.
Admiraron mucho lo que hacían los muchachos Junajpu y
Xbalamke.

Luego entraron a la Casa de Jaguares,
estaba llena de esos animales, la Casa de Jaguares.
—¡No nos coman!
Lo de ustedes está aquí, les fue indicado a los jaguares.
Enseguida arrojaron huesos a los animales;
y éstos se pusieron a pelear sobre los huesos.
—¿Acaso no están acabados?
¿Se habrán comido ya sus corazones?
Hasta al fin se dejaron vencer,
son sus huesos los que están siendo triturados, dijeron los centinelas.
Todos ellos estaban contentos por eso;
pero no estaban muertos.
Estaban muy bien al salir de la Casa de Jaguares.
—¿Qué clase de gente es ésta?
¿De dónde vienen?, se preguntaron todos los de Xibalba.

Luego entraron en medio del fuego,
una Casa de Fuego,
sólo fuego había adentro.
Tampoco se quemaron.
Sólo troncos rollizos,
sólo leña ardía allí.
Estaban saludables cuando amaneció.

Lo que se esperaba, era que murieran pronto en medio de lo que
iban pasando;
pero no ocurría así,
y esto iba desconsolando a los de Xibalba.

Los pusieron luego adentro de la Casa de los Murciélagos.
Sólo murciélagos habitaban esa casa,
una casa llena de murciélagos de la muerte,[165]
unos animales grandes,
cuyos hocicos eran afilados,
                    su instrumento de muerte;
que de una vez acababan con lo que les llegaba enfrente.
Estuvieron, pues, allí adentro de esa casa,
sólo que durmieron adentro de sus cerbatanas.
No fueron decapitados[166] por los que estaban en la casa.
Pero allí mismo se dejaron derrotar,
uno de ellos, por un murciélago de la muerte que llegó desde arriba.
Pero esto lo hicieron sólo para demostrar quiénes eran ellos,
porque tenían a quién pedir sabiduría.
Toda la noche, pues, los murciélagos estuvieron haciendo bulla:
—¡Kilitz'
kilitz'!, decían,
            y repetían durante toda la noche.
De pronto el ruido se detuvo,
ya no se movieron los murciélagos;
pero allí estaba uno, encaramado sobre la punta de la cerbatana.
Dijo entonces Xbalamke:
—Junajpu: ¿cuánto miras tú que falta para el amanecer?
—¡A saber cuánto falta!
¡Voy a ver!, contestó éste.
Tanto quería ver que sacó la cabeza de la cerbatana,
        quería ver el amanecer;
y al instante le cercenó la cabeza un murciélago de la muerte
                    quedó decapitado el cuerpo de Junajpu.
—¿Qué pasó?

¿No ha amanecido?, preguntó Xbalamke.
Pero ya no se movía Junajpu.
—¿Qué ha pasado?
¿Se habrá ido Junajpu?
¿Qué has hecho?
Pero ya no se movía,
sólo resollaba.
Esto desesperó a Xbalamke.
—¡Ay![167] Ya nos dejamos vencer, exclamó.
Y allá, sobre el campo de pelota fueron a colocar la cabeza
según lo dispuesto por Jun Kame y
                              Wuqub Kame.
Estaban muy contentos todos los de Xibalba por la cabeza de Junajpu.

Enseguida él llamó a todos los animales
al pizote,
al jabalí,
a todos los pequeños animales,
        los grandes animales.
En la noche,
todavía era de madrugada cuando les preguntó sobre su comida:
—¿Cuál es la comida de cada uno de ustedes?
A esto los voy a mandar:
¡Traigan para acá lo que comen!, les dijo Xbalamke.
—¡Está bien!, dijeron, cuando se fueron a traer lo suyo,
                              luego regresaron todos.
Hubo quienes sólo cosas podridas fueron a traer como comida,
hubo quienes sólo hojas de milpa fueron a traer,
hubo quienes sólo piedras fueron a traer,
hubo quienes sólo tierra fueron a traer.
Era variada la comida de los pequeños animales
                    los grandes animales.[168]
El último venía empujando algo
se había quedado el pizote:
un chilacayote fue a traer
    le venía dando vueltas con su trompa.

Y esto se utilizó como reemplazo de la cabeza de Junajpu.
De inmediato le labraron los ojos.
El cerebro para que pensara, vino del Cielo.[169]
Fue el mismo Uk'u'x Kaj,
          Jun Raqan el que había venido
                el que había bajado a la Casa de los
                       [Murciélagos.
Y aunque no fue fácil completarle la cara,
quedó muy bien,
incluso su piel adquirió una hermosa apariencia
y hasta llegó a hablar.
En eso ya quería amanecer
ya estaba teñido de rojo el horizonte
—¡Ennegrécelo otra vez!, Abuelo, le fue dicho a la deidad del
                       [amanecer.[170]
—¡Está bien!, dijo el anciano y lo tiznó.
Enseguida oscureció otra vez.
Cuatro veces tiznó el horizonte aquel abuelo.
"Está tiznando el tacuacín", dice ahora la gente
cuando se tiñe el horizonte de rojo y azul
y así estableció su existencia.
—¿Estará bien?, le fue preguntado a Junajpu.
—¡Sí, está bien!, contestó.
Y empezó a girar la cabeza
como si realmente fuera su cabeza.
Después, tomaron decisiones,
          se pusieron de acuerdo.
—Tal vez no debes jugar
únicamente haz como que lanzas,
seré yo quien lo haga todo, le dijo Xbalamke.
Luego le dio instrucciones a un conejo:
—Te pondrás allí, a la orilla del campo de juego,
allí vas a estar,
en medio de la siembra de tomates,[171] le fue dicho al conejo por
                       [Xbalamke.
—Cuando llegue la pelota contigo

debes salir corriendo,
yo haré lo demás, le fue dicho al conejo cuando fue instruido en la
[noche.
Luego amaneció,
allí estaban bien de salud cada uno de ellos.

Comenzaron a jugar de nuevo,
estando ya colocada la cabeza de Junajpu sobre el campo de juego:
—¡Hemos vencido!
¡Están acabados!
¡Ríndanse!
Están derrotados, les fue dicho.
Aún así gritó Junajpu:
—Tiren la cabeza como pelota, les dijo.
—Ya no siente dolor,
nos golpearemos a nosotros mismos.
Luego lanzaron la pelota los Señores de Xibalba
salió a su encuentro Xbalamke
la pelota fue a dar directamente a su cinturón donde la hizo rebotar
enviándola de una vez fuera del campo de juego,
en uno
dos rebotes llegó al tomatal;
al instante salió el conejo
se fue brincando,
atrás se fueron persiguiéndolo los de Xibalba.
En tumulto ruidoso,
gritando se fueron detrás del conejo.
Acabaron por irse todos los de Xibalba.

De inmediato los muchachos fueron a traer la cabeza de Junajpu,
pusieron el chilacayote de Xbalamke
asentaron el chilacayote sobre el campo de juego.
La cabeza de Junajpu era ya su verdadera cabeza
y los muchachos se pusieron muy contentos.
Mientras tanto, todavía seguían buscando la pelota los de Xibalba.
Enseguida los muchachos fueron a traer la pelota al tomatal

y los llamaron de una vez:
—¡Regresen!
Aquí está nuestra pelota,
¡Ya la encontramos!, dijeron.
Ya la tenían allí cuando regresaron los de Xibalba.
—¿Dónde estaba que ni la vimos?, dijeron éstos.
Luego se pusieron a jugar otra vez,
y fue parejo el juego para ambas partes.
Enseguida, el chilacayote fue apuntado por Xbalamke
el chilacayote se partió de una vez al caer al campo de juego,
trayendo a luz sus pepitas delante de ellos.[172]
—¿Adónde lo fueron a traer?
¿Dónde está quien lo trajo?, preguntaron los de Xibalba.
Y así fueron vencidos los Señores de Xibalba por parte de Junajpu y
Xbalamke.
En medio de grandes pruebas estuvieron;
pero no murieron a pesar de todo lo que les hicieron.

He aquí entonces su memoria,
la muerte de Junajpu y
Xbalamke.
Ésta es su memoria,
su muerte la que contaremos.
Cuanto les fue dicho lo hicieron,
todos los sufrimientos
los tormentos que les hicieron pasar;
pero no murieron de las pruebas de Xibalba,
ni fueron vencidos por todos los animales voraces que hay en Xibalba.

Enseguida mandaron a llamar a dos adivinos
como los que leen el futuro;
éstos son sus nombres: Xulu y
Pak'am.[173]
Ambos eran sabios.
—Si les preguntan los Señores de Xibalba

                    sobre nuestra muerte,
pues, ellos están discutiendo el porqué no hemos muerto y
                          porqué no hemos sido vencidos,
después de pasar sus tormentos,
ni sus animales pudieron con nosotros.
Ésta es, pues, la señal que tenemos en nuestros corazones:
la hoguera de piedra es su instrumento de nuestra muerte.
¿Acaso no se han reunido todos los de Xibalba?
Pero la verdad es que no vamos a morir.
Éstas son, pues, las instrucciones que les vamos a dar:
si les vienen a preguntar sobre nuestra muerte cuando nos quememos.
—¿Qué dicen ustedes, Xulu
                    Pak'am? Si les preguntan:
—"¿No sería bueno arrojar sus huesos al barranco?"
—"No conviene porque así pueden volver a la vida". Han de contestar.
—"¿No estaría bien si los colgamos a un árbol?", les han de preguntar
                                        [enseguida.
—"Así no estaría bien,
así los van a volver a ver". Han de contestar.
Cuando les digan por tercera vez:
—"Esto es lo que es bueno:
tiraremos sus huesos al río". Si les dicen esto ellos.
—"¡Así conviene que mueran!
Y mejor si se molieran sus huesos en una piedra,
como se muele la harina de maíz;
uno por uno hay que molerlos.
Luego hay que arrojarlos al río,
donde cae la fuente que parte hacia las pequeñas montañas y
                    hacia las grandes montañas". Han de
                                        [decir cuando
pongan en práctica nuestros consejos.
                    lo que les hemos dicho, dijeron el pequeño
                              [Junajpu[174] y
                                Xbalamke.

Cuando dieron esas instrucciones,
era porque ya sabían que iban a morir.

En eso se preparaba una gran hoguera de piedras
como hoguera para cocinar la dulce bebida, hicieron los de Xibalba,
utilizaron grandes ramas.
Enseguida vinieron los mensajeros,
                los que debían acompañarlos;
                los mensajeros de Jun Kame y
                        Wuqub Kame.
—"¡Que vengan!
Iríamos con los muchachos,
pero mejor que vengan a ver lo que cocinamos para ellos". Dicen los
                                    [Señores,
muchachos, les fue dicho.
—¡Está bien!, contestaron éstos.
Se fueron rápido,
y llegaron a la orilla de la hoguera.
Allí, entonces, quisieron forzarlos a jugar:
—¡Saltemos sobre nuestra dulce bebida!
Que sean cuatro veces las que pasemos encima,
uno después de otro, muchachos, les fue dicho por parte de Jun Kame.
—No traten de engañarnos con eso.
¿Acaso no sabemos de nuestra muerte, Señores?
¡Vean esto!, dijeron.
Luego, poniéndose frente a frente,
extendieron sus brazos los dos y
se lanzaron de cabeza hacia la hoguera.
Allí, pues, murieron los dos juntos.
Contentos se pusieron todos los de Xibalba,
alzándose en vocerío,
alzándose en silbidos:
—¡Los hemos vencido!
¡En realidad, no fue fácil que se entregaran!, exclamaron.

Enseguida fueron llamados Xulu y
                    Pak'am,
a quienes habían dejado sus instrucciones,

y les preguntaron a dónde debían ir sus huesos.
Luego del conjuro de Xibalba,
sus huesos fueron molidos
y los fueron a tirar al río.
Pero éstos no se fueron lejos,
sino directamente se asentaron debajo del agua,
y en jóvenes hermosos se convirtieron,
su apariencia volvió a ser la misma,
y así volvieron a mostrarse.

Al quinto día reaparecieron
y fueron vistos por la gente a la orilla del río,
los dos tenían la apariencia de hombres peces,[175]
cuando fueron vistos por los de Xibalba.
Los fueron a buscar, entonces, a las orillas de los ríos,
y al día siguiente se mostraron como dos pordioseros:
con harapos se vistieron,
con harapos se cubrían,
con harapos se tapaban.
Nada impresionaba de ellos cuando fueron vistos por los de Xibalba.
Era diferente lo que hacían ahora:
sólo el baile del pujuy,
     el baile de la comadreja;
sólo el baile del armadillo.
sólo el del ciempiés;[176]
sólo el de zancos bailaban ahora.
Además, hacían grandes prodigios:
quemaban una casa,
como si de verdad ardiera,
y de inmediato volvía a ser la misma.
Muchos de Xibalba se admiraban por esto.
Luego se autosacrificaban
moría uno de ellos;
se quedaba como si estuviera muerto.
Primero se mataban a sí mismos
y de inmediato volvían a la vida.

Impresionados estaban los de Xibalba con lo que hacían.
Todo esto que hacían
era el principio de la derrota de los de Xibalba.

Llegó enseguida la noticia de sus bailes a oídos de los
[Señores Jun Kame y
Wuqub Kame.

Al escucharlo preguntaron:
—¿Quiénes son esos dos mendigos?
¿Es verdad que causan tanto deleite?
—Realmente son muy hermosos sus bailes.
¡Todo lo que hacen!, contestó [el que había llevado la noticia].¹⁷⁷
La información que llegó con los Señores
la escucharon deleitable.
Enseguida, pidieron a sus mensajeros,
a sus mandaderos ir a llamarlos.
—"¡Que vengan a hacerlo acá,
para que lo veamos,
para que nos maravillemos de ellos,
y los admiremos! Dicen los Señores". Han de decirles, les fue dicho
a los mensajeros.
Llegando éstos con los bailarines
transmitieron el mensaje de los Señores.
—¡No nos gustaría!
Porque francamente nos da vergüenza.
¿No sería vergonzoso que nosotros entráramos a la casa de los
Señores?
Porque nuestra apariencia es muy mala.
¿No son acaso grandes nuestros ojos por la pobreza?
¿No se han dado cuenta que sólo somos bailadores?
¿Qué les podríamos decir a nuestros compañeros de pobreza
que quedan con el deseo de ver nuestros bailes,
y que se entusiasman con nosotros?
Eso no lo vamos a lograr con los Señores.
Así, pues, no queremos hacerlo, mensajeros, dijeron Junajpu y

De todos modos se los llevaron a la fuerza:
con castigos,
con sufrimientos;
a las malas se fueron.
No fue fácil que empezaran a caminar;
varias veces los forzaron,
iban y venían los mensajeros delante de ellos,
        los enviados a traerlos.
Así se fueron donde los Señores.

Llegaron, pues, ante los Señores,
se presentaron con humildad,
bajaron su cabeza al llegar;
se humillaron,
se doblaron,
se postraron;
se mostraron sencillos con sus harapos,
en realidad parecían pordioseros cuando llegaron.

Enseguida les preguntaron por su patria[178] y
        su pueblo de procedencia.
Les preguntaron también por su madre y
        su padre:
—¿De dónde vienen?, les fue dicho.
—Nunca lo hemos sabido, Señor,
no conocimos a nuestra madre ni
        a nuestro padre.
Éramos muy pequeños cuando ellos murieron,
        [contestaron únicamente,
        no revelaron nada.
—¡Está bien!
Presenten lo que hacen para que veamos.
¿Qué es lo que quieren que les demos en pago?, les preguntaron.
—¡No queremos nada!
En realidad tenemos miedo, le dijeron al Señor.

—¡No tengan miedo!
¡No tengan vergüenza!
Bailen:
que sea primero el baile donde se sacrifican a sí mismos;
luego quemen mi casa,
hagan todo lo que saben hacer.
Queremos verlos,
esto era nuestro deseo al mandarlos a traer,
y como son pobres les daremos su pago, les dijeron.

Entonces empezaron con sus cantos y
                              sus bailes.
Enseguida llegaron todos los de Xibalba,
se amontonaron los espectadores.
Todo lo bailaron:
bailaron la danza de la comadreja,
bailaron la danza del pujuy,
bailaron la danza del armadillo.
En eso les dijo el Señor:
—¡Sacrifiquen a mi perro,
luego revívanlo!, les fue dicho.
—¡Bien!, dijeron.
Enseguida sacrificaron al perro,
y luego volvió a la vida.
Realmente estaba contento el perro
cuando volvió a la vida;
meneaba su cola
cuando volvió a la vida.
Dijo entonces el Señor:
—¡Quemen ahora mi casa!, les fue dicho.
Cuando quemaron la casa del Señor,
estaba repleta de todos los Señores;
pero no se quemaron.
Al momento la volvieron a dejar igual;
ni un instante se consumió la casa de Jun Kame.
Esto lo admiraron mucho todos los Señores,

al igual que lo que bailaban.

Estaban contentísimos.

Luego les fue dicho por el Señor:

—¡Maten ahora a una persona!

¡Sacrifíquenla; pero que no muera!, les fue dicho.

—¡Está bien!, contestaron.

Al momento sujetaron a una persona,

y enseguida la sacrificaron,

             levantaron en alto el corazón extraído de esa persona;

             lo exhibieron ante los Señores.

Esto maravilló a Jun Kame y

                Wuqub Kame.

De inmediato hicieron volver a la vida a esa persona.

Rebosaba de alegría su corazón

cuando volvió a la vida.

Esto asombró a los Señores.

—¡Sacrifíquense ahora ustedes!

Que los veamos.

¡En realidad, nuestros corazones desean ver ese baile!, dijeron los

                                  [Señores

—¡Está bien, Señor!, contestaron.

Enseguida se autosacrificaron:

fue despedazado el pequeño Junajpu por parte de Xbalamke.

Uno por uno fueron esparcidas sus piernas y

                   sus brazos;

fue separada su cabeza,

y llevada a cierta distancia.

Fue extraído su corazón

y mojado fue puesto sobre hojas de milpa.

Al ver esto se pusieron fuera de sí[179] todos los Señores de Xibalba.

Ya sólo uno de ellos continuaba bailando: Xbalamke.

—¡Levántate!, dijo entonces.

Y al instante volvió a la vida,

ambos se regocijaron por esto,

asimismo se alegraron los Señores,

como si ellos mismos lo estuvieran haciendo.
Estaban emocionados los corazones de Jun Kame y
                                Wuqub Kame;
que sentían como si ellos mismos estuvieran bailando.
De pronto sus corazones se llenaron de deseo,
                                de ansiedad por los bailes del
pequeño Junajpu y
        Xbalamke.
De ahí que salieran estas palabras de Jun Kame y
                                Wuqub Kame:
—¡Hagan lo mismo con nosotros!
¡Sacrifíquennos!, dijeron.
—¡Uno a uno, sacrifíquennos!, dijeron Jun Kame y
                                Wuqub Kame al
                                        [pequeño Junajpu y
                                                Xbalamke.

—¡Está bien!
¡Volverán a la vida!
¿Acaso hay muerte para ustedes?[180]
Nosotros sólo venimos a divertirlos,
ustedes son los Señores de sus vasallos,
                                de sus hijos, les dijeron a los Señores.
Al primero que sacrificaron fue al cabecilla de los Señores:
Jun Kame llamado,
Señor de Xibalba.
Ya estaba muerto Jun Kame,
cuando tomaron a Wuqub Kame.
Pero no fueron vueltos a la vida.
De inmediato salieron huyendo los de Xibalba
al ver muertos a los Señores.
Les sacaron el corazón,
fueron sacrificados los dos.
Esto se hizo para castigarlos.
Tan rápido como había muerto uno de los Señores,
sin haberlo vuelto a la vida;

el otro Señor se humilló,
                  lloró delante de los bailadores;
                  no lo aceptaba,
                  no lo entendía:
—¡Tengan lástima de mí!, dijo al darse cuenta de lo que ocurría.
Terminaron huyendo todos sus vasallos,
                                   sus hijos a un gran barranco.
En un solo lugar se aglutinaron en ese gran abismo;
allí estaban amontonados
cuando encontraron incontables hormigas,
que se les arremolinaron en el barranco
y fue como si los hubieran arreado de allí.
Cuando volvieron,
se vinieron a entregar todos.
Se humillaron,
llegaron gimiendo.
Así, pues, fueron vencidos los Señores de Xibalba;
sólo por prodigios,
y sólo por la autotransformación que hicieron.

Hasta entonces revelaron sus nombres,
                  y se ensalzaron a sí mismos ante todos los de Xibalba:
—¡Oigan nuestros nombres:
los vamos a decir!
Les diremos también los nombres de nuestros padres.
He aquí quiénes somos:
somos el pequeño Junajpu y
                  Xbalamke, por nombre.
Y nuestros padres, que ustedes mataron, se llamaban
                                        [Jun Junajpu y
                                        Wuqub Junajpu.
¡Nosotros, pues, les hemos hecho pagar los tormentos,[181]
                                        los sufrimientos de nuestros
                                        [padres!
Nosotros también sufrimos todos los tormentos que ustedes nos
                                        [hicieron.

De esa cuenta vamos a acabar con todos ustedes.
¡Los vamos a matar!
Ya no hay quién los pueda salvar, les fue dicho.
Enseguida se humillaron,
            lloraron todos los de Xibalba:
—¡Tengan compasión de nosotros, Junajpu y
                              Xbalamke!
Es cierto que actuamos mal en contra de sus padres, como dicen;
los que están enterrados en el "sacrificadero del campo de juego",
                                        [reconocieron.
—¡Está bien, pues!
Ésta es nuestra palabra que vamos a decirles.
Oigan todos ustedes de Xibalba:
puesto que ya no serán grandes sus días
ni los de su descendencia;
tampoco ya no serán grandes las ofrendas que reciban.
Ya sólo un poco de sangre coagulada,
ya no habrá sangre limpia para ustedes.[182]
Sólo comales,
sólo ollas viejas,
sólo trastos inservibles;
ya sólo, pues, de las criaturas de los pajonales
            de las criaturas de los despoblados comerán.[183]
No será de ustedes ninguna de las hijas nacidas en claridad
                  de los hijos nacidos en claridad.[184]
Sólo los que se menosprecian serán de ustedes;[185]
esos son los que tienen culpa,
        los que pelean,
        los que se entristecen,
        los que se afligen.
¡Donde haya culpa, pueden entrar!
Ya no atacarán repentinamente a toda la gente.
¡Sólo serán invocados sobre sangre coagulada!, les fue dicho a todos
los de Xibalba.
Así fue, entonces, como empezó su desaparición,
y la negación a ser invocados.

Aunque no eran grandes sus días en la antigüedad,
sólo quería conflictos esta gente de antaño.
Realmente no eran divinos sus nombres en la antigüedad,
sólo que causaban espanto sus caras horribles.

Provocaban enemistad,
eran traidores,[186]
incitaban al mal y
a la discordia.
Eran diestros para esconder sus intenciones,
eran hipócritas,
malvados,[187]
engañadores,
opresores, les decían.[188]
Tenían pintadas las caras cuando se les encontraba.
Así fue entonces la pérdida de su grandeza y
de su poder.
Su dominio ya no volvió a ser grande.
Esto, por obra del pequeño Junajpu y
Xbalamke.

Mientras tanto lloraba e
invocaba su abuela frente a las matas de maíz,
las que ellos dejaron
[sembradas.
Retoñaron las matas de maíz,
luego se secaron.
Esto ocurrió cuando se quemaron en la hoguera.
Cuando volvieron a retoñar esas matas,
su abuela efectuó una ceremonia:
quemó copal ante las cañas,
esto, en memoria de sus nietos.
Se contentó el corazón de su abuela que por segunda vez retoñaran
[las cañas.
De ahí que fueran deificadas por su abuela,

y fue cuando las nombró: En medio de la casa,
                         En medio de la cosecha,
                         Cañas vivas,
                         Lecho de tierra; fueron los nombres
que llegaron a tener.

Así, pues, las denominó: En medio de la casa,
                         En medio de la cosecha;[189]
porque en medio de la casa sembraron aquellas matas.
Así mismo las denominó: Lecho de tierra,
                         Cañas vivas;[190]
porque sobre tierra aplanada sembraron las matas.
Así también las llamó Cañas vivas,
porque aquellas cañas retoñaron.
Estos nombres fueron puestos por Ixmukane
a lo que habían dejado sembrado Junajpu y
                         Xbalamke
para que precisamente fueran recordados por su abuela.

En relación con sus progenitores
Los que antiguamente habían muerto, Jun Junajpu y
                         Wuqub Junajpu.
Ellos pudieron ver los rostros de sus padres allá en Xibalba
y hablaron sus padres con ellos después que vencieron a Xibalba.

He aquí cómo arreglaron a sus padres:
reconstruyeron los restos de Wuqub Junajpu,
allá los fueron a juntar en el "sacrificadero del campo de juego",
pero ya sólo su cara fue necesaria.
Le pidieron que nombrara todas sus partes:
sólo su boca,
    su nariz,
    sus ojos, logró mencionar.
Ya muy poco pudo decir.
Y aunque su boca ya no pudo nombrar sus otras partes,

al menos había sido escuchada otra vez.
Así fue como aceptaron dejar los corazones de sus padres
que quedaron allá en el "sacrificadero del campo de juego".
—Aquí serán invocados.
¡Así va a ser!, les dijeron sus hijos, cuando consolaron sus corazones.
—Lo primero sea lo de ustedes,
serán los primeros en ser honrados por las hijas nacidas en claridad
por los hijos nacidos en claridad.
Sus nombres no serán olvidados.
¡Que así sea!
Les dijeron a sus padres, cuando consolaron a sus corazones.
—¡Nosotros sólo hemos hecho pagar su muerte,
su desaparición;
las penas,
los tormentos que les hicieron!
Éste fue, pues, su mensaje de despedida,
después que habían vencido a todos los de Xibalba.
Luego ascendieron para acá, en medio de la claridad.
De inmediato ascendieron al Cielo:
uno fue el Sol
y el otro fue la Luna.
Entonces se iluminó la bóveda del Cielo,
la faz de la Tierra,
en el Cielo se establecieron.

Luego subieron los cuatrocientos muchachos muertos por Sipakna.
En sus compañeros se convirtieron;
en estrellas del Cielo se volvieron.

CAPÍTULO CUARTO

He aquí el principio de cuando se pensó en la creación humana y
de cuando se buscó la naturaleza de su cuerpo.

Dijeron entonces Alom
              K'ajolom;
              Tz'aqol
              Bitol;
              Tepew Q'ukumatz, así llamados:
—Se acerca el amanecer.
¡Que se termine la obra!
Que aparezcan los que sustentan,
              los que nutren;
              las hijas nacidas en claridad,
              los hijos nacidos en claridad.
¡Que aparezca la humanidad,
la gente sobre la faz de la Tierra!, dijeron.
Llegaron para juntarse,
y celebraron consejo en medio de la oscuridad,
              en el amanecer.
Cuando buscaron
y discutieron,
reflexionaron,
y meditaron, aquí.
De esa manera surgió la idea clara,
              diáfana;

encontraron y
decidieron qué se necesitaba para el cuerpo humano.
Ya faltaba poco para que aparecieran el Sol,
                              la Luna,
                              las estrellas sobre Tz'aqol,
                                        Bitol.

De Paxil
de K'ayala', así llamados[191]
vinieron las mazorcas amarillas,
          las mazorcas blancas.
Éstos son los nombres de los animales
los que trajeron el alimento: la zorra[192]
                         el coyote;
                         la cotorra,
                         el cuervo.
Fueron cuatro animales los que trajeron noticia
                         [de las mazorcas amarillas
                          de las mazorcas blancas.
Ellos venían de Pan Paxil,
y fueron los que enseñaron el camino a Paxil.
Allí encontraron el alimento,
los ingredientes para el cuerpo de la gente creada,
                         la gente formada.
Agua se usó para la sangre,
                 en sangre humana se convirtió
maíz fue lo utilizado por Alom
                 K'ajolom.
Se pusieron contentos al encontrar un lugar de abundancia[193]
lleno de fragancias,
abundante en mazorcas amarillas y
                 mazorcas blancas,
abundante también en pataxte y
                 cacao;
de incontables zapotes,
                 anonas,[194]

jocotes,
nance,
matasanos y
miel.
Estaba rebosante de alimento este pueblo de Pan Paxil
                              Pan K'ayala', así
                                            [llamado.
Había comida,
había de todas clases: pequeños alimentos,
                       grandes alimentos;
                       pequeñas plantas,
                       grandes plantas;
los que enseñaron el camino fueron los animales.

A continuación fueron molidas las mazorcas amarillas,
                       las mazorcas blancas;
Nueve molidas[195] le dio Ixmukane,
comida fue la utilizada
y junto con el agua de masa se originaron las extremidades,
                       la fuerza humana.[196]
Esto lo dispusieron Alom,
                    K'ajolom;
                    Tepew Q'ukumatz, así llamados.
Luego pusieron en la palabra[197] su creación,
                       la construcción de nuestras primeras
madres y
padres.
Sólo fueron mazorcas amarillas
           mazorcas blancas su carne;
sólo de masa de maíz fueron las piernas
                       los brazos humanos;
los de nuestros padres primigenios.
Fueron cuatro los humanos creados,
sólo masa de maíz fue utilizada en la creación de sus carnes.

Éstos son los nombres de las primeras gentes creadas y
formadas:
La primera persona fue Balam Ki'tze',
la segunda fue Balam Aq'ab;
la tercera fue Majuk'utaj y
la cuarta fue Ik'ibalam.[198]
Éstos son, pues, los nombres de nuestras primeras madres y
padres.

Sólo fueron creados,
sólo fueron moldeados, se dice.
No tuvieron madre,
no tuvieron padre.
Sólo de los varones hablamos.[199]
No hubo mujer quien los diera a luz
y tampoco fueron engendrados por Tz'aqol,
Bitol;
Alom,
K'ajolom.

Sólo fue por prodigio,
sólo por portento fueron creados,
fueron construidos por Tz'aqol,
Bitol;
Alom,
K'ajolom;
Tepew Q'ukumatz.

Y cuando la creación dio su fruto,
aparecieron los humanos:
hablaron y
platicaron;
vieron y
escucharon.
Caminaron y
tocaron las cosas.
Eran muy buenas gentes,
eran hermosas sus facciones varoniles.

Tuvieron respiración
y podían ver;
al punto se extendió su mirada
alcanzaron a ver
alcanzaron a conocer todo lo habido debajo del Cielo.
Cuando miraban, al instante observaban y
                                  contemplaban la bóveda del Cielo,
                                        la faz de la Tierra.
Nada los obstruía,
todo lo podían ver;
no tenían que caminar para ver lo que hay debajo del Cielo
sólo debían estar donde estaban, para ver.
Su conocimiento llegó a ser grande,
su mirada traspasaba los árboles,
                     las piedras;
                     los lagos,
                     el mar;
                     las montañas,
                     los valles.
En verdad eran personas dotadas, Balam Ki'tze',
                               Balam Aq'ab,
                               Majuk'utaj e
                               Ik'ibalam.
Entonces les preguntaron, el Creador y
                     el Formador:
—¿Qué sienten de su existencia?
¿Acaso no pueden ver?
¿Acaso no pueden escuchar?
¿Acaso no está bien su lenguaje,
como su manera de andar?
¡Miren, pues,
observen lo que hay debajo del Cielo!
¿Acaso no son claras las montañas,
                     los valles que miran?
¡Compruébenlo otra vez!, les fue dicho.
Enseguida terminaron de ver todo lo habido debajo del Cielo

y después agradecieron a Tz'aqol
                    Bitol:
—¡En verdad, dos veces gracias
                    tres veces gracias!
Porque hemos sido creados
y nos han sido dadas nuestras bocas
                    nuestras caras.
Hablamos,
escuchamos;
meditamos,
y nos movemos.
Nos sentimos muy bien,
hemos conocido lo que está lejos
                    lo que está cerca.
Asimismo hemos visto lo que es grande
                    lo que es pequeño debajo del Cielo, y
                                sobre la Tierra.
Gracias a ustedes hemos sido creados,
                    hemos sido construidos
                    hemos sido formados,
                    hemos sido originados. ¡Tú, abuela nuestra
                                Tú, abuelo nuestro!,
                                        [dijeron dando
gracias por su creación y
su formación.
Acabaron por conocerlo todo,
vieron las cuatro esquinas
        los cuatro lados;
        la bóveda del Cielo,
        la faz de la Tierra.

Pero esto no lo oyeron con gusto el Creador y
                                el Formador.
—No está bien lo que han dicho nuestras criaturas,
                    nuestras obras:
"Hemos entendido todo, lo que es grande

lo que es pequeño", han dicho.

De ahí que entraran de nuevo en consejo Alom
                                        K'ajolom
—¿Qué hemos de hacer ahora con ellos?
Su vista sólo debe alcanzar lo que está cerca,
sólo deben ver un poco de la faz de la Tierra.
No está bien lo que dicen.
¿Acaso no son simple creación,
                    simple formación, por nombre?
¿Acaso se anticipa que ellos también serán dioses?
Si todavía no han procreado,
            ni se han multiplicado.
¡Que se hagan la siembra y
                el amanecer!
Ahora que todavía no son muchos.
¡Que así sea!
Modifiquémoslos un poco,
eso es lo que hay que hacer,
porque no está bien lo que hemos encontrado.
¿Acaso van a ser iguales a nosotros,
porque lejos llega su conocimiento,
porque lo miran todo?, esto fue lo dicho por Uk'u'x Kaj,
                                        Jun Raqan
                                        Ch'ipi Kaqulja
                                        Raxa Kaqulja;
                                        Tepew Q'ukumatz:
                                        Alom
                                        K'ajolom;
                                        Xpiyakok
                                        Ixmukane;
                                        Tz'aqol
                                        Bitol; así llamados.
Enseguida cambiaron la naturaleza de su creación
                        de su formación.
Sus ojos fueron empañados por parte de Uk'u'x Kaj,

fueron opacados como cuando se echa el aliento sobre la faz de un
[espejo,
se puso borrosa su visión.
Ya sólo podían ver lo que estaba cerca
sólo era claro lo que estaba a su alrededor.

Así fue, entonces, la pérdida de su sabiduría
junto con todos los conocimientos de los cuatro
[humanos.
El origen y
el principio.
Así fue, pues, la creación
la formación de nuestros primeros abuelos
de nuestros padres, por parte de
[Uk'u'x Kaj,
Uk'u'x Ulew.

Entonces existieron sus compañeras,
las que serían sus esposas.
Los mismos dioses las pensaron también.
Como si fuera en un sueño las recibieron.
Verdaderamente eran hermosas las mujeres que estaban con
[Balam Ki'tze',
Balam Aq'ab,
Majuk'utaj e
Ik'ibalam.
Con sus esposas al lado, realmente despertaron a la vida;
al instante se alegraron sus corazones por sus compañeras.
Éstos son, entonces, los nombres de sus esposas:
Kaqapaloja'[200] es el nombre de la esposa de Balam Ki'tze',
Chomija'[201] es el nombre de la esposa de Balam Aq'ab,
Tz'ununija'[202] es el nombre de la esposa de Majuk'utaj,
Kak'ixaja'[203] es el nombre de la esposa de Ik'ibalam.
Éstos son, pues, los nombres de sus esposas,
las que eran Señoras principales,

las que dieron origen a la gente de los pueblos pequeños,
de los pueblos grandes.

Éste es nuestro origen,
el de nosotros, la gente k'iche'.
Muchos también llegaron a ser los adoradores,
los penitentes.[204]
Ya no solamente eran ellos cuatro,
pero ellas cuatro fueron las madres de nosotros la gente k'iche'.

Diferentes eran los nombres de cada uno de ellos
cuando se multiplicaron allá en el Oriente,
muchos llegaron a ser los nombres de la gente:
Tepew Oloman,[205]
K'ojaj,
K'enech Ajaw,[206] se llamaban otros,
y se multiplicaron allá en el Oriente.
Se sabe también del principio de los Tamub,
de los Ilokab;[207]
que juntos salieron del mismo lugar de donde sale el Sol.
Balam Ki'tze' era el abuelo,
el padre de las nueve casas grandes de los Kaweq.
Balam Aq'ab era el abuelo,
el padre de las nueve casas grandes de los Nija'ib.
Majuk'utaj era el abuelo,
el padre de las cuatro casas grandes de los Ajaw
[K'iche'.[208]

Tres linajes distintos existieron,
pero no está en el olvido el nombre de los abuelos,
de los padres;
los que procrearon
los que se propagaron allá donde sale el Sol.
Además, vinieron los Tamub,
los Ilokab junto con las trece ramas de pueblos,
trece casas reales:[209]

los Rabinaleb,
los Kaqchikeleb,
los Ajtz'ikinaja que incluye a los Saqajib y
a los Lakamib;
los Kumatz,
los Tujal Ja,
los Uch'abaja,
los Ajch'umilaja,
los Ajkibaja,
los Ajbatenaja,
los Akul Winaq,
los Balamija',
los Kanchajeleb,
los Balam Kolob,[210]
éstos son sólo los principales pueblos,
son las ramas de los pueblos, como les decimos.
Sólo los principales hemos nombrado.

Muchos otros se originaron de cada una de estas ciudadelas;[211]
pero no hemos escrito sus nombres.
Ellos también se multiplicaron allá en el Oriente.
Llegó a ser mucha gente,
en la oscuridad se multiplicaron.
Todavía no había nacido el Sol,
ni la luz cuando se multiplicaron.
En un solo lugar estuvieron todos,
en gran número existían y
caminaban allá en el Oriente.
Todavía no mantenían
no sustentaban [a sus deidades];
sólo alzaban la vista hacia el Cielo,
tampoco sabían a dónde ir.
Por mucho tiempo permanecieron así
mientras estuvieron confortables.[212]

Había gente de piel oscura,

gente de piel clara,[213]
era una gran variedad de gente y
una gran cantidad de idiomas de la gente;
que miraban desde la orilla donde estaban hacia el Cielo.

Había gente de la montaña
que no había sido vista.
Todavía no tenían casa,
y se mantenían errantes en las pequeñas montañas,
                            en las grandes montañas.
"Como si fueran locos", decían
cuando despreciaban a la gente de la montaña, se cuenta.
Allá vieron la salida del Sol,
y una sola era la lengua de todos.[214]

Todavía no se invocaba a las estelas;[215]
tenían muy presente las palabras de Tz'aqol,
                            Bitol;
                    de Uk'u'x Kaj,
                            Uk'u'x Ulew, decían.

Sólo esperaban con ansiedad la siembra del amanecer,
se mantenían rogando,
sus palabras eran reverentes,
ellos eran reverentes,
eran obedientes,
eran respetuosos.
Elevaban su vista hacia el Cielo,
pedían por sus hijas
            por sus hijos:
—¡Ay!, Tz'aqol,
            Bitol
¡Míranos,
escúchanos!
No nos abandones,

no nos desampares.
Tú, divinidad en el Cielo,
              en la Tierra.
Corazón del Cielo,
Corazón de la Tierra.
Danos nuestra señal
        nuestra descendencia mientras haya Sol,
                        mientras haya claridad.[216]
Cuando sea la siembra,
cuando amanezca:
ubícanos en muchos caminos verdes,
                        veredas verdes.
Que sea en valles planos
        en pueblos planos.
Muy buenos valles
muy buenos pueblos.
Que sea buena la vida y
                la existencia que nos otorgues.
Tú, Jun Raqan
Ch'ipi Kaqulja
Raxa Kaqulja;
Ch'ipi Nanawak
Raxa Nanawak;[217]
Wok
Junajpu;[218]
Tepew Q'ukumatz:
Alom
K'ajolom;
Xpiyakok
Ixmukane;
Abuela del Sol
Abuela de la claridad.
¡Cuando sea la siembra,
cuando amanezca!, decían cuando ayunaban e
                                invocaban;
esperando con ansiedad el amanecer,

esperando ver la salida del Sol.
Contemplaban al lucero de la mañana,[219]
            la gran estrella en el nacimiento del Sol,
            la que enciende la bóveda del Cielo y
                        la superficie de la Tierra,
            la que guía a la humanidad creada,
                        a la humanidad formada.
Dijeron entonces Balam Ki'tze',
            Balam Aq'ab,
            Majuk'utaj e
            Ik'ibalam:
—¡Esperemos que amanezca!, dijeron.
Ellos eran grandes sabios,
varones entendidos,
eran respetuosos,
eran obedientes,[220] así se les decía.
Todavía no había estelas que protegieran a nuestras primeras madres,
                        a nuestros primeros padres.
Pero se cansaron sus corazones de esperar al Sol.
Ya eran muy numerosos los pueblos
incluida la gente mexicana,[221]
y los adoradores,
los penitentes.
—¡Vámonos!
Vamos a buscar y
vamos a ver si hay quién cuide nuestra descendencia.[222]
Al encontrarlos, quemaremos ante ellos.
De la manera en que estamos,
no tenemos quién vele por nosotros, dijeron, pues, Balam Ki'tze',
                        Balam Aq'ab,
                        Majuk'utaj e
                        Ik'ibalam.

Y habiendo escuchado noticias de una ciudadela,
se dirigieron hacia allá.

Éste es el nombre del lugar²²³
hacia donde se fueron Balam Ki'tze',
                            Balam Aq'ab,
                            Majuk'utaj e
                            Ik'ibalam
junto con los Tamub e
                Ilokab:
Tulán
Suywa;²²⁴
siete cuevas,
siete barrancos, se llamaba aquella ciudadela²²⁵ donde llegaron,
                                    donde recibieron
                                        [sus deidades.

Llegaron, entonces, todos a Tulán,
era incontable la gente que llegó,
caminaban en multitud
y en orden les fueron dadas sus deidades.
Siendo los primeros Balam Ki'tze',
                            Balam Aq'ab,
                            Majuk'utaj e
                            Ik'ibalam quienes estaban contentos.
—Esto es lo que buscábamos.
¡Lo hemos encontrado!, dijeron.
El primero en aparecer fue Tojil, nombre de la deidad;²²⁶
que fue llevado a cuestas por Balam Ki'tze'.
Luego apareció Awilix, el nombre de la deidad,²²⁷
que cargó Balam Aq'ab.
Jaqawitz,²²⁸
es el nombre de la deidad que recibió Majuk'utaj;
Nik'aqaj Taq'aj²²⁹
es el nombre de la deidad que recibió Ik'ibalam.
Allí estaban los compañeros de los k'iche'es,
los Tamub también recibieron [su deidad]
fue el mismo Tojil para los Tamub,
tenía nombre lo recibido por los abuelos

los padres de los Señores Tamub, como
[sabemos ahora.
Los terceros fueron los Ilokab,
también fue Tojil el que recibieron los abuelos
los padres de los Señores, así lo
[sabemos ahora.

De esta manera, entonces, se denominan los tres grupos k'iche'es.
No se separaron porque tenían una misma deidad:
[Tojil para los k'iche'es,
Tojil para los Tamub e
Ilokab;
uno solo era el nombre de su deidad
y por eso no se separaron los tres grupos k'iche'es.
Era en verdad grande la naturaleza de los tres: Tojil,
Awilix y
Jaqawitz.
Luego entraron todos los demás pueblos:
los Rabinaleb,
los Kaqchikeleb,
los Ajtz'ikinaja,
y la gente mexicana, como se llaman ahora.
Allí fue donde se alteró el idioma de los pueblos,
sus idiomas empezaron a diferenciarse.
Ya no se entendían bien entre sí, cuando salieron de Tulán.
Allí fue entonces, donde se apartaron unos de otros:
algunos siguieron hacia el Oriente,
pero muchos más se vinieron para acá.
Sólo con pieles se cubrían,
todavía no vestían muy buenas ropas,
sólo con pieles de animales se adornaban.
Eran pobres,
no tenían nada;
pero era prodigiosa su naturaleza cuando salieron
[de Tulán
Suywa;

Siete cuevas
Siete barrancos,
como se dice en el antiguo texto.[230]

Caminaron en grandes grupos para llegar a Tulán;
todavía no había fuego.
Nada más estaban los de Tojil
la deidad de los pueblos,
el primero en crear el fuego.
No está claro cómo lo produjo,
ya estaba ardiendo su fuego cuando lo vieron Balam Ki'tze',
Balam Aq'ab.
—¡Ay!, todavía no ha aparecido nuestro fuego.
¡Nos moriremos de frío!, exclamaron.
Entonces habló Tojil:
—¡No se aflijan!
Tendrán el suyo.
El fuego del que hablan, se apagará, les dijo, pues, Tojil.
—¿No es verdad que tú eres dios?
el que nos mantiene
el que nos sustenta
¡Tú, nuestro dios!, dijeron, agradeciendo lo
[dicho por Tojil.
—¡Está bien!
En verdad soy su dios.
¡Que así sea!
Soy su señor.
¡Que así sea!
Les fue dicho a los adoradores,
a los penitentes, por parte de Tojil.
Así fue como se entusiasmaron esos pueblos,
estaban contentos por su fuego.

En eso comenzó a caer una gran lluvia,
todavía ardía el fuego de los pueblos,

cuando cayeron grandes cantidades de granizo sobre todos los pueblos,
que su fuego se apagó por el granizo.
Se quedaron otra vez sin fuego.
Entonces pidieron otra vez por su fuego Balam Ki'tze',
$\qquad\qquad\qquad\qquad$ Balam Aq'ab:
—¡Tú, Tojil,
de verdad nos estamos muriendo de frío!, le dijeron a Tojil.
—¡Está bien!
No se aflijan, dijo Tojil.
De inmediato sacó fuego,
dando vueltas dentro de su sandalia.[231]

Enseguida se alegraron Balam Ki'tze',
$\qquad\qquad\qquad$ Balam Aq'ab,
$\qquad\qquad\qquad$ Majuk'utaj e
$\qquad\qquad\qquad$ Ik'ibalam;
y luego se calentaron.

Pero continuaba apagado el fuego de los otros pueblos
y se estaban muriendo de frío;
enseguida comenzaron a llegar
los que pedían por su fuego a Balam Ki'tze',
$\qquad\qquad\qquad$ Balam Aq'ab,
$\qquad\qquad\qquad$ Majuk'utaj e
$\qquad\qquad\qquad$ Ik'ibalam.

Ya no soportaban el frío
$\qquad\qquad\qquad$ ni el granizo;
estaban temblando
y tiritando,
ya no tenían vida;
les temblaban las piernas y
$\qquad\qquad$ los brazos;
las manos las tenían tiesas, cuando vinieron:
—No nos avergonzamos ante ustedes
sólo les pedimos un poco de su fuego, dijeron al llegar.

Pero no fueron atendidos.
Ante esto, aquellos pueblos echaron maldiciones.
Ya era diferente la lengua de Balam Ki'tze',
                              Balam Aq'ab,
                              Majuk'utaj e
                              Ik'ibalam.

—¡Ay! ¿Dónde hemos dejado nuestra lengua?
¿Qué es lo que hemos hecho?
¡Nos hemos perdido!
¿Dónde fuimos engañados?
Era una sola nuestra lengua cuando fuimos a Tulán.
Y era uno solo nuestro lugar de origen,
                    nuestro lugar de creación.
¡No está bien lo que hemos hecho!, exclamaron todos los pueblos
bajo los árboles
bajo los bejucos.
De pronto apareció una persona[232] delante de Balam Ki'tze',
                              Balam Aq'ab,
                              Majuk'utaj e
                              Ik'ibalam.
Dijo entonces este mensajero de Xibalba:
—De verdad que éste es su dios,
el que han buscado,
el que representa la memoria de su creador
                    de su formador.
No les den fuego a los pueblos
hasta que ellos no den algo a Tojil
no acepten lo que ellos les ofrezcan.
Pidan lo que pertenece a Tojil,
          de él depende lo que ellos deben dar por recibir fuego,
                              [dijo el de Xibalba.
Éste tenía alas,
como las alas de un murciélago.
—Yo soy enviado de quienes los crearon
               de quienes los formaron, dijo el de Xibalba.

Se pusieron contentos,
se engrandecieron en sus corazones, Tojil,
                                    Awilix,
                                    Jaqawitz, ante lo dicho por el
de Xibalba.
Pero al instante se esfumó de su presencia,
no se vio cómo desapareció.²³³

De nuevo llegaron los pueblos,
estaban muriéndose de frío;
caía un granizo espeso,
una lluvia negra,²³⁴
y granos de hielo.
Era insoportable el frío en que se encontraban,
                            se encorvaban,
                                    iban entumecidos por el frío todos
los pueblos cuando llegaron donde estaban Balam Ki'tze',
                                    Balam Aq'ab,
                                    Majuk'utaj e
                                    Ik'ibalam.
Era inmensa la aflicción de sus corazones,
se cubrían la boca
se cubrían la cara.²³⁵

Llegaron, pues, los suplicantes²³⁶ delante de Balam Ki'tze',
                                    Balam Aq'ab,
                                    Majuk'utaj e
                                    Ik'ibalam:

—¿Acaso no nos tienen lástima?
Les pedimos un poco de su fuego.
¿Acaso no se encontró
no se reveló
que era una sola nuestra casa y
        una sola nuestra patria
cuando ustedes fueron creados
cuando ustedes fueron formados?

¡Tengan misericordia de nosotros!, dijeron.
—¿Qué nos darán ustedes a cambio
para que les tengamos misericordia?, les fue preguntado entonces.
—¡Está bien!
Les daremos plata, contestaron los pueblos.
—No queremos plata, dijeron Balam Ki'tze',
                                      Balam Aq'ab.
—¿Qué es lo que en verdad quieren?
¿Si lo podemos saber?, preguntaron de nuevo los pueblos.
—¡Está muy bien! Vamos a preguntarle a Tojil,
y luego se los diremos, les respondieron.
Enseguida le preguntaron a Tojil:
—¿Qué es lo que deben dar los pueblos, tú, Tojil,
los que han venido a pedir tu fuego?, le preguntaron, pues,

                                      [Balam Ki'tze',
                                      Balam Aq'ab,
                                      Majuk'utaj e
                                      Ik'ibalam.

—¡Está muy bien!
"¿Querrán dar[237] sus costados
                sus sobacos?
¿Querrán sus corazones, abrazarme, yo que soy Tojil?
Si no quieren,
entonces no les daré su fuego, dice Tojil",
                                      deben decirles.
"Esto todavía no ocurrirá
no es ahora que deben dar sus costados
                        sus sobacos. Manda a decir",
                                      Les dice.
Ésta fue la respuesta a Balam Ki'tze',
                        Balam Aq'ab,
                        Majuk'utaj e
                        Ik'ibalam.
Luego ellos transmitieron las palabras de Tojil.
—¡Está bien!
Que se amamante,

y está bien que lo abracemos, dijeron entonces,
cuando toleraron
y aceptaron la palabra de Tojil.
No lo pensaron:[238]
—¡Está bien!, dijeron de inmediato.
Recibieron el fuego,
y se calentaron.
Pero hubo un grupo que sólo se robó el fuego en medio del humo,
fueron los de la Casa del Murciélago,
Chamalkan,[239] se llamaba la deidad de los Kaqchikeleb
y era un murciélago su imagen.
Cuando pasaron entre el humo
lo hicieron suavemente y se llevaron el fuego.
Los Kaqchikeleb no pidieron por su fuego y
tampoco se dejaron vencer;
los demás pueblos sí fueron derrotados
cuando aceptaron que lo de su costado
                    lo de su sobaco, fuera extraído.
Ésta es, pues, "la extracción" de la que habló Tojil.
Cuando serían sacrificados los pueblos en su presencia,
cuando les arrancarían sus corazones de los costados
                    de los sobacos.
Pero esto todavía no se había comenzado a hacer,
cuando Tojil adivinó la toma de poder y
                    majestad por Balam Ki'tze',
                    Balam Aq'ab,
                    Majuk'utaj e
                    Ik'ibalam.

Allá de donde venían, Tulán,
                    Suywa,
no comían,
en unidad guardaban ayuno;
así se mantenían mirando la aurora
esperando la salida del Sol,
se turnaban para ver la gran estrella,

llamada Ik'oq'ij.
La que sale antes que el Sol,
cuando nace el Sol;
la hermosa estrella de la mañana.

Siempre dirigían la vista hacia el Oriente
cuando estuvieron allá en Tulán
                                    Suywa, por nombre,
de donde vinieron sus deidades.
No fue realmente aquí donde recibieron su poder y
                                    su autoridad.
Fue allá donde fueron derrotados[240] y
                    sometidos los grandes pueblos,
                            los pequeños pueblos;
cuando fueron sacrificados ante Tojil;
y le ofrendaron su sangre
                su sangre coagulada,
                su costado,
                sus sobacos toda la gente.
De Tulán vino entonces, al instante su poder,
como la gran sabiduría que llegaron a adquirir
                            [en medio de la oscuridad,
                            en medio del amanecer.

Luego se vinieron,
partieron de allá,
abandonaron el Oriente.
—Éste no es nuestro hogar,
vámonos, para ver dónde nos hemos de establecer, dijo, entonces,
Tojil.
En verdad les hablaba a Balam Ki'tze',
                    Balam Aq'ab,
                    Majuk'utaj e
                    Ik'ibalam.
—¡Pero antes tienen que agradecer!

Deben sangrarse las orejas,
punzarse los codos.
¡Hagan su penitencia!
Ésta es su manera de agradecer a los dioses.
—¡Está bien!, respondieron y se sangraron las orejas.
Lloraron en su canto
su partida de Tulán.
Lloraron con sentimiento cuando se vinieron,
cuando abandonaron Tulán.
—¡Ay! No es aquí donde veremos el amanecer,
cuando nazca el Sol,
el que alumbra la faz de la Tierra, dijeron.
Luego se vinieron
solamente acampaban a la orilla de los caminos,
sólo que algunas gentes se quedaban donde dormían.
Otros pueblos se levantaban de nuevo
y siempre miraban a la estrella,
la que precede al Sol.
Ésta era la señal del amanecer en sus corazones,
cuando salieron de allá del Oriente.
En unidad pasaron por Nim Xo'l,²⁴¹ como se le llama ahora.
Luego llegaron sobre una montaña.
Allí se juntó toda la gente k'iche' con los otros pueblos.
Allí, pues, llegaron todos a celebrar consejo.
Esa montaña se llama ahora Chi Pixab²⁴²
así se llama la montaña donde se juntaron.
Allí, se identificaron unos a otros:
—¡Yo soy, quien está aquí!
Soy gente k'iche'.
¡Tú ahí!,
Tamub ha de ser tu nombre, les fue dicho a los Tamub.
Luego dijeron:
—Tú Ilokab,
Ilokab ha de ser tu nombre.
Que no desaparezcan las tres ramas k'iche'es,

es una sola nuestra palabra,²⁴³ dijeron cuando se pusieron sus
[nombres.

Luego fueron nombrados los Kaqchikeleb:
Kaqchikeleb fue su nombre;
asimismo, los Rabinaleb
que fue el nombre que adquirieron.
No se ha perdido hasta hoy
también a los Ajtz'ikinaja, como se llaman ahora.
Éstos fueron los nombres que se pusieron entre sí.

Tuvieron que llegar allí
a esperar el amanecer,
a observar la salida de la estrella,
la que se anticipa al nacimiento del Sol.
—De allá venimos,
sólo que nos hemos separado, se dijeron entre sí.
Afligían a sus corazones las grandes penas que venían pasando,
no había comida,
no había sustento.
Sólo olían la raíz de sus bastones,
y así se imaginaban que comían;
no se alimentaban mientras venían.

No está claro cómo cruzaron el mar,
como si no hubiera mar pasaron;
sólo sobre unas piedras pasaron
allí estaban las piedras en la arena,
y le pusieron por nombre
Piedras en Hilera
Arenas Arrancadas, llamaron al lugar por donde pasaron el mar.²⁴⁴
Estaban separadas las aguas donde pasaron.
Sus corazones estaban afligidos cuando celebraron consejo,
no tenían nada que comer,
sólo algo para beber hecho de una sola clase de maíz.
Allí, pues, cargados hasta la cima de la montaña llamada Chi Pixab,

llevaban consigo a Tojil,
                    Awilix y
                    Jaqawitz.
Ayuno completo observaba Balam Ki'tze' junto con su esposa.
Kaqapaloja' se llamaba la esposa.
Lo mismo hacía Balam Aq'ab con su esposa,
Chomija', llamada.
También Majuk'utaj mantenía ayuno completo junto con su esposa,
Tz'ununija' llamada;
e Ik'ibalam
con Kak'ixaja', que era el nombre de su esposa.
Ellos eran, pues, los que ayunaban en la oscuridad
                              en el amanecer.
Era grande su pesar cuando estuvieron en la montaña Chi Pixab,
llamada ahora.
Y allí hablaron de nuevo sus dioses.

Esto es lo que dijeron, entonces, Tojil,
                    Awilix,
                    Jaqawitz a Balam Ki'tze',
                              Balam Aq'ab,
                              Majuk'utaj e
                              Ik'ibalam.
—¡Debemos irnos,
debemos marcharnos!
Éste no es lugar donde debemos estar,
en un lugar escondido deben ubicarnos.
¡Ya se acerca el amanecer!
¿No sería una desgracia para ustedes si somos capturados por los
                                        [guerreros?
Construyan lugares donde podamos estar disponibles para ustedes,
                                        [adoradores y
                                        penitentes.
A cada quien en su lugar deben ubicarnos, dijeron, cuando hablaron.
—¡Está bien!
Nos marcharemos de aquí,

iremos a buscar unos bosques, contestaron todos.
Enseguida cada quien empezó a cargar con su deidad.
Así llevaron a Awilix a un barranco,
"barranco escondido" lo llamaron;
era un gran barranco en medio del bosque,
"Lugar de Awilix" se llama ahora donde se quedó.
Fue escondido en el barranco por parte de Balam Aq'ab.
En orden de ubicación, éste fue el primero.

Luego dejaron a Jaqawitz sobre una gran pirámide[245]
"Jaqawitz" se llama la montaña ahora;
la cual terminaron de habitar,
allí se quedó su dios llamado Jaqawitz.
Asimismo se quedó Majuk'utaj con su deidad,
el segundo de los dioses que escondieron;
pero no fue en un bosque donde quedó Jaqawitz,
sino en un cerro desmontado fue escondido Jaqawitz.

Luego siguió Balam Ki'tze'
vino a un gran bosque,
para esconder a Tojil, vino Balam Ki'tze'.
"Pa Tojil" se llama ahora esa montaña.
Luego nombraron aquel escondite en el barranco como: "medicina
[de Tojil".

Estaba lleno de serpientes,
estaba lleno de jaguares,
                cascabeles,[246] y
                barbamarillas.
Allí en la montaña los dejaron,
fueron escondidos por los adoradores y
                        penitentes.
Juntos se quedaron Balam Ki'tze',
                Balam Aq'ab,
                Mujuk'utaj e
                Ik'ibalam.
En unidad esperaron el amanecer

allí, sobre la montaña llamada Jaqawitz.

A poca distancia estaba el dios de los Tamub
                        con los Ilokab,
Amaq' Tam[247] se llamaba el lugar donde estuvo el dios de los Tamub
y allí les amaneció.
Amaq' Uq'in k'at[248] se llama el lugar donde les amaneció a los Ilokab,
y allí estuvo el dios de los Ilokab,
a corta distancia entre la montaña.

Allí también estaban todos los Rabinaleb,
                        los Kaqchikeleb,
                        los Ajtz'ikinaja;
todos los pueblos pequeños y
            pueblos grandes.
Juntos se detuvieron,
en unidad les amaneció;
en unidad esperaron la salida de la gran estrella,
                        Ik'oq'ij, por nombre.
—La que sale antes que el Sol, cuando amanece, dijeron.
En unidad, pues, estuvieron Balam Ki'tze',
                        Balam Aq'ab,
                        Majuk'utaj, e
                        Ik'ibalam.
No dormían,
ni tenían descanso.
Había una gran ansiedad en sus corazones,
                        en sus vientres por la aurora,
                                por el amanecer.
Encima de eso, sintieron vergüenza,
los embargó una gran tristeza,
            una gran angustia porque el sufrimiento los abrumaba.
Así se encontraban.
—No es un lugar agradable a donde hemos venido.
¡Ay! Si tan sólo pudiéramos ver el nacimiento del Sol.
¿Qué hemos hecho?

Éramos iguales en nuestra patria,
y nosotros la abandonamos, decían, cuando hablaban entre sí,
                    en medio de la tristeza,
                    en medio de la pesadumbre y
                    en medio del llanto, cuando hablaron.
Sus corazones estaban desesperados por ver el amanecer.

Los que ya estaban tranquilos eran sus dioses, en los barrancos,
                                        en los bosques;
entre bromelias,
entre musgo gris²⁴⁹ se encontraban.
No los colocaron sobre pedestales de madera.
Al principio hablaban Tojil,
                    Awilix y
                    Jaqawitz.

Lo grandioso de sus días y
la grandeza de su ánimo,
            de su espíritu estaban sobre todos los dioses de los otros
                                        [pueblos.
Eran muchos sus prodigios
        muchas sus maneras de alcanzar,
                    de ganar con asombro,
                        con miedo, su lugar en el
                                        [corazón
de los pueblos, cuyo ánimo había sido calmado por Balam Ki'tze',
                            Balam Aq'ab,
                            Majuk'utaj e
                            Ik'ibalam;
quienes no tenían animosidad hacia los dioses que habían traído,
                        que habían cargado
                                        [cuando
salieron de allá de Tulán,
                    Suywa,
allá, donde sale el Sol.

Allí estaban, pues, en el bosque:
en el amanecer de Tojil
            de Awilix,
            de Jaqawitz, como se le llama ahora.
Allí, pues, fueron gratificados,
            amanecieron nuestros abuelos,
                 nuestros padres.

Ahora vamos a contar el amanecer,
            el aparecimiento del Sol,
                 de la Luna y
                 de las estrellas.

Esto fue, pues, el amanecer,
            el aparecimiento del Sol,
                 de la Luna y
                 de las estrellas.
Grande fue la alegría de Balam Ki'tze',
            Balam Aq'ab,
            Majuk'utaj e
            Ik'ibalam cuando vieron
al lucero de la mañana,
apareció de primero;
resplandecía cuando salió,
venía adelante del Sol.
Enseguida desenvolvieron su incienso,
                el que habían traído del Oriente;
sus corazones se regocijaron cuando desenvolvieron las tres
variedades,[250]
muestra de su agradecimiento.
Mixtam pom era el nombre del incienso que traía Balam Ki'tze';
Kawistan pom era el nombre del incienso que traía Balam Aq'ab;
Kabawil pom se llamaba el incienso que traía Majuk'utaj.
Los tres traían su incienso,
y esto fue lo que quemaron en dirección de la salida del Sol.

Lloraron de felicidad cuando les amaneció,
quemaron su incienso,
      su preciado incienso.
Luego lloraron porque todavía no habían visto,
          no habían contemplado el nacimiento
del Sol.
Enseguida salió el Sol.
Se contentaron los pequeños animales,
      los grandes animales;
se levantaron de la orilla de los ríos
          de los barrancos;
subieron a la cima de los montes
y a un solo lugar dirigieron su mirada
hacia el lugar donde salió el Sol.
En eso rugieron los pumas,
      los jaguares;
pero primero cantó el pájaro,
      k'eletzu,[251] por nombre.
De verdad que se alegraron todos los animales
y extendieron sus alas el águila,
      el zopilote blanco;[252]
      las aves pequeñas,
      las aves grandes.
Mientras tanto estaban arrodillados los adoradores,
      los penitentes;
grande era su alegría como la de los adoradores y
      los penitentes de los Tamub e
          Ilokab;
      como la de los Rabinaleb,
      Kaqchikeleb y
      Ajtz'ikinaja;
      como la de los Tujal Ja',
      Uch'abaja,
      Ajkibaja,[253]
      Ajbatenaja;
      como la de los Yaki Tepew,[254] y

como cuanto pueblo existe hoy.
Era incontable la gente,
un solo amanecer tuvieron todos los pueblos.
Enseguida se secó la superficie de la tierra a causa del Sol,
semejante a una persona era el Sol cuando se manifestó;
tenía una faz ardiente
y esto secó la superficie de la Tierra.
Antes que saliera el Sol era húmeda
                              era cenagosa la superficie de la Tierra,
antes que saliera el Sol.
Pero el Sol se levantó
semejante a una persona,
no se aguantaba su calor.
Pero sólo se manifestó al nacer
y sólo su reflejo es el que quedó.

"No es realmente el mismo Sol que alumbra", se dice en su texto
                                                    [antiguo.
De inmediato, también, fueron convertidos en piedras Tojil,
                                        Awilix y
                                        Jaqawitz;
          al igual que las imágenes de los pumas,
                        de los jaguares,
                        la serpiente cascabel,
                        la serpiente barbamarilla.
Pero Saqik'oxol[255] se ocultó en el bosque cuando aparecieron
                                        [el Sol,
                                        la Luna,
                                        las estrellas
todos los demás se convirtieron en piedras.
Si no, tal vez nosotros no estaríamos vivos a causa de los animales
                                                    [voraces:
el puma,
el jaguar;
la serpiente cascabel
la serpiente barbamarilla.

Sin Saqik'oxol tal vez no tendríamos nuestra gloria hoy,
si no hubieran sido petrificados los primeros animales por el Sol.[256]
Cuando éste apareció,
se llenaron de felicidad los corazones de Balam Ki'tze',
                            Balam Aq'ab,
                            Majuk'utaj e
                            Ik'ibalam;
se alegraron grandemente cuando amaneció.
Pero no era mucha la gente que allí estaba,
eran pocos los que se encontraban sobre la montaña Jaqawitz.[257]
Allí amanecieron,
allí quemaron sus ofrendas,
allí les amaneció.
De donde sale el Sol habían venido,
ésas eran sus montañas y
            sus valles;
de allá habían venido Balam Ki'tze',
                    Balam Aq'ab,
                    Majuk'utaj e
                    Ik'ibalam, así llamados.
Fue allí donde se multiplicaron en esa montaña,
que luego se constituyó en su ciudadela;
allí, pues, estaban cuando vieron aparecer el Sol,
                                la Luna,
                                las estrellas;
            cuando amaneció,
            cuando se iluminó la faz de la Tierra y
                        todo lo que hay debajo del Cielo.
Allí también comenzaron su canto llamado Qamuqu,
lo cantaron,[258]
lo que era el lamento de sus corazones,
                de sus vientres.
Así decían en su canto:
—¡Ay de nosotros!
Nos perdimos en Tulán;
allá nos dividimos,

allá dejamos a nuestros hermanos mayores
                a nuestros hermanos menores.
¿Dónde habrán visto ellos el Sol?
¿Dónde habrán estado cuando amaneció?, preguntaron
                                [a los adoradores,
                                a los penitentes
de los Yaki.
—Porque era también Tojil la deidad de los yaki,
Yolkwat
Quetzalcóatl, por nombre;²⁵⁹
que dejamos allá en Tulán
                allá en Suywa.
Ellos salieron junto con nosotros,
fueron nuestros compañeros de partida, dijeron entre sí.
Se acordaron de sus hermanos mayores
                de sus hermanos menores,
los Yaki, a quienes les amaneció allá,
                                en México, como se llama ahora.
Había también una parte de la gente que se quedó allá en el Oriente,
los Tepew Oloman, por nombre.
—Los que dejamos allá, dijeron.
Grande era la aflicción de sus corazones allí sobre Jaqawitz.
Lo mismo sentían los de los Tamub e
                Ilokab;²⁶⁰
sólo que ellos estaban en el bosque.
Pueblo de los Tam se llama donde les amaneció a los adoradores
                                a los penitentes
de los Tamub, junto con su deidad que también era Tojil.
Sólo un nombre tenía la deidad de las tres ramas de la gente k'iche'.
Así, pues, era el mismo nombre de la deidad de los Rabinaleb,
aunque cambia un poco: *Jun Toj*, se le dice;
éste es el nombre de la deidad de los Rabinaleb;
pero eso nada más se dice,
porque era igual su idioma al idioma de los k'iche'es.²⁶¹
Ahora bien, lo que se diferencia es el idioma de los Kaqchikeleb,
                                [porque

era diferente el nombre de su deidad cuando salieron de Tulán
Suywa:

Sotz'i Ja Chimalkan se llama su deidad,
pero ésa es la única diferencia de la que se habla ahora;
y también derivado del nombre de su deidad
adquirieron el nombre sus linajes: Ajpop Sotz'il
Ajpop Xajil; así llamados.[262]
Así como su deidad también se diferenciaron sus idiomas,
esto ocurrió cuando se los entregaron allá en Tulán.
Por aquellos iconos de piedra varió también su idioma
cuando salieron de Tulán en medio de la oscuridad.
Pero una sola fue la siembra,
el amanecer para todos los pueblos.
Y ya tenían nombres las deidades de cada grupo.

Ahora hablaremos de su estancia y
de su permanencia allí sobre la montaña.
En un solo lugar estaban los cuatro: Balam Ki'tze',
Balam Aq'ab,
Majuk'utaj e
Ik'ibalam, así llamados.
Sus corazones lloraban por Tojil,
Awilix y
Jaqawitz, a quienes habían dejado
entre bromelias,
entre musgo gris.
Ésta fue, pues, su ceremonia,
el origen de la veneración de Tojil.
Cuando llegaron ante la presencia de Tojil y
de Awilix,
los fueron a ver,
los fueron a invocar,
y también agradecieron ante su presencia la llegada de la aurora.
Ellos ya estaban contraídos[263] en piedra allí en el bosque,

sólo fue su espíritu[264] el que habló, cuando llegaron

[los adoradores y
los penitentes

ante Tojil.
No traían grandes presentes,
quemaron sólo trementina,
          sólo sedimento de resina,
               junto con pericón, para esa ceremonia a sus deidades.
Entonces habló Tojil
pero sólo fue su espíritu el que transmitió sus ideas

[a los adoradores y
a los penitentes.

Dijeron entonces cuando hablaron:
—Realmente estas montañas y
          estos valles serán nuestros
nosotros también nos hemos vuelto de ustedes.
Es grande nuestro día y
grande nuestro nacimiento porque toda la gente es suya,
                    todos los pueblos.
Nosotros sólo somos acompañantes de sus ciudadelas
y por eso vamos a darles instrucciones:
no revelen nuestra existencia ante los pueblos
cuando causemos aflicción[265] porque de verdad que ya son muchos

[en existencia.

Así que no debemos ser capturados por ellos.
Mientras tanto ofrézcannos las criaturas de los pajonales
                    de los juncos[266]
como las crías[267] de venado
          las crías de las aves;
vengan a entregarnos un poquito de esa sangre.
¡Tengan piedad de nosotros!
Que queden las pieles de venado,
cuídenlas porque servirán para engañar
déjenlas arrancadas.
Que el venado sea
la representación nuestra que ustedes enseñen a los pueblos.

Cuando les pregunten ¿dónde está Tojil?
enséñenles los envoltorios de piel de venado,[268]
y ustedes tampoco se enseñen.
Asimismo, hay otra cosa que tienen que hacer
y esto los engrandecerá.
Derroten a todos los pueblos;
que traigan su sangre
su sustancia ante nosotros.
Ellos tienen que venir a abrazarnos
ellos ya nos pertenecen,[269] dijeron, pues, Tojil

                                            Awilix y
                                            Jaqawitz.

Tenían apariencia juvenil cuando se les miraba
                        cuando se ofrendaba ante ellos.
Enseguida comenzó la cacería de crías de pájaros
                             de crías de venado;
con empeño comenzaron la búsqueda los adoradores y
                                  los penitentes.

Y cuando encontraban los pájaros y
                        crías de venado,
enseguida iban a untarles la sangre de venado y
                            de pájaros a la boca de piedra
de Tojil
de Awilix.
En cuanto la sangre había sido bebida por las deidades
de inmediato hablaban las piedras cuando llegaban los adoradores y
                                  los penitentes;
                        cuando iban a quemar sus
                                  [ofrendas.
De igual manera hacían delante de los Envoltorios Sagrados:
quemaban trementina
quemaban también pericón amarillo y
                      pericón blanco.[270]
Había un Envoltorio Sagrado por cada una de las deidades
que era traído a la cumbre de la montaña.

Pero ellos no habitaban sus casas durante el día,
sólo entre montañas caminaban.
Y lo que comían era sólo larvas de abejorros
                    sólo larvas de avispas y
                    sólo larvas de abejas que buscaban.
Esto no era buen alimento
        ni buena bebida.
Tampoco parecían claros los caminos a sus casas,
y tampoco parecía claro dónde estaban sus esposas.

Mientras tanto eran muchos los pueblos
cada cual se había reunido,
                se había asentado;
cada división de esos pueblos pululaba por los caminos
                        y era claro por donde caminaban.
En cuanto a Balam Ki'tze',
            Balam Aq'ab,
            Majuk'utaj e
            Ik'ibalam no se sabía dónde estaban.

Pero cuando veían a los pueblos pasar por los caminos,
era cuando se ponían a gritar desde la cumbre de las montañas,
lanzando aullidos de coyote
gritos de zorra;
e imitaban los rugidos del puma y
                    del jaguar cuando veían a los pueblos caminar
en multitud.
—Es sólo un coyote el que aúlla,
        sólo una zorra;
es sólo un puma
    sólo un jaguar, decían los pueblos.
Era como si no fueran gentes en la mente de los pueblos;
pero era su manera de engañar a esos pueblos.
Tenían un propósito
y ciertamente no querían espantar a los pueblos con lo que hacían;
tenían un objetivo para imitar el rugido del puma

el rugido del jaguar.
Cuando miraban, pues, a una persona sola
o sólo a dos caminar, habrían querido
[desaparecerla.
Cada día, cuando regresaban a sus casas al lado de sus esposas,
sólo larvas de abejorros
larvas de avispas y
sólo larvas de abejas traían;
y esto es lo que les daban a sus esposas.
Cada día, cuando iban ante la presencia de Tojil,
Awilix y
Jaqawitz, decían en sus
[corazones:
—Ellos son Tojil
Awilix y
Jaqawitz;
y sólo sangre de venado
de pájaro les ofrendamos;
mejor puncemos nuestras orejas,
nuestros codos para pedir nuestra fortaleza,
nuestro vigor a Tojil
Awilix y
Jaqawitz.
¿Quiénes se encargarán de la muerte de los pueblos?
¿Acaso uno por uno los hemos de matar?, dijeron entre sí.

Luego fueron ante Tojil,
Awilix y
Jaqawitz.
Allí se punzaron las orejas
los codos delante de las divinidades.
Sirvieron su sangre,[271]
la vaciaron en la boca de las piedras.
Pero en realidad, ya no eran de piedra,
cada uno de ellos parecía joven cuando llegaban,
se alegraban, con la sangre de los adoradores y

de los penitentes.
Luego vino la señal de lo que debían hacer:
—¡Deben derrotarlos!
Es la salvación de ustedes.
Esto viene decidido desde Tulán cuando nos trajeron, les fue dicho.
Hablaban de cuando habían ofrecido la piel en el lugar llamado
[Silisib,²⁷²
con su sangre;
lo que sería una lluvia de
[sangre.
Esto se convirtió en ofrenda para Tojil,
Awilix y
Jaqawitz.
He aquí cómo comenzó el robo de la gente
de los pueblos por parte de
[Balam Ki'tze',
Balam Aq'ab,
Majuk'utaj e
Ik'ibalam.

Luego vino la matanza de los pueblos:
agarraban a aquellos que caminaban solos
que caminaban en par;
así no se notaba su desaparición.
Enseguida los iban a sacrificar ante Tojil,
Awilix.
Después iban a regar sangre en los caminos
y la cabeza la dejaban rodando en los caminos.
Decían entonces los pueblos:
—¡Un jaguar ha comido!, decían esto porque parecían
[huellas de jaguar,
las huellas que
ellos dejaban.
Ellos no se mostraban;
pero era mucha la gente que habían robado;

y no fue sino hasta muy tarde que se dieron cuenta los pueblos.
—Si son Tojil
                Awilix quienes se meten con nosotros;
sólo busquemos a los adoradores y
                        a los penitentes hasta donde están sus casas,
¡Sigamos sus huellas!, dijeron entonces todos los pueblos cuando
celebraron consejo.
Luego empezaron a seguir las huellas de los adoradores y
                                de los penitentes;
pero éstas no eran claras.
Sólo huellas de venado,
sólo huellas de jaguar era lo que veían.
No se veían las huellas de ellos,
no se encontraban por ningún lado.
Las primeras huellas eran de cuadrúpedos
así parecían sus huellas;
esto era para confundirlos.
Sus caminos no estaban claros:
aparecían nubes,
se formaba un temporal,
aparecía lodo;
o se formaba una llovizna.

Esto era todo lo que los pueblos veían delante de ellos,
sus corazones se cansaron de buscarlos y
                        de perseguirlos porque era grande
el ser de Tojil,
        Awilix y
        Jaqawitz.
Y así estuvieron por largo tiempo sobre la montaña,
en la orilla de los pueblos mataban.
Así fue como comenzó el rapto,
                la escogencia de los sacrificados.[273]
Cuando agarraban a gente de los pueblos por los caminos
las sacrificaban ante Tojil,
                Awilix y

                    Jaqawitz;
protegiendo a sus propios hijos aquí sobre la montaña.
Tojil,
Awilix y
Jaqawitz,
los tres tenían apariencia de jóvenes,
                    cuando caminaban,
eran sólo el espíritu de las piedras.
Había un río donde se bañaban,
y solamente en la orilla del agua aparecían.
Este lugar se llamaba "el baño de Tojil",
así fue como aquel río adquirió su nombre.
Muchas veces los veían los pueblos
pero desaparecían de inmediato cuando eran vistos por esos pueblos.

Luego se tuvo noticia de dónde estaban Balam Ki'tze',
                    Balam Aq'ab,
                    Majuk'utaj e
                    Ik'ibalam.

Y fue, entonces, cuando celebraron consejo los pueblos
para darles muerte.
Pero primero pensaron los pueblos sobre la manera de vencer a
                              [Tojil,
                    Awilix y
                    Jaqawitz.
Todos los adoradores y
        los penitentes hablaron ante los pueblos;
se habían reunido,
se habían llamado todos, entre sí;
no hubo un solo grupo,
        ni dos grupos, que faltara.[274]
Todos se juntaron entre sí y
        se organizaron entre sí, cuando celebraron consejo.
Dijeron, pues, cuando se preguntaron unos a otros:

—¿Será tan difícil vencer a los Kaweq
                    a la gente k'iche'?
Por causa de ellos se están acabando nuestras hijas,
                              nuestros hijos;
no está claro cómo desaparecen a la gente:
¿Y si nos acaban con esos raptos?
¡Que así sea: si es tan grande el poder de Tojil
                              Awilix y
                              Jaqawitz; que sea Tojil
                                   [nuestra deidad!
¡Capturémoslos, entonces!
No dejemos que acaben con nosotros.
¿Acaso no constituimos una multitud?
Mientras que los Kaweq no son muchos, dijeron, cuando se reunieron
                                             [todos.
Pero algunos dijeron, dirigiéndose a los pueblos cuando hablaron:
—¿Quién ha visto que se bañan a orillas del río, todos los días?
Si ellos son Tojil
              Awilix y
              Jaqawitz,
sería mejor derrotarlos primero a ellos.
Y ahí mismo comenzaría la derrota de los adoradores y
                              de los penitentes.
De inmediato dijeron otros al tomar la palabra:
—¿Pero cómo hemos de derrotarlos?
Luego dijeron:
—Que ésta sea nuestra manera de vencerlos:
como tienen apariencia de muchachos cuando se les mira a la orilla
                                        [del río,
que vayan entonces dos doncellas, verdaderamente muy hermosas,
radiantes de belleza, las doncellas;
de manera que no puedan reprimir sus deseos hacia ellas, dijeron.
—¡Está muy bien!
Busquemos, pues, a dos doncellas preciosas, dijeron y buscaron entre
                                        [sus hijas.
Verdaderamente eran bellísimas las doncellas,

luego les dieron instrucciones a las doncellas:
—¡Deben irse, hijas nuestras!
¡Vayan a lavar estas chamarras al río!
Y si ven a los tres muchachos,
desnúdense ante ellos.
Y si sus corazones las desean,
¡atráiganlos!
Y si ellos dicen: "Quisiéramos llegar a ustedes",
—"Está bien", han de responderles.
Y cuando les pregunten:
—"¿De dónde vienen?
¿Hijas de quiénes son?" cuando esto digan,
—"Somos hijas de los Señores" han de responderles.
Deben traernos alguna señal,
cualquier cosa que ellos les den.
Si ellos desearan poseerlas
de veras, entréguense a ellos.
Y si ustedes no quieren entregarse,
las mataremos, entonces.
Nuestros corazones estarán satisfechos cuando traigan una señal,
ésa será la prueba en nuestros corazones de que ellos las poseyeron,
                                            [dijeron, pues,
los Señores cuando instruyeron a las doncellas.
Eran dos,
éstos son sus nombres: Ixtaj, se llamaba una doncella,
                Ixpuch', se llamaba la otra doncella.

Eran, pues, dos, Ixtaj e
            Ixpuch', por nombre.[275]
Las que mandaron al río
            al baño de Tojil,
                    Awilix y
                    Jaqawitz.
Esto fue lo que acordaron todos estos pueblos.

Y luego se marcharon,
las ataviaron muy bien,
de verdad iban muy hermosas cuando se fueron hacia allá,
donde se bañaba Tojil.
Parecía como que iban a lavar, cuando se fueron.
Por su lado, estaban contentos los Señores por sus dos hijas que habían
enviado.
En cuanto llegaron a la orilla del río,
de una vez se pusieron a lavar,
y se desnudó cada una de las dos.
Estaban embrocadas sobre las piedras cuando las encontraron
                                    [Tojil,
                                    Awilix y
                                    Jaqawitz.
Ellos llegaron a la orilla del río
y apenas les llamó la atención las dos doncellas que estaban lavando.
Ante esto las doncellas se avergonzaron cuando llegaron los de Tojil.[276]
No se despertó el deseo de los de Tojil por las dos doncellas.
Enseguida les preguntaron:
—¿De dónde vienen?, les fue dicho a las dos doncellas.
Les volvieron a preguntar:
—¿Qué quieren para venir acá a orillas de nuestro río?, les fue dicho.
—Nosotras sólo fuimos mandadas por los Señores a venir acá.
"Vayan a ver a los de Tojil,
hablen con ellos", nos dijeron los Señores.
Asimismo "traigan señal de su palabra si los miran". Nos fue dicho.
Así dijeron las dos doncellas cuando dieron a conocer su objetivo.

Lo que querían los pueblos,
es que las doncellas fueran poseídas por los espíritus de los de Tojil.
Dijeron entonces Tojil,
            Awilix y
            Jaqawitz cuando volvieron a hablar con Ixtaj e
                                    Ixpuch',
así llamadas, las dos doncellas:

—¡Está bien!

Que vaya señal de nuestra plática con ustedes.

Esperen un poco.

Eso entregarán a los Señores, les fue dicho.

En eso ya estaban en consulta los adoradores y
                                    los penitentes.

Y les dijeron a Balam Ki'tze',
                Balam Aq'ab,
                Majuk'utaj e
                Ik'ibalam:[277]

—Pinten tres lienzos.[278]

Escriban el signo de su ser para que llegue a los pueblos.

Esto se tiene que ir con las dos doncellas que están lavando.

Entréguenselos a ellas, les fue dicho a Balam Ki'tze',
                                    Balam Aq'ab y
                                    Majuk'utaj.

Enseguida se pusieron a pintar cada uno de los tres.

El primero en pintar fue Balam Ki'tze': el jaguar fue su signo,
                                    esto fue lo que pintó sobre
                                                        [el lienzo.

Luego siguió Balam Aq'ab: el águila fue su signo,
                                esto fue lo que pintó sobre el lienzo.

Cuando pintó Majuk'utaj: un enjambre de abejorros,
                            un enjambre de avispas fue su signo,
                                            su escritura,
                                esto fue lo que pintó sobre el lienzo.

Terminada la representación de cada uno de los tres,

doblaron las tres piezas que habían pintado.

Enseguida fueron a entregar los mantos a Ixtaj e
                                    Ixpuch', así llamadas.

Dijeron entonces Balam Ki'tze',
                Balam Aq'ab y
                Majuk'utaj:

—¡Ésta es la prueba de su conversación!

Cuando lleguen ante de los Señores:

"De verdad hablaron los de Tojil con nosotras" han de decir.

"He aquí la prueba que hemos traído" han de decirles.

"Que se cubran con los lienzos que les entreguen", les fue dicho a las doncellas, cuando les dieron instrucciones.

Ellas se fueron enseguida,
llevando consigo los lienzos pintados.

Cuando llegaron,
de inmediato se alegraron los Señores al verlas;
colgaban de sus brazos lo que habían ido a pedir las doncellas.
—¿No vieron a los de Tojil?, les fue preguntado.
—¡Sí, los vimos!, contestaron Ixtaj e
                         Ixpuch'.
—¡Eso estuvo muy bien!
¿Cuál es la prueba que han traído,
si es eso verdad?, dijeron los Señores.
Era como la prueba de transgresión [de las deidades],[279] para los
                                                  [Señores.
Fueron extendidos, entonces, los lienzos por parte de las doncellas.
Uno, lleno de jaguares,
Otro, lleno de águilas[280] y
el otro, con enjambres de abejorros,
                     de avispas, lo pintado en los lienzos.
Eran resplandecientes.
Enseguida les entró el deseo por aquellos lienzos,
se los pusieron encima.
No hizo nada el jaguar,
ésa fue la primera pintura que se puso encima uno de los Señores.
Cuando se puso otro de los Señores el segundo lienzo pintado,
                         el que tenía el águila pintada,
se sintió muy bien el Señor envuelto en el lienzo
y empezó a dar vueltas delante de los demás,
lo desplegaba delante de todos los demás.
Luego, otro Señor se puso el tercer lienzo pintado,
el de los abejorros y
        las avispas se echó encima;
y de inmediato fueron picadas sus carnes por los abejorros y

las avispas.

Era inaguantable,
era insoportable la picadura de los insectos;
que empezó a gritar el Señor a causa de los insectos
que eran sólo imágenes pintadas sobre el lienzo.
Eran las figuras de Majuk'utaj.
Hasta con la tercera representación fueron vencidos.

Enseguida fueron reprendidas las doncellas por parte de los Señores;
Ixtaj e
Ixpuch', así llamadas.
—¿Qué clase de lienzos son estos que han traído?
¿Dónde los fueron a traer?
¡Son ingratas!, les fue dicho a las doncellas cuando las regañaron.
Así fueron vencidos de nuevo todos los pueblos por los de Tojil.

Lo que ellos querían era que los de Tojil hubieran poseído[281] a
                                                    [Ixtaj e
                                                    Ixpuch'.
Que ellos se hubieran vuelto fornicantes,[282]
en el corazón de los pueblos: ellas habrían sido su tentación.[283]

Pero no se logró esa derrota porque Balam Ki'tze',
                        Balam Aq'ab y
                        Majuk'utaj eran hombres
                                        [prodigiosos.
De nuevo celebraron consejo todos los pueblos:
—¿Hasta cuándo los vamos a soportar?
En verdad se ha vuelto grande su condición, dijeron al juntar sus
                                                    [pensamientos.
—Mejor ¡invadámoslos,
        matémoslos!
¡Armémonos de arcos,
        de escudos!
¿Acaso no somos numerosos?
¡Que no haya uno

ni dos que quede de ellos!,[284] dijeron cuando celebraron consejo.
Entonces se armaron todos los pueblos,
eran masas de guerreros cuando se juntaron todos los pueblos,
                                        los matadores.
Mientras tanto estaban Balam Ki'tze',
                        Balam Aq'ab,
                        Majuk'utaj e
                        Ik'ibalam;
ellos estaban sobre la montaña,
Jaqawitz es el nombre de la montaña donde se encontraban.
Estaban allí para salvar a sus hijos sobre la montaña.
No era mucha gente,
no era una multitud,
        como la muchedumbre de los pueblos.
Sólo una pequeña parte de la cumbre de la montaña tenían bloqueada
y por eso se dispuso su muerte por parte de los pueblos,
se juntaron todos,
celebraron consejo,
y se organizaron todos.

He aquí, pues, que se reunieron entre sí, todos los pueblos;
iban armados de arcos y
                de escudos, todos ellos.
Era incontable la riqueza de sus ornamentos,
era hermoso el aspecto de todos los jefes,
                        de todos los varones.
En verdad éstas eran sólo palabras de ellos,
en verdad en cautivos se volverían.
—En cuanto a Tojil,
él es una deidad,
y si a él debemos adorar,
entonces, vamos a capturarlo, dijeron entre sí.
Pero esto ya lo sabía Tojil,
                lo sabían también Balam Ki'tze',
                                Balam Aq'ab y

Majuk'utaj.
Ellos oían cuanto se planificaba porque no dormían,
                                estaban alertas desde que se
armaron todos de guerreros.
Enseguida se levantaron todos los guerreros,
pensando invadir de noche, se marcharon;
pero no llegaron,
en el camino se quedaron dormidos todos esos guerreros,
y así fueron derrotados otra vez por Balam Ki'tze',
                                Balam Aq'ab y
                                Majuk'utaj.
En un solo lugar se habían quedado dormidos en el camino,
ya no sentían nada,
cayeron en un sueño profundo, todos.
De ahí comenzaron a arrancarles las cejas
                        los bigotes;
luego desataron los adornos de metal de sus cuellos,
                junto con sus penachos y
                        sus collares;
del puño de sus jabalinas sólo tomaron el metal.[285]
Esto lo hicieron para escarmentarlos,
para burlarse de ellos y
para darles muestra de la grandeza de la gente k'iche'.
En cuanto despertaron,
de inmediato quisieron tocar su penachos
                al igual que los puños de sus jabalinas;
pero ya no había metal en esas jabalinas y
tampoco estaban sus penachos.
—¿Quién nos ha despojado?
¿Quién se está burlando de nosotros?
¿De dónde salen
quienes nos han robado nuestros metales?, se preguntaron todos los
                                            [guerreros.
—¿No serán los mismos malvados que roban gente?
¡Que esto no quede así!
¡No tengamos miedo de ellos!

Hay muchos espacios por donde invadir su pueblo;
y allí volveremos a ver nuestros metales.
¡Recuperemos lo nuestro!, dijeron todos los pueblos.
Pero sólo eran palabras de todos ellos.
Entre tanto, estaban muy confiados los adoradores y
                                        los penitentes que estaban sobre
la montaña.
Sin embargo, estaban haciendo grandes planes Balam Ki'tze',
                                        Balam Aq'ab,
                                        Majuk'utaj e
                                        Ik'ibalam.
Cuando lo decidieron Balam Ki'tze',
                    Balam Aq'ab,
                    Majuk'utaj e
                    Ik'ibalam, construyeron una cerca[286] a la orilla
de su ciudadela.
Sólo con tablas,
sólo con estacas cercaron los alrededores de su ciudadela.
Luego hicieron unos muñecos,
                    como gente, parecía su obra;
luego los colocaron en fila allí,
                    sobre la empalizada.

Pero también los armaron con escudos y
                    con flechas,
les pusieron los penachos de metal en sus cabezas,
se los pusieron siendo sólo muñecos y
                    sólo gente de madera;
utilizaron los metales de los pueblos,
                    aquellos que habían ido a quitarles en el camino.
Con esto fueron adornados los muñecos.
Con esto terminaron cercando los alrededores de la ciudadela.
Y enseguida fueron a consultar sobre sus planes, a Tojil:
—¿Nos matarán?
¿Y si somos vencidos?, expresaron sus corazones delante de Tojil.[287]
—¡No se aflijan!

¡Yo estoy aquí!
Esto es lo que deben usar contra ellos.
¡No tengan miedo!, les fue dicho a Balam Ki'tze',
                              Balam Aq'ab,
                              Majuk'utaj e
                              Ik'ibalam cuando les fueron
dados los abejorros y
        las avispas.
Esto fue lo que fueron a traer,
los traían cuando regresaron.
Enseguida los pusieron dentro de cuatro grandes tinajones
                        los cuatro que estaban alrededor de la
                                        [ciudadela.
Encerraron a los abejorros y
            a las avispas dentro de los tinajones.
Éstas eran sus armas en contra de los pueblos.

Pero eran observados a distancia,
espiados e
inspeccionada su ciudadela por agentes de los pueblos.
—¡No son muchos!, dijeron éstos.
Pero sólo fueron a ver a los muñecos,
                a los maniquís que parecían menear
                                    [sus flechas y
                                    sus escudos.

De verdad, tenían apariencia de hombres,
de verdad, tenían apariencia de combatientes cuando los vieron los
                                        [pueblos.
Se pusieron contentos todos los pueblos
porque no era significativa la cantidad que vieron;
en cambio esos mismos pueblos conformaban multitudes,
era incontable la gente,
            los guerreros y
            los matadores;
los que iban a matar a Balam Ki'tze',

Balam Aq'ab y
Majuk'utaj, quienes se encontraban sobre
la montaña,
Jaqawitz se llamaba el lugar donde estaban.

Ahora, cómo fueron invadidos es lo que vamos a contar.
Allí estaban, pues, Balam Ki'tze',
Balam Aq'ab,
Majuk'utaj e
Ik'ibalam.
Estaban juntos sobre la montaña con sus esposas y
sus hijos cuando vinieron
todos los guerreros,
todos los matadores.
No eran menos de dieciséis mil
ni veinticuatro mil[288] hombres que rodearon la ciudadela.
Haciendo bulla y
armados de flechas y
de escudos;
se golpeaban las bocas para gritar,
vociferaban;
hacían ruido con las manos,
hacían bulla;
alborotando y
silbando llegaron al pie de la ciudadela.
Pero aún así, no se amedrentaron los adoradores ni
los penitentes.
Éstos sólo los miraban desde la orilla de la cerca,
ya estaban en fila con sus esposas,
con sus hijos.
Estaban muy confiados,
porque eran puras palabras las de los pueblos.
Aquéllos empezaron a subir las faldas de la montaña,
cuando ya les faltaba muy poco,
todavía no habían entrado a las puertas de la ciudadela;

ellos destaparon los tinajones,
los cuatro que estaban alrededor de la ciudadela;
y cuando salieron los abejorros y
                          las avispas, parecían una humareda,
cuando salieron de cada uno de los tinajones.
Los guerreros fueron abatidos por los insectos que
se prendían en sus ojos y
se prendían en sus narices,
              en sus bocas,
              en sus piernas,
              en sus brazos.
Dondequiera que iban los atacaban,
dondequiera que iban [los guerreros] los encontraban por puños.[289]
En todos lados había abejorros y
                          avispas que se prendían a picarles sus ojos.
Tuvieron que cuidarse de los insectos arremolinados sobre cada una
de las gentes.
Estaban aturdidos por los abejorros y
                          las avispas que ya no pudieron empuñar
sus arcos,
ni sus escudos.
Se encogían sobre el suelo,
se encorvaban,
caían en las faldas de la montaña.
Y cuando ya no sentían nada, fueron atacados con flechas y
                                    heridos con hachas.
Ya sólo palos sin punta usaron Balam Ki'tze' y
                          Majuk'utaj;
e incluso sus esposas entraron a matar.

Ya sólo regresaron algunos,
y fue cuando empezaron a huir todos los pueblos.
A los que encontraron primero, los acabaron,
                                    los mataron;
no fue poca la gente que murió.
A los que aún no morían,

a los que pensaban perseguir,
los insectos se encargaron de ellos.
Ya no representaron ninguna amenaza:[290]
ni con flechas
ni con escudos fueron muertos.

Cuando estuvieron abatidos todos los pueblos,
ya sólo les quedó humillarse, a esos pueblos, ante Balam Ki'tze',
                                                    Balam Aq'ab y
                                                    Majuk'utaj:
—¡Tengan piedad de nosotros,
no debemos morir!, suplicaron.
—¡Está bien!
Aunque su destino es morir,
serán tributarios[291] mientras haya Sol,
                    mientras haya claridad, les fue dicho.
Así fueron derrotados todos estos pueblos
                    [por nuestras madres primigenias
                    nuestros padres primigenios.
Esto lo consiguieron allí sobre la montaña,
Jaqawitz, denominada hasta hoy.
Éste fue el primer lugar donde se establecieron,
allí fue donde se multiplicaron y
                    aumentaron;
                    tuvieron hijas,
                    tuvieron hijos sobre el monte Jaqawitz.
Ya estaban contentos después de haber derrotado a todos los pueblos,
a los que habían vencido sobre la cumbre de la montaña.
Así fue como tuvieron que hacer para derrotar a los pueblos,
                    a todos los pueblos.
Luego sus corazones estuvieron tranquilos.
Les comunicaron a sus hijos que el tiempo se acercaba,
                    que iban a morir;
después de muchos intentos en que los quisieron matar.

Ahora es donde contaremos la muerte de Balam Ki'tze',
                                    Balam Aq'ab,
                                    Majuk'utaj e
                                    Ik'ibalam, así llamados.
Ellos ya presentían su muerte,
                    su desaparición cuando les dieron consejos a sus
                                                            [hijos.
Ellos no estaban enfermos;
no estaban fatigados,
ni sin aliento cuando dejaron sus recomendaciones a sus hijos.
Éstos son los nombres de sus hijos:
fueron dos los que engendró Balam Ki'tze':
K'oka'ib se llamaba el primero,
K'oqawib se llamaba el segundo;[292]
éstos eran los hijos de Balam Ki'tze', abuelo y
                                    padre de los Kaweq.
Fueron también dos los que engendró Balam Aq'ab,
y éstos son sus nombres:
K'o'akul se llamaba el primer hijo,
K'o'akutek le decían al segundo hijo de Balam Aq'ab, de los Nija'ib.[293]
Sólo uno engendró Majuk'utaj:
K'o'ajaw[294] se llamaba.
Fueron tres los que tuvieron hijos,
pero Ik'ibalam no tuvo hijos.[295]
Verdaderamente ellos eran adoradores y
                                    penitentes.
Éstos son, pues, los nombres de sus hijos,
a los que dejaron sus instrucciones.

En un solo lugar estaban los cuatro,
se pusieron a cantar,
sus corazones estaban tristes,
lloraban sus corazones en su canto,
Qamuqu[296] se llamaba el canto
                            que cantaron.
Luego instruyeron a sus hijos:

—¡Hijos nuestros, nosotros nos vamos
nosotros regresamos!
Sabias palabras,
sabios consejos les dejamos.
También a ustedes los vamos a dejar en estas lejanas montañas,
¡Esposas nuestras!, les dijeron a sus esposas.
A cada quien aconsejaron.
—Regresaremos a nuestro pueblo.
Ya está alineado nuestro Señor Venado,[297]
ya se refleja en el Cielo.
Sólo vamos a emprender el regreso,
nuestra misión está cumplida,
nuestros días están completos.
Sentirán nuestra presencia;
¡No nos olviden,
no nos borren de su memoria!
Cuiden de sus hogares,
de la patria donde se establezcan.[298]
¡Que así sea!
Sigan entonces su camino,
y verán el lugar de donde vinimos,[299] dijeron cuando los aconsejaron.

Luego Balam Ki'tze' dejó señal de su existencia:
—Esto es para hacerme peticiones lo que dejo a ustedes.
¡Éste es su poder!
Les he dejado mis instrucciones,
mi consejo, dijo entonces cuando dejó la señal de su
[existencia.
Pisom Q'aq'al,[300] le decían.
No se sabía su contenido porque estaba envuelto,
no se podía desatar tampoco,
no se notaba su costura porque ninguno vio cuando lo envolvieron.
De esta manera dejaron sus instrucciones cuando desaparecieron allí,
sobre la cumbre de la montaña Jaqawitz.
No fueron vistos después[301] por sus esposas

ni por sus hijos.
No está clara su desaparición
cuándo desaparecieron.[302]
Pero sí está claro lo que dejaron instruido,
y el Envoltorio se volvió sagrado para ellos.
Era la memoria de sus padres.
De inmediato empezaron a quemar ofrendas delante de la memoria
de sus padres.

Fue entonces cuando comenzó la generación de los Señores,
los que le sucedieron a Balam Ki'tze';
de donde se originaron los abuelos y
                              padres de los Kaweq.
Esto nunca lo olvidaron sus hijos,
K'oka'ib y
K'oqawib, por nombre.
Así, pues, fue la muerte de los cuatro,
los que fueron nuestros abuelos primigenios,
                   nuestros padres primigenios;
cuando desaparecieron
cuando quedaron sus hijos allí,
sobre la cumbre de la montaña Jaqawitz,
donde permanecieron sus hijos por un tiempo.

Ya había caído,
ya estaba sometida la grandeza de todos los pueblos,
ya no tenían ningún poder;
sólo estaban allí,
sólo se juntaban todos entre sí, cada día.

Para conmemorar a sus padres,
grande era la gloria del Envoltorio, para ellos.
Nunca lo desataron
lo mantenían con ellos
Envoltorio Sagrado lo llamaban cuando ensalzaban y

nombraban lo que
mantenían oculto;
lo que les fue dejado por sus padres,
lo que era señal de su existencia.
Así, pues, fue la desaparición
el fin de Balam Ki'tze',
Balam Aq'ab,
Majuk'utaj e
Ik'ibalam
Las primeras gentes que vinieron de allá, de la orilla del mar
de donde sale el Sol.
En un tiempo muy antiguo llegaron acá.
Cuando murieron ya eran muy ancianos,
los adoradores y
los penitentes, como se les nombra.

RO'
CAPÍTULO QUINTO

Luego dispusieron irse hacia donde sale el Sol,
pensaron cumplir con las recomendaciones de sus padres.
No los habían olvidado,
ya hacía mucho tiempo que habían muerto sus padres;
los pueblos les dieron esposas,
éstos se convirtieron en sus suegros cuando tomaron esposas los tres.
Dijeron, pues, al marcharse:
—¡Nos vamos al Oriente,
de allá vinieron nuestros padres!, dijeron cuando tomaron camino
los tres varones.
K'oka'ib se llamaba uno, el hijo de Balam Ki'tze',
en nombre de todos los Kaweq.
K'o'akutek se llamaba el hijo de Balam Aq'ab,
en nombre de los Nija'ib.
K'o'ajaw se llamaba el otro, el hijo de Majuk'utaj,
en nombre de los Ajaw K'iche'.
Éstos son, pues, los nombres de los que se fueron a la orilla del mar,[303]
eran tres cuando partieron,
pero tenían sabiduría,
y tenían conocimiento;
su condición no era la de gente común.
Dejaron aconsejados a todos sus hermanos mayores
                              sus hermanos menores.
Estaban contentos al partir:

—¡No moriremos,
      regresaremos!, dijeron cuando se fueron los tres.
Y sólo pasaron por [la orilla] del mar cuando llegaron allá al Oriente,
                            cuando fueron a recibir los
símbolos de autoridad.
Éste es, pues, el nombre del Señor,
"Señor del Oriente", ante quien llegaron.

Se presentaron ante el Señor,
Nakxit[304] se llamaba el gran Señor,
la única autoridad,
con muchos poderes.
Él fue quien les dio los símbolos del poder,
                  todos los emblemas.
Fue cuando les entregaron los símbolos de Señor del Consejo
                          de representante del
                                [Consejo;[305]
fue cuando trajeron las insignias del poder y
                    de autoridad para el Señor del
                            [Consejo
                        el representante
del Consejo.
Nakxit les entregó completos los emblemas de su autoridad,
y éstos son los nombres:
palio[306] y
el trono;
flauta de caña,
y un tambor pequeño;[307]
polvo resplandeciente,
arcilla amarilla;[308]
los colmillos de puma,
los colmillos de jaguar;[309]
cabeza
patas de venado;[310]
brazaletes de cuero,

brazaletes de conchas de caracol;[311]
calabacilla para tabaco,
escudilla real;[312]
plumas de guacamaya,
plumas de garza real.[313]
Todo esto trajeron de regreso.
Fue también cuando trajeron de la orilla del mar la escritura de Tulán,
la escritura de
[Suywa];
como le dicen a lo que está en [sus signos]
en sus escritos.[314]

Luego, pues, llegaron acá,
a la ciudadela llamada Jaqawitz.
Allí se juntaron todos los Tamub,
los Ilokab;
se reunieron todos los pueblos,
se pusieron contentos cuando regresaron K'oka'ib,
K'o'akutek,
K'o'ajaw;
y aquí reasumieron el gobierno de los pueblos.
Se alegraron los Rabinaleb,
los Kaqchikeleb,
los Ajtz'ikinaja;
al revelárseles la señal de las insignias de la grandeza del Señorío.
Grande, pues, se volvió la existencia de los pueblos,
que antes no se había alcanzado sin la revelación de su autoridad.
Allí estaban en Jaqawitz,
y se encontraban con ellos todos los que habían venido del Oriente.
Por mucho tiempo permanecieron aquí sobre la cumbre de la
[montaña,
y en conjunto hacían un gran número;
aquí también murieron las esposas de Balam Ki'tze',
de Balam Aq'ab y
de Majuk'utaj.

Luego se vinieron,
dejaron abandonada su montaña.
Empezaron a buscar otra montaña dónde establecerse.
Fueron incontables las montañas donde estuvieron;
las ensalzaron,
les pusieron nombres.
En estos lugares se juntaron y
        se fortalecieron nuestras primeras madres,
          nuestros primeros padres, decían
los ancestros;
cuando contaban y
cuando relataban el abandono de su primera ciudadela llamada
            [Jaqawitz.

Llegaron, entonces, al lugar
donde fundaron la ciudadela llamada Chi K'ix.[315]
Por mucho tiempo permaneció allí cada una de las divisiones
de los pueblos,
tuvieron hijas y
tuvieron hijos.
Allí estuvieron cuando conformaban cuatro territorios;[316]
pero era uno solo el nombre de todo el pueblo.
Casaron a sus hijas,
        a sus hijos,
sólo las regalaban;
sólo por favores y
sólo por regalos daban a sus hijas;
lo aceptaban y
hacían lo que era bueno para su existencia.

Revisaron después cada una de las divisiones del pueblo.
Éstos eran los nombres de lo que conformaba Chi K'ix:
Chi Chaq',
Jumeta Ja,
K'ulba,

Kawinal,[317] se llamaban las montañas donde se detuvieron.

Pero también examinaron las montañas y
                    las ciudadelas;
buscaban un lugar habitable
porque ya eran muy numerosos todos ellos;
aun cuando ya habían muerto los que fueron a traer el señorío al
                                    [Oriente,
ya eran muy ancianos cuando llegaron a cada una de estas ciudadelas.
No se acostumbraron en los lugares por donde estuvieron,
pasaban penas y
            aflicciones.
Hasta mucho tiempo después encontraron su ciudadela
                            [nuestros abuelos y
                            nuestros padres.

Éste es, pues, el nombre del pueblo a donde llegaron:
Chi Ismachi' es el nombre de la montaña,
                de la ciudadela donde estuvieron.[318]
Allí, pues, se establecieron,
y allí fue donde desarrollaron su poder;
construyeron edificios de cal y
                canto[319] durante esta cuarta generación de
                            [Señores;
Así decían K'onache',[320] y
            Belejeb Kej el Q'alel Ajaw cuando gobernaban K'otuja e
            Istayul,[321]
así llamados el Ajpop y
                Ajpop K'amja quienes gobernaron allí en Chi Ismachi'.
Ésta la constituyeron en una hermosa ciudadela,
sólo fueron tres casas grandes las que había allí en Chi Ismachi',
todavía no estaban las veinticuatro casas reales.
Sólo eran tres las casas reales:
una casa real de los Kaweq,
una casa real de los Nija'ib y

una casa real de los Ajaw K'iche';
pero sólo eran dos casas reales las que gobernaban[322]
a las dos divisiones de la ciudadela.
Y allí estaban en Chi Ismachi', viviendo en unidad,
　　　　　　　　　　no tenían maldad y
　　　　　　　　　　tampoco animadversión.
Tenían un gobierno pacífico,
no tenían pleitos,
ni levantamientos;
estaban en calma,
el bien de su pueblo ocupaba sus corazones;
no había envidia,
y tampoco maldad en lo que hacían.
Su gloria era modesta,
todavía no eran admirables,
todavía no eran poderosos.

Luego trataron de hacerlo
empuñando escudos allí en Chi Ismachi';
una muestra de poder fue lo que hicieron,
señal de su gloria y
señal de su grandeza.

Cuando vieron esto los Ilokab
se generó una guerra por parte de los Ilokab;
quienes quisieron venir a matar al Señor K'otuja,
ellos querían tener un Señor aliado,
quisieron probar con Istayul.
querían los Ilokab enseñarle a cometer un crimen.[323]
Pero su confabulación en contra de K'otuja fracasó,
y sobre ellos se revirtió.
Para comenzar, no murió el Señor [K'otuja] como querían los Ilokab
y así fue como se originaron los levantamientos,
　　　　　　　　　　los tumultos y
　　　　　　　　　　la guerra.
Atacaron primero la ciudadela,

marcharon sobre ella los guerreros de la muerte;
lo que querían era que los k'iche'es desaparecieran de una vez,
deseaban gobernar sólo ellos.
Pero fue a ellos a quienes fueron a traer,
                    los capturaron y
                    los hicieron prisioneros;
fueron muy pocos los que se salvaron.
De ahí comenzaron los sacrificios,
fueron sacrificados los Ilokab delante de los dioses;
éste fue el castigo de su culpa, instituida por el Señor K'otuja.
Muchos otros fueron esclavizados
            otros capturados y
            otros puestos en servidumbre.
Sólo fueron a entregarse para ser vencidos
por haber comenzado la guerra en contra del Señor,
                        en contra del campo y
                            la ciudadela.[324]
La desaparición,
la destrucción del señorío k'iche' deseaban sus corazones;
pero esto no lo consiguieron.

Así, pues, comenzó el sacrificio de la gente delante de los dioses,[325]
cuando se libró la guerra de los escudos,
que a su vez dio origen a la fortificación de la ciudadela de
                                [Chi Ismachi'.
Allá comenzó la gloria, porque realmente era grande el poder de los
Señores k'iche'es;
eran únicos en prodigios estos Señores.
No había quién los humillara,
tampoco alguno que pudiera con ellos.
Fueron los creadores de la grandeza del señorío
que se originó allí en Chi Ismachi'.

Allí también aumentó la vergüenza de los dioses,[326]
el terror comenzó de nuevo,
se llenaron de espanto todos los pueblos;

---

                    los pequeños pueblos
                    los grandes pueblos
que presenciaron la llegada de prisioneros de guerra
que eran sacrificados,
que eran muertos por el
                    [poder y
                    majestad del Señor K'otuja
                              del Señor Istayul con los Nija'ib y
                                        los Ajaw K'iche'.
Sólo eran tres ramas de la familia que estuvieron allí,
en Chi Ismachi', como se llamaba la ciudadela.
Y allí comenzaron los banquetes,
                    las bebidas por sus hijas cuando las pedían
en matrimonio.[327]
Era la forma de ayuda mutua de las tres Casas Grandes, como ellos
las llamaban.
Allí, pues, tomaban sus bebidas y
allí comían sus alimentos en intercambio por sus hermanas y
                                        por sus hijas.
Había alegría en sus corazones cuando esto hacían;
comían y
bebían adentro de las Casas Grandes:
—De esta manera agradecemos y
damos gracias por la señal,
                    por nuestra descendencia;
ésta es muestra de nuestro consentimiento para
                              [que sean esposas y
                              sean esposos, decían.

Allá se designaron y,
allá se pusieron nombres los linajes:
los pueblos aliados,[328]
los principales se nombraron:
—Somos compañeros nosotros los Kaweq,
          nosotros los Nija'ib y
          nosotros los Ajaw K'iche', dijeron los tres linajes y
                              las tres Casas Grandes.

Por mucho tiempo, permanecieron aquí en Chi Ismachi',
hasta que encontraron y
hasta que vieron otra ciudadela
dejaron abandonada Chi Ismachi'.

Luego se levantaron y vinieron
a la ciudadela de Q'umaraq Aj[329] como la llamaban los k'iche'es.
Fue entonces cuando vinieron los Señores K'otuja y
                              Q'ukumatz,
                    así como los demás Señores.
Había habido cinco cambios y
cinco generaciones de gente desde el origen de la luz,
                         origen de los pueblos;
                         origen de la vida y
                              de la humanidad.
Aquí, pues, construyeron muchas casas y
aquí también construyeron los templos para sus deidades,
en medio de la ciudadela los ubicaron, cuando vinieron y
                              cuando se establecieron.

Luego se ocuparon en engrandecer su señorío
ya eran muchos y
la población era numerosa.
Fue cuando pensaron de nuevo en sus Casas Grandes,
se reunieron y
se dividieron porque surgieron las discordias.
Se envidiaban por el precio de sus hermanas,
                    de sus hijas, porque ya no les presentaban
                                        [bebidas.[330]
Éste fue, pues, el origen de su separación,
fue cuando se voltearon unos contra otros
     cuando se arrojaron los huesos,
                    las calaveras de los muertos.[331]
Se distanciaron entre sí,
y fue cuando se dividieron en nueve linajes;

terminando así la pelea por las hermanas,
                    por las hijas;
y fue cuando se dispuso dividir el señorío,
en veinticuatro Casas Grandes se constituyó.
Hacía mucho tiempo que habían llegado todos a esta ciudadela,
cuando se completaron las veinticuatro Casas Grandes aquí,
en esta ciudadela de Q'umaraq Aj,
que vino a ser bendecida por el Señor obispo;[332]
después, fue abandonada.

Allí se habían engrandecido
allí habían adquirido esplendor sus tronos y
                    sus sitiales;
se habían dividido, conforme su poder, cada uno de los Señores.
Hasta nueve linajes llegaron a conformarse:
nueve señoríos de los Kaweq,
nueve señoríos de los Nija'ib,
cuatro señoríos de los Ajaw K'iche',
dos señoríos de los Saqik.[333]

Se habían vuelto numerosos y
también eran muchos los que seguían a cada uno de los Señores,
y éstos eran los primeros entre sus vasallos y
                    sus hijos;
eran masas,
multitudes familiares por cada uno de los Señores.

Ahora diremos los nombres de cada uno de los Señores,
                    de cada una de las Casas Grandes.
Éstos son, pues, los títulos de los Señores Kaweq:
éstos eran los Señores principales:
Ajpop,
Ajpop K'amja,
Ajtojil,
Ajq'ukumatz,

Nim Ch'okoj Kaweq,
Popol Winaq chi T'uy,
Lolmet Kejnay,
Popol Winaq pa Jom Tzalatz',
Uchuch K'amja.[334]
Éstas eran, entonces, las autoridades al frente de los Kaweq,
eran nueve Señores,
cada quien tenía una Casa Grande
que después habrían de crecer.

Éstos son los títulos de los Señores Nija'ib,
éstos eran los Señores principales:
Ajaw Q'alel,
Ajaw Ajtzik Winaq,
Q'alel K'amja,
Nima K'amja,
Uchuch K'amja,
Nim Ch'okoj Nija'ib,
Awilix,
Yakolatam Utza'm Pop Saqlatol,
Nima Lolmet Ye'oltux.[335]
Éstas eran, pues, las nueve autoridades al frente de los Nija'ib.

Éstos son los de los Señores k'iche'es,
éstos son los nombres de sus principales:
Ajtzik Winaq,
Ajaw Lolmet,
Ajaw Nim Ch'okoj Ajaw,
Ajaw Jaqawitz.[336]
Eran cuatro las autoridades al frente de los k'iche'es,
con sus respectivas Casas Grandes.

Y dos linajes eran de los Señores Saqik
Tz'utuja,
Q'alel Saqik;[337]
era una sola Casa Grande,

con dos Señores.

Así, pues, se completaron los veinticuatro Señores y
las veinticuatro Casas Grandes que llegaron a conformarse.
Fue entonces cuando aumentó el poder
                                    la majestad entre los k'iche'es;
su poderío,
su majestad creció y
                el peso de los k'iche'es se hizo sentir,
cuando se hicieron las construcciones de cal y
                                        canto en el campo y
                                                la ciudadela.
Vinieron, entonces, los pequeños pueblos
                        los grandes pueblos
fuese el título de sus Señores,
vinieron a engrandecer a los k'iche'es;
fue cuando se originó la gloria
                        la majestad;
cuando se construyeron las casas de las deidades y
                        las casas de los Señores.
Pero no lo hicieron ellos,
no se habría trabajado y
tampoco se habrían construido sus casas y
tampoco se habrían construido las casas de sus dioses,
de no ser porque habían aumentado sus vasallos,
                                    sus hijos.
No los tenían que convencer
no los iban a secuestrar o
                arrebatar;
porque cada uno de ellos era súbdito de los Señores.
También se habían vuelto numerosos sus hermanos mayores,
                                    sus hermanos menores;
se juntaron sus responsabilidades de vida,
se ocupaban en atender peticiones, cada uno de los Señores.
De verdad eran muy amados,
de verdad eran muy respetados los Señores.

Era tenido en gran respeto su día,
el día de nacimiento de los Señores por sus vasallos,
                              por sus hijos;
cuando aumentaron los habitantes del campo y
                              la ciudadela.
Pero tampoco era que sólo venían a entregarse todos los pueblos,
ni que hubieran guerras en sus campos y
                              sus ciudadelas;
sino fue por el prodigio de los Señores,
irradiaban poder el Señor Q'ukumatz y
                el Señor K'otuja.

De verdad que llegó a ser prodigioso el Señor Q'ukumatz:
por siete días subía al Cielo,
por otros siete días iba a estar en Xibalba;
por otros siete días tomaba forma de serpiente
y verdaderamente se transformaba en serpiente;
otros siete días asumía la cualidad de águila y
otros siete días la cualidad de jaguar,
de verdad su imagen se transformaba en águila,
                              en jaguar.
Otros siete días se transformaba en sangre reposada
                    y no había más que sangre
                              [reposada.

Verdaderamente tenía una naturaleza prodigiosa este Señor
que llenó de espanto a los otros Señores.
Se esparció la noticia,
todos los Señores de los pueblos supieron de la naturaleza prodigiosa
de este Señor.
Éste fue el principio y
          el engrandecimiento de los k'iche'es,
esto ocurrió cuando Q'ukumatz dio muestras de su grandeza.
Su memoria no se ha olvidado en la mente de sus nietos y
                              de sus hijos.
En ninguna otra parte había acontecido esto,

que un Señor tuviera una naturaleza tan prodigiosa;[338]
aunque esto lo hizo sólo para dominar a todos los pueblos,
sólo dio muestras de su ser.

Así terminó siendo uno la cabeza de todos los pueblos.
Él era de la cuarta generación,
el prodigioso Señor llamado Q'ukumatz,
quien asimismo era Ajpop y
                        Ajpop K'amja.
Quedaron, pues, sus sucesores y
                  sus descendientes,
que tuvieron poder y
            majestad;
y cuando engendraron,
sus hijos llegaron a ser más numerosos.
Fueron engendrados Tepepul[339] e
                        Istayul,
quienes sólo cumplieron con su señorío,
fueron la quinta generación,
que a su vez engendraron la siguiente generación de Señores.

Éstos son los nombres de la sexta generación:[340]
eran dos grandes Señores,
eran gloriosos:
K'ikab se llamaba el uno
Kawisimaj se llamaba el otro.[341]
Hicieron grandes cosas K'ikab y
                        Kawisimaj;
ellos extendieron el dominio k'iche' porque, de verdad, eran de
naturaleza prodigiosa.
Ellos destruyeron y
fragmentaron los campos y
                  ciudadelas de los pueblos pequeños,
                        de los pueblos grandes;
los lugares vecinos desde la antigüedad.
Entre ellos, la que era la patria de los Kaqchikeleb,

lo que ahora se conoce como Chuwila;[342]
y también la patria de los Rabinaleb,
lo que se conoce como Pa Maka';[343]
la patria de los Kawkeb,[344]
la de los Saqkabaja.[345]
También ciudadelas como las de los Saqulewab,[346]
                    de los de Chuwi' Meq'ena',[347]
                    Xelajuj,[348]
                    Chuwa Tz'aq,[349]
junto con los de Tz'oloj Che'.[350]
Ellos aborrecían a K'ikab,
le hicieron la guerra;
pero ellos fueron vencidos y
        fueron destruidos los campos y
                    las ciudadelas de los Rabinaleb,
                            de los Kaqchikeleb y
                            de los de Sakulewab.
Cayeron,
fueron derrotados todos los pueblos.[351]
Los soldados de K'ikab llevaron la muerte hasta lejanos lugares.
Cuando un grupo o
dos grupos no llevaban el tributo que correspondía;
caían sus ciudadelas
hasta que llevaban sus tributos ante K'ikab y
                            Kawisimaj.
Sus linajes eran desangrados,
            eran flechados en contra de los árboles;
hasta reducir a nada su gloria y
                su origen.[352]
Sus proyectiles no dejaron ciudadela sin destruir,
al instante las arrasaban hasta sus cimientos.
Era como cuando golpea el trueno para despedazar una roca.

Del miedo,
llegaban los pueblos delante del árbol de trementina[353]

llevando como señal de sus ciudadelas lo que ahora es una montaña
[de piedras.
Sólo algunas de esas piedras no están cortadas
las otras están como si hubieran sido partidas con hacha.
Allá está en la costa, Petatayub[354] se llama,
se ve claramente hoy en día,
la miran todas las gentes que pasan por allí,
es testimonio de la valentía de K'ikab.
No pudieron matarlo y
tampoco vencerlo;
porque de verdad era un hombre valiente
y obtuvo el tributo de todos los pueblos.
Enseguida celebraron consejo todos los Señores
y fue cuando cortaron el acceso a los barrancos,
a los poblados,[355]
a las ciudadelas caídas de todos los pueblos.

Fue entonces cuando salieron los centinelas
los vigías de guerra;
organizaron a los que controlaban linajes y
habitantes de aquellos lugares.
—Por si regresan
y quieren ocupar sus ciudadelas, dijeron reunidos en consejo todos
los Señores.
Luego presentaron su objetivo:
—Ésta será como nuestra defensa,
esto será como nuestros linajes;
que se convierta en nuestra empalizada
en nuestra fortaleza.
Que sea muestra de nuestro valor,
de nuestra hombría, dijeron todos los Señores
[cuando se
asignaron puestos a cada linaje para enfrentar a los enemigos.
Fue cuando fueron instruidos,
cuando fueron nombrados a ocupar los territorios de los pueblos.
—Vayan porque ahora éstos ya son nuestros territorios.

¡No tengan miedo!
Si todavía hay enemigos que lleguen en contra de ustedes a querer
[matarlos,
vengan pronto a avisarnos,
para ir a matarlos,[356] les dijo, entonces, K'ikab cuando instruyó
[a todos
en presencia del Q'alel
      del Ajtzik Winaq.

Entonces se marcharon los llamados Punta de flechas,
                            Punta del arco.[357]
Entonces se repartieron los abuelos,
                los padres de toda la gente k'iche'.
Estaban en cada uno de los montes,
pero sólo como guardias de los montes
      sólo como guardianes de las flechas,
                de los arcos y
         como vigías de guerra, se fueron.

No amanecían en ningún lugar y
tampoco tenían una deidad[358]
sólo bloqueaban los alrededores de las ciudadelas,
marchándose así todos los de Wila
              los de Chulimal,
                  de Saqiya'
                  de Xajbakyej,
                  de Chitemaj,
                  de Wajxalajuj,[359]
asimismo los de Kabraqan
        los de Ch'abi Q'aq'
        los de Junajpu,[360]
junto con los habitantes de Maka'
        los habitantes de Xayabaj,
        los habitantes de Saqkabaja,
        los habitantes de Siyaja,
        los habitantes de Meq'ena'

los habitantes de Xelajuj.[361]

Hacia los valles
hacia las montañas salieron los guardias de la guerra,
                los guardias de esos territorios;
cuando partieron por orden de K'ikab,
              de Kawisimaj,
el Ajpop,
el Ajpop K'amja;
el Q'alel,
el Ajtzik Winaq.
Eran cuatro los Señores que mandaban y
                que vigilaban a los guerreros enemigos.
K'ikab,
Kawisimaj se llamaban los dos Señores de los Kaweq,
Ke'ema era el nombre del Señor de los Nija'ib;
Achaq' Iboy era el nombre ante los Ajaw K'iche'.[362]
Éstos eran, pues, los nombres de los Señores que mandaban y
                que enviaban
                    [mensajeros;
fue cuando se marcharon sus vasallos y
           sus hijos a las montañas,
              a cada una de las montañas.
Habiéndose ido, lo primero que trajeron fueron cautivos
              trajeron prisioneros
                [ante K'ikab,
                  Kawisimaj,
                  Q'alel y
                  Ajtzik Winaq.
Tuvieron que hacer guerra los Punta de flechas,
            los Punta del arco;
haciendo cautivos,
haciendo prisioneros.
En hombres valientes se constituyeron aquellos enviados
              que aumentaron en número;
y asimismo recibieron muchas gratificaciones por parte de los Señores

cuando venían a entregar a sus prisioneros,
a sus cautivos.

Después, entraron en consejo los Señores,
el Ajpop,
el Ajpop K'amja,
el Q'alel,
el Ajtzik Winaq y esto fue lo que se dispuso:
—Sólo tomemos a los primeros cuando haya que dignificar el linaje
de los vigilantes.
¡Yo soy el Ajpop!
¡Yo soy el Ajpop K'amja!
Ajpop será mi dignidad,
mientras que la tuya, Ajaw Q'alel.
¡Que sean dignos los dignificables!,[363] dijeron, pues, todos los Señores
cuando celebraron consejo.
De la misma manera actuaron los Tamub y
los Ilokab,
igual fue la condición de las tres divisiones k'iche'es
cuando nombraron y
ennoblecieron a los principales entre sus vasallos e
hijos.
Así, pues, fue el resultado de la consulta.
Pero no fue aquí en el K'iche' donde esto se inició,
tiene nombre el lugar donde iniciaron a los principales entre
[vasallos e
hijos;
cuando llamaron a cada quien a sus montañas,
en un solo lugar se reunieron: Xe' Balax
Xe' K'amaq' se llama la montaña
donde fueron elevados en rango
cuando recibieron sus cargos
y esto ocurrió aquí en Chulimal.[364]

Así, pues, fue la promoción,
el nombramiento y
la distinción de los veinte Q'alel,

de los veinte Ajpop nombrados
por el Ajpop,
    el Ajpop K'amja;
por el Q'alel,
    el Ajtzik Winaq.
Todos fueron reconocidos:
el Q'alel,
el Ajpop,
los once Nima Ch'okoj.
el Q'alel Ajaw,
el Q'alel Saqik,
el Q'alel Achij,
el Rajpop Achij
el Rajtz'alam Achij
el Utza'm Achij fueron los títulos conferidos a los guerreros[365]
cuando fueron promovidos y
        nombrados en sus puestos,
        en sus asientos.

Ellos fueron los principales entre vasallos e
             hijos de la gente k'iche',
vigías y
escuchas de los Punta de flechas.
      los Punta del arco;
que cercaron la empalizada
      la muralla alrededor de los k'iche'es.

Asimismo lo hicieron los Tamub y
      los Ilokab;
nombraron y
promocionaron a los principales entre sus vasallos e
           hijos que tenían en cada
una de sus montañas.
Éste es, pues, el origen de los Q'alel,
      de los Ajpop;
de las dignidades que existen ahora en cada uno de esos lugares.

Así fue el origen,
cuando se replicó la organización de los Ajpop,
de los Ajpop K'amja,
la organización de los Q'alel,
de los Ajtzik Winaq.

Ahora vamos a nombrar las casas de las deidades
aunque las casas tenían el mismo nombre de esas deidades:
el gran templo de Tojil se llamaba un edificio,
era la casa de Tojil por parte de los Kaweq.
Awilix se llamaba el edificio
dedicado a Awilix por parte de los Nija'ib.
Jaqawitz se llamaba en turno el edificio,
dedicado a la deidad de los Ajaw K'iche'.
Tz'utuja que todavía se puede ver y
ahora se llama K'ajbaja,[366]
es un gran edificio.
Allí estaban los iconos de piedra
venerados por los Señores k'iche'es y
venerados por todos los pueblos.
Los pueblos primero hacían sus ceremonias delante de Tojil
y después honraban al Ajpop y
al Ajpop K'amja;
viniendo a presentar sus plumas de quetzal y
sus tributos ante ellos,
ante los Señores.
Aquellos mantenían y
proveían al Ajpop y
al Ajpop K'amja
que habían conquistado sus ciudadelas.
Eran grandes Señores,
eran gente prodigiosa
eran Señores portentosos Q'ukumatz y
K'otuja;
también eran Señores portentosos K'ikab y

Kawisimaj.

Ellos sabían si había que hacer guerra,
todo estaba claro para ellos.
Podían ver si habría mortandad,
        si habría hambre,
        si habría que pelear.
Lo sabían muy bien,
porque tenían dónde verlo,
había un libro,
Popol Wuj llamado por ellos.[367]
Pero no sólo de esa manera eran Señores,
eran grandes en esencia y
eran grandes sus ayunos.
Era su manera de agradecer su propia creación
        de agradecer su señorío.
Por largo tiempo ayunaban y
            hacían penitencia delante de sus deidades.
Ésta era la manera de su ayuno:
por nueve cuentas de veinte[368] ayunaban,
por otras nueve hacían penitencia y
            hacían ceremonias.
Por otras trece cuentas de veinte ayunaban y
    otras trece hacían penitencia[369] y
                ceremonias delante de Tojil,
                    delante de sus deidades.

Sólo zapotes,
sólo matasanos,
sólo jocotes comían,
no tenían nada hecho de maíz para comer.
De nuevo entraban a diecisiete cuentas de veinte en penitencia y
            otras diecisiete en ayuno,[370]
                    sin nada para comer.
Verdaderamente observaban grandes abstinencias
y ésta era la señal de su condición de Señores.
Tampoco dormían con mujer,

se mantenían solos cuando ayunaban.
Sólo en la casa de las deidades estaban cada día,
venerándolas,
quemándoles ofrendas y
haciendo penitencia.
Allí permanecían fuera en el anochecer o,
                        en el amanecer;
lloraban sus corazones y
lloraban sus vientres cuando pedían por la tranquilidad
                        por la vida de sus vasallos,
                              de sus hijos y
                        por sus propios señoríos.
Levantaban sus rostros hacia el cielo,
y ésta era su petición a sus deidades cuando hacían sus rogativas.

Ésta era, pues, la súplica de sus corazones:
—¡Que amanezca!, tú de los cinco días,[371]
tú, Jun Raqan,
tú, Corazón del Cielo y
            de la Tierra,
tú, proveedor de la abundancia y
            del alimento;[372]
tú, dador de hijas
       de hijos.
Desparrama,
deja caer[373] lo que es verde
       lo que es maduro.
Concédeles vida y
          desarrollo a nuestras hijas,
             a nuestros hijos.[374]
Que se multipliquen,
que crezcan los que te sostengan,
          los que te guarden;
          los que te invoquen en los caminos,
               en las veredas;

en los ríos
en los barrancos;
debajo de los árboles,
debajo de los bejucos.

Dales sus hijas,
        sus hijos.
Que no haya desgracia,
            desastre,
            infortunio,
            desventura
que nadie los engañe detrás,
                    ni delante.
Que no lleguen a ser juzgados,
que no se hieran,
que no sean abusados,
que no sean condenados por la justicia.[375]
Que no caigan en la bajada del camino
            en la subida del camino.
Que no haya obstáculo,
            ni tropiezo detrás,
            ni delante de ellos.
Ubícalos en el camino verde,
        en la vereda verde.[376]
Que no tengan desgracia,
            ni desastre;
            por tu culpa
            por tu conjuro.
Que sea buena la existencia de los que te dan sustento,
                de los que proveen en tu boca y
                        en tu presencia.

¡Tú, Corazón del Cielo,
tú, Corazón de la Tierra,
tú, Envoltorio Sagrado,
tú, también, Tojil,
        Awilix,
        Jaqawitz;

bóveda del Cielo,
superficie de la Tierra;
las cuatro esquinas,
los cuatro lados!
¡Que sólo haya claridad,
que sólo haya paz[377] ante tu boca,
                          ante tu presencia, tú, divinidad!

Así, pues, eran los Señores
cuando ayunaban durante nueve cuentas de veinte,
                          trece cuentas de veinte y
                          diecisiete cuentas de veinte.
Durante muchos días de ayuno lloraban sus corazones
                          [por sus vasallos
                          por sus hijos;
                          por todos: esposas y
                                    descendientes;
cuando prestaban su servicio cada uno de los Señores.
Ésta era su manera de ofrendar por la tranquilidad
                          por la vida y
          su manera de ofrendar por el señorío.
Esto era el señorío del Ajpop,
          el Ajpop K'amja,
          el Q'alel,
          el Ajtzik Winaq.
De dos en dos entraban en ayuno y
          se cambiaban para llevar la carga del pueblo
                          y de toda la gente k'iche'.
De un solo lugar se originó la tradición,
          el origen de sustentar y
                    de proveer.
Por este solo origen de la tradición,
lo mismo hicieron los Tamub,
          los Ilokab;
          junto con los Rabinaleb,
                    los Kaqchikeleb,

                    los Ajtz'ikinaja,
                    los Tujal ja',
                    los Uch'abaja.
De un solo tronco se extendió esta tradición k'iche'[378]
              y los demás también la hicieron suya.

Pero no sólo fue así que gobernaban,
no sólo fue así nada más que recibieron a los que los alimentaban,
                              a los que los sostenían;
No fueron sólo sus ayunos
              las penitencias que hicieron.[379]
Tampoco sólo fueron a arrebatar[380]
              a robar su señorío,
                    su poder,
                    su majestad.
Y no sólo así, nomás, fueron abatidos los barrancos,
                    las ciudadelas
de los pequeños pueblos,
de los grandes pueblos;
sino éstos pagaron un gran precio:
trajeron turquesa,[381]
trajeron metales;
trajeron granos de jade
              granos de piedras preciosas medidas en manos,
                              en puños.[382]
Trajeron penachos hechos de plumas verdes;[383]
éstos fueron los tributos de todos los pueblos.
Lo que se trajo ante la presencia portentosa de los Señores Q'ukumatz,
                                        K'otuja;
              ante la presencia de K'ikab y
                    de Kawisimaj,
el Ajpop,
el Ajpop K'amja,
el Q'alel,
el Ajtzik Winaq.
No fue poco lo que hicieron y

no fueron pocos los pueblos que derrotaron;
de muchas ramas de los pueblos llegaba el tributo al K'iche'.
Con muchas penas se llegó a esto y
                 se estableció por parte de los Señores.
No fue de inmediato que creció su poder,
fue Q'ukumatz quien dio origen a la grandeza del señorío.
Así fue, pues, como comenzó su engrandecimiento y
                       el engrandecimiento del K'iche'.
Y ahora vamos a enumerar la generación de los Señores
asimismo, vamos a dar los nombres de todos los Señores.

Éstas son, pues, las generaciones
                 la secuencia de todos los Señores
desde que vieron el amanecer, Balam Ki'tze'
                  Balam Aq'ab,
                  Majuk'utaj e
                  Ik'ibalam;
nuestros primeros abuelos,
nuestros primeros padres cuando apareció el Sol,
                     aparecieron la Luna y
                        las estrellas.
Éstas son, pues, las generaciones
                 la secuencia de los Señores.
Vamos a comenzar desde sus raíces,
de cómo fueron entrando los Señores,
cuando llegaban
cuando se sucedía cada generación de Señores;
los antepasados,
los Señores de las ciudadelas,
todos y cada uno de los Señores.
Aquí, pues, es cómo fueron manifestándose cada uno de los Señores
Aquí, pues, es cómo fueron sucediéndose uno por uno los Señores
                           [k'iche'es.
Balam Ki'tze' fue el origen de los Kaweq,
K'oqawib, segunda generación de Balam Ki'tze'.[384]

Balam K'onache' fue quien estableció los títulos Ajpopol,
                    fue de la tercera generación.

K'otuja e
Istayul conformaron la cuarta generación.

Q'ukumatz y
K'otuja, origen de los Señores prodigiosos, fueron la quinta
                                                    [generación.

Tepepul e
Istayul[385] fueron sextos en el orden.

K'ikab y
Kawisimaj séptimo cambio en el señorío,
                    fueron prodigiosos.

Tepepul e
Istayul fueron la octava generación.

Tekum[386] y
Tepepul, novena generación.

Wajxaqib K'am[387] y
K'ikab, décima generación de Señores.

Wuqub No'j y
Kuwatepech[388] fueron en el orden, los undécimos Señores.

Oxib Kej y
Belejeb Tz'i' la duodécima generación de Señores.[389]
Ellos estaban gobernando cuando vino Donadiu[390]
y fueron torturados por los castellanos.[391]

Tekum y
Tepepul fueron tributarios ante los castellanos,
ellos habían sido engendrados[392] y fueron la treceava generación
de Señores.

Don Juan de Rojas y
don Juan Cortés, decimocuarta generación de Señores,
ellos fueron hijos de Tekum y
                    Tepepul.

Éstas son, pues, las generaciones,
                el orden del Señorío de los Ajpop
                                Ajpop K'amja de los
Kaweq K'iche'.

196

Y ahora nombraremos de nuevo a sus linajes,
éstas son, pues, las Casas Grandes de cada uno de los Señores
que siguen al Ajpop y
                    al Ajpop K'amja.
Ésta es la denominación de los nueve linajes de los Kaweq,
                    de las nueve Casas Grandes.
Éstos son los títulos de los Señores de cada una de esas Casas Grandes:
Ajaw Ajpop tenía su Casa Grande,
                    Granero era el nombre de esa Casa Grande.[393]
Ajaw Ajpop K'amja,
Casa de Pájaros se llamaba su Casa Grande.
Nim Ch'okoj Kaweq tenía su Casa Grande.
Ajaw Ajtojil tenía su Casa Grande.
Ajaw Ajq'ukumatz tenía su Casa Grande.
Popol Winaq Chi T'uy tenía su Casa Grande.
Lolmet Kejnay tenía su Casa Grande.
Popol Winaq pa Jom Tzalatz' tuvo, pues, su Casa Grande.[394]
Tepew Yaki tenía su Casa Grande.[395]
Éstos son los nueve linajes de los Kaweq.
Y eran numerosos los vasallos y
                    los hijos que seguían a estas nueve Casas Grandes.

He aquí lo de los Nija'ib,
también eran nueve las Casas Grandes.
Pero primero diremos la descendencia de los Señores.
Era una sola su raíz desde antes del origen del Sol,
                    antes de la luz para la humanidad.
Balam Aq'ab, primer abuelo y
                    padre.
K'o'akul y
K'o'akutek, segunda generación.
K'ochajuj y
K'otz'ibaja, tercera generación.[396]
Belejeb Kej, cuarta generación.[397]

K'otuja, la quinta generación de Señores.

Batz'a fue, pues, la sexta generación.³⁹⁸

Istayul fue, pues, la séptima generación.

K'otuja, en turno, fue octavo en el orden de los Señores.

Belejeb Kej, noveno en el orden.

Ke'ema, le decían en turno, al de la décima generación.³⁹⁹

Ajaw K'otuja, la undécima generación.

Don Cristóbal, como le decían,

gobernó en tiempos de los castellanos.

Don Pedro de Robles es el actual Ajaw Q'alel.

Éstos son, pues, todos los Señores descendientes de los Ajaw Q'alel.

Ahora nombraremos los títulos de los Señores de cada una de
las Casas Grandes:

Ajaw Q'alel,

el primer Señor ante los Nija'ib, tenía su Casa Grande.

Ajaw Ajtzik Winaq tenía su Casa Grande.

Ajaw Q'alel K'amja tenía su Casa Grande.

Nima K'amja tenía su Casa Grande.⁴⁰⁰

Uchuch K'amja tenía su Casa Grande.

Nim Ch'okoj Nija'ib tenía su Casa Grande.

Ajaw Awilix tenía su Casa Grande.

Yakolatam tenía su Casa Grande.

[Nima Lolmet Ye'oltux tenía su Casa Grande]⁴⁰¹

Éstas son, pues, las Casas Grandes ante los Nija'ib,

así se denominaban los nueve linajes de los Nija'ib, así llamados.

Eran bastantes las ramificaciones familiares de cada uno de
estos Señores,

sólo a los primeros hemos mencionado.

He aquí, pues, los del Ajaw K'iche'.

Éste fue el abuelo,

      el padre:

Majuk'utaj, la primera persona.

K'o'ajaw era el nombre del Señor de la segunda generación.

Q'aq' Laqam,⁴⁰²

K'okosom,[403]
Komajkun,[404]
Wuqub Aj,[405]
K'okamel,[406]
K'oyabakoj,[407]
Winaq Ba[la]m.[408]
Éstos son los Señores ante los Ajaw K'iche'.
Éstas fueron las generaciones y
              la secuencia.

Éstos son, pues, los nombres de los Señores de las Casas Grandes;
sólo había cuatro Casas Grandes.
Ajtzik Winaq Ajaw, nombre del primer Señor, tenía su Casa Grande.
Lolmet Ajaw, segundo Señor, tenía su Casa Grande.
Nim Ch'okoj Ajaw, tercer Señor, tenía su Casa Grande.
Jaqawitz, el cuarto Señor, tenía su Casa Grande.
Cuatro eran las Casas Grandes ante los Ajaw K'iche'.[409]

Había también tres Nim Ch'okoj,
que eran como padres ante todos los Señores K'iche'.
En unidad se conformaron estos tres maestros de la palabra,
los dadores de vida,
las que son madres de la palabra,
los que son padres de la palabra.
Grande entre pocos era la naturaleza de los tres maestros de la palabra:
gran maestro de la palabra ante los Kaweq[410] [era el primero],
[gran maestro de la palabra] ante los Nija'ib era el segundo,
gran maestro de la palabra era el tercer Señor ante los Ajaw K'iche'.
Eran, pues, tres los maestros de la palabra,
cada uno representando un linaje.

Esto es, entonces, la esencia de los k'iche'es
porque ya no hay dónde verla.
Antes había [un libro],
antiguamente [escrito][411] por los Señores,

pero ha desaparecido.

Así, pues, se completa todo lo relacionado al K'iche'.
que ahora se llama Santa Cruz.

NOTAS

1. Literalmente el "constructor" y "creador". *Tz'aq* y *bit* son raíces verbales "construir" y "crear".*Tz'aq* quiere decir "construcción" y *bit* "creación". El sufijo *-ol*, en ambos sustantivos, es marcador agentivo.

2. Alom viene de *ali*, "niña", y *k'ajolom* viene de *k'ajol*, "niño" o "hijo de varón". La partícula *-om* es un agentivo que hace referencia a su calidad de mujer que "concibe" y al varón que "engendra", respectivamente. Éstos son adjetivos que hacen referencia a la pareja creadora en una lectura antropomórfica.

3. Literalmente, éstas son metáforas para decir "cazador tacuacín, cazador coyote". En otra parte del texto se identifica a *wuch'*, "tacuacín", como la deidad que oscurece el Cielo antes del amanecer. Recinos (1953: 82) asocia a Junajpu Wuch' como "dios del amanecer" y a Junajpu Utiw como "dios de noche".

4. En estas líneas los adjetivos *saqi nim*, "blanco grande", están omitidos del segundo verso paralelo; pero líneas más adelante aparecen completos. Aquí la referencia zoomórfica es más directa y aclara que son la pareja de ancianos (tiempo) que acompañan el proceso de creación. Son los mismos que acompañan a Junajpu y Xbalamke a vencer a Wuqub Kak'ix. Recinos (1953: 82) relaciona a *Saqi Nim Sis* como "diosa madre" y a *Saqi Nim Aq* como su "consorte".

5. El texto k'iche' dice Tepew Q'ukumatz. Tepew es una palabra náhuatl que significa "conquistador" o "victorioso" y se compone de los términos *te-*, "gente", y *-pew*, "conquistar" (Campbell, 1983), que en este caso es el adjetivo, y Q'ukumatz es el nominal. La

expresión ha sido traducida como "majestad" (Edmonson, 1971: 4) y "soberana" (D. Tedlock, 1996: 63). En este contexto es una metonimia de Quetzalcóatl. Q'ukumatz es mi escritura porque Recinos lo escribe *Gucumatz*. Para mayor claridad, Recinos dice: "es la versión quiché de *Kukulcán*, el nombre maya de *Quetzalcóatl*" (Recinos, 1953: 82) y que significa "majestuosa serpiente emplumada".

6. Esto viene de *ajraxa laq, ajraxa tzel*, metáfora asociada a lo plano y verde de la Tierra y de la bóveda cósmica. *Laq* literalmente es "plato", y *tzel* es recipiente de forma redonda. Esto quiere decir: los guías espirituales mitológicos que ofrecen ceremonias a la Tierra y al Cielo. El color azul está asociado a la bóveda del Cielo.

7. *Mamom* viene de *mam*, "abuelo"; es el consorte mitológico de *Iyom*, "comadrona".

8. Conforme a Ximénez (1967: 9) Ixmukane quiere decir "entierro o fosa". Recinos (1953: 83) dice que estos nombres equivalen a "los dioses mexicanos Cipactonal y Oxomoco, los sabios que según la leyenda tolteca inventaron la astrología judiciaria y compusieron la cuenta de los tiempos, o sea el calendario". Edmonson (1971: 5) asocia estos nombres a los términos náhuatl *yexpoacoc* y *yexomocane* que traduce como "bisabuelo", "bisabuela" y agrega que es extraño que al nombrar a esta pareja el nombre masculino vaya primero, contrario al orden usual k'iche'; por lo que sugiere revertir el orden en una eventual reconstrucción de estos nombres.

9. En el folio 1r del manuscrito de Ximénez, se lee *Popo Vuh* y de ahí don Adrián Chávez propuso el término *Pop* considerando que "la segunda 'o' de *Popo* es falsa" (Chávez, 1978: en "Explicación necesaria"). Sin embargo en el folio 54r del mismo manuscrito se lee *Popol Vuh*. Ver explicación en la introducción.

10. El manuscrito dice literalmente *Ilbal saq*, que es una aposición al nombre *Popol Wuj*, y que literalmente quiere decir "instrumento para ver con claridad"; esto es, el libro que contiene la mitología y la historia k'iche'. Sobre la frase *petenaq Ch'aqa palow*, comparto la traducción de Edmonson (1971: 7), quien dice que *Ch'aqa palow* quiere decir "del lado del mar"; y no "del otro lado del mar". Los argumentos históricos se pueden fundamentar en las siguientes bases lingüísticas. Domingo de Basseta en las oraciones (a-b) y Varea en (c-d) proporcionan los siguientes datos:

(a) *chaca haa ubic* "de la otra parte del río";
(b) *chaca haa uloc* "de esta parte del río";

(c) *ch'aqa apo*   "de la otra parte de allá";

(d) *ch'aqa pe*   "de esta parte de acá".

En k'iche' los direccionales son *ubik*, de "aquí para allá", y *uloq*, de "allá para acá"; aunque el segundo algunas veces se puede omitir sin que la oración sea agramatical, como en este ejemplo del *Popol Wuj*. Compárese:

Chak'ama' uloq le chikop   "trae el animal (de allá para acá)".

Chak'ama' ubik le chikop   "lleva el animal (de aquí para allá)".

Chak'ama' le chikop   "trae el animal" y en última instancia: "acéptalo" (como regalo o compraventa); pero no precisamente equivale a decir "llevarlo de aquí para allá".

En los siguientes ejemplos, la ausencia del direccional *bik*, en contraste con los ejemplos anteriores, produce una oración agramatical.

Katok uloq o Katok   "Entra" o "adelante" (siempre de afuera o de allá para acá).

Katel ubik   "Sal" (de aquí para allá).

Katel   Es una frase agramatical.

De esta cuenta, la oración *Petenaq ch'aqa palow* en el *Popol Wuj* quiere decir "del lado del mar" o "de la orilla del mar"; lo cual se corrobora con lo que se dice en el *Memorial de Sololá: Chi uqajibal k'a q'ij xojpe wi pa Tulan, ch'aqa palow* ("del poniente venimos a Tulán, a este lado del mar") (mi traducción).

En una ubicación geográfica, si del poniente maya se llega a Tulán, no hay mar de por medio; más bien, se llega a la costa marítima. Carmack (1983a: 212) ha sugerido que "el Tulán quiché tal vez se hallara en la región de la Costa del Golfo y no en la parte central de México" y D. Tedlock (1996: 16) argumenta que ese lugar del "oriente" es Chichén Itzá, y que en ese lugar los ancestros k'iche'es habrían recibido el texto o parte del manuscrito jeroglífico del *Popol Wuj*. Enrique Florescano por su parte (2000: 339) dice: "Mi interpretación de que la Tulán Suyuá del *Popol Vuh* es Chichén Itzá, se apoya en los siguientes datos. En el posclásico, la capital política más importante del sureste era Chichén Itzá; esta ciudad también está situada al oriente de los altos de Guatemala." Esta idea de peregrinación del poniente al oriente está relacionada con expansiones primigenias. Kaufman (en Campbell y Kaufman, 1990:

55) ha propuesto que alrededor del año 2200 a. C. el proto-maya se hablaba en Los Cuchumatanes (poniente en este caso), y que alrededor del año 1000 a. C. la gente se expandió por el río Usumacinta hacia Petén (oriente). En otras palabras, la gente se originó o partió del poniente hacia el oriente y luego se cuentan los lugares recorridos de regreso. No es que hayan cruzado el mar.

11. Ésta es una lectura literal de *qamujibal* "nuestra oscuridad" en referencia a la parte mitológica hasta la salida del Sol.

12. Este tipo de expresiones que aquí se traducen como *así llamado, así nombrado, así se dice* son frases que cierran el discurso. Edmonson (1971: xii) las equipara a las comillas. En el presente caso, se está cerrando la descripción del libro que los autores k'iche'es están copiando.

13. Literalmente "sus cuatro estacas". Ésta es una metáfora que asocia el cosmos con un campo de siembra donde hay una estaca en cada una de las esquinas.

14. Aquí se está haciendo referencia a la cuerda con que aún se miden los terrenos. *Umej* del manuscrito ha sido traducido como "la mitad"; pero significa "doblez", como la dobladura de los cortes que visten las mujeres mayas.

15. En el texto k'iche' se dice *kaj ulew, cho palo*, literalmente: "cielo tierra" y "lago mar", metonimias para referirse al cosmos y a todas las aguas de la Tierra, respectivamente.

16. Esta manera de contar un hecho pasado, en este caso el silencio primigenio, es una de las características del discurso k'iche': se cuenta en tiempo presente un hecho ya acontecido.

17. Aquí se anticipa que los dioses que estaban envueltos en plumas y que se encontraban en el agua, son nombrados como "Majestuosa Serpiente Emplumada".

18. El texto k'iche' dice *saqtetoj e k'o wi* donde *saqtetoj* quiere decir "luz que sale de entre las plumas" donde estaban envueltos. Ésta es una lectura inversa fundada en Basseta quien traduce *saqtetoj* como "la claridad que entra por los risquieros", es decir entre los resquicios. Asimismo, el texto literalmente dice que estaban "enterrados" entre plumas verdes y azules. La palabra *q'uq'* significa quetzal, pero también así se llaman sus plumas. *Raxon* es otra ave de plumas color azul que está asociada al quetzal. En el diccionario de Basseta se dice: "*Q'uq'*: la pluma verde y el pájaro que le cría. *Raxon*: pluma azul y el pájaro".

19. Aquí se aclara por qué se dice "Serpiente Emplumada". Es por la luz o blancura que escapa de entre las plumas de quetzal en medio de la oscuridad. Si vemos a esta ave de frente, debajo de sus plumas verdes tiene unas blancas y en k'iche' la palabra para "luz" es la misma que para "blanco". La metáfora, entonces, está asociada al ave.

20. Recinos (1953: 86) traduce "hablaron entre sí *Tepew* y *Gucumatz*" cuando el texto k'iche' dice que quien habló con ellos fue Uk'u'x Kaj.

21. El manuscrito dice Uk'u'x Kaj, literalmente "Corazón del Cielo"; huracán que Ximénez traduce como "un pie" debido a que la palabra se compone de *jun*, "uno", y *raqan*, "su-pie". Sin embargo, el significado de *raqan* es más amplio, en el diccionario de Coto se utiliza para designar cosas grandes, largas o altas. De hecho, en Coto, la palabra para decir "gigante" está asociada a *hu rapah r'aqan*. De ahí que Brinton (1890: 123) sugiere que esa palabra hace referencia a la fuerza y poder de las tormentas tropicales, conocidas como huracanes. Es más, Brinton propone que ese término maya pasó a las Antillas donde la escucharon los navegantes europeos y luego pasó a formar parte del vocabulario de las lenguas indoeuropeas. *Kaqulja* es "rayo", que implica la luz (relámpago) y trueno, mientras que *koyopa* significa la luz pero sin sonido o relámpago visto a distancia. *Ch'ip* se dice "al último" de las hijas o hijos y *raxa* quiere decir "verde, tierno, fresco" o como agrega Ximénez: "cosa hermosa". De esa cuenta Kaqulja Jun Raqan equivale a "Rayo huracán" o sea fuerza poderosa; Ch'ipa Kaqulja (más adelante se escribe *ch'ipi*), literalmente significa "Rayo más joven", fuerza en potencia, y Raxa Kaqulja, "Rayo hermoso", como la hermosura de su contraparte envueltos en plumas de quetzal en el mar reposado. Nótese que a "Corazón del Cielo" se le identifica como "Huracán", que implica su fuerza acuática en un espacio donde sólo existía el mar y el Cielo y luego se enumeran tres manifestaciones de esa fuerza.

22. Esta identificación de tres manifestaciones de "Corazón del Cielo" ha dado pie a argumentar una influencia cristiana en el texto, lo que no se descarta tomando en cuenta que la copia de que se dispone fue hecha por un cura doctrinero. En la parte final del libro desaparece una cuarta deidad Nik'aj Taqaj, que corresponde al linaje de Ik'ibalam. Sin embargo, de la época precolombina y conforme a datos epigráficos también se encuentra la "triada de Palenque"

(Schele y Miller, 1986: 48-51) que de ninguna manera puede ser considerada influencia cristiana. Empero, con la posible alteración del texto por parte de Ximénez, que puede demostrarse con oraciones mal construidas o copiadas, en este caso se está hablando de una fuerza superior que se manifiesta en tres formas y no necesariamente de una "trinidad". La forma del verso, sin embargo, evidencia que se está hablando de una cuatriedad. El manuscrito, textualmente, dice: *rumal ri uqux cah huracán ubí, caculha huracán nabe, ucab cut chipa caculha, roxchic raxa caculha*. En el formato de la presente versión, cuya traducción genera esta nota, el texto k'iche' quedaría así:

...*rumal ri Uk'u'x Kaj Jun Raqan ubi',*
    Kaqulja Jun Raqan nabe,
    ukab k'ut Ch'ipa Kaqulja,
    rox chik Raxa Kaqulja

Aquí puede verse que la palabra Jun Raqan es común a los dos primeros versos y *kaqulja* al segundo par. Mi interpretación es, sin embargo, que si bien son tres las manifestaciones de "Corazón del Cielo", su identificación se hace en cuatro versos.

23. La pregunta en el texto k'iche': *Jupa ta chawaxoq, ta saqiroq puch?*, está en forma imperativa. Esto quiere decir que los dioses, después de decidir la creación humana sólo se preguntan por el momento propicio para hacerlo. La "siembra" y el "amanecer" son expresiones paralelas en el *Popol Wuj*, que están asociadas a la siembra de luz en el Cielo y al surgimiento de vida en la Tierra.

24. *Juyub taqaj*, literalmente "montaña-valle", es otra metonimia para referirse a la "superficie de la Tierra". Éste es un cognado del *tzuul taq'a* de los q'eqchi'es y que líneas abajo conforma un verso paralelo con "Tierra".

25. Aquí se identifican cuatro nombres. Esto clarifica lo dicho en la nota 22 que son tres las manifestaciones de "Corazón del Cielo". Entre otros ejemplos prehispánicos están la identificación de las tres estrellas que conforman la constelación de Orión (ver D. Tedlock, 1996: 236-7), las tres estrellas que carga la tortuga en un detalle del *Códice de Madrid* (ver Freidel, Schele y Parker, 2000: 78), y en el mismo *Popol Wuj* son nombrados tres semidioses del mal que tuvieron que ser destruidos: Wuqub Kak'ix, Sipakna y Kabraqan.

26. Uk'u'x Ulew, "Corazón de la Tierra", es la contraparte de "Corazón del Cielo".

27. La creación de venados y pájaros, es una figura que implica la creación de todos los animales. En líneas más adelante se identifica a otra clase de animales, que equivalen a los "guardianes" de los montes.

28. Literalmente "su oficio", pero por contexto se entiende que a los animales se les condena a ser alimento de otros.

29. Aquí es explícito que se está hablando de un ser único de barro. Si ésta fuera una alusión a la creación bíblica, como otros han argumentado, sería en todo caso una referencia burlesca a los seres de barro.

30. Aquí se está haciendo referencia a la función de Xpiyakok e Ixmukane como ajq'ijab o guardadores primigenios de la cuenta de los días, y la utilización del tz'ite' como medio de adivinación.

31. A falta de un mejor término en español, se utiliza la palabra "sacerdote" para identificar a oficiantes religiosos que a la vez eran conocedores del movimiento de los astros y por eso conocedores de la cuenta de los días.

32. Las palabras k'iche'es *k'uwal* y *yamanik* las presenta Pantaleón Guzmán como "diamante" o "esmeralda", a cada una de ellas, y juntas como "riquezas".

33. El texto k'iche' dice *ajtoltekat,* que no necesariamente identifica a los toltecas como pueblo sino a una profesión. Esto se deduce de las líneas anteriores. Recinos (1953: 92) anota, además, que "Los toltecas, en efecto, fueron grandes maestros en la platería". Edmonson (1971: 22) traduce esta línea como "artesanos", y D. Tedlock (1996: 69) como "maestro artesano".

34. Frijol rojo que es fruto del árbol de pito *(Erythrina corallodendron Urb).* Este árbol, como bien dice Recinos (1953: 92), es utilizado en algunos lugares "para formar cercados"; en algunas regiones de la costa sur se sigue usando como cerco. Su fruto se sigue usando en ceremoniales de adivinación.

35. El texto k'iche' dice *chi raqan* y ha dado lugar a diversas interpretaciones. Recinos y Chávez lo traducen como parte del nombre de Ixmukane y otros lo traducen literalmente como "a sus pies". Sin embargo, estoy de acuerdo con D. Tedlock (1996: 234) quien, siguiendo la interpretación de don Andrés Xiloj, lo traduce como alguien que presta asistencia. En este caso, la sacerdotisa Ixmukane asiste a Xpiyakok en la ceremonia de adivinación.

36. Literalmente "corazón". Recinos (1953: 94) traduce como "no tenían alma".

37. El texto k'iche' dice *kikomajil*, sinónimo de "su sangre".

38. Sibaque es el junquillo con que se elaboran los petates. De acuerdo con Edmonson (1971) el sibaque (*Typha angustifolia*) se usa para hacer petates. De acuerdo con Recinos ésta es la "espadaña" y en pie de página agrega: "planta de la familia de las tifáceas, muy usada para la fabricación de esteras llamadas en el país petates tules". También se usa como pita para amarrar los tamales.

39. El texto k'iche' dice *k'otk'owach*, literalmente "escarbador de cara". *Kamasotz'*, "murciélago decapitador", que en páginas posteriores le corta la cabeza a uno de los héroes gemelos. *Kotzbalam*, "jaguar masticador", derivado de *kotz*, "mejilla", conforme a Ximénez, *balam*, "jaguar", con lo cual debe entenderse que era el jaguar que masticaba sus mejillas y sus carnes. *Tukumbalam*, "jaguar batidor", que desparramó los huesos y nervios de los hombres de madera.

40. Aquí se le identifica como *kamalotz'* y cuando se habla de los héroes gemelos como *kamasotz'*. Soy de la opinión que aquí hay un error de Ximénez. En lugar de copiar *kamasotz'* escribió *kamalotz'*.

41. Literalmente el "jaguar de sus mejillas". Kotz significa "mejilla" de acuerdo con Ximénez y el nombre de este jaguar es *kotzbalam*, "mejilla jaguar".

42. Literalmente un "aguacero negro"; pero que significa una lluvia que dura muchos días y noches.

43. Este término ha sido un problema para los traductores porque Ximénez (folio 5r) no fue claro en transcribir las palabras *tzi*, "nixtamal", y *tz'i'*, "perro". Por contexto y porque "perro" y "piedra de moler" no conforman la misma categoría gramatical, es que la palabra en k'iche' debe ser *tzi*, "nixtamal", que sí está asociado a "piedra de moler" como los dos pareados precedentes que conforman cada uno la misma categoría gramatical.

44. Este pareado aclara la nota anterior: "perros" y "chompipes" (pavos) conforman un verso paralelo por la categoría animal. En el pro-tomaya, *ak'* quería decir "chompipa" (England, 1994: 157) y luego esa palabra k'iche' pasó a identificar a la gallina. Este ejemplo es semejante a *kej*, "venado", que se transpuso a "caballo" y se adoptó el término náhuatl *mazatl* para identificar al venado. Ahora a los chompipes se les nombra *no's*. Lo interesante en estos términos es que el término *castilian* o *kaxlan* se antepone a los sustantivos para identificar a lo venido de Castilla (España), vg. *kaxlan wa*, "pan"; *kaxlan tzij*, "idioma español"; incluso en náhuatl aparece la palabra

castillantotolim, o *castillan totolim*, "pollo, gallo, gallina" (Dakin y Lutz: 1996).

45. Joli, juk'i son sonidos onomatopéyicos que hacen referencia al proceso de fricción sobre las piedras de moler.

46. Tres piedras entre las cuales se forma el fuego para cocinar y tradicionalmente alrededor del cual se juntaban las familias para comer. Conforme a D. Tedlock (1996: 236), éste parece ser el origen de la creación de la constelación Orión. Schele (2000: 75-77) también sostiene el mismo punto.

47. Literalmente "Siete Guacamaya", siendo el numeral 7 parte del nombre como sucede en Wuqub Kame, "Siete Muerte", Wuqub Junajpu, "Siete Junajpu", etcétera. *Kak'ix* es guacamaya (Basseta, Pantaleón de Guzmán). A Wuqub Kak'ix se le asocia también con la "Osa Mayor" como está traducido en el diccionario de De León (1955: 33), lo cual coincide con el número de estrellas que integran dicha constelación y cuya luz es efectivamente tenue. Recuérdese aquí que conforme al mito k'iche', el Cielo está siendo literalmente "sembrado" de astros por los dioses.

48. Esa referencia a la gente de madera que fue inundada, indica que Wuqub Kak'ix era la única luz que les proveía de claridad. Nótese además la conexión o "traslape" de ambos mitos.

49. En nota anterior decía que Pantaleón de Guzmán reporta *k'uwal* y *yamanik* como "esmeralda" o "diamante"; pero juntas equivalen a "riquezas".

50. El texto k'iche' dice: *rax kawakoj chi abaj* que literalmente quiere decir: "de verde/azul están ataviados con piedras...", una referencia implícita a las incrustaciones de jade practicadas por la antigua odontología maya.

51. Literalmente "Un Cerbatanero". *Jun* es uno, *-aj* es el agentivo y *pu* es apócope de *pub*, "cerbatana".

52. Una interpretación de este nombre es "Pequeño Jaguar-venado" donde el prefijo *x-* indica el diminutivo, *balam* es "jaguar" y *ke* es apócope de *kej* que significa "venado". Sin embargo, D. Tedlock (1996: 239) presenta una interesante traducción al identificar *balam* con "jaguar" y "oculto"; *Q'e*, "Sol" en su fase nocturna de acuerdo con la tradición q'eqchi'. *Balamq'e*, "dios Sol (el-Sol-de noche va como tigre al oriente...)" (Haeserijn, 1979: 53), lo que a su vez se confirma al final del relato mitológico. El primer gemelo se convierte en Sol y el segundo en la Luna, lo cual puede entenderse propiamente como el "Sol escondido durante la noche" o su reflejo porque

en k'iche' a la Luna también se le identifica como "Sol nocturno". Nótese además que es Xbalamke quien reconstruye la cabeza de Junajpu, y eso ocurre durante la noche, y que en q'eqchi', *po* es "Luna" o "mes" con lo cual existiría un juego de sonidos con la sílaba final del término Junajpu.

53. Esta palabra viene del náhuatl *cipactli*, "caimán o lagarto" (Campbell, en Carmack y Morales, 1983: 85), cuyas características son identificadas más adelante.

54. Literalmente: "temblor", "terremoto", lo cual coincide con sus características de destructor de montañas y volcanes. *Kab* en yucateco, además de significar "miel" como en otros idiomas mayas, también equivale a "fuerza, rigor o intensidad fuerte de algún fenómeno". *Kab* también significa "tierra", en yucateco (*Diccionario maya*). Lo anterior quiere decir que Kabraqan, como puede interpretarse "dos piernas", es un nombre asociado a la "tierra" donde provoca sustos y otras veces daños severos.

55. Chimalmat es palabra k'iche'; *chi* es preposición y *malmatik* es verbo que indica correr detrás de algo. D. Tedlock (1996: 241) asocia a Chimalmat con la "Osa Menor", lo cual concuerda con su pareja Wuqub Kak'ix, "Osa Mayor".

56. Todos estos nombres son de volcanes. El *Chi q'aq'*, que literalmente quiere decir "donde hay fuego", es generalmente identificado como el volcán de Fuego; el Junajpu siempre ha sido identificado como el volcán de Agua; pero es más probable que éste sea el volcán de Acatenango, como D. Tedlock (1996: 241) sugiere, y que Pekul, que literalmente quiere decir "peñasco derrumbado", sea el volcán de Agua; aunque también se conoce con este nombre al volcán Santo Tomás. El *ya' xcanul* que Ximénez transcribe como *Yaxcanul* y que Recinos (1953: 100) identifica como el volcán Santa María, es probablemente otro volcán. *Ya'* en kaqchikel o tz'utujil, *ja'* en k'iche', quiere decir "agua" y *xkanul* es nombre genérico de volcán; en consecuencia *ya' xkanul* puede entenderse como "volcán en el agua". En este sentido, *ya' xkanul* apunta a uno de los volcanes del lago Atitlán. Recinos (1953: 100) dice que ese volcán es el que se conoce como *Gagxanul* en kaqchikel y en su versión del *Memorial de Solalá* (Recinos, 2003: 59-61) se dice que *Gagxanul* es el volcán a donde Q'aq'awitz y Saqitz'unun habrían ido a traer el fuego. Parece más lógico que ese volcán sea uno de los del lago Atitlán y no el Santa María, ubicado en territorio k'iche', porque además en ese mismo pasaje del *Memorial de Solalá* se dice: "Marcháronse

de allí y llegaron a *Cecic ynup*, así llamado, y se fueron remando por el lago". Con respecto al *Makamob*, muy probablemente sea el "cerro quemado" y *Julisnab* puede ser el que antiguamente fue el volcán de Almolonga, destruido hace miles de años y del cual geológicamente sólo queda un "agujero" donde actualmente se ubica el pueblo de Almolonga, Quetzaltenango, como textualmente implica la palabra *jul* en el texto k'iche'. *Is*, literalmente, quiere decir "pelos" y a la vez puede entenderse como "retoños" y *nab* que conforme a Basseta es *neb* y que significa "poner en ringleras o amontonar", lo cual concuerda con la fila de cerros o "retoños" que se encuentran alrededor de lo que antiguamente habría sido el volcán de Almolonga.

57. En la copia k'iche' de Ximénez erróneamente se identifica a este gemelo como Jun Junajpu, en lugar de Junajpu.

58. Literalmente estos nombres quieren decir "gran jabalí blanco" y "gran pizote blanco", nombres zoomórficos que según Recinos (1953: 102) representan a la pareja creadora; aunque es más probable que esos nombres estén asociados a porciones del tiempo, como Junajpu Wuch, Junajpu Utiw, identificados por Recinos (1953: 82) como "dios del amanecer" y "dios de la noche", respectivamente.

59. Esto de "curar" es un eufemismo para lo que se dice en la siguiente línea.

60. En el texto k'iche' estas dos líneas están unidas por el juego de palabras *xkam*, "murió", y *xuk'am*, "recuperó". Este uso de paronomasia es usual en el texto.

61. En este punto del manuscrito en la parte k'iche', folio 8r, se encuentran 10 líneas y media tachadas. Lo tachado efectivamente corresponde a otro pasaje y no a la muerte de Wuqub Kak'ix. Corresponde al momento en que los 400 muchachos tiran el tronco sobre Sipakna, lo cual se encuentra exactamente en el siguiente folio, 9r.

62. Comparto el criterio de Recinos (1953: 104) cuando dice que este número es una manera colectiva "para indicar un gran número, un montón".

63. Aquí otra paronomasia. En el texto k'iche' se juega con las palabras *ki'*, que quiere decir "dulce", y *ki*, "maguey"; pero cuyo resultado es "amargo". Se está haciendo referencia al licor derivado del maguey.

64. Una especie de bromelia de hojas rojas que crece sobre árboles.

65. Conforme a Recinos (1953: 108) esa montaña "se levanta al poniente del pueblo de Rabinal, en la región del río Chixoy".

66. La expresión "mientras haya Sol, mientras haya claridad" equivale a "eternidad".

67. Esta manera de hacer fuego es distinta a la producción de fuego por parte de Tojil.

68. Tierra blanca como yeso.

69. Con esta expresión, los gemelos también reiteran el deseo de los dioses por la creación humana. No es, pues, tan "oscura" como algunos traductores han afirmado.

70. En esta frase el nombre de Wuqub Junajpu no aparece en el manuscrito, pero por contexto se deduce que es un error de copia. La oración está en plural y sólo aparece el nombre de Jun Junajpu; aunque dos frases más adelante y en otras partes del relato ambos nombres están escritos. Wuqub Junajpu es el hermano de Jun Junajpu. *Junajpu* o *ajpu* es un día en el calendario maya.

71. *Batz'* es también un día del calendario y *chowen* es su equivalente en idioma yucateco.

72. Ixbaqiyalo se compone de los siguientes términos: *ix-* marcador femenino; *baq*, hueso; *ya* o *ja'*, "agua"; y *lo*, término dubitativo. D. Tedlock (1996: 250) traduce este término como "Mujer Garza".

73. En el texto k'iche' dice *ulaqel* y en Basseta se dice que *laqo* significa "juntar", y *laqanik* "cosa junta, como los casados". En consecuencia, *ulaqel* puede entenderse como en edad para unirse o casarse. Recinos (1953: 114) traduce estas líneas como: "no tenía mujer, era soltero".

74. Recuérdese aquí que antiguamente *ajtz'ib* significaba escribir o pintar, por lo que la referencia puede ser a cualquiera de estas dos artes.

75. Esta ave, *wok* en k'iche', no puede ser un gavilán, águila o cuervo como otros han traducido. Gavilán es *xik*; águila, *k'ot*; cuervo, *joj* en k'iche'. Comparto el criterio de D. Tedlock (1996: 91): esta ave es un halcón.

76. *Kame* es un día del calendario. De nuevo, aquí aparecen los números 1 y 7 que a mi parecer equivalen a inicio y fin. Cuando se combinan los 13 números del calendario con los 20 nombres de los días, comenzando con el número 1, indefectiblemente se termina con el 7. En términos matemáticos, la suma de 1 y 7 es igual a 8, *wajxaqib*, el número convencional que equivale al todo. De aquí una razón por la que el ciclo de 260 días comienza con el día *batz'* y con el número 8.

77. Es interesante observar aquí que, irónicamente, entre los lacandones Jesucristo "era asociado frecuentemente con uno de los temibles Señores de la Muerte" (Bruce, 1983: 275).

78. Estos nombres, por contexto, pueden derivarse de *xikik' ri upatan* que, literalmente, quiere decir "ensangrentar es su oficio". Esto viene de *kik'*, "sangre" y *kik'irisaj*, "ensangrentar". Un apócope de esa expresión sería *xikik' ri patan* —> *Xiki ri pat*. Este nombre es paralelo a Kuchuma Kik' cuya traducción literal sería "aflicción o dolor de sangre". *Chuma* se deriva de *chumunik*, "dolerse, afligirse" (Basseta), aunque Ximénez lo traduce como "sangre junta".

79. Literalmente se dice: "la sangre que enferma a la gente".

80. Estos nombres derivan de *puj*, "pus"; *q'ana*, "amarillo", y el agentivo *aj* que indica oficio o profesión.

81. *Chuq'anal* literalmente quiere decir "amarillez".

82. *Ch'amiy* o *ch'amiya*, con -a final como inserción vocálica, quiere decir "vara" o "cetro", símbolo de autoridad. *Baq* es "hueso" y *jolom* es "cabeza", pero en este caso es "calavera". Estos nombres equivalen a "Señor de la Vara de Hueso", "Señor de la Vara de Calavera".

83. Literalmente los nombres de estos Señores son: "Señor de la Basura" y "Señor Apuñalador". Sin embargo y por contexto Ajal Mes equivale a causante de desgracia, por provocar enemistad. La palabra clave en el texto k'iche' es *tza* que es sinónima de *labal* y quiere decir "enemistad" o "guerra" (Basseta); en q'eqchi' el término *tza* quiere decir "demonio" (Sam Juárez, *et al.*, 2003). En el texto k'iche' se dice *tza mes*, que tiene un significado literal de "enemistad de basura", es decir enemistad surgida de la nada y que trae como consecuencia la muerte.

84. Literalmente "gavilán" y "mecapal". En el texto de Ximénez se lee *xic*, "gavilán". La palabra *patan* también puede significar "oficio" o "mecapal". El texto k'iche' sugiere aquí el segundo significado, no sólo porque el mecapal oprime la frente de quien lleva una carga, sino porque en el mismo texto existe un paralelismo entre *patan* como "mecapal" y *kitelela' on* derivado de *telej*, "cargar".

85. En una traducción literal, esto quiere decir: "cada quien con su mecapal, con su carga al hombro", lo que equivale a cada quien con su oficio y responsabilidad.

86. Conforme al texto k'iche', literalmente se está hablando de "golpear" la garganta y el pecho.

87. El término k'iche' es *bate* y generalmente ha sido traducido como "argolla" o "anillo". En el diccionario de Vico se dice "argolla para la garganta", en Basseta se dice que *bate* es el "árbol con que hacen barbasco", y *batenta*, se identifica como "quicios de la puerta"; es decir, los goznes y seguramente las piedras redondas con agujero donde se instalaba la parte de la puerta que permitía abrirlas y cerrarlas. Por analogía, y conforme a estudios sobre el juego de la pelota se deduce que *bate* es una pieza de cuero u otro material flexible que cubría el torso de los jugadores y que servía para desviar la pelota (ver Ekholm, 1991: 243-49). Susan Gillespie en esa misma colección de ensayos señala que esa indumentaria era utilizada en la mitad del cuerpo, "la única parte permitida para tocar la pelota" (1991: 338). De ahí mi traducción de *bate* como "cinturones". Los protectores de cuero que se identifican en la línea anterior, eran seguramente las faldillas que cubrían los genitales.

88. El texto k'iche' dice *wachsot*, que puede desglosarse en *wach*, "frente", y *sot* o *su't*, "pañuelo", que debe entenderse como turbante o el pañuelo protector que se amarraban en la cabeza.

89. Una traducción literal de *rajpop achij* sería "varones" u "hombres encargados de la estera". D. Tedlock (1996: 93) lo traduce como un título con rango militar: guardianes militares de la estera.

90. El nombre del segundo mensajero, *Jun Raqan Tukur*, literalmente "tecolote de una pierna", puede también significar "tecolote gigante". El cuarto mensajero, *Jolom Tukur*, literalmente "cabeza de tecolote", puede también entenderse como "tecolote calavera" como traduce D. Tedlock (1996: 94). Estos cuatro mensajeros de Jun Kame y Wuqub Kame, "1 muerte" y "7 muerte", llegan a llamar a Jun Junajpu y a Wuqub Junajpu para ir a Xibalba, lugar donde mueren. De aquí podría derivar la creencia de que cuando canta un tecolote, es porque está anunciando la muerte.

91. En el texto k'iche' se identifica a este lugar como *nim xob karchaj*, sitio que Recinos (1953: 119) identifica como "La gran Carchah". Este lugar también se nombra en *El Título de Totonicapán* (1983: 217) como *Ch'uti cho chiri' nimsoy charchaq*, "un lago pequeño allí en Nimsoy Carchaj", sitio sobre el cual Robert Carmack escribe: "Parece ser una referencia al lugar de Verapaz que actualmente se conoce como San Pedro Carchá". D. Tedlock (1996: 255) ubica el pequeño lago como el lugar conocido ahora como "Las Islas". Todo lo anterior para indicar que aquel campo de juego se encontraba

en una "gran hondonada" a inmediaciones del actual San Pedro Carchá.

92. El padre es Xpiyakok. Ésta es la primera vez que se habla de la muerte de uno de estos seres divinos.

93. Literalmente, dicen a Jun Batz' y Jun Chowen "mantengan el calor en el corazón de su abuela", lo cual mantiene el paralelismo en estos versos.

94. Este lugar es obviamente tenebroso y difícil de pasar. D. Tedlock (1996: 256) sugiere que podrían ser las cuevas de Semuc Champey.

95. Aquí se describe lo difícil que era pasar por ese lugar. En el texto k'iche' se dice literalmente que el lugar estaba lleno de estacas puntiagudas y Ximénez lo traduce como "palos puntiagudos". El lugar seguramente estaba lleno de espinas grandes.

96. Esta identificación de "agua podrida" es porque en el texto k'iche' en folio 14r y folio 23v en la transcripción de Ximénez se hace mención de los mismos ríos. Si bien en la primera identificación se transcribió *puch* por *puh*, es obvio que la referencia es hacia el mismo río que Ximénez traduce la segunda vez como "río de materia".

97. Debe entenderse por "antorcha" a unas rajas de ocote que sirven para alumbrar. El ocote se extrae del pino colorado, que para mayor calidad y conforme tradición antigua, se corta del lado de donde sale el Sol.

98. Literalmente, un chay, o sea, una pieza afilada.

99. El texto k'iche' dice *xkiqaq'up*, que es un error de copia por *kix-qaq'up* —como en la línea anterior que dice *xkisachik* por *kix-sachik*— y que en una traducción literal quiere decir "vamos a quebrarlos". Ésta es una metáfora que asocia a la persona o a la familia con el tronco de un árbol que hay que "quebrar" para que desaparezca. Esta figura también se encuentra en el *Xajoj Tun* o *Rabinal Achi*, donde K'iche' Achi amenaza a Job Toj con acabar con sus "raíces" y su "tronco". Bretón (1999: 145) efectivamente traduce esa metáfora como fin de "linaje ancestral".

100. Literalmente, "quedará oculta su cara".

101. El texto k'iche' dice *pusbal chaaj*. *Pusbal* quiere decir "lugar del sacrificio", y *chaaj*, "juego de pelota". En líneas más adelante se vuelve a identificar el mismo lugar como el espacio en que está el árbol donde van a colocar la cabeza de Jun Junajpu.

102. *Crescentia cujete*.

103. El nombre de la doncella se compone de los siguientes términos: *ix-* es el prefijo femenino y también es diminutivo; *kik'* es "sangre"; pero *ik'* también quiere decir luna. D. Tedlock (1996: 260) lo traduce como "sangre luna". Según mi parecer, podría traducirse mejor como "joven sangre luna".

104. Ésta es una metáfora para decir "entras a la vida". Ixkik' estando ya embarazada constituye parte esencial del proceso de creación divina. Ella proviene del reino de la muerte, Xibalba, y por eso al subir a la superficie terrestre literalmente entra al reino de la vida. Recinos traduce esa oración como "confía en mi palabra", Chávez como "formas parte de la verdad" y Tedlock como "guarda la palabra".

105. Aquí se refiere a los pensamientos o sabiduría de los dos hermanos, Jun Junajpu y Wuqub Junajpu. Esta frase es muy importante porque el narrador habla en plural y aunque la calavera que embaraza a Ixkik' sea la de Jun Junajpu y la cabeza de Wuqub Junajpu esté enterrada junto a su cuerpo, ambos son responsables de la paternidad de los futuros gemelos. Es más, al terminar el relato a quien tratan de revivir los gemelos es efectivamente a Wuqub Junajpu, no a Jun Junajpu, con lo que completa la idea de una paternidad compartida y aceptada por los hijos.

106. Literalmente, "cuando vio que ya tenía hijo".

107. La oración literalmente dice: "... a quien conozca su cara", lo cual es cierto;puesto que fue la calavera confundida entre las ramas del árbol lo que embarazó a Ixkik'.

108. El texto k'iche' dice *tzel* que equivale a una jícara grande o recipiente con forma redonda. Basseta traduce *tzel* como "jícara de chiapa grande, y batea para lavar los pies".

109. El texto k'iche' dice *mawi chutzinik,* una expresión coloquial que quiere decir: "todavía no está", donde *utzinik* literalmente quiere decir "acabar, terminar". El contenido se refuerza con el verso paralelo que continúa en la línea siguiente y donde explícitamente Ixkik' dice "no me maten".

110. En estas líneas se está jugando con las palabras *tzaqix,* literalmente "dejar caer", y *utz'aqik,* "su construcción", dándose a entender que los Señores de Xibalba le van a dar vueltas al corazón entre sus manos sin dejarlo caer, hasta llegar a aparentar que ellos son los que le dan la forma a ese músculo.

111. En estas líneas la palabra *jolomax* ha sido difícil de traducir por parte de diversos autores y por inferencia la han considerado

sinónimo de "sangre" o "sangre de árbol", la savia. Sin embargo, líneas más adelante se identifica que la savia del árbol de donde se extrajo el líquido que suplantó el corazón de Ixkik' se denomina *jolomax*. En el diccionario de Coto encontramos que las palabras *jolom*, "cabeza", y *wi'*, literalmente "encima", se utilizan como sinónimas y que *wi'* se le llama también a la nata que se forma sobre determinados líquidos. Utilizando esta sinonimia de manera inversa, se refuerza la idea de que *jolomax* equivale a la "savia" o en todo caso a la "nata" que se forma sobre la savia. En consecuencia, lo que la doncella está anticipando en estas líneas es que lo que se va a presentar a los Señores de Xibalba, no es su sangre, sino la sangre o savia de un árbol.

112. El nombre en k'iche' es *ch'u'j kaq che'*, donde *ch'u'j* puede significar "loco", "rabioso" y también "grana" como se encuentra en el diccionario de Basseta. *Kaq* es "rojo" y *che'* quiere decir "árbol". Estoy de acuerdo con Recinos (1953: 129) al denominarlo "árbol rojo de grana". A este árbol se le conoce comúnmente como "árbol de sangre" y antiguamente se le extraía la savia como colorante. Se le conoce también como "árbol de drago" o "sangre de dragón". Estrada Monroy (1973: 274) en sus notas finales al texto de Ximénez también agrega: "El nopal en que se cría el gusano de la grana".

113. Aquí se está hablando de Ixmukane, la abuela de Jun Batz' y Jun Chowen. Ixmukane efectivamente es la madre de Jun Junajpu, padre de estos dos hermanos. Ixbakiyalo, la madre de Jun Batz' y Jun Chowen, como se dijo anteriormente, ya había muerto.

114. Aquí Ixmukane se refiere cariñosamente a sus hijos Jun Junajpu y Wuqub Junajpu como si fueran sus últimos hijos cuando en efecto fueron sus únicos hijos. El término *ch'ipa* o *ch'ipi* en el *Popol Wuj* se refiere al último o al más pequeño de los hijos y en el español guatemalteco se utiliza la expresión "chipi" para referirse a esos últimos descendientes.

115. La palabra en k'iche' es *tzijel*, que derivada de *tzij*, "palabra", literalmente quiere decir "la palabra nueva" o "noticias de alguien"; pero también puede ser un derivado de *tzijo*, "encender". En ese sentido, los hijos son la "palabra" renovada de una persona o la llama "encendida" de su memoria. De aquí mi traducción por "descendencia".

116. En esta línea, cuando Ixkik' dice *iwila'*, literalmente "ustedes verán", se involucra entre los recipientes del mensaje a los medio hermanos mayores de los que lleva en el vientre. Aunque está hablando con

su suegra, incluye entre su audiencia a Jun Batz' y Jun Chowen hacia quienes inmediatamente se mueve la narración.

117. La palabra tapiscar significa cosechar el maíz, cuando el producto está ya maduro.

118. Conforme al discurso k'iche', el narrador no sólo cuenta la historia como un hecho pasado sino "ubica", "transporta" al lector al lugar de los hechos. Éste se marca con el locativo *chiri'*, "aquí", en lugar de *chila'*, "allá".

119. Aquí debe entenderse un terrón o grupo de 4 ó 5 plantas de maíz sembradas en un mismo hoyo. No una sola planta, como literalmente podría traducirse. Se siembra el maíz en grupitos de 4 ó 5 granos de maíz, luego se limpia y "calzan" las plantas para que no las bote el viento. Por eso, llegado el tiempo y cuando la milpa está creciendo se pueden ver volcancitos de tierra al pie de las 4 ó 5 plantas a lo largo de los terrenos.

120. Éstos son nombres de deidades femeninas que cuidan la siembra de maíz y cuyos nombres se derivan del calendario; aunque en orden invertido. Ixtoj significa "diosa del día de pago", e Ixq'anil "madurez", en referencia al fruto del maíz cuando está listo para ser cosechado. D. Tedlock (1996: 264-265) explica esta inversión del nombre de los días en términos del carácter lunar de Ixkik'. Por aparte, la invocación a la deidad del cacao, Ixkakaw, hace referencia a ese producto como moneda y como ofrenda en referencia directa al día toj, "día de pago".

121. Ixtziya' vuelve a hacer referencia al maíz como producto ya cocinado. *Ix-* es el marcador femenino, *tzi*, "nixtamal" y *ya'* "agua". De esa cuenta Ixtziya' significa deidad de la "comida de maíz". En el diccionario de Basseta encontramos la siguiente entrada: "*tziyah ri ixim pa chah:* cocer el maíz con la ceniza". Desde el punto de vista poético, Ixkakaw e Ixtziya' forman otro verso paralelo.

122. Como en otras partes del *Popol Wuj*, se están estableciendo algunos días del calendario. En este caso el día *k'at*, "red", por eso, Ixmukane, que es la sacerdotisa primigenia, supo leer el significado de ese prodigio y aceptó a Ixkik', como nuera.

123. El texto k'iche' dice *kichaq'*, literalmente "sus hermanos menores". Éste puede ser un error de copia, porque en k'iche' es *qatz*. Hablando de Jun Batz' y Jun Chowen que en realidad son "sus hermanos mayores", en cuyo caso en el plano retórico se puede estar "minorizando" a esos hermanos mayores y por eso se utiliza la expresión contraria.

124. Literalmente, esta línea dice: "como muchachos parecíamos en sus corazones". La palabra k'iche' *ala* significa "muchacho, niño"; pero también "súbdito" o "esclavo" como en *qalabom*, término compuesto de *q-*, marcador posesivo de primera persona plural, "nuestro"; *ala*, "muchacho", *alab* o *alabom*, "muchachos". En Basseta tenemos la expresión *qalabom*, (así) "llaman los Señores a sus súbditos".

125. Literalmente "árbol amarillo", *q'an* es "amarillo" y *te'* es un arcaísmo proveniente del protomaya. Su cognado k'iche' es *che'*, "árbol". Este arcaísmo se suma a *kan*, "serpiente", que actualmente se dice en k'iche' *kumatz*.

126. En el texto k'iche' dice *wex*, palabra que ha sido traducida generalmente como "calzones" (vg. Recinos); sin embargo para identificar esa prenda existe la palabra *skaw*. Chávez (1978: 37) traduce *wex* como "banda" y D. Tedlock (1996: 106) como "pants". En los diccionarios de Basseta y Ximénez, *wex* y *tok* son sinóminos y se traducen como "bragas". En el diccionario q'eqchi' del PLFM encontramos el término *wex*, que equivale a los pantalones.

127. El texto k'iche' dice *rax kiwach*, "sin vergüenzas". En Basseta encontramos la expresión *"Rax vach*: sin vergüenza".

128. Estas dos expresiones literalmente quieren decir "me habrán echado a perder, me habrán puesto de cabeza".

129. Una traducción literal a la expresión k'iche' *kiq'ij* es "día de ellos", que ha sido traducido como "suerte" (Recinos), "destiny" (D. Tedlock), etcétera. En Basseta encontramos el término *uquihil* como "su tiempo".

130. En el texto k'iche' se denomina *Junajpu k'oy* a esta melodía que después se convierte en baile.

131. Estoy de acuerdo con D. Tedlock (1996: 107 y 267), quien traduce "the skinny little things below their bellies" en referencia a los genitales de los micos.

132. El texto k'iche' dice *ma k'ama chikijoq'ik chi ke*, expresión contraria a cubrir de pelos o paja una cosa. En ese sentido, se está hablando de que sus caras estaban cubiertas de pelos, que no estaban rasurados.

133. En el manuscrito, la oración k'iche' dice *mixek'obik* donde la raíz verbal es *k'ob-*, "vanidad", "alabanza", como en el pasaje de Wuqub Kak'ix donde se dice *kuk'obisaj wi rib*, "se envanecía".

134. En el texto k'iche' se dice *mixkina*, que Ximénez traduce como "azadón" y Basseta como "el azadón de palo".

135. El texto k'iche' dice *xmucur* que, conforme al diccionario de Pantaleón de Guzmán, quiere decir "la tórtola". En k'iche' contemporáneo y según hablantes de Santa Catarina Ixtahuacán, a esta ave se le nombra ahora *xbuqur*.

136. La expresión es literal y correctamente ha sido traducida como burla o engaño. El texto k'iche' dice: *kojmich'owik*, donde la raíz verbal *mich'o* quiere decir "escardar" y en este contexto literalmente es "tomar el pelo".

137. El texto k'iche' dice *yak* y generalmente ha sido traducido como "gato de monte". En el diccionario de Basseta *yak* se identifica como "zorra, que es la que come las gallinas". Identificación que concuerda con lo que hace *utiw*, "coyote". En términos de categoría lingüística, *yak* y *utiw* cumplen la misma función y en consecuencia refuerzan el contenido de la copla léxica que conforman. Thor Janson (2001: 95) tiene una ilustración de *gray fox*, "zorro gris", que identifica como "gato de monte".

138. Ésta es una traducción literal de lo que en el texto k'iche' se lee: *tik'il uk'u'x aq'ab*, una metáfora para decir "medianoche". En líneas más adelante, también se lee *tik'il q'ij*, "el sol está alzado", para decir "mediodía".

139. Ésta es una salsa hecha a base de tomates asados y chile molido. Según el *Diccionario de guatemaltequismos*, éste es un "aderezo compuesto de tomate, chile, cebolla, cilantro y sal".

140. Las oraciones *Esto han de decir, cuando lleguen* con las que se abre y cierra el mensaje, constituyen la figura literaria conocida como *enmarque*. Es más, las expresiones *dicen los Señores*, conforman un *enmarque interno*. De ahí que la cita entre citas, es decir el mensaje, va entre comillas.

141. Tamasul es una palabra náhuatl que significa "sapo".

142. Esta expresión es literal y semejante a lo dicho por el ratón cuando fue capturado por los muchachos. Frase semejante dirán el sapo y el halcón en líneas siguientes. Por aparte, este mensaje va metafóricamente envuelto en cuatro "sobres" o sea los mensajeros: el piojo, el sapo, la serpiente y el halcón.

143. Éste es un juego de palabras: el ave se llama wak y en su canto dice: *wak k'o, wak k'o*, que literalmente quiere decir "aquí estoy, aquí estoy...". Conforme a D. Tedlock (1996: 270), es una especie de halcón cazador de serpientes.

144. Literalmente "¿Quién es quien llora?", pero se entiende que el ave "llora/canta" para atraer la atención.

145. Comparto el criterio de D. Tedlock (1996: 271) que traduce *lotz kik'* como "blood of sacrifice". *Lotz* o *lotzo* se refiere a incisiones para extraer sangre o "abrir la hinchazón madura o postema" como dice Basseta. *Kik'* es "sangre".

146. *Aj* literalmente significa "caña", la planta de donde nace el maíz; pero sabemos que el maíz se siembra por puñados de 4 ó 5 granos.

147. Literalmente el texto k'iche' dice *retal qatzij*, "señal de nuestra palabra"; pero por el contexto, debe entenderse como señal de la existencia.

148. En la copia k'iche' de Ximénez se lee *molaí* y esto ha sido transcrito como *molay*. Es muy probable que la í en Ximénez sea *j* para decir *molaj*, como aquí se transcribe y que quiere decir "reunión" o "grupo" de aves, personas, animales, etcétera. En yucateco también encontramos los términos *mola'*, *molaj*, *molay* como derivados de *mol* o *molo-*, raíz verbal que indica "junta, reunión", etcétera. Estas aves serían los azacuanes, como las identifica Bárbara Tedlock (1992: 185-186). Los azacuanes son las aves migratorias que pasan antes de la época de lluvia y por eso se les llama también *torol jab*, "que abren el período de lluvia". Estas aves regresan al Norte cuando el invierno termina. Aunque los azacuanes son una clase específica de aves falconiformes, la gente los identifica indistintamente con águilas, gavilanes, halcones, garzas, etcétera.

149. Es interesante ver aquí que los caminos no se identifican en el orden cuando sus padres llegaron a ese lugar. Ahí se hablaba de los caminos según el orden cósmico con que se nombran los cuatro lados del Universo: Oriente, Poniente, Norte y Sur. Aquí se habla del camino negro "poniente", blanco "norte", rojo "oriente" y verde, que es el "centro" y que sustituye al color amarillo "sur". Se sigue una oposición de colores comenzando con el negro, camino que marcó la muerte de sus padres, luego viene el blanco, el rojo y el verde, siendo este último el "camino de la vida" y centro del orden cósmico maya. De aquí que el orden con que se nombra a los caminos en este pasaje, tiene una intencionalidad subyacente: no perecer, como efectivamente sucede. D. Tedlock (1996: 273) sugiere que como en este pasaje no se especifica el camino que tomaron los muchachos para llegar a los Señores de Xibalba, es probable que hayan tomado ese camino verde, el "camino de la vida", como los ancestros piden para sus hijos en la segunda invocación. Mi criterio es, sin embargo, que aunque se nombra aquel camino, sí tomaron el camino negro

porque siguieron la ruta de su mensajero, *xan*, y saludan a los Señores en el orden exacto que aquel animal los va picando.

150. Éste es el nombre del zancudo que enviaron a perforar la tinaja de la abuela.

151. En el manuscrito de Ximénez la expresión *naqui* en la columna k'iche' está tachada, sin embargo lo traduce como "¿Qué es...?", y esto es seguido por otros traductores.

152. De acuerdo con el orden con que se nombra a los Señores de Xibalba, debe ir el nombre de Xikiri Pat, ausente en el texto k'iche', a quien además se le identifica como quien pregunta al sexto Señor de Xibalba que es picado. Si no es error de copia es elipsis; pero debe identificarse porque es el orden con que los muchachos escuchan y repiten esos nombres.

153. De nuevo, aquí se omite el nombre de este Señor de Xibalba. Por contexto y conforme a la nota anterior se agrega en esta traducción.

154. Nótese aquí que los nombres de los Señores de Xibalba no son exactamente iguales a los nombrados con anterioridad. Ajal Mes y Ajal Toq'ob son sustituidos por Kik' Re, "dientes sangrantes", y Kik' Rixk'aq, "garras sangrantes". Recinos (1953: 149, nota de pie de página 176) dice: "Es verdad que entre uno y otro episodios media una generación y esos cambios son naturales... En la composición de todos estos nombres entra muy bien a propósito la palabra *quic* (sangre)."

155. Ésta es una manera de derrotar al otro. Sabiendo su nombre se conocen sus virtudes y debilidades. Por eso lo reiterativo de hablar sobre la revelación de nombres. De ahí que en la actualidad, el día de nacimiento conforme al calendario maya se guarda con celo. Este hábito cultural, también lo practican los indígenas de América del Norte, quienes tienen un nombre público y otro secreto.

156. Concuerdo con D. Tedlock (1996: 273) cuando dice que la referencia a "muñecos de madera" es a todos los allí sentados, no sólo a los dos primeros. Asimismo, que por parte de Xibalba era de esperar carcajadas de burla, como cuando llegaron Jun Junajpu y Wuqub Junajpu. Ahora, en cambio, la sorna es contra los Señores de Xibalba.

157. En el texto k'iche' se dice *q'ala* que viene de *q'alaj*, "aclarar", y es equivalente a *saqirik*, "blanquear, alumbrar el día", que es el saludo para "buenos días". Es probable que hayan utilizado la expresión *q'alaj* en lugar de *saqarik* porque en Xibalba no alumbra el Sol y también como burla, ya que *q'alaj* también significa "está claro" en el sentido de que para los muchachos estaba claro lo que ocurría.

Líneas más adelante, el mensajero de Jun Kame utiliza la expresión *saqirik*, no *q'ala*.

158. El texto k'iche' dice literalmente *mata xkanaj ubi' kumal*, "que no se les quedaran sus nombres"; pero por la razón dada sobre lo secreto del nombre, traduzco "es que no se enteraran de sus nombres".

159. El texto k'iche' dice *juch'il*, derivado de *juch'*, "raya", o decoraciones que seguramente tenía la pelota. No es "gusano", como traducen Ximénez, Villacorta, Recinos.

160. Ésta es una expresión cargada de sorna por parte de los muchachos. Ellos ya sabían lo que la pelota de Xibalba contenía adentro: un pedernal para matarlos. Cuando los padres de los muchachos están en Xibalba, se identifica el juego de la pelota, en ese lugar, como "pedernal blanco", y que la pelota era un "chay redondo".

161. Estos versos que conforman un cuarteto, han sido traducidos como "ramos" o "manojos" de flores e incluso, el cuarto verso como "un ramo de grandes peces", según la retraducción del francés al español por Miguel Ángel Asturias y J. M. Gonzalez de Mendoza de la versión de Georges Raynaud (1927: 56). En la copia de Ximénez se dice *muchij, muchit*, derivado de *muchu*, "desmenuzar"; no a *much'*, "chipilín", como regularmente ha sido traducido. Por aparte, nótese que los pétalos de flores están asociados a los cuatro colores del cosmos maya: rojo, blanco, amarillo. El color negro, que sería el siguiente, es sustituido por "grandes". Esto sucede porque en tercetos y cuartetos, uno de los versos rompe el paradigma para dar fluidez a la narración. En este caso, el cuarto verso cambia con lo que sería esperado: "pétalos negros". Lo de "grandes peces" deriva de que el texto k'iche' dice *k'a ri nima'q*, lo que fue tomado como *kar nima'q* que literalmente podría equivaler a "peces grandes"; pero de todas maneras es agramatical porque en k'iche' el adjetivo antecede al sustantivo, o sea, tendría que decir: *nima'q kar*.

162. Ésta es una paronomasia en el texto k'iche'. Están en *Chayim ja*, "Casa de los Chayes", y las hormigas son denominadas *chay sanik*, *ch'eken sanik*, "hormigas cortadoras, hormigas vencedoras". Se juega con las palabras *chay, chayim* y *ch'eken* para llegar a un fin, que es ganarle a los de Xibalba. Este juego de palabras también se escucha en *cha'*, "decir", y *cha(y)* sobre lo cual Brasseur (1972: 383) escribió: "La belleza que los indios ven en la constante repetición de palabras y en el volver sobre el mismo sentido, los hace encontrar a menudo significados diferentes, lo que depende mucho

de la pronunciación más o menos acentuada y del conjunto de la frase".

163. Éstos son nombres onomatopéyicos de dos aves nocturnas que habitan a ras del suelo. Conforme a Pantaleón de Guzmán, xpurpuweq y pujuy son sinónimos y quieren decir "mochuelo", que en algunos diccionarios se asocia a búho y a lechuza; pero estas aves son distintas. La que aquí se nombra como xpurpuweq sería la que otros traducen como "chotacabra" o "cuerpo-ruin" (vg. Recinos y Chávez). Pujuy viene del yucateco y se le nombra como "gallina ciega", otra ave de mal agüero *(Diccionario maya)* que pertenece a la misma especie anterior.

164. El texto k'iche' dice *xekel*, "colgado", en una expresión de burla a los mandaderos/centinelas allí apostados como mirones. Éstos, en todo caso, habrían sido murciélagos.

165. El texto k'iche' dice *kamasotz'*. En la primera parte, a este animal se le identificó como "murciélago decapitador", que es lo que vuelve a suceder en las siguientes líneas. *Kama* deriva de la raíz verbal *kam-*, "morir", y *sotz'* es "murciélago". De aquí que éstos, son murciélagos de la muerte.

166. Literalmente "no fueron picados"; sin embargo, líneas más adelante, Junajpu es decapitado. Ésta es la razón por la que aquí se traduce: "no fueron decapitados".

167. La expresión *aqaroq*, literalmente quiere decir "¡que amanezca!, ¡que se haga la claridad!", se deriva de *saqaroq*, la forma imperativa de *saqarik*, saludo que se usa al amanecer. Aqaroq es entonces una exclamación que se usa para dirigirse a las divinidades o como en este caso una manifestación de dolor o pena que puede traducirse como "¡Oh, ay, salve!", etcétera.

168. En el texto k'iche' la palabra *ch'uti*, "pequeño", está omitida. Éste seguramente es un error de copia. En líneas anteriores, el verso pareado "pequeños animales, grandes animales" está completo y por eso se agrega aquí el adjetivo "pequeños".

169. Esta oración ha sido traducida, con variación, como "Muchos sabios vinieron del Cielo" (Recinos, Chávez, Raynaud, Brasseur) siguiendo a Ximénez quien tradujo "y muchísimos sabios vinieron de el Cielo". El texto k'iche' dice *Tzatz chi ajna'oj chikaj xpe wi*, y aunque *tzatz* significa "muchos" también significa "sesos", porque viene de *tzatzq'or* (véase diccionario de Ximénez).

170. *Wuch'* quiere decir "tacuacín" y así también se nombra "el momento que precede al amanecer" (Recinos, 1953: 82). En las primeras líneas

del *Popol Wuj* se identifica a Junajpu Wuch' como "deidad del amanecer" y de ahí que en este pasaje se le pide "tiznar" de nuevo el Cielo. En ese sentido, disiento de Recinos (1953: 160) que siguiendo a Ximénez traduce y argumenta que en estas líneas *wuch'* debe traducirse como "zopilote".

171. Ximénez traduce correctamente "en el tomatal", que debe entenderse como siembra de tomates. Brasseur y Recinos traducen "encinal". Villacorta y Rodas (1927: 277) como "hueco del tejado". Chávez como "chicharral". La planta de tomate, como dice el texto k'iche', es más concordante con el tamaño del conejo. Entre otros trabajos sobre el protomaya citado por England (1994) se encuentra la palabra *pix* (-p) como "tomate, miltomate"; y esa misma palabra k'iche', en el diccionario de Basseta, se traduce "tomate".

172. Esto también podría traducirse como: "trayendo a luz su claridad delante de ellos"; sin embargo, utilizo la palabra literal "pepitas", para aclarar que se trata de un chilacayote y no una tortuga, porque, como dice Edmonson (1971: 124), "turtles don't have seeds".

173. En el diccionario de Basseta encontramos *ajxulu* como "adivino", equivalente a *ajq'ij*. Conforme a Coto (1983: 140), *xulu* son "unos demoñuelos o familiares que se les aparecían junto a los ríos". Conforme a Varea (1997: 358), "al que curaba con estos diablillos, llamaban aj-q'ij, aj-xulu". Todo indica que Xulu es el "sacerdote del agua". Pak'am parece derivar de *pak'alik*, "dar vuelta", "boca arriba", cuyo significado sería darle vuelta a lo que se mira. D. Tedlock (1996: 278) sugiere que *xulu* y *pak'am* son los que conforme a Coto (1983: 13) "adivinan en agua". Esto está asociado a que en este pasaje, los gemelos "vuelven a la vida" como hombres peces.

174. Aquí, como en otras líneas, el texto k'iche' dice *Xjunajpu* donde el prefijo *x-* debe tomarse como diminutivo y marcador afectivo; no como marcador del género femenino *ix-*. Asimismo, es el prefijo *x-* en Xbalamke que en una traducción literal y cuyo nombre completo sería Xbalamkej equivalente a "pequeño jaguar venado". En todo el texto se habla de *k'ajolab*, "hijos varones" (de hombre), nunca se dice *me'al*, "hija de varón" y tampoco se hace referencia a los gemelos como *wal ala*, "hijo de mujer" y menos *wal ali*, "hija de mujer". En la genealogía maya, el hombre y la mujer se refieren a sus hijos con terminología distinta. Es clarísimo que ambos gemelos son varones y para marcar el afecto hacia los jóvenes héroes, quizás debió escribirse sus nombres como *Xjunajpu, Xbalamke*.

175. Esto está relacionado con *karchaj*, "peces de ceniza", como literalmente sería el nombre actual de Carchá, lugar cercano al mitológico campo de pelota del *Popol Wuj*.

176. Conforme a Basseta, *xtz'ul* es el "ciempiés" y lo describe como "baile usado entre los indios, en que uno que baila se pone una daga en la boca; danzan con unas carátulas, y dan vueltas alrededor a tono de conchas de galápagos".

177. Aunque en el texto k'iche' no se dice "el que había llevado la noticia". Se añade aquí por claridad y porque el diálogo así lo insinúa.

178. Literalmente "su montaña"; pero en este contexto debe entenderse como lugar de procedencia, como se utiliza en pasajes más adelante. Al traducir *juyubal* como "patria", sigo a Ximénez.

179. El texto k'iche' dice *keq'abar k'u ri ronojel rajawal,* que quiere decir: "estaban ebrios (de la emoción) todos los Señores..."

180. Ésta es una expresión cargada de sorna, considerando que quienes van a ser sacrificados son los mismos Señores de la Muerte.

181. Ximénez, Brasseur, Raynaud, Recinos y Chávez traducen la palabra k'iche' *pak'ol* como "vengadores", "vengador", que se deriva de *pak'alik* y en este contexto dar vuelta a algo.

182. En este pareado se dice *kik' jolomax*, "sangre coagulada", que en el pasaje donde Ixkik' extrae la savia del árbol de grana, ésta se coagula y se convierte en sustituto de su corazón, se dice *xa kik'*, *xa jolomax*, "sólo sangre, sólo savia coagulada será para ellos". De aquí que se está haciendo referencia a aquella "sangre coagulada". En el verso siguiente se dice *ch'ajom kik'*, que literalmente quiere decir "sangre lavada", pero en sentido negativo.

183. La copla léxica *k'im* y *tolob* también aparece en el Xajoj Tum. *K'im* es "pajón", y *tolob*, probablemente está relacionado con *toloba*, "despoblar" conforme a Basseta, y a *tolom*, "cosa desierta", conforme a Ximénez, en referencia a la hierba que crece en esos lugares.

184. Aquí se está haciendo referencia a la futura creación humana.

185. Recinos (1953: 170) reconoce la dificultad de traducir esta frase. El hecho es que la palabra *no'j, na'oj* en el manuscrito k'iche' como puede significar "sabiduría", "consejo" y un día del calendario, también equivale a la expresión "no importa" (Basseta), según la pronunciación y escritura. En consecuencia, el significado de "no importa", se traduce aquí como "los que se menosprecian", por el reflexivo que tiene la frase en k'iche'.

186. Literalmente "los que son como los tecolotes", pero según Ximénez y Basseta es una figura para decir "traidores". Por aparte, Recinos (1953: 171) siguiendo a Brasseur sugiere que las expresiones *ajtza*, *ajtukur* de estas dos últimas líneas, puedan estar haciendo referencia a los itzá y a pobladores de San Miguel Tucurú.

187. El texto k'iche' dice: *q'eqa' il, saqil* que literalmente quiere decir "ennegrecidos", "blanqueados" o que puede entenderse como con "sentimientos negros y blancos" y que aquí se traduce como "hipócritas" y *saqil* o *aqil* como "malvados".

188. El texto k'iche' dice *ajlatz'ab* donde *aj-* es agentivo, *latz'*, "estrecho" y el sufijo *–ab* marca el plural que termina significando "opresores".

189. El texto k'iche' dice *nik'aj ja, nik'aj bichok*. *Nik'aj* es "centro" o "en medio"; *ja*, "casa" y *bichok* probablemente se derive de *bichoj*, que es cuando la caña de milpa se dobla para que la mazorca se termine de secar y no se pudra con la lluvia. En Ximénez se encuentra la entrada *bich*, "desgranar como maíz". En una extensión de significados, esto quiere decir en medio de la época de cosecha. Nótese además que en estas líneas hay una metátesis entre las palabras *ja*, "casa" y *aj*, "caña" como señala Bárbara Tedlock (1992: 118). Esto puede estar asociado a que la casa es el lugar de habitación y las cañas son señal de vida.

190. La inversión de estos nombres tal vez se deba a error de copia, o a una duplicidad de la frase "Cañas vivas" que luego se repite y se aclara el porqué de ese nombre. Antes se dijo "Cañas vivas, Lecho de Tierra". En k'iche', los modificadores tienen la misma estructura sintáctica *k'asam aj, ch'atam ulew*. *K'asam* viene de *k'asalik*, "vivo", y *ch'atam* de *ch'at*, "cama" o "lecho" donde se sembró la milpa.

191. Estos lugares mitológicos han sido asociados a diversos sitios, conforme a Recinos (1953: 174) Bancroft opinaba que estaban en la región de Palenque y el Usumacinta y de acuerdo con Brasseur en la región de Tabasco. D. Tedlock (1996: 288) propone que este lugar es una montaña ubicada cerca de la carretera Panamericana, en la frontera de México y Guatemala. El nombre Paxil efectivamente, como argumenta D. Tedlock (1996: 288), puede derivarse de la raíz verbal *paxi-*, "quebrar", y *k'ayala'* de *k'ayil*, "amargura" y *a'*, "agua". El estudio sobre el tema por Navarrete (2000) también apunta a aquella región como el origen del maíz. El nombre Paxil se ha mitologizado y de esa cuenta aparece la historia del origen del maíz en distintas áreas.

192. Ver nota 137.

193. Literalmente una "buena montaña", pero montaña es asociada a lugar de procedencia, por lo que debe entenderse como pueblo, lugar, región o sitio.

194. El texto k'iche' dice *k'awex*, que Basseta traduce como "anona de tierra fría" y Pantaleón de Guzmán como "anona agria".

195. Ximénez y Recinos, entre otros, traducen "nueve bebidas", cuando literalmente se refiere a "nueve molidas" o a que Ixmukane molió "nueve veces" el maíz amarillo y blanco. Estas "nueve veces" también equivalen a los nueve ciclos lunares que aproximadamente dura la gestación humana. Agradezco esta observación a don Mateo Sam.

196. El texto k'iche' dice *uq'abche'al*, literalmente "ramas, brazos de" para decir extremidades; y *uq'anal*, literalmente "grasa", pero que significa "vigor, fuerza". Esta copla pareciera incongruente pero si se piensa que la fortaleza humana se expresa a través de los brazos y las piernas, adquiere sentido.

197. El texto k'iche' dice *xkikoj pa tzij*, literalmente: "los pusieron en la palabra", una metáfora para decir "les dieron vida". Esta misma expresión la encontramos cuando Jun Junajpu le dice a Ixkik': *katok pa tzij*, literalmente: "entras a la palabra" (ver nota 104); pero que en realidad significa "entras a la vida" como efectivamente sucede cuando la madre de los héroes gemelos sale de Xibalba y sube a la superficie terrenal para dar a luz a los que derrotan al reino de la muerte.

198. Estos nombres quiere decir: "jaguar de la sonrisa dulce" o "jaguar de mucha sonrisa"; "jaguar nocturno", "quien no esconde nada" y "jaguar luna". Balam es nombre genérico de "jaguar", y Ki'tze' puede estar derivado de *ki'*, "dulce" o *k'i*, "mucho" y *tze'* es "sonrisa". D. Tedlock (1996: 289) llama la atención sobre este nombre por su resemblanza con el término *k'iche'*, "muchos árboles". Con respecto al segundo nombre, *aq'ab* es "noche", y también podría identificar al jaguar negro. El tercero, Majuk'utaj se estaría derivando de una expresión negativa que significa: "quien no esconde nada". Ximénez lo traduce como "no acepillado" (versión de 1962: 86), Edmonson (1971: 148) como "No hay", y D. Tedlock (1996: 146) como "Ahorita no". Del cuarto nombre, Ik'ibalam ha de derivarse de *ik'*, "luna". D. Tedldock (1996: 146) traduce este último nombre como "Jaguar Oscuro" con base en el idioma chol en el que *ik'* significa "oscuro, negro".

199. Esta línea está muy bien explicada por Recinos (1953: 177, nota 248), quien dice: "No tenían nombre de familia. No tenían ascendientes. Eran el principio de la estirpe humana. O sea que no tienen patronímico, o nombre de familia."

200. En la copia de Ximénez se transcribe *caha paluna* en k'iche' y *caha paluma* en la versión en español. El adjetivo *caha* corresponde a *kaq-a*, "rojo" con la *-a* final como inserción vocálica. En *El Título de Totonicapán* (Carmack y Mondloch, 1983: 8r) encontramos el nombre escrito como *cakapaluma*. Soy del criterio que el segundo término puede ser *palo ha*, que en transcripción contemporánea sería *paloja'*, "agua de mar", y que el nombre completo es una metáfora "agua roja del mar" en referencia al color del horizonte marítimo cuando apenas empieza a salir el Sol y el color rojo del cielo tiñe al mar y se refleja con sus aguas. Tedlock lo interpreta como *paluma*, "tortuga de agua", basado en Pantaleón de Guzmán y Tomás Coto quienes traducen *palama* como "galápago". Ximénez (1962: 88) lo traduce como "agua parada que cae de lo alto" y con variantes se ha interpretado como "lluvia del cielo cayendo en el mar" (vg. Villacorta y Rodas, 1927: 409).

201. Chomija' deriva de *chom*, "hermosa", más la *-i* como inserción vocálica derivada de la escritura jeroglífica y *ja'*, "agua". Es decir "Agua Hermosa" o como Ximénez (1962: 88) lo interpreta: "agua hermosa y escogida".

202. Esto quiere decir "Colibrí de Agua". *Tz'unun* más la *-i* como inserción vocálica quiere decir "colibrí", y *ja'*, "agua".

203. "Guacamaya de Agua". Esto viene de *kak'ix*, "guacamaya", más la *-a* como inserción vocálica y *ja'*, "agua". Como puede verse, estos cuatro nombres están asociados al agua como fuente de vida y a una asociación vital. Si los primeros hombres fueron construidos de maíz, producto de la tierra, las mujeres provienen de lugares cercanos al agua. Por aparte, estos nombres están asociados a linajes. Edmonson (1971) interpreta estos cuatro nombres como asociados a *ja*, "casas" o linajes; mientras que D. Tedlock (1996) asocia el primero y el tercero a *ja'*, "agua", y el segundo y cuarto a *ja*, "casa". En esto, comparto el criterio de Ximénez en asociar los cuatro nombres con el "agua".

204. Estas líneas vienen de *ajk'ixib* de la raíz verbal *k'ixik* o *k'ixibik* que Basseta traduce como "respetar, tener vergüenza", en alusión a los dedicados a la adoración divina. Por eso, entre otros, Edmonson (1971: 154) lo traduce como "worshippers", Recinos (1953: 180)

"sacerdotes" y D. Tedlock (1996: 149) "penitentes". La segunda palabra *ajk'ajib* viene de *k'ajij,* literalmente "escarmentar"; pero por contexto hace referencia a actos de penitencia. Por lo que se dice en líneas siguientes y otros pasajes, se entiende que los primeros cuatro varones eran *ajq'ijab,* es decir personas que llevaban la cuenta de los días.

205. *Tepew* es palabra náhuatl que quiere decir "victorioso". Recinos (1953: 180) propone que es "una de las tribus de origen tolteca que emigraron junto con los quichés". *Tepew,* sin embargo, como en Tepew Q'ukumatz es un adjetivo de *oloman,* también palabra náhuatl que quiere decir "lugar de hule" (Campbell, 1983). Es decir, Tepew Oloman no son dos pueblos distintos como Recinos propone, sino uno solo. Tedlock (1996: 291) sugiere que ese pueblo pudo ser hablante de pipil, que alguna vez ocupó el valle del Motagua.

206. *K'ojaj* es palabra k'iche' que literalmente quiere decir "enmascarar". En Basseta encontramos la palabra *cohah* como "el cerco de la luna" que parece ser la contrapartida velada y lunar de los K'enech Ajaw que viene del yucateco *k'inich,* patronímico para decir "ojos o cara de sol" y *k'inich ahaw,* "señor-cara-de-sol", "un aspecto de Itzamná, dios maya de la creación" (Barrera Vázquez, 1980: 403). Conforme a D. Tedlock (1996: 291) el término K'enech Ajaw podría referirse a los Itzá y Mopán. *K'ojaj* puede ser, entonces, la contrapartida de un pueblo asociado al culto del Sol. En el diccionario yucateco también encontramos que *k'ohoba* es "enmascararse" y "disfrazarse de brujo", e *itz* precisamente significa brujería que usualmente se practica a la luz de la Luna.

207. De acuerdo con D. Tedlock (1996: 344 y 358) los Tamub e Ilokab eran linajes aliados a los propiamente llamados k'iche'es; para Carmack y Mondlock (1983: 215), los Tamub son el "Segundo grupo quiché (después de los Nima Quichés)".

208. Aquí hay que hacer notar que conforme *El Título de Totonicapán* (Carmack y Mondloch, 1983: 175 y 177) se dice que Ik'ibalam "era un joven [no casado, se entiende] cuando vino de donde sale el sol" y que "murió en su juventud". En una interpretación literal, puede tomarse lo dicho en ese título o de manera alternativa, que Ik'ibalam no tuvo descendencia. Esto explicaría el porqué el cuarto "padre primigenio" comienza a desaparecer en la historia y cuyo lugar llega a ser asumido por dos Señoríos de Saqik como se identifica en el capítulo quinto de esta traducción.

209. El texto k'iche' dice *oxlajuj tekpan*. *Oxlajuj* quiere decir 13 y *tekpan* es una palabra náhuatl que quiere decir "casa o palacio real" (Karttunen, 1992: 217).

210. Los Rabinaleb obviamente son los k'iche'es de Rabinal y lugares circunvecinos; y los Kaqchikeleb, son los kaqchikeles. El nombre Ajtz'ikinaja, literalmente "los de la casa de pájaros" o Ajtz'ikinajay, "linaje de la casa de los pájaros" (Orellana, 1984: 81). Conforme a Recinos (1953: 181) éstos tuvieron "por capital la ciudad lacustre de Atitlán" y de acuerdo con Edmonson (1971: 156) son los de Santiago Atitlán. La interpretación "casa de pájaros" se la autoatribuyen los habitantes de Santiago Atitlán; aunque también es posible interpretar ese nombre como "los de los pájaros de agua" por su afinidad con Tz'ununija', "Colibrí de Agua", nombre antiguo del vecino pueblo de San Pedro La Laguna. Con respecto a los Saqajib y Lamakib soy del criterio que éstos eran dos grupos o pueblos aliados o dependientes de los de Santiago Atitlán. Saqajib probablemente es una referencia a los pájaros que anuncian el amanecer o de manera más literal "los blanqueadores" y en todo caso Sak'ajib, "los madrugadores"; y no identifica al actual pueblo de Salcajá como Brasseur, Recinos y Tedlock, entre otros, sugieren. Esto se refuerza con el hecho de que *lamanik* muy probablemente se derive de *lamaj* que en Basseta se traduce como "cardenal" o como "señal de un golpe con palo". Esto quiere decir que si *lamaj* no es el nombre del cardenal, puede serlo del pájaro carpintero; pero de cualquier manera asociado a pájaros, como nombre de una rama de los Ajtz'ikinaja. Aunque de acuerdo con Carmack (1973: 60) los Lamaquib eran la parcialidad que luego llegó a llamarse "Santo Tomás" de Sacapulas. Esta asociación me parece muy alejada; aunque puede tener cierto sustento por el hecho de que Sacapulas está en la ribera del río Chixoy. El siguiente nombre es Kumatz, cuyo origen común ha de haber sido donde se habló el proto-maya y sus descendientes se ubican ahora mayoritariamente en los alrededores de María Tecum en Sololá. Tujal Ja, "baños de vapor", es asociado al actual pueblo de Sacapulas. Los Uch'abaja, "los de la casa de las flechas", han de ser los padres originarios de los Chavajay, que ahora habitan en las orillas del lago Atitlán. Los Ajch'umilaja, "los de la casa de las estrellas", han de ser los ascendientes de los Ch'umil, habitantes de Sololá. De los Ajkibaja no se tiene referencia. Los Ajbatenaja, literalmente "los de la casa de las argollas o cinturones", utilizados en el juego de la pelota. Sus descendientes con mucha probabilidad

son los Baten de Totonicapán. Los Akul Winaq cuyos descendientes han de ser los habitantes del valle Akul en la región Ixil. Los Balamija', "jaguar de agua", es muy probable que sean los ascendientes de los habitantes de lo que ahora se conoce como Santa Cruz Balanyá en Chimaltenango. Los Kanchajeleb, que D. Tedlock (1996: 293) traduce como los "guardianes de los despojos de guerra", los ubica en el área de Sacapulas. Los Balam Kolob, "jaguares del lazo", aunque según otras fuentes también provienen de Sacapulas, de acuerdo con Carmack (1983: 264) en su estudio sobre *El Título de Totonicapán*, "los Ak'aab y Balam Colob de nuestro título y *El Título de C'oyoi* parecen haberse hallado cerca del valle de Quetzaltenango. Existe actualmente el apellido Colob entre los indígenas de Cantel de este valle". En efecto, los Colob actualmente escrito *Colop* proceden de Cantel, Quetzaltenango. Son trece pueblos, entonces, y no quince, porque los Saqajib y Lamakib son parte de la casa real de los Ajtz'ikinaja. El origen territorial primario de todos estos linajes pudo estar asociado a la región norte de Sacapulas si se toma en cuenta que conforme datos lingüísticos, el proto-maya se hablaba en aquella área.

211. El texto k'iche' dice *tinamit*, que viene del náhuatl *tenamitl*, "cerca o muro de ciudad" (Karttunen, 1992: 224), "pueblo fortificado" (Campbell, 1983). En términos más descriptivos también se dice *siwan tinamit* para indicar una ciudad fortificada entre barrancos.

212. Adrián Chávez (1978: 68), traduce esta línea como "luego se establecieron aquí en 'los magueyes'", de donde él deriva la etimología de la palabra *ki-chè*. No comparto esta traducción por las siguientes razones: 1) se está hablando del oriente, donde efectivamente abundan los magueyes; pero geográficamente no corresponde al territorio k'iche'; 2) la cláusula k'iche' en el texto de Ximénez dice: *ta xqohe pa qui chiri* que en la columna en español se traduce: "y allí mesmo estuvieron en aquella dulzura". La frase *pa qui* significa un estado, una situación; no un lugar. Para significar lo que Chávez traduce, la cláusula k'iche' tendría que estar escrita *ta xqohe chiri pa qui*. Comparto el criterio de Edmonson (1971: 158), quien traduce esa misma cláusula: "while they were there in comfort". Por aparte hay que reconocer que en Ximénez hay inconsistencia para diferenciar las palabras "maguey", "mucho" y "dulce" que en escritura contemporánea son *ki, k'i, ki'* respectivamente.

213. El manuscrito k'iche' habla de "gente negra", "gente blanca", que como dice Recinos (1953: 181) no debe entenderse de manera literal

porque: "Evidentemente el autor se propuso dar la idea de la multitud de gentes diferentes y extrañas entre sí, negras y blancas, es decir, de piel clara y de piel oscura, y de la variedad de lenguas que existían en el Oriente".

214. Esto pareciera contradictorio, luego que en líneas anteriores se habló de la gran cantidad de idiomas. Pero la unidad de idioma a la que alude en esta línea, se refiere a la familia k'iche' o como Recinos (1953: 181) dice: "Los quichés, sin embargo, mantenían su unidad étnica y su lengua común en medio de aquella Babilonia". Por aparte, esto de la gente de la montaña probablemente sea una auto referencia k'iche', quienes como dice D. Tedlock (1996: 293 y 2003: 275) son descritos más adelante como cazadores de venados y pájaros para demostrar que los k'iche'es surgieron de una condición humilde.

215. El texto k'iche' dice che'-abaj, "árbol-piedra", en referencia directa a las estelas. Esto, como dice Tedlock (1996: 293 y 2003: 275), es uno de los varios indicios de que la gran ciudad del Este donde la gente k'iche' recibió sus deidades patronales, era un sitio maya clásico.

216. En el texto k'iche' se dice qetal, qatzijel pareado que en el diccionario de Coto aparece como descendencia. Las expresiones "mientras haya sol, mientras haya claridad" se refieren a eternidad o una manera de decir: "mientras haya vida".

217. Conforme a Campbell (1983), nanawak vendría del náhuatl y quiere decir "cerca del agua". Para Schultze Jena (citado por Tedlock, 1996: 294) Nanawak puede ser el dios azteca Nanahuatl o Nanahuatzin, quien lanzó el rayo para abrir la montaña donde se encontró el maíz.

218. Estas otras dos deidades también son nuevas entre el panteón k'iche'. Wok, como dice Recinos (1953: 182), "era el mensajero de Huracán que llegaba a presenciar el juego de pelota de Hun-Hunahpú y Vucub-Hunahpú". Y los nombres de los dos sacrificados en Xibalba y luego establecidos como deidades a ser invocadas por sus hijos en el capítulo anterior, ya aparecen aquí como Junajpu.

219. Esto es Venus, cuyo nombre en k'iche' es Ik'oq'ij que en una lectura derivada de ikol o yakol q'ij puede traducirse como la estrella "que levanta al sol" pero también puede ser leído como ik'oq'ij, "luna-sol", donde la vocal de en medio es una inserción vocálica que facilita la silabificación.

220. Aquí la copla es *ajk'ixib, ajnim,* se traduce como "respetuosos, obedientes". Es distinta a *ajk'ixib, ajk'ajib* que antes y en líneas adelante se traduce: "adoradores, penitentes". Como se ha dicho, *ajk'ix* significa "respetar, tener vergüenza". En este caso, tiene el primer significado porque va asociado a *ajnim* que quiere decir "obediente".

221. El texto k'iche' dice *yaki,* palabra derivada del náhuatl *yahki* que significa "fueron" y de acuerdo con Campbell (1983) es un linaje k'iche'. Conforme al *Calepino en lengua cakchiquel* de Francisco de Varea, *yaki wineq* es "persona mexicana". Recinos (1953: 183) propone que eran los antiguos toltecas.

222. En una traducción literal esto sería "nuestra señal" pero como en la invocación anterior, esa "señal" equivale a descendencia.

223. Literalmente "montaña", pero que equivale a lugar o "patria" como traduce Ximénez en otros pasajes.

224. Éste es un nombre mítico asociado al lugar donde los señores principales adquirían sus símbolos de poder. Si bien Tulán viene del náhuatl, no necesariamente se refiere a la Tula de Guerrero como comúnmente se especula y ha sido aclarado en nota 10. En términos lingüísticos, Tulán también está asociado a *tolan,* que quiere decir "lugar abandonado". Tedlock argumenta que el lugar donde los padres primigenios k'iche' recibieron a sus "dioses" es Copán y el lugar donde la segunda generación peregrinó a recibir su parafernalia del poder es Chichén Itzá. Esto último se fundamenta, además, en que en el *Chilam Balam de Chumayel* (Roys, 1967: 83) se habla de *Nacxit,* uno de los nombres de Quetzalcóatl.

225. Ésta es una referencia a aquel lugar mítico y como dice D. Tedlock (1996: 296) muchos lugares mayas fueron construidos sobre cuevas naturales y donde no las había, se hicieron cuevas artificiales como en el caso de Utatlán.

226. El nombre Tojil deriva del día *toj* del calendario maya que significa "día para ofrendar", "día para pagar" por el verbo *tojo,* "pagar". Esta deidad del fuego estableció un "pago" por el fuego y también está asociada a los truenos y relámpagos que producen las tormentas tropicales conocidas como *jun raqan,* "huracán" en español.

227. Edmonson propone que Awilix puede originarse de *ix,* "jaguar", y que el nombre significaría "Señor Jaguar"; D. Tedlock (1996: 297), sin embargo, argumenta que equivale a "Señor Golondrina", derivado del término q'eqchi' *kwilix* y del chol *wilis chan,* "golondrina".

En el diccionario q'eqchi' de Haeserijn (1979) efectivamente está la palabra *kwilix*, "golondrina".

228. Soy del criterio que este nombre es Jaqawitz y no *Jakawitz* como usualmente se ha transcrito. Jaqawitz está compuesto de *jaq-* que en varios idiomas mayas quiere decir "abierto" y *witz*, "cerro". Esto concuerda con lo que en líneas más adelante se describe en k'iche' como *saqijuyub*, "cerro desmontado" o sin árboles. Es decir, el nombre de esta deidad está identificado con el lugar de ubicación. Es más, considero que en la antigüedad el nombre era *Saqawitz* porque *saq* es la palabra protomaya para decir blanco o desmontado y que Ximénez copió como *acavitz* y otras veces como *hacavitz*. En *El Título de Totonicapán* ese nombre está transcrito como *jaɛawitz* y en el *Memorial de Sololá* como *ɛaɛawitz* "cerro de fuego".

229. Este nombre, literalmente, significa "en medio del valle".

230. El manuscrito k'iche' dice: *cha' chupam ojer tzij* que en una traducción literal es "dice dentro la antigua palabra", pero cuyo significado es "antiguo texto" en referencia al contenido, al menos mitológico, de la versión original o parte de aquel original del *Popol Wuj* que también es compartida con otros pueblos mayas de Yucatán. La parte histórica, como vemos, todavía estaba en desarrollo y no podría ser parte de aquel antiguo texto.

231. Esto obviamente se refiere a la producción de fuego a base de la frotación de pequeñas piezas de leña. Sin embargo, en el caso de Tojil, como manifestación de Jun Raqan, "un pie", es explícito que produjo el fuego con ese único pie utilizando su sandalia como base. Ximénez traduce esta línea como "dando vueltas en su zapato".

232. Aquí y entre paréntesis, aparece una inserción latina que dice: "Demonium loquens eis", lo cual es un agregado de Ximénez dentro del texto k'iche' y que en la columna en español traduce como "demonio que les hablaba". Esta asociación demoníaca por parte de Ximénez debe derivarse de que en el *Popol Wuj* se habla de un personaje alado, como un murciélago venido de Xibalba, lugar que Ximénez traduce como "infierno".

233. Es interesante anotar aquí lo dicho por Recinos (1953: 188). Este personaje alado llega de Xibalba y se "presenta como un enviado del Creador y Formador, pero hay motivo para sospechar de su identidad". Lo anterior quiere decir que Recinos tampoco consideraba que ese personaje era enviado de los dioses creadores.

234. Ésta es una metáfora para decir "temporal" o largos períodos de lluvia intermitente.

235. El texto k'iche' dice *chik'imaj*, donde el verbo es *k'imaj*, "cubrir", derivado de *k'im*, "pajón". En Basseta la entrada *k'im* se traduce como "zacate" y *k'imaj uwi' ja*, "cubrir la casa de zacate". En este sentido, la expresión en el *Popol Wuj* significa que ante el intenso frío, los que llegaron a pedir fuego se "cubrían" o "frotaban" la boca y la cara con las manos.

236. En el texto k'iche' se dice *eleεom*, que Ximénez (folio 37r) traduce "ladrones". Sin embargo y por contexto, comparto la opinión de Recinos en cuanto a que esto puede ser un error de copia de Ximénez. No se está hablando de "robar" sino de "suplicar". Recinos (1953: 188) dice "del verbo quiché *elahic*, rogar, suplicar, humillarse, se forma el sustantivo *elahom*, que da la idea que aceptamos en este lugar y que parece más conforme con el sentido del pasaje de que se trata".

237. El verbo k'iche' es *tu'nik*, "mamar", metáfora que significa "remover" el corazón. Lo que aquí se está anticipando es que los pueblos deberán entregar víctimas para sacrificios donde se extrae el corazón.

238. He aquí otra expresión que refuerza la nota anterior. El texto k'iche' dice *mawi xkiyalaj chik*, donde *yalaj*, posible error de copia o variación dialectal de *yaluj*, constituye la clave de interpretación. *Yaluj* quiere decir "detenerse, tardarse" (Basseta). Es decir, que no se "detuvieron a pensar" en las consecuencias y en la línea siguiente se dice literalmente que de inmediato aceptaron aquel compromiso. De ahí que traduzca "no lo pensaron" en lugar de "no se detuvieron" o "no se tardaron", que considero transmite mejor la idea de lo que está sucediendo.

239. El nombre *chamal-kan* posiblemente derive de *cha'omal*, "hermosa" (Coto), y *kan*, "serpiente", en proto-maya.

240. El texto k'iche' dice *xch'ataj wi*, que puede ser un error de copia por *xch'akataj wi*, "fueron derrotados" o "vencidos".

241. Nim Xo'l, "gran hondonada". D. Tedlock (1996: 342) propone que ese lugar es el mismo *Nim Xob Karchaj* que estaría cerca o en el mismo pueblo conocido ahora como San Pedro Carchá, en Alta Verapaz.

242. Literalmente, "lugar del consejo".

243. Ésta es una traducción literal, pero la palabra *tzij*, como dice Recinos (1953: 192), "tiene varias acepciones: palabra, opinión, historia, suerte o destino". En este caso se está hablando de una historia en

común a lo cual habría que agregar "vida", como se dijo en nota 197 cuando los dioses creadores le dan vida a sus criaturas de maíz.

244. Esto de "pasaron el mar" no debe tomarse de manera literal. Es una figura para explicar el paso entre determinados lugares que se anegan en la época de lluvia, o como dice D. Tedlock (1996: 301): "En efecto, los nombres describen una calzada como las que cruzan lagos o áreas temporalmente inundadas para conectar varios sitios mayas de las tierras bajas".

245. El texto k'iche' dice *kaqja*, literalmente "casa roja"; pero de acuerdo con Varea (1997) en cuyo diccionario está la palabra *kaqjay* que quiere decir: "montecillos redondos de piedra y tierra seca que hacían los antiguos". En el diccionario de Ximénez, está la palabra *cachal* que seguramente debió transcribirse como *caqhai*, y que el mismo Ximénez traduce como "cerros hechos a mano, a manera de cuestas". En la siguiente línea se agrega que ese "cerro" o "montaña" se llama ahora Jaqawitz. En varios idiomas mayas además la palabra *witz* quiere decir "cerro" o "montaña". Y como agrega D. Tedlock (1996: 302): "no es sorprendente que el término para pirámide fuera (literalmente) 'casa roja' considerando que las pirámides mayas (y los templos de encima) estaban pintadas de rojo, al menos hasta el período clásico".

246. Conforme el diccionario de Pantaleón de Guzmán, *sochoj* es la "víbora de cascabel".

247. Literalmente "pueblo de los Tam[ub]" o "parcialidad de los Tamub" como dice Carmack (1983: 220), quien agrega "se localiza en una falda del cerro Telecuché en cantón Cruz Ché de Santa Cruz de Quiché". *Amaq'* quiere decir "pueblo o ciudad" (Basseta).

248. En *El Título de Totonicapán* se dice que los Ilokab estuvieron en un cerro llamado *"Uq'uin"*, que Carmack (1983: 220) identifica como "una aldea en el noreste del pueblo de San Pedro Jocopilas" y también señala que en ese lugar hay un sitio arqueológico. La palabra *uq'in* puede provenir de *q'inom*, "jocote", y *k'at*, literalmente "red", es un día del calendario maya. En consecuencia, el nombre del lugar podría estar asociado al inicio de una cuenta cíclica relativa al día *k'at*.

249. El texto k'iche' dice *atz'yaq* que en una acepción general es "ropa" o "trapo" pero por contexto, es la variedad de musgo que crece sobre los árboles y que se asemeja a una cabellera gris (Recinos, 1953: 196). En el diccionario de Basseta, encontramos esta palabra *atz'yaq che'*, como "paxte"; pero entendiéndose esto también como

un artefacto de baño en Guatemala, se utiliza la expresión general de musgo. Estas líneas indican que a los dioses los colocaron entre "pie de gallo", como se conoce a la bromelia, y entre musgo gris.

250. Éstas son variedades de incienso. *Pom*, en k'iche', y *copal-li*, en náhuatl. Conforme a Recinos (1953: 197), *mixtan* viene de Mictlán, que equivale al inframundo que se confirma en el diccionario náhuatl de Karttunen (1983). *Kawistan* es también asociado por Tedlock a un término náhuatl. En la actualidad, sin embargo, algunos *ajq'ijab* asocian cuatro variedades de *pom* con los cuatro lados del mundo: *Mixtam pom* (oriente); *Kawistan pom* (poniente); *Kabawil pom* (norte) y *Porowal pom* (sur).

251. El texto k'iche' dice *k'eletzu*. *K'el* es "cotorra" y *tzu* "flauta". Es decir, una cotorra parlanchina.

252. Conforme a Recinos (1953: 198) éste sería el "rey zope", que se distingue "por la combinación de sus plumas negras y blancas".

253. En esta parte del texto se dice *Kiba Ja*, pero antes se les identificó como Ajkibaja. La identificación en esta página carece del agentivo *aj-* que indica oficio o profesión.

254. *Yaki*, como se dijo antes, significa "mexicano" y *tepew* es una palabra náhuatl que significa "conquistador o victorioso". Aquí sin embargo no se hace referencia a ellos como "victoriosos mexicanos" porque en ese caso la nominación sería *tepew yaki*, como corresponde a la sintaxis k'iche'. Aquí se está diciendo que también los *ajq'ijab* de ellos, vieron la salida del Sol e inmediatamente, se agrega: "como cuanto pueblo existe hoy".

255. Éste es el "dueño" de las montañas y "guardián" de los animales. En el *Memorial de Sololá* (Otzoy, 1999: 105, 161) se dice textualmente: *xa wi wawe' in k'o wi, xa in ruk'u'x juyu'*: "aquí es mi lugar, soy el corazón de la montaña". Su ropa era del color de la sangre derivado seguramente del calor provocado durante el nacimiento del Sol y su representación actual es la imagen colorada que carga consigo el *ajitz* en el "baile de la conquista". De Saqik'oxol, dice el texto k'iche', *xa xuchap chi uk'a rib pa che'*... que en una traducción literal sería: "se agarró de las ramas de los árboles", que debe entenderse como escapar para no ser petrificado como los demás.

256. Esto significa que después de la petrificación inicial, si no fuera por el "guardián" de los animales voraces, tampoco habría alivio ni vida.

257. Esto ratifica lo dicho sobre los *yaki tepew* y la gente "incontable" expresada en líneas anteriores. Un solo amanecer tuvieron todos los pueblos, no que todos se encontraban en Jaqawitz.

258. *Qamuqu* está compuesto de *qa-*, "nuestro", y *muqu*, "mirar" o "enterrar", que equivale hasta donde la vista puede llegar. Recuérdese que la vista de los padres primigenios podía atravesar árboles, piedras, etc. Es decir, el nombre de este canto se refiere a la procedencia u origen.

259. En este punto estoy de acuerdo con D. Tedlock (1996: 305-6), quien dice que el equivalente de Tojil no es Yolkwat ni Quetzalcóatl sino Tezcatlipoca y que en todo caso, esta comparación tiene un contenido político.

260. Aquí se está hablando de los "sacerdotes" de esos pueblos, como se ratifica unas líneas más adelante. No de los pueblos en sí.

261. En términos lingüísticos, el idioma de los habitantes de Rabinal es k'iche'.

262. El manuscrito k'iche' dice *ajpo* por *ajpop*, "Señores de la estera", y *xa* por *xajil* (conforme a Edmonson 1971: 184). Estas denominaciones, en el texto k'iche', están escritas en kaqchikel.

263. Literalmente, sentados con las rodillas junto a la barbilla y convertidos en piedra. Por eso se dice en la línea siguiente que sólo su espíritu hablaba. En Basseta encontramos la entrada *wonoba rib* como "encogerse y juntar como las rodillas con la barba". Esta posición también se ve ilustrada en algunos códices.

264. Sin entrar a discutir el nahualismo entendido como la transformación de personas en animales, también existe el concepto de que dentro de los objetos hay un ser vivo. Así, en el *Calepino en lengua cakchiquel* (Varea, 1997: 209-10) se dice: "creen que había cosa viva dentro del árbol, piedra o monte que hablaba..." Por esto traduzco aquí *nawal* como "espíritu", la representación juvenil de estos dioses, como se dice más adelante.

265. El texto k'iche' dice literalmente *kojq'aq'anij*, que sintácticamente es problemático. Unos lo traducen como voz activa (Ximénez, Recinos, Chávez, etc.) en cuyo caso sería *kojq'aq'anik*. Otros en voz pasiva (Edmonson, Tedlock, etcétera) en cuyo caso sería *kojq'aq'anix rumal*. Lingüísticamente hablando, creo que es un error de copia de Ximénez y la oración debe ser *kojkiq'aq'anij*, "ellos tienen aflicción por nuestra causa". Una oración transitiva con la misma estructura sintáctica sería *kojkichajij*, "ellos nos cuidan". Tojil está anticipando el dolor a causar.

266. En el *Popol Wuj* el nominal de este verso paralelo aparece como *k'im, torob* y en el *Rabinal Achi* como *k'im, tolo*.

267. Literalmente, las "hembras de venado", las "hembras de aves". En el *Calepino en lengua cakchiquel* (Varea 1997: 209-10) *xnam* es "la venada hembra".

268. Comparto el criterio de D. Tedlock (1996: 307-8) que *k'u'kej* significa la piel de venado en la que se envuelve o "se esconde" lo sagrado. En este caso significa el "envoltorio sagrado" de cada una de las deidades, como se dice y traduce en líneas adelante.

269. Ésta es una referencia a la promesa que hicieron los pueblos cuando a cambio del fuego "aceptaron" la extracción de sus corazones.

270. El texto k'iche' dice *jolom okox*, que en una traducción literal es "cabeza de hongo"; sin embargo Ximénez identifica estas palabras como hierba y no como hongo. D. Tedlock (1996: 307-8) propone que es la variedad blanca del pericón, que regularmente es amarillo. Por claridad, se agrega lo del color "amarillo" en esta traducción.

271. El texto k'iche' dice *xkiwaquj* y conforme a Basseta, *waq* quiere decir "bebida de los dioses". En este sentido, ellos "sirvieron la bebida de los dioses".

272. Esto de "cuando habían dado la piel" es un eufemismo para referirse al pacto de cuando los pueblos, a excepción de los kaqchikeles, habían aceptado la extracción de corazones a cambio del fuego. El lugar donde esto se pactó y que antes no había sido nombrado se llama Silisib que viene del verbo *silobik* que significa "meneo" o "tembladera" (Basseta), que explica muy bien el hecho de cuando los pueblos temblaban de frío y por el terror que se avecina.

273. El texto k'iche' dice *echalami q'at* donde *chala*, conforme a Basseta, quiere decir "escoger entre muchos" y *q'at* quiere decir "cortar" o "sacrificar".

274. Ésta es la famosa frase que Recinos tradujo como "Que todos se levanten, que se llame a todos, que no haya un grupo, ni dos grupos de entre nosotros que se quede atrás de los demás". En primer lugar, ésta no es una cita sino parte de la narración. La cita viene más abajo y ésta es una aposición a lo que los narradores están contando. Ximénez traduce estas líneas en los siguientes términos: "y fueron todos llamados y convocados, y ni una, ni dos de las tribus se quedó"; es decir, se está hablando en tercera persona plural, "ellos"; no en primera de plural, "nosotros".

275. En *El Título de Totonicapán* (Carmack y Mondloch, 1983: 180) se proporciona un tercer nombre: *Q'uibatsunjá*. De hecho estos nom-

bres quieren decir: *ixtaj*, "niña" en kaqchikel; *ixpuch'*, "tierna" en k'iche' como cuando una fruta todavía no está madura. El marcador femenino en ambos casos es *ix-*. Ahora bien, con respecto al tercer nombre de estas jovencitas, comparto parcialmente el criterio de Recinos (1953: 209); aunque en lugar de traducir "la bien arreglada o acicalada" soy del criterio de traducirlo literalmente. Esto es: "ramilletes del agua", análogo a *batz'un kotz'i'j*, "ramillete de flores"; es decir, en los tres nombres se está expresando: niñez, inmadurez y frescura.

276. Aquí debe advertirse que se está hablando en plural y sólo se menciona a Tojil. Es decir y como en otros casos, la tercera persona singular puede significar tercera persona plural; aunque aquí el marcador verbal es explícitamente plural: *x-e-opon*, aspecto/tiempo, tercera persona plural-verbo "llegar"; es decir "ellos llegaron" por lo que debe entenderse Tojil, Awilix y Jaqawitz. Por esto traduzco el sujeto singular como "los de Tojil", para indicar que se está hablando de las tres deidades.

277. Recinos (1953: 210) tiene razón al advertir en pie de nota 333, que aquí aparece el nombre de Ik'ibalam, pero que luego son solamente los otros tres los que pintaron los lienzos o mantas.

278. En esta sección se utiliza el verbo *tz'ibaj* que actualmente significa "escribir", pero que en la antigüedad también significaba "pintar" y he aquí otra prueba. En Basseta encontramos que *tz'ibaj* quiere decir "pintar, escribir". De hecho, pintar es una forma de escribir. Por aparte, traduzco lienzo en lugar de manto, porque la tela donde se pinta se denomina lienzo.

279. El texto k'iche' habla de "transgresión" (otros lo traducen como "pecado") y por lo general se ha asumido que se está hablando de las doncellas; pero por contexto sabemos que para los Señores, lo que llevaban las doncellas era prueba de que las deidades las habían poseído y eso significaba el principio de su derrota.

280. Nótese que unas líneas antes, se dijo que Balam Ki'tze' y Balam Aq'ab pintaron una unidad de su ser y aquí aparecen como multitud; como la pintura de Majuk'utaj. La única explicación que se puede dar, es el poder mágico de los autores de esas obras o que éste es otro error de copia en el manuscrito.

281. En la copia de Ximénez del *Popol Wuj* se dice textualmente *quiibal* y en su diccionario encontramos las entradas *quil* y *quilbej* que traduce como "embarazar". Soy del criterio de que estas palabras se derivan de la raíz *qui'al* o en la ortografía contemporánea *ki'al*

que quiere decir "jugo" y en este caso "flujo masculino". En el diccionario de Basseta también encontramos otra palabra para "semen" y es *vaal* que a su vez puede significar "jugo" de diversas especies. Es decir y en una traducción literal, semen es el "jugo masculino". En el diccionario de Coto, encontramos *yaal* como propiamente "semen" y la misma palabra sólo que transcrita como *ya'al* en el diccionario español-cakchiquel-inglés de Blair *et al.*, se traduce como "jugo". Ximénez, además, traduce esa línea como "Y lo que querían era que se fuesen el Tojil, tras las dos doncellas". Esa misma línea es traducida por otros como "tentar a Tojil" o que éste "cortejara" o se "divirtiera" o tuviera "placer" con las doncellas. Villacorta y Rodas (1927) se acercan un poco más al traducir: "lo que ellos querían era que *Tojil* se hubiera rendido ante *Ixtaj* e *Ixpuch'* y las hubiera poseído"; Burgess y Xec (1955: 236) dicen: "Lo que ellas deseaban [las tribus] era que se hubieran ido los deseos de Tojil hacia *Xta'j* y *Xpuch'*." Chávez (1978: 89) lo traduce como: "lo que querían era que Tojil hubiera poseído a Shtaj y a Shpuch." Y es que el objetivo de los pueblos, como hemos visto antes, es que estas deidades cayeran sexualmente. Pero esto tiene un propósito político: conseguir una alianza. En el *Rabinal Achi*, por ejemplo, al enemigo prisionero se le piensa como posible hijo político o como cuñado.

282. Esa línea forma un verso paralelo con la línea anterior donde se encuentra inserto el verso paralelo que identifica a Ixtaj e Ixpuch', y se sigue hablando de los de Tojil. No de las doncellas como la gran mayoría de traductores han leído. Se está hablando de las deidades como "fornicantes". Esta línea es traducida también por Burgess y Xec (1955: 236) como: "y hubieran llegado a ser fornicarios". Es decir, los dioses, el objetivo a derrotar por los pueblos. De aquí, pues, que ha sido un grave error de traducción a partir de Ximénez, hablar de que lo que deseaban los pueblos es que ellas se convirtieran en "rameras", porque se está hablando de Tojil, Awilix y Jaqawitz. Edmonson (1971: 201) en pie de página dice sobre esta línea que Ximénez, "refiere esto a las jovencitas, pero es seguro que los gobernantes quichés eran los que debían ser seducidos a manifestar una indecente y mágica sexualidad peligrosa". Por aparte, en el diccionario de Basseta aparece *woloqotilaj ixoq* como "ramera" y *joxol ixoq* como "puta". Esta segunda acepción ha de haber llevado a confusión para atribuirles a las doncellas, una actividad pensada para hacer caer a las deidades.

283. Con esta línea se cierra esta descripción del deseo de los pueblos hacia los de Tojil. Aquí se deja claro que lo que los pueblos querían, era tentar a aquellos seres divinos.

284. Aquí se confirma lo dicho anteriormente en relación con este llamado de guerra. Aquí sí es cita textual y se está hablando de una eliminación total de los enemigos, en este caso, los padres primigenios de los k'iche'es. Recinos (1953: 212) traduce: "Que no haya uno, ni dos de entre nosotros que se quede atrás" cuando lo que el texto k'iche' dice, es que no sobreviva ni uno ni dos, de "ellos". Ximénez traduce correctamente el sujeto de esta expresión: "No ha de quedar ni uno, ni ninguno de ellos". Edmonson (1971), Chávez (1978), Tedlock (1996) también lo traducen correctamente como "ellos" y no "nosotros".

285. Textualmente quiere decir "bastones" pero siendo instrumentos de guerra, lo traduzco como jabalinas. Recinos lo traduce como "picas". Esto del metal en aquellos instrumentos parece una transposición histórica. Antes se dijo que cuando cruzaron tierras anegadas de agua y no tenían nada que comer, "Sólo olían la raíz de sus bastones". Los bastones y estandartes prehispánicos estaban adornados con plumas y conchas (ver *Cosmos maya*, 2000: 297-324). En el *Título C'oyoi* se habla de *Tekum Umam* como "Señor de los bastones y estandartes" como una manera de identificar su autoridad. El hecho de hablar de metal puede estar asociado a las "varas" coloniales que los autores k'iche'es del documento vieron en el siglo XVI o pudo ser una interpretación de Ximénez.

286. El texto k'iche' dice *k'oxtun*, que en el diccionario de Basseta se traduce como "cerca, muralla, castillo" mientras que en Coto, como "cerca o muro". Por la descripción que se da, que sólo fueron tablas y estacas, se entiende que fue un cerco. Es más, en el texto k'iche' se dice *xchikejbej*, traducido aquí como "cercaron" y que se deriva de la raíz verbal *keje* o *kejoj* que en Basseta se encuentra como "cercar con palos".

287. Estas dos líneas están omitidas en la traducción de don Adrián Chávez; no así en su transcripción k'iche'.

288. En el diccionario de Ximénez, *chui* se traduce como la "talega o bolsa, número 8,000". De ahí que *kachuy* en la ortografía actual equivale a "dos veces 8,000" es decir 16,000 y *oxchuy* 24,000. Sin embargo en su traducción del *Popol Wuj* esa numeración aparece como "no sólo venían ni uno, ni dos". Aquí, como en la cuenta de

los 400 muchachos que equivale a "un montón", se está hablando de una multitud enorme de guerreros.

289. Por claridad, en estas líneas se ha agregado "los guerreros", los sujetos de ataque conforme a la oración pasiva de los versos que anteceden. En estas dos líneas, sin embargo, las oraciones son activas y se está narrando que donde ellos iban, "corrían" para ser más explícitos, se encontraban con insectos por todos lados y por puños. El texto k'iche' dice *kichapa'*, "agarraban", pero debe entenderse que en el embate y aunque sin intención sus manos se topaban con insectos. Con respecto a que los "encontraban por puños", me fundamento en el *Calepino en lengua cakchiquel* (Varea, 1997) que dice que la raíz verbal *maj*, de donde propongo que se deriva *kimaja* del texto k'iche', quiere decir también "tomar ajuntando apuñados del suelo, o, de una cesta para echar en otra..." Esta traducción se fortalece, cuando enseguida se dice que los insectos estaban en todos lados y cuando se dijo que "parecían una humareda".

290. En esta línea, la palabra *achijilal* generalmente ha sido traducida como "valentía", que tiene sentido en una oración afirmativa; pero en una negativa como lo es en este caso, significa "amenaza". En términos descriptivos se podría también traducir: "no fue un acto de valentía lo hecho".

291. En el diccionario de Basseta, *patan* es "tributo", además de servicio y oficio. El texto k'iche' dice *ajpatan*, "tributarios" o "contribuyentes".

292. Con respecto a estos nombres, comparto el criterio de D. Tedlock (1996: 313) quien propone que *k'o* en estos nombres puede ser una abreviación de *k'o rab, ruxlab* que Coto traduce como "autoridad". En ese sentido, *k'oka'ib* puede traducirse como "noble dos" y *k'oqawib*, "noble investido".

293. Con respecto a los nombres de los hijos de Balam Aq'ab, Edmonson (1971: 211) propone que vienen del náhuatl. *Akul* es el nombre del pueblo k'iche' enclavado a las orillas del territorio Ixil. Sobre estos nombres, dice Brasseur de Bourbourg (1972: 413) "En *Qo-acul* y *Qo-acutec* se encuentran los nombres de dos familias o tribus radicadas en el país quiché, en lugares que se llaman todavía así".

294. De nuevo se sigue la ortografía contemporánea y K'o'ajaw como traduce D. Tedlock (1996: 174), es "Señor noble".

295. En *El Título de Totonicapán* (1983: 187) se dice también que Ik'ibalam murió siendo joven y que Tz'utuja del linaje Saqik llega a sustituirlo.

296. Éste es el nombre del mismo canto de cuando salió el Sol y se preguntaron por sus demás hermanos.

297. Este día, en el calendario maya, es uno de los cuatro cargadores del tiempo. Conforme a Recinos (1953: 217), éste "es un símbolo de desaparición y despedida".

298. Aquí el texto k'iche' literalmente dice "montaña", pero el concepto es más amplio y por eso Ximénez y Burgess y Xec lo traducen como "patria".

299. Estas líneas tienen dos lecturas, una simbólica que se refiere al lugar después de la muerte y otra literal que confirman la propuesta de que los padres primigenios de los mayas se originaron en el área de Los Cuchumatanes, luego peregrinaron al oriente. Ver nota al principio de este texto sobre la frase "de la orilla del mar".

300. "Envoltorio Sagrado", *pisom* quiere decir "envuelto" y *q'aq'al* "poder", "majestad" conforme al diccionario de Basseta quien lo escribe como sinónimo de la palabra de origen náhuatl, *tepewal*. *Q'aq'al* se deriva de *q'aq'*, "fuego". Recuérdese que cuando Tojil creó el fuego, los primeros en recibirlo adquirieron poder sobre los otros. Una traducción alterna sería "envoltura del poder" o como traduce Chávez (1978: 94) "Envoltura de la fortaleza"; pero siendo un objeto de carácter espiritual o religioso, lo traduzco como "Envoltorio Sagrado".

301. El texto k'iche' dice *xemuqtaj* que puede también interpretarse como "enterrados", sin embargo la raíz verbal *muqu* también puede significar "mirar" como en el nombre del canto Qamuqu. Por contexto, es más congruente "no fueron vistos" antes que "no fueron enterrados".

302. Aquí debe entenderse "desaparición" como sinónimo de muerte, como líneas adelante se explicita.

303. En *El Título de Totonicapán* se dan dos versiones de esta peregrinación, lo interesante a señalar aquí es que en la primera versión se menciona a México, que como dice Carmack (1983: 225) "Tal como el *Popol Vuh*, el *Título Totonicapán* localiza el lugar de origen quiché, al oriente de México. Es difícil saber exactamente qué lugar tenían en mente al decir México, pero parece que lo localizaban al otro lado del mar". Lo anterior refuerza, en primer lugar, el argumento lingüístico planteado en las primeras páginas de esta traducción que cuando el *texto* k'iche' dice *ch'aqa palo* quieren decir "a la orilla del mar" porque México no está "al otro lado del mar". En segundo lugar, cuando se habla de "pasaron el mar", como se

dice líneas más adelante, no debe interpretarse de manera literal; sino una manera poética como propone D. Tedlock (1996: 301).

304. Conforme a Recinos (1953: 220) este nombre es una abreviación de "*Topiltzin Acxitl Quetzalcoatl,* el célebre rey tolteca que obligado a abandonar sus dominios del norte emigró a fines del siglo X a tierras de Yucatán (el Oriente de las crónicas antiguas), fundó la ciudad de Mayapán y repobló la de Chichén Itzá, civilizó la península y terminada su misión se marchó por donde vino". Edmonson y Tedlock coinciden en el origen náhuatl del nombre y lo asocian a Quetzalcóatl.

305. El texto k'iche' dice *ajpopol,* que ha sido traducido como "jefe", "señor" o "rey" (Recinos, 1953: 220), Carmack y Mondloch (1983: 228); y *ajpop q'amja'il* como el "segundo príncipe reinante" (Recinos, 1953: 220), que también comparten Carmack y Mondloch. En mi opinión, el segundo título se refiere más a una función de cancillería y que D. Tedlock (1996: 179) traduce como "Keeper of the Reception House Mat". En *El Título de Totonicapán,* cuando se habla del matrimonio de Q'uqumatz K'otuja con la joven Ixlem, del Señorío de los Malaj, perteneciente a los tz'utujiles, se dice que *Cuatro Pop K'amja* fueron a recibirla.

306. El texto k'iche' dice *mu'j,* literalmente "sombra". En *El Título de Totonicapán* (Carmack y Mondloch, 1983) se dice que el *Ajpop* tenía cuatro palios de plumas sobre su trono, el *Ajpop K'amja* tres palios; el *Nima Rajpop Achij* dos palios y el *Ch'uti Rajpop Achij* un palio.

307. El primer instrumento de este pareado, *subaq,* ha sido traducido de manera literal como "flauta de hueso" (vg. Recinos y Tedlock) o como "hueso nasal" por Edmonson (1971: 218). En el diccionario de Coto, sin embargo, se dice que *su'baq* "es otro género de flautilla que tocan con los tamboriles, llaman *aj,* que es de carrizo". Es decir, la flauta en general se llama *su'* pero la de carrizo o caña se llama *aj* o *su'baq;* aunque puede ser también, que *su'baq,* literalmente "flauta de hueso", haya sido efectivamente un instrumento hecho de ese material. El segundo instrumento de este pareado es *cham-cham* que siguiendo a Coto puede interpretarse como un pequeño tambor, porque es improbable que sea "tambor" en virtud de que antiguamente la palabra para este instrumento era *q'ojom* que ahora se utiliza para decir marimba.

308. Este pareado se refiere a cosméticos con los cuales, como dice Coto (1983: 62), "antiguamente se solían embarnizar los rostros: titil,

ȝan abah". El primer término en el texto k'iche' es *tatil*, que en Basseta y Coto aparece como *titil*. El segundo, *q'an abaj*, literalmente quiere decir "piedra amarilla"; pero ha de haber sido una arcilla, seguramente equiparable al tizate que es de color blanco. En la traducción de Burgess y Xec se dice entre paréntesis sobre este pareado: "polvos de color para consagrar caciques".

309. Este pareado ha sido traducido como "garras de león, garras de tigre" (vg. Recinos); pero como sabemos, aquí no había leones ni tigres; sino pumas y jaguares. Por aparte, el manuscrito dice *tzicuil*, que ha sido traducido como "garras"; sin embargo, la palabra parece derivarse del término compuesto *tz'i'equlil* donde *tz'i'e* significa "colmillo" (Basseta) y *tz'i'ey* (en Coto y Pantaleón de Guzmán) y *qulil* "collar de camisa", según traduce Basseta. Es decir, se está hablando de "colmillos" que se llevan como "collar".

310. En este pareado, la palabra *pich* es "pie de dos uñas" conforme al diccionario de Ximénez y "los pies de cualquier animal de cuatro pies de las rodillas abajo" conforme al *Calepino en lengua cakchiquel* (Varea, 1997).

311. Este pareado parece ser el equivalente a *nuchinq'u, nuk'alqab* del *Rabinal Achi. Nuchinq'u*, conforme al diccionario de Basseta, son "unos brazaletes de hueso" y *k'alqab* conforme a Ximénez son "joyas y manillas". En el *Popol Wuj*, sin embargo, el primer verso de este pareado es *makutax*, que proviene del náhuatl *mah, que* quiere decir "mano" y -*cuetlax*, es "cuero" (Campbell, 1983: 84). Edmonson (1971: 218) traduce este verso como "brazalete de piedras preciosas"; y D. Tedlock (1996: 180) como "brazalete de cuero". Los dos versos del pareado posiblemente se refieren entonces, a un tipo de brazalete de cuero sobre el cual pendían conchas de caracol que al moverse hacían ruido y de ahí la raíz verbal duplicada en *tatam* en el segundo verso.

312. Este pareado parece provenir del yukateko y del náhuatl. En el texto k'iche', el primer verso dice *k'us bus*; pero en el diccionario maya (Barrera Vásquez, 1995: 72) *buxil k'utz* es también unas "calabacitas silvestres para guardar tabaco molido". Con respecto al segundo verso, *kaxkon* muy probablemente venga de *caxitl*, "escudilla, plato, taza, vajilla", conforme a Karttunen (1983: 26). Y porque estos enseres eran de la clase dirigente, traduzco el segundo verso como "escudilla real".

313. El primer verso de este pareado, *chiyom*, sigue la traducción de Recinos cuyo fundamento parece sustentarse en el segundo verso

venido de la palabra náhuatl *aspatulul*, "garza grande", con el cual conforma un verso paralelo.

314. En estas líneas se ha agregado Suywa como aparece en otras partes del texto como verso paralelo de Tulán y que en esta parte de la copia del texto k'iche' se omite como probable error de copia. Asimismo en la copia de Ximénez aparece dos veces *chupam* "en" o "adentro" sin que en la primera esté escrito el nominal y en el segundo aparece *kitzij*, literalmente "sus palabras". En otra parte del texto hemos visto que al relatarse la salida de Tulán, Suywa, se habla de un "antiguo texto" y por eso aquí se traduce "sus escritos" en vez de "sus palabras". Con respecto a "signos", que ha de referirse a la escritura jeroglífica, concuerdo con D. Tedlock (1996: 317) quien dice que la única palabra posible derivada de otras partes del texto es *ketal*, "sus signos, que en este contexto debe referirse a los caracteres de la escritura de Tulán". Recinos (1953: 222) traduce estas líneas en los siguientes términos: "las pinturas, como le llamaban aquello en que ponían sus historias". Estas pinturas o texto con escritura jeroglífica, como se ha dicho antes, ha de ser parte del texto original del *Popol Wuj* que en otras partes se identifica como un antiguo libro.

315. Literalmente "lugar de las espinas" y que conforme al estudio de Alain Ichon (en Carmack y Morales Santos, 1983: 237-246) sería el sitio *Kawinal* ubicado en ambas márgenes del río Blanco a unos tres kilómetros antes de confluir con el río Negro o Chixoy, en jurisdicción de Cubulco, Baja Verapaz.

316. El texto k'iche' dice *juyub*, literalmente "montañas" en referencia a las cuatro secciones en que se dividía la ciudadela de Chi K'ix, como se identifica más adelante.

317. El primero de estos cuatro nombres, *Chi Chaq'* <chaqi'j, ha sido traducido como "lugar seco" (vg. Edmonson y Tedlock); pero también puede ser *Chi ch'aq* <ch'aqi "lugar mojado" en referencia directa a alguno de los sitios ubicados a la orilla del río que atraviesa el lugar. El segundo sitio es *Jumeta Ja'* "corteza de río" que también puede leerse como *Jumeta Ja*, "casa de corteza de árbol". El tercero es *k'ulba* <k'ulba't, "monjón" o "límite", y *Kawinal* es propiamente el nombre de aquel sitio arqueológico y que puede leerse como *ka-* "dos" y *winal* cognado yukateko del k'iche' *winaq* "persona", equivale a "2 cuentas de 20", es decir "cuarenta".

318. Chi Ismachi', "lugar de las barbas", ubicada al sur de Q'umaraq Aj o Utatlán.

319. Literalmente, "tizate" pero hace referencia al polvo blanco derivado del tizate como medio de construcción.

320. K'onache' hijo de K'oqawib con la esposa de su hermano K'oka'ib era de la tercera generación por la línea de los Kaweq y Belejeb Kej era de la cuarta generación por la línea de los Nija'ib'. La cuarta generación por los Kaweq la conformaban K'otuja e Istayul. Recinos (1953: 225) dice que Istayul era hijo de Balam-Conache.

321. Este nombre viene del náhuatl, *ista*, "blanco, sal", y *yul* deriva de -*yo: l*, "corazón" (Campbell, 1983).

322. Esta línea ha sido difícil de traducir por diversos autores, debido a que al margen del manuscrito k'iche', se leen las palabras *cumatzil pro. nim ha*. De donde *cumatzil* ha sido literalmente traducido como "dos serpientes", vg. por Brasseur de Bourbourg. Ximénez sólo traduce *nim ha* como "casa grande" pero en su diccionario aparece la palabra *cumatz* como "culebra en general" o "anguila" y *cumatzilah vinac, cucumatz* llamaban en su gentilidad a dios. En mi opinión, la palabra *cumatzil* deviene de la frase *cumatzilah vinac* que en una acepción amplia querría decir "gobernar" o "administrar" en referencia directa a una autoridad sobrenatural como Q'ukumatz.

323. En *El Título de Totonicapán* (Carmack y Mondlock, 1983) también se habla de este episodio de manera más detallada y ahí se identifica a K'otuja del *Popol Wuj* como Q'ukumatz K'otuja. Se dice que los Ilokab quisieron enemistar a ambos Señores con mentiras; pero fueron descubiertos y castigados. El nombre K'otuja viene de *k'o*, "noble", y *tuja* de *tuj*, "temascal" o "baños de vapor" donde acostumbraba bañarse K'otuja. Conforme a Carmack y Mondlock (1983: 249) esos baños podrían ser los que hoy se conocen como Pachitac en Quiché.

324. Literalmente, "barranco, ciudadela"; proviene de *siwan, tinamit*, una metonimia para referirse a "pueblo" en alusión a las antiguas ciudadelas fortificadas y rodeadas de barrancos para prevenir ataques. La traducción "campo y ciudadela" es alternativa. La figura "barranco, ciudadela" es semejante a *kaj ulew*, "cielo tierra", para referirse a "cosmos" y al concepto q'eqchi' *tzuul tak'a*, literalmente "cerro y valle", para significar "la superficie de la Tierra" (Haeserijn, 1979: 345).

325. Aquí obviamente se hace referencia a Tojil, Awilix y Jaqawitz.

326. Chávez (1978: 99) traduce esta línea como "Aquí aumentó la vergüenza de Dios". El manuscrito dice *xnimar wi uk'ixik kabawil*.

327. Comparto el criterio de Recinos (1953: 227) en cuanto a que la frase k'iche' *ta xkisi'j uloq* que literalmente habla de hacer leña, es una referencia a la costumbre antigua mediante la cual el pretendiente tenía que llevar leña a la casa de la novia. No así con su traducción de "orgías" por la palabra *uqaja'* que hace referencia a la presentación o al acto de compartir bebidas espirituosas. Nótese que si en la parte mitológica se habló de bebida alcohólica como *ki'*, "dulce", o *ki*, "maguey", aquí ya se utiliza la palabra *ja'* como en la actualidad, que no sólo hace referencia al agua sino también a bebidas alcohólicas.

328. Comparto el criterio de D. Tedlock (1996: 291-2) sobre que la referencia de *wuk'* no proviene de "siete tribus" como traduce Recinos, sino de "aliados". De otra manera, no tendría razón que esos mismos "aliados" combatieran a los k'iche'es. *Wuk'* literalmente quiere decir "conmigo".

329. El manuscrito dice *Cumar caah* aunque en *El Título de Totonicapán* también se le identifica como *chi ʒumar caah* de ahí que se traduzca como "lugar de las cañas podridas". D. Tedlock (1996: 320) hace una propuesta interesante, a la que me adhiero, al decir que el nombre es *Q'umaraq Aj* en el sentido de que *q'umaraq* es la forma plural del adjetivo que califica a *aj*, "cañas". A este lugar se le conoce también con el nombre náhuatl de Utatlán.

330. Recinos (1953: 229) está en lo correcto al anotar que esto significa que "Ya no se reunían para comer y beber como lo hacían en Izmachí cuando concertaban las bodas de sus hijas e hijos".

331. Ésta es una metáfora para indicar que la memoria de los muertos había sido disturbada.

332. Aquí se habla del obispo Francisco Marroquín, quien llegó a bendecir aquella ciudadela en 1539 y luego fue abandonada.

333. El linaje Saqik conforme *El Título de Totonicapán* vino a sustituir al de Ik'ibalam, que no dejó descendencia. Ese título literalmente dice: "Señor Sakic Ts'utujá el sustituto de Iquí Balam" (Carmack y Mondlock, 1983: 189). Entre estos dos linajes parece haber una conexión lingüística: *saqik* puede provenir de *saq*, "claro, blanco"; *ik'*, "luna", "luna clara", mientras que el nombre de Ik'ibalam, como se dijo en capítulo aparte, significa "jaguar luna".

334. Éste es el orden jerárquico de los Señores. Ajpop, "el de la estera", era el principal, donde la palabra *pop*, "petate", representaba el poder máximo, seguido del Ajpop K'amja, "receptor de la estera". Los términos *ajpop* como hacen referencia a "petate" también

pueden ser una metáfora, como sugiere D. Tedlock (1996: 315) para referirse a los miembros de la casa del consejo, que en el diccionario de Basseta se identifica como *popol ja*. El término *k'amja* viene de *k'amo*, "recibir", y *ja*, "casa"; puede significar receptor o sucesor del poder como sugiere Recinos (1953: 230), pero, a la vez, un puesto de cancillería como se infiere en *El Título de Totonicapán*. Ajtojil, era el encargado del culto a Tojil; el cuarto en rango es Ajq'ukumatz, encargado del culto a Q'ukumatz, seguido por el Nim Ch'okoj Kaweq, el "principal de los maestros de ceremonias de los Kaweq". *Chocoh* conforme al diccionario de Ximénez significa "bodas o convites" y en el *Calepino en lengua cakchiquel* la palabra *chokola'* se dice que es el cacao que se bebe entre todos, es decir que aunque en este segundo diccionario se utiliza la palabra de origen náhuatl *chocolatl* se está haciendo referencia a reuniones familiares donde los encargados de dirigirlas eran los *ch'okoj*. Al final del *Popol Wuj* se dice, además, que los transcriptores del manuscrito fueron tres *nim ch'okoj*, o sea que además de ser diestros en el lenguaje verbal también lo eran en el lenguaje escrito. El sexto en rango era el Popol Winaq chi T'uy que probablemente era el "ministro tesorero" como dice Recinos (1953: 231); el séptimo, Lolmet Kejnay, "recolector de impuestos", como plantea también Recinos (1953: 231); y porque *lolmay* en el diccionario de Coto, se traduce como "embajador" o enviado de los principales y entre otros asuntos "lleva los tributos". El octavo en rango era el Popol Winaq pa Jom Tzalatz', que de nuevo hace referencia al consejo y *jom* hace referencia al campo de juego de pelota y *tzalatz'* a su construcción lateral inclinada; es decir, a lo que ahora sería un "ministro de deportes". La novena en rango era por lo visto una mujer, *uchuch k'amja* habría sido la "asesora" o "consejera de cancillería". Para Estrada Monroy (1973: 284) sería "la anciana consejera" y como Chávez (1978: 101) comenta: "indica que también las mujeres gobernaban".

335. El primero de estas nueve autoridades se llamaba Ajaw Q'alel siendo la primera palabra "señor" y *q'alel* derivada de *q'alaj*, "claridad", o sea el "Señor que ve las cosas con claridad" o de *q'aq'*, "fuego", por lo que significa poder. Esto ha sido traducido como "Señor capitán" (Edmonson, 1971: 231) y "Señor ministro" (D. Tedlock, 1996: 185). Carmack (1983: 228), sin embargo, dice: "El K'alel era un cargo con funciones judiciales". El segundo sería el "Señor pregonero" o "vocero", deviniendo su título de Ajtzij Winaq como está en *El Título de Totonicapán*; el tercero, el ministro o capitán

en función de canciller, luego viene el Nima K'amja, "principal en línea de sucesión" y la quinta sería la "asesora" o "consejera de cancillería". El sexto el "maestro de ceremonias de los Nija'ib", el séptimo es el sacerdote encargado del culto a Awilix. El octavo, Yakolatam Utza'm Pop Saqlatol, probablemente se refiera al "encargado de los puntos de avanzada" viniendo su nombre de *yako*, "levantar", *utza'm*, "orillas" o "límites"; *pop*, "petate" o la gente entrelazada en esa comunidad y *saqlatol* que viene de *saq*, "claridad". El noveno sería el "recolector de impuestos".

336. El primero era el encargado de los avisos o "pregonero", el segundo era el "recolector de impuestos", el tercero el "maestro de ceremonias" y el cuarto el encargado al culto a Jaqawitz.

337. El primer título viene de *tz'utuj*, "flor del maíz" (Basseta) y *tz'utuja*, significaría "casa de la flor del maíz". Carmack (1983: 236) lo identifica como "un señor autóctono que vivía entre las montañas al este del primer centro quiché de Jakawits". El segundo es el "capitán" o "ministro de los Saqik".

338. Edmonson (1971: 234) ofrece una traducción muy sugerente de estas dos líneas, él traduce "tal vez nada de lo que esto hizo fue real [se refiere a las transformaciones de Q'ukumatz] porque este señor tenía una esencia mágica". Cierto o no, que éstos fueron hechos reales, deben recordarse los poderes mágicos de Junajpu y Xbalamke.

339. Este nombre proviene del náhuatl, *tepetl*, "montaña" (Kartunnen, 1992) y *-po: l*, "grande" (Campbell, 1983).

340. Aquí hay un error en la identificación de las generaciones, que se corrige más adelante. En el folio 52 recto del manuscrito, se adelanta una secuencia a las generaciones; pero en los folios 55 recto y verso se corrige diciendo que constituyen la séptima generación.

341. Tradicionalmente el primer nombre se ha escrito como *Kikab*, pero puede leerse como K'ikab, literalmente "el de mucha dulzura"; *K'iqab*, "el de muchas manos", como traduce D. Tedlock (1996: 324); *Kik'ab*, "sangres", como interpreta (Edmonson 1971: 234). Edmonson, además, sugiere que puede derivar del mam *kikap* que corresponde al día *No'j* del calendario maya. El segundo nombre, *Kawisimaj*, puede derivar de *kow-*, "duro", y *simaj*, "puntiagudo". En el diccionario de Basseta encontramos otro derivado muy sugerente: *usimajil ch'ab*, "el palillo que ponen en las flechas en lugar de hierro".

342. Chuwila, literalmente "en las ortigas", que traducido al náhuatl es Chichicastenango, nombre actual de dicho municipio.

343. Pa Maka', literalmente "donde se recoge agua" es lo que actualmente se conoce como el antiguo sitio donde se ubicó Zacualpa, a dos kilómetros al sureste del actual pueblo (D. Tedlock 1996: 357).

344. Aunque el manuscrito dice *caoqueb,* la palabra en forma pluralizada hace referencia a *kawke* que conforme a Recinos (1953: 234) probablemente sea lo que ahora se conoce como Santa María Cauqué y Santiago Sacatepéquez.

345. Esto es el actual pueblo de San Andrés Sajcabajá.

346. Ésta es la forma plural de Saqulew, "tierra blanca". Se refiere a lo que ahora se conoce como Zaculeu, territorio mam.

347. Esto es Totonicapán y literalmente Chuwi' Meq'ena' quiere decir "sobre el agua caliente".

348. Es el actual municipio de Quetzaltenango.

349. Es el actual municipio de Momostenango.

350. Esto es el actual pueblo de Santa María Chiquimula, Totonicapán.

351. El manuscrito dice *xpak'a'ik,* que literalmente quiere decir "les dieron vuelta".

352. El texto k'iche' literalmente dice: "su día" y "su nacimiento" conforme al calendario maya.

353. Esta línea tiene una lectura alternativa, "que los pueblos efectuaban ceremonias", *q'ol che',* que dice el manuscrito, es el "árbol de trementina" que sirve para hacer copal. En ese sentido se estaría hablando del acto que se hace con el derivado de ese árbol y no de un lugar específico.

354. Este nombre viene del náhuatl *petlatl,* "petate", y *ayotl,* "tortuga" (Karttunen, 1992), éste es el pueblo de Ayutla (Recinos, 1953: 235), hoy conocido como ciudad Tecún Umán. Ayutla es aún un lugar de romería para habitantes del occidente del país; pero sospecho que el origen de este ritual está asociado a este hecho de origen prehispánico.

355. Ésta es de nuevo una lectura alternativa a *siwan, tinamit,* literalmente "barranco, ciudadela". Se está hablando de un acordonamiento de las ciudadelas caídas.

356. D. Tedlock (1996: 326) está en lo correcto: aquí es plural y no es K'ikab el que dice: "yo iré a matarlos". Por contexto se entiende que son tres líderes, K'ikab por los Kaweq, el (Ajaw) Q'alel por los Nija'ib y el Ajtzik Winaq por los Ajaw K'iche' que están dando las órdenes. En el manuscrito están las dos versiones, *nu-,* que es primera persona singular y entrelineado *qa-,* primera persona plural. El error consiste en que el copista no tachó el *nu-* y por eso

se ha leído en singular. De otro modo, no tiene sentido el entrelineado.

357. Aquí hay que advertir que literalmente se está hablando de *ch'ab*,
"arco", y *k'am*, la "cuerda" del mismo arco. La palabra flecha
conforme al diccionario de Basseta es *ralch'ab*, literalmente "hijo
del arco". Sin embargo, en esta parte del texto k'iche' también se
habla de *uchi' ch'a(b)*, *uchi' k'am* que literalmente quiere decir
"punta del arco" y "punta de la cuerda". Por asociación, entonces,
traduzco "punta de flechas", "punta del arco", que han de haber
sido los que encabezaban esa misión.

358. Esto quiere decir que no llevaban iconos sagrados ante quienes
ofrendar como lo hicieron los primeros seres creados.

359. El manuscrito dice *Wila*, que se refiere a Chuwila, "Chichicastenango"; *Chulimal* conforme a Estrada Monroy (1973: 286), es
un caserío ubicado entre San Sebastián Lemoa y Chichicastenango.
Sobre este nombre sugiere D. Tedlock (1996: 327) que *lima* proviene
de *lemowa'*, "espejo de agua", como se conoce a la laguna de aquel
lugar. *Saqiya'*, literalmente "agua blanca", debe ser de origen
kaqchikel por el sustantivo *ya'* cuyo cognado k'iche' es *ja'*, "agua",
y que conforme a Edmonson (1971: 238) queda cerca de Chichicastenango al igual que *Xajbakyej*, "lugar de la danza del venado".
Estrada Monroy (1973: 286) dice de este último, que es el actual
caserío *Xalbaquiej* ubicado "entre Xepocol y Chicalte, en sus cer-
canías pasa el río Xalbaquiej, llamado también Sepelá". Los lugares
Chitemaj, "donde se fabrican bancas de madera", y *Wajxalajuj* por
Wajxaqlajuj, "dieciocho", no están localizados aunque Estrada
Monroy (1973: 286) propone por *Chitemaj* el lugar llamado *Chitem*,
cerca de Lanquín pero esto parece muy alejado de los otros lugares
hasta aquí mencionados.

360. Kabraqan conforme a Recinos (1953: 236) sería el actual Cabricán
de Quetzaltenango; sin embargo y por contexto podría ser éste el
nombre prehispánico del volcán de Agua que en las primeras páginas
se identifica como Pekul, que quiere decir "peñasco derrumbado"
y que sería una descripción por el derrumbe del 11 de septiembre
de 1541. Ya en nota 56 se ha propuesto que Junajpu sería el nombre
del volcán de Acatenango y que el *Chi q'aq'* "donde hay fuego"
que aquí se le identifica como *Ch'abi q'aq'* "lanzador de flechas de
fuego" sería el volcán de Fuego.

361. Este otro grupo de pueblos, Maka', como ya se identificó en líneas
anteriores, es el antiguo sitio de Zacualpa; Xayabaj sería el actual

pueblo de Joyabaj (Recinos 1953: 236); Saqkabaja es San Andrés Saqkabaja; Siyaja, la antigua "Santa Catarina Ixtaguacán"; Meq'ena' es Totonicapán y Xelajuj, "Quetzaltenango".

362. Ke'ema literalmente quiere decir "tejido" y Achaq' Iboy literalmente "hermano menor armadillo" como Chávez traduce. El manuscrito dice *achac* por lo que debe ser *uchac*—> *uchaq'* literalmente "su hermano menor". Es decir el nombre propio del (Ajaw) Q'alel de los Nija'ib era Ke'ema y el del Ajtzik Winaq de los Ajaw K'iche' era Uchaq' Iboy.

363. En el manuscrito encontramos las palabras *q'alel* cuyo significado está asociado a "poder" (ver nota 335), *-qalem* y *-qalej*. Las dos últimas provienen de *eqalem*, "dignidad" o "nobleza" (Basseta).

364. Esto significa que los cargos de los nuevos líderes de los pueblos, se otorgaron en un área cercana a Lemoa y no en Q'umaraq Aj. Las montañas nombradas como Xe' Balax y Xe' K'amaq' estarían ubicadas cerca de lo que hoy se conoce como San Sebastián Lemoa.

365. El texto habla de 20 nombramientos y por algún error sólo aparecen 19, once Nima Ch'okoj que son los maestros de ceremonias y ocho puestos más. El nombre faltante puede ser el de un Q'alel, que como hemos visto antes son identificados como "capitanes" o "ministros". Por deducción, el primer Q'alel es el de los Kaweq, luego se habla de los Ajaw (K'iche'), otro por los Saqik. El que faltaría sería el Q'alel de los Nija'ib. El Q'alel Achij sería el comandante general y no de linaje por su identificación con los *achij*, "guerreros". El Rajpop Achij habría sido un puesto político dentro del rango militar, seguido del Rajtz'alam Achij y del Utza'm Achij. El primero sería el encargado de los límites territoriales porque *tz'alam* se refiere a las "empalizadas" que bordeaban las ciudadelas. El segundo sería el de los puntos de avanzada porque Utza'm significa "nariz" o "límite" de algún lugar.

366. Tz'utuja, como ya se dijo antes, quiere decir "casa de la flor de maíz" y K'ajbaja significaría "casa del sacrificio".

367. Ésta es una clara referencia al libro o parte de aquel documento prehispánico en forma de códice, donde se podían ver y leer eventos que podían repetirse.

368. Comparto el criterio de Edmonson (1971: 243) que dice que *winaq* ha sido generalmente traducido como "hombre" cuando el sentido debe ser "veinte". En consecuencia "nueve cuentas de veinte" equivale a 180 días que es la mitad de un *tun* o sea la mitad del año de 360 días.

369. Aquí de nuevo es la referencia al calendario de 260 días (13 x 20). Estos largos períodos eran de ayuno y abstinencia, como se dice en las siguientes líneas.

370. Esta cuenta está relacionada con dos segmentos del calendario de Venus (ver D. Tedlock, 1996: 206 y 330).

371. El manuscrito dice literalmente *acarroc atoob vquih*, cuya transcripción en el alfabeto contemporáneo es *Aqaroq at oob uq'ij*. En relación con el término *aqaroq*, ya se dijo antes, es una exclamación que significa "¡ay, oh, salve!" y que es una manera imperativa de *saqarik*, para indicar "¡Que amanezca!" o "¡Que se haga la claridad!". En relación con el *atoob* ha sido traducido por Ximénez como "hermosura" y *uq'ij* es la forma posesiva de "su día". En todo caso *atoob uq'ij* querría decir "cuyo día es hermoso" o como el mismo Ximénez traduce "hermosura de su día". Para que sea "hermosura del día" como traduce Recinos (1953: 239), por ejemplo, el adjetivo *atoob* sería el poseído y no el sustantivo *q'ij*; en ese caso, la frase sería *ratob q'ij*. Sin embargo, comparto más los criterios de Edmonson (1971: 244) quien traduce "tú de los cinco días" y de Burgess y Xec (1955: 286) que traducen "tú de cinco glorias". *Atoob* debe provenir de *at job*, "tú cinco", y *uq'ij*, "sus días". En esta forma *at job uq'ij*, una frase sintácticamente bien estructurada, quiere decir: "tú de los cinco días" en referencia directa al calendario de Venus cuyos ciclos como estrella de la mañana, conforme al *Códice de Dresde*, comienzan en cinco distintos días de los veinte que tiene el calendario maya. Aquí debe recordarse que antes del nacimiento del Sol, lo único que podía verse en el firmamento era Ikoq'ij, Venus, y ésta era la estrella que se mantenían viendo los padres primigenios. Esto significa que este saludo inicial, literalmente, quiere decir: "¡Que amanezca!, tú de los cinco días"; pero cuyo significado es una presentación a las divinidades que se mencionan de inmediato. Por aparte, en esta invocación de nuevo se hace referencia a la divinidad en segunda persona, *tú*, cuando en cualquier rogativa los mayas se refieren a la divinidad en segunda persona honorífica *usted*. Por esto tiene razón Chávez (1978: 108) al decir: "que el texto indígena fue alterado" y esto, seguramente, sólo pudo haber sido hecho por fray Francisco Ximénez.

372. La copla *q'anal, raxal* y en líneas más adelante *araxal aq'anal* siempre ha sido asociada a riqueza. En una lectura literal *q'anal* es lo "amarillo", "maduro" y que equivale a la cosecha abundante, *raxal* es lo "verde" de las plantas que equivale al alimento. En

consecuencia, lo que está pidiendo no es riqueza sino abundancia de alimentos.

373. El manuscrito dice *Chatz'iloj, Chamaq'ij uloq araxal, aq'anal* que en traducción literal quiere decir "desparrama, avecinda acá tu verde, tu amarillo". *Chatz'iloj* viene de *tz'il* "sucio" y en una lectura extensiva sería "desparramar" porque el siguiente verbo imperativo *chamaq'ij* viene de *amaq'*, "pueblo", y *amaq'elabik*, según Basseta, quiere decir avecindarse. *Amaq'ij* en consecuencia sería una manera de decir "ubica acá". De esa cuenta traduzco "desparrama, deja caer..."

374. En el manuscrito se habla en tercera persona singular; sin embargo en el discurso k'iche' esto puede significar la tercera persona plural. De esa cuenta traduzco "nuestras, nuestros" en lugar de "mis".

375. Estas cuatro líneas conforman dos versos paralelos, uno externo y otro interno; sin embargo hay otra característica muy interesante. Las dos primeras líneas están en voz pasiva y las dos últimas en voz antipasiva. La copla externa la conforman *pajik*, "ser juzgados", *q'atowik*, "ser condenados", viene de *q'at*, "cortar", y "juzgado" o "tribunal" se dice *q'atbal tzij*, literalmente "lugar donde se corta la palabra". Ximénez (folio 54v) correctamente tradujo [que no] "sean juzgados en tribunal alguno". El verso paralelo interno lo conforman *me sokotajik, me joxowik*, "que no se hieran, que no sean abusados". La frase *Me joxowik* generalmente ha sido traducida como "que no forniquen", pero para eso la estructura sintáctica debería estar en voz activa, es decir *me joxonik*, en términos sintácticos *joxo-n-ik*. En el manuscrito sin embargo encontramos *joxo-w-ik* donde la -*w* marcador de la voz antipasiva significa que "ellos", los hijos, son el objeto de la acción, no los actores. En consecuencia, "no se hieran, no sean abusados" conforma una copla bien estructurada; mientras que "no se hieran, no forniquen" se aparta de la sintaxis k'iche'.

376. Literalmente "camino verde, vereda verde", metáfora para referirse al "camino de la vida". En el pasaje donde Junajpu y Xbalamke llegan a Xibalba, hay cuatro caminos donde el camino de color amarillo que encontraron sus padres, es sustituido por el "camino verde" que significa el "camino de la vida" y por eso ellos no perecen en aquel lugar. Éste es el camino, la vereda que piden los padres para bienestar de sus hijos.

377. Literalmente se está diciendo "que sólo el pueblo (o nación) sea lo que esté en tu boca, en tu presencia"; pero el paralelismo entre *saq*,

"claridad, blanco, llano", y *amaq'*, "pueblo, nación", lleva al concepto de llanura, metáfora que equivale a tranquilidad o "paz" como Ximénez tradujo.

378. Esta oración ha sido traducida como "escuchar", "oír" por *xikin* que literalmente quiere decir "oreja"; sin embargo por el sustantivo precedente, *che'el*, "palo" o "garrote", se entiende que es "extensión" de ese tronco de origen. En Basseta encontramos, por ejemplo, las palabras *xikin ati't*, "bisabuela", *xikin mam*, "bisabuelo".

379. En el texto k'iche' se lee *kiwa'im, uk'aja*. En líneas anteriores hemos visto esta copla como "ayuno, penitencia". Si bien el nominal para ayuno sería *mewa'im* donde el *me-* precisamente es el negativo de comida, y que en esta parte del texto se dice *kiwa'im*, "su comida", pienso que fue error del copista no haber insertado ese negativo, *me-* para decir *kimewa'im*. El otro término, *k'aja*, quiere decir "escarmentar" y por contexto se ha traducido como penitencia.

380. El texto k'iche' dice *xkitz'uba* siendo el verbo *tz'ub'aj*, "besar", "chupar", "succionar". Lo que aquí se está diciendo es que no sólo fueron a "succionar" o a extraer su señorío. Al traducirlo como "arrebatar", comparto el criterio de Burgess y Xec.

381. El manuscrito habla de *xit* que en el diccionario de Pantaleón de Guzmán se identifica como "la piedra muy verde como turquesa".

382. Aquí comparto el criterio de D. Tedlock (1996: 332): se hace referencia a medidas. *Kajq'ab* literalmente hace referencia a "cuatro dedos de la mano" y *tuwik*, como traduce Basseta: "es el puño cerrado y levantado el dedo pulgar; es una medida". Estas dos medidas han de ser sinónimas y todavía se usa en la actualidad cuando se habla de "mano" que equivale a cinco unidades. Con respecto a "granos" el manuscrito dice *raqan* que literalmente significa "su pie" pero en el diccionario de Coto también se dice que una manera de decir "Gotear gotillas pequeñas, como cuando empieza a llover" es *raqan jab*. Es decir, *raqan* son "gotas" pero para nuestro contexto se entiende mejor si se habla de "granos" antes que de "gotas". Ahora bien, con respecto a los "granos" de esas piedras preciosas, el manuscrito dice *k'uwal, yamanik* que en el diccionario de Pantaleón de Guzmán se traduce como "diamante, esmeralda" y "esmeralda, diamante" respectivamente. En el texto k'iche', seguramente, se está hablando de jade y una variedad de esa piedra.

383. Aquí comparto el criterio de Edmonson (1971: 247) sobre que a este pareado le hace falta *q'uq'*, "plumas de quetzal", como se lee en el folio 1v de la transcripción de Ximénez y que aquel autor

tradujo como: "plumas verdes". *Raxon* es el segundo verso que identifica "plumas azules". *K'ubul* significa sentado o ubicado; *chaktik* se conforma de *chak*, "trabajo", y *tik-*, "sembrar". Es decir, en un verso completo se estaría hablando de plumas verdes y azules debidamente trabajadas y ubicadas en un espacio que no puede ser más que penachos o "guirnaldas" como traduce Recinos.

384. Recinos (1953: 242, nota 417) acertadamente hace ver que en esta parte del texto se omite el nombre de K'oka'ib, primer hijo de Balam Ki'tze', y atribuye esto a un posible error de copia. Sin embargo, es posible también que se nombra K'oqawib, porque él es el padre de Balam K'onache'.

385. El manuscrito tiene *ztayub*, *ztayul* y *xtayu* en la 4ta., 6ta. y 8va. generación, respectivamente.

386. El nombre Tekum conforme al diccionario de Ximénez, hace referencia a "ciertas cigarras" y conforme a Tirado quiere decir "mariposa negra".

387. Este nombre k'iche' hace referencia a un día del calendario, *wajxaqib*, "ocho", y *k'am*, "cuerda", que conforme a Brasseur de Bourbourg (1972: 429) es traducción k'iche' del náhuatl *Chicuey-Malinalli*. En náhuatl, *malina* quiere decir "torcer cordel encima del muslo" (Karttunen, 1992), y conforme a Edmonson (1971) y D. Tedlock (1996) equivale al día E del calendario k'iche'.

388. Éste es otro nombre de origen náhuatl derivado de *coatl*, "serpiente", y *pechoá*, "se encorva" (Karttunen, 1992), es decir "serpiente que se encorva". Brinton (1890: 86) traduce *coatepetl* como "Serpent-Mount, or Snake-Hill" a quien Edmonson (1971: 249) sigue en su traducción como "Snake mountain". Asumo que de aquí se deriva el nombre del actual municipio de Coatepeque.

389. Éstos ya son nombres propios del calendario maya, Oxib Kej, "tres venado", Belejeb Tz'i', "nueve perro".

390. Tonatiuh conforme al diccionario de Karttunen (1992) quiere decir "el Sol" y nos refiere a *tóna* que quiere decir "hacer calor o Sol". Probablemente, el sobrenombre de Pedro de Alvarado no se refiera al color de su cabello, como tradicionalmente se ha dicho, sino a su práctica de "quemar" a sus víctimas.

391. El texto k'iche' dice *xejitz'axik*, "fueron ahorcados"; sin embargo el *Memorial de Sololá* (Recinos, 2003: 100) dice que fueron sometidos a tormento y "quemados por Tunatiuh". Es decir, empalmando las dos versiones, primero fueron "colgados", y "torturados" para

sacarles la confesión con la que Alvarado justificó la ejecución. Sobre este tema, ver D. Tedlock (2000).

392. El manuscrito dice *xek'ajolan*, "ellos engendraron", en lugar de *xek'ajolax*, "fueron engendrados". Por contexto, la forma pasiva es la que corresponde en esta línea.

393. *K'uja* quiere decir "troje", lugar donde se almacenan las mazorcas.

394. Varios traductores incluyen la palabra *xcuxeba*, Ximénez entre ellos, como parte del nombre de este "consejero en el juego de pelota" como lo identifica Brasseur de Bourbourg (1972: 339); sin embargo, esa palabra probablemente se deriva de *xk'oje' ba*, que quiere decir: "tuvo pues".

395. En otra parte del texto, cuando se habla de la salida del sol, se identifica a los Yaki Tepew como un pueblo, y aquí Tepew Yaki es un título. Por aparte, en esta enumeración de Casas Grandes hay dos incongruencias como señala Edmonson (1971: 250). En la primera enumeración (ver págs. 178 y 179 en esta traducción), la quinta posición la ocupa el Nim Ch'okoj Kaweq mientras que en este listado aparece en la tercera posición. La novena posición de los Señores en el primer listado lo ocupa Uchuch K'amja, y aquí es sustituida por Tepew Yaki.

396. El nombre de estos Señores deviene de, como hemos visto antes, *k'o* que es *"noble"*, y *chajuj* probablemente se origina de *chaj*, "ocote, pino", para indicar "el que enciende" y *tz'iba-ja* es de la "casa de la pintura" o de "la escritura".

397. Este nombre Belejeb Kej es un nombre de un día del calendario maya, "nueve venado".

398. Batz'a proviene de *batz'-ja*, "casa de mono", siendo *batz'*, "mono", un día del calendario maya.

399. En el folio 53r del manuscrito se le identifica como *queema* y en el folio 56r como *quema* que antes se tradujo como "tejido".

400. En el manuscrito esta línea se encuentra repetida en el sexto lugar de esta lista. Aquí se omite dicha repetición. Ver nota siguiente.

401. Conforme a la lista brindada en el folio 51r éste sería un título que se encuentra repetido como *Nima K'amja* en el sexto lugar, mencionado en la lista del folio 56r del manuscrito.

402. Q'aq' puede ser "fuego" o *kaq*, "rojo", *laqam*, "bandera" conforme Basseta.

403. Probablemente quiera decir "honorable mojado". *K'o*, "honorable", y *kosom*, "mojado", derivado de *cozo* que conforme a Basseta quiere

decir "mojar". Edmonson (1971: 253) lo traduce como "Jefe Golpeado".

404. *Komaj*, "sangre", y *kun*, raíz verbal de "curar", probablemente quiere decir "médico de los males de sangre".

405. Día del calendario, "7 caña".

406. "Honorable mortal". *K'o*, "honorable", y *kamel*, "mortal".

407. Este nombre, como dice Edmonson (1971: 253), probablemente es un apodo. *K'o*, "honorable", *yabakoj* significaría "puma enfermo". *Yabakoj* es también el nombre antiguo de Cuyotenango, Suchitepéquez.

408. Comparto el criterio de Edmonson (1971: 253) que aquí debe ser Winaq Balam, "persona jaguar", en lugar de *Bam* (que no tiene ningún sentido). Esta traducción conforma un verso paralelo con el nombre precedente, "puma".

409. Aquí se omite la identificación de los dos últimos linajes, el de los Saqik que en el folio 51r se les nombra como Tz'utuja y Q'alel Saqik.

410. En la columna k'iche' de la copia de Ximénez se omite por error *chuwach Kaweqib*, pero se restablece en su traducción en español donde dice "de los caviquib". Ver folio 56v.

411. Estas dos líneas son semejantes a lo descrito en el primer folio. Si allá se dijo *k'o nabe wujil*, "había un libro antiguo", aquí sólo se dice *k'o nabe* y se omite *wujil*. Si allá se dijo *ojer tz'ibam*, aquí sólo se dice *ojer*. Aparentemente el desconsuelo de los transcriptores era tan grande que ya no tuvieron ánimo de reiterar lo escrito al principio y tal vez el final del texto debió ser: *k'o nabe wujil,/ ojer tz'ibam puch* como está en el folio 1r y *Popol Wuj ubi' kumal* conforme al folio 54r pero que ya no hay dónde verlo conforme al folio 1r. De cualquier manera, los autores k'iche'es están haciendo saber su desconsuelo por un texto que se estaba perdiendo.

Bibliografía

Aveni F., Anthony (ed.)
1992   *The Sky in Mayan Literature*. New York: Oxford University Press.

Barrera Vásquez, Alfredo y Rendón, Silvia
1978   *El libro de los libros de Chilam Balam*. México: Fondo de Cultura Económica.
1995   *et al. Diccionario maya. Maya-español, español-maya*. México: Editorial Porrúa.

Basseta, Domingo de
s.f.   *Vocabulario en Lengua Quiché* (ca. 1698). En la Bibliothèque Nationale, Paris. Paleografía de William Gates (1921), en la J.P. Harrington Colection en la National Anthropological Archives, Smithsonian Institute, Washington, D.C.

Berendt, Karl Hermann
(s.f.)   *Calendario de los indios de Guatemala Kiché*. Copia del manuscrito de 1772 en la University Museum Library, University of Pennsylvania, Philadelphia.

Berlin, Adele
1992   *The Dynamics of Biblical Parallelism*. Bloomington and Indianapolis: Indiana University Press.

Blair, Robert W. *et al.*
1981   *Diccionario español-cakchiquel-inglés*. Provo, Utah: Brigham Young University.

Brasseur de Bourbourg, Charles Etienne
1862   *Rabinal-Achi ou le drame-ballet du tun*. Collection de Documents
        dans les Langues Indigenes, 2, pt. 2. Paris: Arthus Bertrand.
1972   *El Popol Vuh*. Guatemala: Editorial Universitaria.

Breton, Alan
1999   *Rabinal Achi. Un drama dinástico maya del siglo XV*. Guatemala:
        Centro Francés de Estudios Mexicanos y Centroamericanos.

Bright, William
1990   "With one lip, with two lips: Parallelism in Nahuatl". En *Lan-
        guage*, Journal of the Linguistic Society of America. Vol. 66, No.
        3, septiembre de 1990.

Brinton, Daniel G.
1890   *Essays of an Americanist*. Philadelphia: Porter and Coates.
1969   *The Annals of the Cakchiquels*. Reimpresión de la edición de
        1885 por AMS Press, Inc. New York.

Bruce, Robert D.
1983   "El Popol Vuh y el libro de Chan K'in". En *Nuevas Perspectivas
        sobre el Popol Vuh*, editado por Robert M. Carmack y Morales
        Santos, Francisco. Guatemala: Editorial Piedra Santa. Págs. 273-
        292.

Burgess, Dora M. y Xec, Patricio
1955   *Popol Wuj*. El Noticiero Evangélico, Quetzaltenango.

Campbell, Lyle
1983   "Préstamos lingüísticos en el *Popol Vuh*". En *Nuevas perspectivas
        sobre el Popol Vuh*, editado por Robert M. Carmack y Morales
        Santos, Francisco. Guatemala: Editorial Piedra Santa. Págs. 81-86.

Campbell, Lyle y Kaufman, Terrence
1990   "Lingüística Mayance: ¿Dónde nos encontramos ahora?". En
        Lecturas sobre la lingüística maya. Editado por England, Nora
        y Elliot Stephen. Guatemala: Centro de Investigaciones Regiona-
        les de Mesoamérica. Págs. 51-58.

Cardoza y Aragón, Luis
1979   *Rabinal-Achí: el Varón de Rabinal*. México: Editorial Porrúa.

Carmack, Robert M.
1973   *Quichean Civilization: The Ethnohistoric, Ethnographic, and
        Archaeological Sources*. Berkeley: University of California Press.

1979   *Evolución del Reino Quiché*. Guatemala: Editorial Piedra Santa.
1981   *The Quiché Mayas of Utatlán*. Norman: University of Oklahoma Press.

Carmack, Robert M. y Mondloch, James L.
1983   *Título de Totonicapán*. Texto, traducción y comentario. Edición facsimilar. Instituto de Investigaciones Filológicas. México: Centro de Estudios Mayas, Universidad Nacional Autónoma de México.
1989   *El Título de Yax y otros Documentos quichés de Totonicapán, Guatemala*. Edición facsimilar, transcripción, traducción y notas. Instituto de Investigaciones Filológicas. Centro de Estudios Mayas, Universidad Nacional Autónoma de México.

Carmack, Robert M. y Morales Santos, Francisco
1983   *Nuevas perspectivas sobre el Popol Vuh*. Guatemala: Editorial Piedra Santa.

Chávez, Adrián Inés
1978   *Pop Wuj. Poema Mito-histórico Kí-chè*. Traducción directa del manuscrito. Guatemala: Centro Editorial Vile.
s.f.   *Kí-chè Tzib, escritura kí-chè y otros temas.*

Coe, Michael D.
1973   *The Maya Scribe and His World*. New York: Grolier Club.
1987   *The Maya*. Cuarta edición. London: Thames and Hudson Ltd.

Coto, Thomás de
1983   *Vocabulario de la Lengua Cakchiquel*. Editado por René Acuña. México: Universidad Nacional Autónoma de México.

Dakin, Karen y Lutz, Christopher H.
1996   *Nuestro pesar nuestra aflicción*. México: Universidad Nacional Autónoma de México y Centro de Investigaciones Regionales de Mesoamérica.

Davies, William D. y Sam Colop, L. E.
1990   "K'iche' and the Structure of Antipassive". En *Language,* Journal of the Linguistic Society of America. Vol. 66, No. 3, septiembre de 1990.

Edmonson, Munro S.
1967   "Narrative Folklore". En *Handbook of Middle American Indians*. Vol. 6 editado por Robert Wauchope y Manning Nash. Austin: University of Texas Press. Págs. 357-368.

1971   *The Book of Counsel: The Popol Vuh of the Quiche Maya of Guatemala.* Middle American Research Institute. Publicación No. 35. New Orleans: Tulane University.

1982   *The Ancient Future of the Itza: The Book of Chilam Balam of Tizimin.* Austin: University of Texas Press.

1985   "Quiche Literature". En *Literatures,* editado por Munro Edmonson. Supplement to the Handbook of Middle American Indians, Vol. 3. Austin: University of Texas Press. Págs. 107-132.

1986   *Heaven Born Merida and its Destiny: The Book of Chilam Balam of Chumayel.* Austin: University of Texas Press.

1997   *Quiché Dramas and Divinatory Calendars.* Middle American Research Institute. Publicación No. 66. New Orleans: Tulane University.

Ekholm, Susanna M.

1991   "Ceramic Figurines and the Mesoamerican Ballgame". En *The Mesoamerican Ballgame* editado por Scarborough, Vernon L. y Wilcox, David R. Tucson: University of Texas Press. Págs. 241-249.

England, Nora C.

1994   *Autonomía de los idiomas mayas: historia e identidad.* Guatemala: Editorial Cholsamaj.

England, Nora C. y Elliot, Stephen

1990   *Lecturas sobre la lingüística maya.* Guatemala: Centro de Investigaciones Regionales de Mesoamérica.

Estrada Monroy, Agustín

1973   *Popol Vuh.* Edición facsimilar. Paleografía parcialmente modernizada y notas de Agustín Estrada Monroy. Guatemala: Editorial José de Pineda Ibarra.

Finnegan, Ruth

1992   "Oral Poetry". En *Folklore, Cultural Performances, and Popular Entertainments.* Editado por Bauman, Richard. Oxford University Press.

Florescano, Enrique

1999   *Memoria indígena.* México: Editorial Taurus.

Fox, James J.

1977   "Roman Jakobson and the Comparative Study of Parallelism". En *Roman Jakobson: Echoes of his Scholarship.* Editado por

Daniel Armstrong y C.H. Van Schooneveld. Lisse: The Peter Ridder Press.

Freidel, David, Schele, Linda y Parker, Joy
2000   *El cosmos maya. Tres mil años por la senda de los chamanes.* México: Fondo de Cultura Económica.

García Márquez, Gabriel
1997   "Botella al mar para el dios de las palabras". Discurso inaugural en Primer Congreso Internacional de la Lengua Española, Zacatecas, México.

Gillespie, Susan D.
1991   "Ballgame and Boundaries". En *The Mesoamerican Ballgame,* editado por Scarborough, Vernon L. y Wilcox, David R. Tucson: University of Texas Press. Págs. 317-345.

Girard, Rafael
1952   *El Popol-Vuh, fuente histórica.* Guatemala: Editorial del Ministerio de Educación Pública.

Gossen, Gary H.
1985   "Tzotzil Literature". En *Literatures,* editado por Munro Edmonson. Supplement to the Handbook of Middle American Indians, Vol. 3. Austin: University of Texas Press. Págs. 64-106.

Guzmán, Pantaleón de
1984   *Compendio de nombres en lengua cakchiquel.* Editado por René Acuña. México: Universidad Nacional Autónoma de México.

Haeserijn V., Esteban
1979   *Diccionario k'ekchi' español.* Guatemala: Editorial Piedra Santa.

Heidel, Alexander
1949   *The Gilgamesh Epic and Old Testament parallels.* The University of Chicago Press.

Himelblau, Jack J.
1989   *Quiche Worlds in Creation: The Popol Vuh as a Narrative Work of Art.* Culver City: Labyrinthos.

Henne Pontious, David (comp.)
1980   *Diccionario quiché-español.* Guatemala: Instituto Lingüístico de Verano.

Houston, Stephen D.
1989   *Maya Glyphs*. Londres: British Museum Publications.

Ichon, Alain
1983   "Arqueología y Etnohistoria en Cawinal". En *Nuevas perspectivas sobre el Popol Vuh*. Editado por Robert M. Carmack y Francisco Morales Santos. Guatemala: Editorial Piedra Santa. Págs. 237-246.

Jakobson, Roman
1987   *Language in Literature*. Editado por Krystyna Pomorska y Stephen Rudy. Cambridge, Massachusetts: The Belknap Press of Harvard University Press.

Jakobson, Roman y Pomorska, Krystina
1983   *Dialogues*. Cambridge, Massachusetts: The MIT Press.

Janson, Thor
2001   *Maya Nature*. Guatemala: Vista Publications.

Josserand, J. Kathryn
1991   "Narrative Structure of Hieroglyphic Texts at Palenque". En *Sixth Palenque Round Table, 1986*. Merle Greene Robertson, editor general; Virginia M. Field, editor de volumen. Norman and London: University of Oklahoma Press. Págs. 12-31.

Karttunen, Frances
1992   *An Analytical Dictionary of Nahuatl*. Norman and London: University of Oklahoma Press.

León, Juan de
1955   *Diccionario Quiché-Español*. Guatemala: Editorial Landívar.

León-Portilla, Miguel
1986   *Pre-Columbian Literatures of México*. Norman and London: University of Oklahoma Press.

Lounsbury, Floyd G.
1989   "The Ancient Writing of Middle America". En *The Origin of Writing*. Editado por Wayne M. Senner. Lincoln: University of Nebraska Press. Págs. 203-237.

Maynard, Gail y Xec, Patricio
1954   *Diccionario preliminar del idioma Quiché*. Copia mimeografiada.

Mondloch, James L.

1978   *Basic Quiché Grammar*. Albany: Institute for Mesoamerican Studies. State University of New York at Albany.

1981   *Voice in Quiché-Maya*. Disertación doctoral. State University of New York at Albany. Ann Arbor: University Microfilms.

Morales Pellecer, Sergio

2002   *Diccionario de guatemaltequismos*. Guatemala: Artemis Edinter.

Navarrete, Carlos

2000   *Relatos mayas de las tierras altas sobre el origen del maíz: Los caminos de Paxil*. Guatemala: Editorial Palo de Hormigo.

Orellana, Sandra

1984   *The Tzutuhil Mayas: Continuity and Change, 1250-1630*. Norman: University of Oklahoma Press.

Otzoy C., Simón

1999   *Memorial de Sololá*. Guatemala: Edición facsimilar del manuscrito original. Comisión Interuniversitaria Guatemalteca de Conmemoración del Quinto Centenario del Descubrimiento de América.

Raynaud, Georges

1927   *Los dioses, los héroes y los hombres de Guatemala antigua o el Libro del Consejo. Popol-Vuh de los indios quichés*. Traducción del francés al español por Miguel Ángel Asturias y J. M. Gonzalez de Mendoza. Editorial París-América.

Recinos, Adrián

1953   *Popol Vuh: Las antiguas historias del Quiché*. (Segunda edición). México: Fondo de Cultura Económica.

1957   *Crónicas indígenas de Guatemala*. Guatemala: Editorial Universitaria.

2003   *Memorial de Sololá, Anales de los Kaqchikeles y Título de los Señores de Totonicapán*. Novena reimpresión. Guatemala: Editorial Piedra Santa.

Roys, Ralph L.

1967   *The Book of Chilam Balam of Chumayel*. Norman: University of Oklahoma Press.

Sáenz de Santa María, Carmelo (recopilador)

1940   *Diccionario cakchiquel-español*. Guatemala: Sociedad de Geografía e Historia de Guatemala.

Sam Colop, Luis Enrique
1993   "Xajoj Tun vs. Quiché Vinak". En *Encuentro* No. 10. Instituto Guatemalteco de Cultura Hispánica, Guatemala.
1994   *Maya Poetics*. Disertación doctoral. State University of New York at Buffalo. Ann Arbor: University Microfilms.
1999   *Popol Wuj Versión Poética K'iche'*. Guatemala: Pembi-GTZ, Editorial Cholsamaj.

Sam Juarez, Miguel, *et al.*
2003   *Diccionario q'eqchi'*. Guatemala: Proyecto Lingüístico Francisco Marroquín.

Scarborough, Vernon L. y Wilcox, David R.
1991   *The Mesoamerican Ballgame*. Tucson: University of Texas Press.

Schele, Linda and Freidel, David
1990   *A Forest of Kings: the Untold Story of the Ancient Maya*. New York: William Morrow and Company, Inc.

Schele, Linda y Miller, Mary Ellen
1986   *The Blood of Kings: Dynasty and Ritual in Maya Art*. Fort Worth, TX: Kimbell Art Museum.

Schultze Jena, Leonhard S.
1944   *Popol Vuh: Das heilige Buch der Quiché-Indianer von Guatemala*. Stuttgart y Berlin: W. Kohlhammer.

Tedlock, Barbara
1983   "El C'oxol: un símbolo de la resistencia quiché a la conquista espiritual". En *Nuevas perspectivas sobre el Popol Vuh*, editado por Robert M. Carmack y Francisco Morales Santos. Guatemala: Editorial Piedra Santa. Págs. 343-357.
1992   *Time and the Highland Maya*. Edición revisada. Albuquerque: University of New Mexico Press.
1999a "Continuities and Renewals in Maya Literacy and Calendrics". En *Theorizing the Americanist Tradition*, eds. Lisa Philips Valentine y Regina Darnell. University of Toronto Press. Págs. 195-208.
1999b "Maya Astronomy: What We know and How We Know it". En *Archaestronomy*, Volume XIV (10). Austin: The University of Texas Press. Págs. 39-58.

Tedlock, Dennis
1983a "Las formas del verso quiché". En *Nuevas perspectivas sobre el Popol Vuh*, editado por Robert M. Carmack y Francisco Morales Santos. Guatemala: Editorial Piedra Santa. Págs. 123-132.

1983b   *The Spoken Word and the Work of Interpretation.* Philadelphia: University of Philadelphia Press.

1987   "Hearing a Voice in an Ancient Text: Quiché Maya Poetics in Performance". En *Native American Discourse: Poetics and Rhetoric,* editado por Joel Sherzer y Anthony C. Woodbury. Cambridge: Cambridge University Press. Págs. 140-175.

1992a   "Myths, Math and the Problem of Correlation in Mayan Books". En *The Sky in Mayan Literature,* editado por Anthony Aveny. Oxford University Press. Págs. 247-273.

1992b   "The Popol Vuh as a Hieroglyphic Book", en *New Theories on the Ancient Maya,* editado por Elin C. Danien and Robert J. Sharer. University Museum Symposium Series, vol. 3. Págs. 229-240. The University Museum, University of Pennsylvania.

1993   *Breath on the Mirror: Mythic voices & visions of the living Maya.* San Francisco: Harper.

1996   *Popol Vuh: The Mayan book of the Dawn of Life.* Edición revisada y expandida. A Touchstone Book. Simon and Schuster, Inc.

2000   "La tortura en los archivos coloniales: Encuentro maya con los europeos". En *Mesoamérica* No. 39, Págs. 393-416. Guatemala: Centro de Investigaciones Regionales de Mesoamérica.

2003   *Rabinal Achi: a Mayan drama of War and Sacrifice.* Oxford University Press.

Thompson, J. Eric S.
1960   *Maya Hieroglyphic Writing.* Norman: University of Oklahoma Press.

1972   *A Commentary on the Dresden Codex.* Philadelphia: American Philosophical Society.

Tirado, Fermín Joseph
1787   *Vocabulario de lengua kiche.* Manuscrito en la Tozzer Library. Harvard University, Cambridge.

Townsend, Paul G. (comp.)
1980   *Ritual Rhetoric From Cotzal.* Guatemala: Instituto Lingüístico de Verano.

Varea, Francisco de
1997   *Calepino en lengua cakchiquel.* Guatemala: Universidad Mariano Gálvez de Guatemala.

Vico, Domingo de
s. f.   *Vocabulario de la lengua cakchiquel y quiché (ca. 1550). Manus-*

crito *en Biblioteca Nacional de París*. Fotocopia en Newberry Library de Chicago.

Villacorta C., José Antonio y Rodas N., Flavio
1927   *Manuscrito de Chichicastenango (Popol Buj)*. Guatemala: Tipografía Sánchez & De Guise.

Villacorta C., José Antonio
1962   *El Popol-Vuh en crestomatía quiché*. Tomo I. Guatemala: Editorial José de Pineda Ibarra.

Ximénez, Francisco
1962   *Popol-Vuh*. Guatemala: Editorial José de Pineda Ibarra.
1965   *Historia de la Provincia de San Vicente de Chiapa y Guatemala*. 4 tomos. Guatemala. Editorial José de Pineda Ibarra.
1967   *Escolios a las historias del origen de los indios*. Publicación especial, No. 13. Sociedad de Geografía e Historia de Guatemala.
1985   *Primera Parte del Tesoro de las Lenguas Cakchiquel, Quiché y Zutuhil, en que las dichas Lenguas se traducen a la nuestra, española*. Edición crítica por Carmelo Sáenz de Santa María. Academia de Geografía e Historia de Guatemala. Publ. Esp. No. 30. Guatemala.

Popol Wuj, traducción y notas de Sam Colop se terminó de imprimir en el mes de julio de 2019, año del centenario del nacimiento de Carlos Solórzano Fernández (1 de mayo de 1919 – 30 de marzo de 2011), Premio Nacional de Literatura "Miguel Ángel Asturias", 1989 y Luz Méndez de la Vega (2 de septiembre de 1919 – 8 de marzo de 2012), primera mujer en ganar el Premio Nacional de Literatura "Miguel Ángel Asturias", 1994. F&G Editores, 31 avenida "C" 5-54 zona 7, Colonia Centro América, 01007. Guatemala, Guatemala, C. A. Teléfonos: (502) 2292 3792, (502) 5406 0909 informacion@fygeditores.com www.fygeditores.com